MOZART'S OPERAS

De Wilde: Nancy Storace in 1791

DANIEL HEARTZ

MOZART'S OPERAS

Edited, with contributing essays, by Thomas Bauman

UNIVERSITY OF CALIFORNIA PRESS

Berkeley   Los Angeles   Oxford

University of California Press
Berkeley and Los Angeles, California
University of California Press, Ltd.
Oxford, England
© 1990 by
The Regents of the University of California

Library of Congress Cataloging-in-Publication Data

Heartz, Daniel
Mozart's operas / Daniel Heartz ; edited, with contributing
essays, by Thomas Bauman.
p.   cm.
"A Centennial book."
Includes bibliographical references.
ISBN 0-520-06862-9 (alk. paper)
1. Mozart, Wolfgang Amadeus, 1756–1791.   Operas.   2. Opera.
I. Bauman, Thomas, 1948–   .   II. Title.
ML410.M9H2   1990
782.1′092—dc20   89-20435
                                                        CIP

Printed in the United States of America

1   2   3   4   5   6   7   8   9

A CENTENNIAL BOOK

One hundred books published between 1990 and 1995 bear this special imprint of the University of California Press. We have chosen each Centennial Book as an example of the Press's finest publishing and bookmaking traditions as we celebrate the beginning of our second century.

UNIVERSITY OF CALIFORNIA PRESS

Founded in 1893

CONTENTS

ILLUSTRATIONS

TABLES

PREFACE

*A*nd more than ever now, in these times of turmoil and confusion, do we
need the profound and noble sincerity of *Idomeneo* and the serene spiri-
tuality of *The Magic Flute*"—thus did Edward J. Dent end the second
edition of his book *Mozart's Operas*, completed just after World War II. The subject of the present book is framed by the two operas he singles out, and its simple
title is intended as homage to Dent. My contributing editor and I hope to have
brought to this book a balance of musical, literary, and theatrical concerns such
as inform Dent's urbane and witty study. Our many differences with him have
nothing to do with the stimulation and aesthetic pleasure he always provides. They
reflect, rather, how much the field of study has grown and changed in the second
half of the twentieth century.

Two decisive events in 1986 shaped the conception of this book. At that time I
began writing three substantial essays to mark the bicentennial anniversaries of the
three operas Mozart composed to librettos of Lorenzo da Ponte; these became
Chapters 8, 9, and 14. By 1986, Thomas Bauman had finished his book *W. A. Mozart: "Die Entführung aus dem Serail,"* which I read in typescript, and was doing
extensive research on *Die Zauberflöte*. It occurred to us that if we combined his
expertise on the German-language operas with what I had written and was in the
process of writing on those in Italian, we would have the makings of a uniform
and comprehensive volume devoted to the operas of Mozart's mature years. I selected a few from among several earlier essays on Mozart's operas and rewrote
them, in some cases totally, so as to make them complementary, and added two
completely new ones, the present Chapters 5 and 10. My aim was to paint a
rounded picture of the operatic masterpieces of the composer's last decade. The
two essays by Thomas Bauman, Chapters 4 and 16, newly written for this volume,
were indispensable to completing the picture.

I have been able to provide pertinent visual illustrations largely from my personal collection, formed over many years by seeking out pictures for my own edification and enjoyment and that of my students. The illustrations selected are not merely decorative; they reinforce important points in the text, and receive explanatory commentary.

The ultimate source of my ideas, here gathered, is the classroom experience of trying to bring Mozart's operas to life in the ears and imaginations of students—many generations of students, in fact. At the University of California (from 1960), at the University of Chicago (from 1957), and during terms as guest professor at Princeton and at Cornell, Mozart's operas have always been the central focus of my teaching. Earlier still, during graduate study at Harvard, I recall giving a lecture in the Mozart year of 1956 on *Don Giovanni,* which substituted for the expected lecture on the topic of my Ph.D. dissertation, French sixteenth-century dance music. From this it may be safely assumed that *Don Giovanni* has always held a special place in my affections. The essays here that began as program articles for the San Francisco Opera and other opera companies are like classroom presentations in a sense, too, in that they attempt to reach out to a wide public, while keeping in touch with the latest research results of specialists everywhere.

It seems appropriate, then, to dedicate these essays to my students. In so doing I can begin to repay them for so many exhilarating exchanges over the years, and to one of them in particular, the editor of this volume, I can render thanks for his contributing essays and for all the work he did on the way to the finished product.

D.H.
Berkeley, California
1989

EDITOR'S PREFACE

*T*hose who have loved and studied Mozart's operas will no doubt have noticed in many books devoted to these works a tendency toward the condition of the operatic Baedeker. Such books do serve as a useful source of information for each opera—its immediate historical background, a summary of its plot, a description of the music as it unfolds in performance, and (perhaps) a critical evaluation. Yet anyone who has tried to communicate something of the spirit of Mozart's operatic art knows the limits of the number-by-number approach, either as a didactic method in the classroom or as a pattern for provocative readings. The essays offered here explore the operas of Mozart's maturity in ways that are multivariate and thematic rather than exhaustive or systematic.

Not all the titles will be familiar even to those already well acquainted with Professor Heartz's singular and profound contribution to the study of eighteenth-century opera. As they now stand, the eighteen chapters that follow divide equally into three groups: six lightly rewritten (2, 7, 8, 11, 13, and 17), six substantially revised or expanded (1, 3, 6, 12, 15, and 18), and six newly written for this volume (4, 5, 9, 10, 14, and 16).

We have tried to include a generous number of musical examples;[1] in some chapters, even so, the reader may wish to refer to a score of the opera under discussion. For Mozart's operas, the Neue Mozart-Ausgabe has served as our musical source,[2] with the exception of *Così fan tutte* (scheduled for release by the NMA in 1990), for which recourse was had to Georg Schünemann's edition published by C. F. Peters. (In our examples, staccato markings—which appear in Mozart's auto-

---

1. All examples were newly computer set using Leland Smith's SCORE music typography program. The editor wishes to thank Professor Smith for the advice and expertise he has generously provided.

2. *Wolfgang Amadeus Mozart: Neue Ausgabe sämtlicher Werke*, ed. Internationale Stiftung Mozarteum Salzburg (Kassel, 1955–).

graphs variously as dots, strokes, or something in between—are uniformly rendered as dots.)[3]

Quotations from primary and secondary sources generally appear in English with the original text in the notes. Passages from plays and librettos, however, present original text and translation side by side. Unless specifically noted, all translations are our own. In the case of Mozart's letters, we have translated all passages afresh from the complete critical edition of Bauer and Deutsch.[4] Since the sequence of documents in Bauer-Deutsch is chronological, each letter is cited by date only, which appears here either in the body of the text or in the note along with the original version. We have also provided our own translations of passages from Deutsch's documentary biography of Mozart.[5]

Grateful acknowledgment is made to those who have extended permission to reproduce previously published material in original or revised form:

Chapter 1 ("Sacrifice Dramas"), revised from "*Idomeneo* and the Tradition of Sacrifice Drama," *Glyndebourne Festival Programme Book 1985*, pp. 139–45 (Glyndebourne Festival Opera).

Chapter 2 ("The Genesis of *Idomeneo*"), reprinted from "The Genesis of Mozart's *Idomeneo*," *Musical Quarterly* 55 (1969): 1–19 (Macmillan Publishing Company).

3. This seemingly insoluble editorial quandary was the subject of a musicological competition sponsored by the Internationale Stiftung Mozarteum. The essays were published as *Die Bedeutung der Zeichen Keil, Strich und Punkt bei Mozart*, ed. Heinrich Albrecht (Kassel, 1957). For a useful follow-up essay by one of the participants, see Paul Mies, "Die Artikulationszeichen Strich und Punkt bei Wolfgang Amadeus Mozart," *Musikforschung* 11 (1958): 428–55.

4. *Mozart: Briefe und Aufzeichnungen, Gesamtausgabe*, ed. Internationale Stiftung Mozarteum, collected and annotated by Wilhelm A. Bauer and Otto Erich Deutsch, 4 vols. documents, 2 vols. commentary, 1 vol. indices (Basel, 1962–75).

5. Otto Erich Deutsch, *Mozart: Die Dokumente seines Lebens* Neue Mozart-Ausgabe, ser. 10, work group 34, supplement (Kassel, 1961); hereafter referred to as Deutsch, *Dokumente*. An English translation by Eric Blom, Peter Branscombe, and Jeremy Noble was published as *Mozart: A Documentary Biography* (London, 1965).

Chapter 3 ("Mozart's Tragic Muse"), revised and expanded from *Studies in Music from the University of Western Ontario* 7 (1982): 183–96 (University of Western Ontario).

Chapter 6 ("From Beaumarchais to Da Ponte: The Metamorphosis of *Figaro*"), revised and expanded from *San Francisco Opera Magazine: Le nozze di Figaro* (Fall 1986): 26–33.

Chapter 7 ("Setting the Stage for *Figaro*"), reprinted from *Musical Times* 127 (1986): 256–60.

Chapter 8 ("Constructing *Le nozze di Figaro*"), reprinted from *Journal of the Royal Musical Association* 112 (1987): 77–98.

Chapter 11 ("Goldoni, *Don Giovanni*, and the *Dramma Giocoso*"), revised from *Musical Times* 120 (1979): 993–98.

Chapter 12 ("Donna Elvira and the Great Sextet"), revised and expanded from "'Che mi sembra di morir': Donna Elvira and the Sextet," *Musical Times* 122 (1981): 448–51.

Chapter 13 ("Three Schools for Lovers, or 'Così fan tutte le belle'"), reprinted from "Three Schools for Lovers: The Mozart–Da Ponte Trilogy," *About the House* 6, no. 2 (1981): 18–22 (The Friends of Covent Garden).

Chapter 15 ("La Clemenza di Sarastro: Masonic Beneficence in the Last Operas"), revised and expanded from "La Clemenza di Sarastro: Masonic Benevolence in Mozart's Last Operas," *Musical Times* 124 (1983): 152–57.

Chapter 17 ("Mozart and His Italian Contemporaries"), reprinted from "Mozart and his Italian Contemporaries: 'La clemenza di Tito,'" *Mozart-Jahrbuch 1978/79*, pp. 275–93 (Internationale Stiftung Mozarteum).

Chapter 18 ("The Overture to *La clemenza di Tito* as Dramatic Argument"), reprinted, with a new epilogue, from "The Overture to *Titus* as Dramatic Argument," *Musical Quarterly* 64 (1978): 29–49 (Macmillan Publishing Company).

MOZART'S OPERAS

1 · SACRIFICE DRAMAS

*W*hen the score of *Idomeneo* first appeared in print in 1806, the composer-critic Johann Friedrich Reichardt proclaimed it "the purest art work that even our Mozart ever completed."[1] The ideal of purity was linked in the minds of that time with ancient Greek tragedy, which *Idomeneo* revived, in its own way, through the alchemy of Italian opera. It fell, moreover, into a specific kind of tragedy that stretched all the way back to antiquity: the sacrifice drama. Human sacrifice remained an obsessive theme with the ancient Greeks even during Hellenic times, when they were busy reinterpreting the old heroic sagas handed down to them. Murder of one's own kin represented the strongest dramatic stuff of all. It permeated the tragedies dealing with the house of Atreus, which had a history of violent conflicts going back several generations before Agamemnon and Clytemnestra, the parents of Electra, Iphigenia, and Orestes.

Euripides shaped the sacrifice drama more than anyone else with his two plays on the Iphigenia legend. *Iphigenia in Aulis* (performed in 405 B.C.) interprets the story of King Agamemnon, becalmed in northern Greece with his fleet, having made the dire promise to sacrifice his daughter if only the gods would grant favorable winds and propel his armies to Troy. Iphigenia, like Ilia in *Idomeneo*, offers herself as a willing victim in what she believes to be a just cause—the common good. Before going to her death, she exhorts the chorus to dance around the temple and the altar. In another ending to the play, just as the high priest delivers the fatal blow, a mountain hind miraculously replaces Iphigenia, who is carried off to Tauris in Scythia by the goddess Diana. *Iphigenia in Tauris* works on the bitter

Revised from "*Idomeneo* and the Tradition of Sacrifice Drama," *Glyndebourne Festival Programme Book 1985*.

1. "Das reinste Kunstwerk, das selbst unser Mozart je vollendet hat"; *Berlinische Musikalische Zeitung* 2 (1806): 11.

irony that, as high priestess of Diana in a barbarian kingdom, Iphigenia is forced to perform human sacrifices. Fifteen years have passed since Aulis. The Trojan War is over, and the "victors" return with their spoils to gruesome homecomings. Clytemnestra murders Agamemnon and is killed in her turn by Orestes, in league with Electra. Orestes, pursued by the Furies, lands with his friend Pylades at Tauris. Brought to the sacrificial altar, they dispute who will give his life for the other, but of course it is Orestes who must come under the knife of his sister, so that the ultimate degree of pathos may be extracted from the situation. Athena finally restrains Thoas, the Scythian king, allowing all the Greeks to set sail for home. Both *Iphigenia* plays have their parallels with *Idomeneo*, and both contributed to the tradition out of which Varesco and Mozart fashioned their "heroic drama" of 1781.

Racine began the modern tradition of sacrifice drama with his much admired *Iphigénie en Aulide* of 1674. Combining Euripides with the conventions of French classical plays, this work adopts still a third ending, in which another girl, Eriphile, snatches the sword from the high priest and immolates herself in place of her rival, Iphigenia. The playwright Crébillon, searching to find a subject that would allow him to imitate Racine, but not too closely, chose the legend of Idomeneo. In his tragedy *Idomenée* (1703), he took much from Fénelon's brilliant novel *Télémaque* (1699), which recounts the legend in a version where Idomeneo stabs and kills his son, Idamante. Yet for his ending, Crébillon followed Racine: Idamante snatches the sacrificial sword from his father and kills himself.

New plays often suggested new operas, and it was so in this case. The Paris Opéra, having put on a successful *Iphigénie en Tauride* in 1711 (a collaborative effort involving the composer André Campra), commissioned the poet Antoine Danchet to write an *Idomenée* for the following year, to be set to music by Campra. This work was also successful. Danchet's dark and brooding poem became the direct model for Varesco's libretto. In it Idomeneo is a persecuted, disconsolate figure who suffers mightily for his rash vow; ultimately he kills his son, then tries to kill himself. French opera specialized in orchestral storms, and Danchet capitalized on nature in turmoil as an outer metaphor for the turmoil within the characters. It was his idea to have an offstage chorus of shipwrecked mariners as the fleet from Troy bearing Idomeneo tries to land. Bringing Electra to Crete as another desolate survivor of the postwar horrors also appears to have been his invention. It was a masterly stroke, for she personified the woes of the house of Atreus. Indeed, she was a walking symbol of the opera's central issue—the killing of kin that weighs so heavily on both Electra and Idomeneo.

Electra too, like her brother Orestes, is pursued by the Furies, who wreaked vengeance on parricides and tormented them with hissing serpents. Minoan art becomes suggestive here. The snake goddesses of 1600 B.C. remind us of the ancient, ritual significance of serpents. The fresco of three ladies with serpentine hair of 1700 B.C. bears on another point concerning Mozart's Electra, who, in her magnificent final aria, asks the horned vipers and serpents to tear open her heart ("Squarciatemi il core, Ceraste, serpenti"). Varesco found these hideous images in

Dante's *Inferno*, where the Furies are described as having manes of little serpents and horned vipers ("Serpentelli e ceraste avien per crine").[2]

Italian opera began to profit from Racine's *Iphigénie en Aulide* in the early eighteenth century. Zeno made a libretto from it, a typical aria opera with several pairs of lovers and little flavor of antiquity. This was set to music by a number of composers, beginning with Caldara for Vienna in 1718. A more serious preoccupation with the Iphigenia legend awaited the mid-century, when it caught the fancy of rulers, creative artists, and critics in several centers. At Berlin, under the close supervision of Frederick II, who gave his Italian librettists French prose scenarios to work with, Racine's *Iphigénie en Aulide* was made into an opera by Villati, set to music by Carl Heinrich Graun, and brought to the stage in 1748. Forward-looking features of the score included the large amount of orchestrally accompanied recitative, the dispensing with *da capo* repetitions in some arias, several choruses, and the use of a lugubrious processional march when Iphigenia, robed and adorned for the sacrifice, is led in. The last feature was copied in the *Ifigenia in Aulide* that Mattia Verazi and Nicolò Jommelli wrote for Rome in 1751. The Berlin critic Christian Gottfried Krause dedicated his essay on poetry for music to Graun in 1752 and proclaimed Graun's *Ifigenia* a model for modern librettists and composers to follow. Krause admired Sophocles and Euripides, but he did not believe that the horrors of Greek tragedy could be shown on the stage without offending modern sensibilities. There must be a happy outcome, he opined. Yet the antique chorus could and should be revived. He imagined an example related to the sacrifice of Iphigenia in theme:

> Would it not produce the most touching effect if Jephthah were about to discharge
> his oath standing in the middle of the stage, surrounded by a large chorus, with
> murmuring thunder threatening God's punishment were he to fail his duty. In such
> a way could the antique chorus be imitated. The French do it very often, and staff
> their choruses with an unusually strong number of voices.[3]

Another consequence of the Berlin *Ifigenia* was that King Frederick commissioned a painting of the moment of sacrifice from the French royal painter, Carle Vanloo, which became the subject of intense critical debate when it was completed in 1757.[4]

---

2. This line from Dante's *Inferno* is quoted in Kurt Kramer, "Das Libretto zu Mozarts 'Idomeneo': Quellen und Umgestaltung der Fabel," in *Wolfgang Amadeus Mozart. Idomeneo 1781–1981* (Munich, 1981), p. 30.

3. "Muss es nicht die grösste Rührung geben, wenn Jephte mit dem Hohenpriester in der Mitte des Theater steht, und sein Gelübde that; und ihm auf beyden Seiten die stark besetzten Chöre unter einem murmelnden Gedonner die göttlichen Strafen androhen, dafern er sein Gelübde brechen würde. Auf solche Weise lässt sich der Chor der Alten nachahmen. Die Franzosen thun es sehr oft, und besetzen ihre Chöre ungemein stark mit Stimmen"; Christian Gottfried Krause, *Von der musikalischen Poesie* (Berlin, 1752), p. 440.

4. *Carle Vanloo: Premier peintre du roi*, catalog by Marie-Catherine Sahut of an exhibition at Nice, Clermont-Ferand, and Nancy, 1977, no. 158.

Francesco Algarotti was another witness to the success of the Berlin *Ifigenia*. Back in his native Venice in 1753, he wrote the influential and oft-translated treatise *Saggio sopra l'opera in musica* (1755).[5] To it he appended, as an illustration of his precepts, a French libretto for an *Iphigénie en Aulide* that draws close to Euripides in its starkness but still relies on Racine. It ends as Diana descends from the clouds, snatches Iphigenia, and leaves a hind in her place. Tiepolo depicts this version in the greatest of all paintings dedicated to the sacrifice of Iphigenia, which was executed in 1757, following the artist's return to Venice.[6] In the very same year, Diderot was propounding Racine's play as the perfect vehicle for a reform of French opera,[7] a reform that Gluck eventually brought to pass with *Iphigénie en Aulide* for Paris in 1774. Meanwhile, Parisian dramatists and critics were exploring the possibilities of some related sacrifice dramas.

Guymond de la Touche startled patrons of the Comédie Française in 1757 with an *Iphigénie en Tauride* very close to that of Euripides. Racine had left an outline for treating the story, to which he added the typical *galant* intrigues, but he did not complete the play. Guymond restricted the characters to only four: Iphigenia, Orestes, Pylades, and the barbarian Thoas. There is no "love interest." Nothing detracts from the primal tensions between the principals. Diderot and Grimm found much to admire in the force and passion of the situations in the new play, although they did not allow it the exalted level of Euripides for drama or Racine for language.[8] Its operatic consequences were, ultimately, Gluck's masterpiece for Paris in 1779 but, more immediately, the genial opera of a young Italian composer who served as an inspiration to Gluck. Tommaso Traetta got his start in serious opera by rewriting several arias in Jommelli's *Ifigenia in Aulide* for the Roman revival of 1753. As would be the case later with Gluck, one Iphigenia opera led to another. Durazzo, the impresario at the court of Vienna from 1754 to 1764, saw the operatic possibilities in Guymond's play and had it transformed into a libretto by Coltellini for Traetta. The result reached the stages of Schönbrunn Palace and the Burgtheater in 1763.[9] The tragic grandeur and pathos of the choruses in this *Ifigenia in Tauride*, especially the one during which Orestes is conducted into the temple as the sacrificial victim, make it an important milestone on the path leading not only to Gluck's Iphigenia operas, but also to *Idomeneo*.

Flurries of interest in the Iphigenia dramas tended to beget interest in the related theme represented by Idomeneo and his oath. Five years after the Roman *Ifigenia*

5. Francesco Algarotti, *Saggi*, ed. Giovanni da Pozzo (Bari, 1963), pp. 149–223.

6. This work is reproduced and discussed at length by Michael Levey, *Giambattista Tiepolo: His Life and Art* (New Haven, 1986), pp. 230–32.

7. Denis Diderot, *Entretiens sur "Le fils naturel"* (Paris, 1757). The section on opera comes at the very end.

8. Friedrich Melchior von Grimm, *Correspondance littéraire, philosophique et critique par Grimm, Diderot, Raynal, Meister et al.*, ed. M. Tourneux (Paris, 1877–82), 2:392–97 (1 August 1757). On plays treating this subject, see further Robert R. Heitner, "The Iphigenia in Tauris Theme in Drama of the Eighteenth Century," *Comparative Literature* 16 (1964): 289–309.

9. Daniel Heartz, "Traetta in Vienna: *Armida* (1761) and *Ifigenia in Tauride* (1763)," *Studies in Music from the University of Western Ontario* 7 (1982): 65–88.

in Aulide by Jommelli, the same theater saw an *Idomeneo* set to music by Baldassare Galuppi, the leading Venetian composer. Little is known about this opera, and the librettist has yet to be identified, but the score does survive and represents an important advance in dramatic continuity within the composer's serious operas. Paris saw a new play, *Idomenée* by Lemierre, in 1764. It does not seem to have had operatic consequences, but it provoked some telling commentary by Friedrich Melchior von Grimm, a leading opera critic since he arrived in Paris in 1749, and a man on close personal terms with Mozart:

> Our plays are too full of speeches, and the Idomeneo subject is not apt for them. In it everything should be passion and movement. The subject of Jephthah, which is fundamentally the same, has the advantage over Idomeneo of presenting as a victim a devoted girl, which makes the theme more touching. Both subjects are more suitable for opera than for spoken tragedy. They are susceptible of interesting spectacle and a great number of strong and pathetic situations that welcome musical setting.[10]

Mozart may never have seen the *Correspondance littéraire* in which this review appeared, but that is in a sense irrelevant; he saw the author of this strong and well-taken position about the operatic nature of sacrifice drama, and even stayed with him in the summer of 1778, when he was searching widely through French dramatic literature for a suitable tragic subject. He wrote to his father that he thought the older French tragedies were better than the newer ones, an opinion that could be taken as a commentary on the qualitative difference between a work like Danchet's *Idomenée* and that of Lemierre. Certainly he must have discussed such matters with Grimm. Who better than Grimm could advise him on selecting a subject? If, as has been proposed,[11] it was Mozart himself who selected *Idomenée* by Danchet and brought it back with him from Paris, then got Munich to accept the choice, it may well have been the canny Grimm who put him on this track.

The "passion and movement" that Grimm found so lacking in Lemierre's treatment of the Idomeneo legend was not absent from the work of the greatest French visual artists of the time. François Boucher, another royal painter, included a furiously agitated, imperious Neptune in his *Recueil de fontaines*, engraved by Aveline (Fig. 1). These fountains were never intended to become real fountains, thus allowing Boucher all the more scope to show the elemental power of the sea god, ruler with his trident over winds and waves and all the creatures of the marine world. Fragonard, Boucher's greatest disciple, left among his many wash drawings one of an ancient sacrifice showing a swirling figure holding a trident—Neptune—to

10. "Nos pièces sont trop pleines de discours, et le sujet d'Idoménée n'en est pas susceptible: tout y doit être passion et mouvement. Le sujet de Jephté, qui est le même dans le fond, a sur celui d'Idoménée l'avantage de présenter pour victime dévouée une fille, ce qui rend le fond plus touchant. L'un et l'autre de ces sujets sont plus faits pour l'opéra que pour la tragédie. Ils sont susceptibles d'un spectacle très-intéressant et d'un grand nombre de situations fortes et pathétiques et favorables à la musique"; Grimm, *Correspondance littéraire* 5 : 462 (1 March 1764).

11. Daniel Heartz, "Mozart, His Father, and *Idomeneo*," *Musical Times* 119 (1978): 228–31.

FIGURE I

Boucher: Neptune tames the
waves

whom the hooded high priest raises his eyes while the sacrificial victim next to the
altar flings her arms aloft.[12] The artist conveys well the awesome moment of decision between life and death, and a suggestion of temple columns at the right enhances the solemn rapture of all the figures.

Sacrifice drama, defined in terms of passion and movement, reached its highest
fulfillment in opera with the two Iphigenia dramas by Gluck and Mozart's *Idomeneo*. In *Iphigénie en Aulide*, Gluck made concessions to the Parisian mania for inserted ballets. Grimm, a staunch advocate of Italian opera, decried the result. Yet
the work was not as bereft of vocal opportunities for the principal singers as Algarotti's schematic treatment of the same subject, where words and music are kept
to a bare minimum and the emphasis is on pantomime, dance, and spectacle. Gluck
was unhappy that the opera had to end with a long multipartite chaconne in the
French manner (exactly like *Idomeneo*). After the premiere he swore he would write
no more ballet music and thenceforth his operas would end with sung words, as in

12. Illustrated and discussed by Eunice Williams, *Drawings by Fragonard in North American Collections* (Washington, D.C., 1978), pp. 66–67. For an illustration in color, see Pierre Rosenberg, *Fragonard*
(New York, 1988), no. 107, p. 219.

the great Italian tradition. *Iphigénie en Tauride* offered fewer, but better integrated, opportunities for ballets, with its barbaric Scythians on the one hand and its temple scenes on the other. Gluck took advantage of both, musically differentiating the wild abandon of the first in choruses and dances from the solemn, processional strains of the priestesses. He also came closer to the Italian ideal by writing real arias for the four principals. Yet not even a dictatorial figure like Gluck could prevail altogether over Parisian habits: onto his sung conclusion the Opéra tacked Gossec's ballet of *Les Scythes enchaînés*. Still, the integration of drama and music throughout the work converted even an Italophile like Grimm, who declared: "it may not be melodious, but perhaps it is something better: hearing it makes me forget that I am at the opera and lets me believe that I am at a Greek tragedy."[13] Had he had the opportunity to witness *Idomeneo* two years later, he would have seen his prophecy with regard to sacrifice drama fulfilled, and recognized more of his kind of melodiousness in it as well.

Idomeneo matches Gluck's second Iphigenia opera in its balance between choral-balletic spectacle and personal drama. Its ten arias (after cuts made just before the premiere) correspond roughly to the number in *Iphigénie en Tauride*. Ballets do not play so large a part in *Idomeneo* as they do in *Iphigénie en Aulide*, but they were much more important than present-day audiences are apt to realize. Besides the great chaconne at the end (which bears some direct thematic resemblances to Gluck's), there were choreographed sequences in each of the three acts. The march for the disembarkation (No. 8) close to the end of act 1 leads to the five-part *ciaccona* (No. 9), in which Neptune's praises are sung in terms of marine lore—imagery that cries out for simultaneous visual realization in dance. The same is true with the end of act 2, from the march of embarkation (No. 14) and the sea idyll that follows it (No. 15) to the ultimate pantomimes of terror and fleeing, which are spelled out in the original libretto. The third and last march, that of the priests (No. 25)—an afterthought of Mozart's in imitation of Gluck—opens the scene in Neptune's temple, where all movement should be highly stylized and awe-inspiring.

The last act of *Idomeneo* stunned original audiences by its intensity, and it poses great challenges even today. Here Mozart threw himself most personally into the work, putting himself more than anywhere else into competition with Gluck. Only Mozart could have suggested all the departures from Danchet, amounting to no fewer than eight new dramatic situations of a kind in which Gluck had triumphed.[14] The case is so clear, and so extraordinary, as to make one wonder whether Mozart did not consider confronting Gluck outright, by writing an Iphigenia opera. In the event, he drew freely in terms of both drama and music from both of Gluck's Iphigenia operas.

13. "Je ne sais pas, si c'est là du chant, mais peut-être est ce beaucoup mieux. Quand j'entends Iphigénie j'oublie, que je suis à l'Opéra, je crois entendre une tragédie grecque"; Grimm, *Correspondance littéraire* 12:250 (May 1779).
14. This is demonstrated below in Chapter 2, "The Genesis of *Idomeneo*."

The final ballet is only the most obvious musical link. In *Iphigénie en Aulide*, Gluck used the solo oboe in such a fashion that it became a kind of timbral leitmotif for the sacrificial victim. Mozart does the same by providing poignant held tones on the solo oboe above the progressions when Idomeneo, just before the immensely powerful sacrifice chorus "O voto tremendo" (No. 24), confesses that the victim is Idamante.[15] Here Mozart fuses the "Idamante motif" with a minor second idea, which we shall call the "*duol* motif" (it is sung using this word in No. 10a, m. 50). The fusion of these motifs is so crucial he used it to form the ending of the overture (Ex. 1.1A–B). In the chorus, the way the bass line winds around the main tone with dissonant upper and lower neighbor tones is distinctly Gluckian (cf. the opening chorus of *Alceste*, Paris version).

Perhaps the finest music in *Iphigénie en Aulide* comes after Diana relents; the four principals utter little cries, calling out one another's names, and then sing a quartet of breathless wonderment, "Mon coeur ne saurait contenir l'excès de mon bonheur extrême" ("My heart cannot contain the excess of my delirious happiness"). Mozart used the same hesitant stammering of called names after the voice of Neptune's oracle is heard (No. 28), releasing the king from his vow. Originally another quartet was to have come next, just as in Gluck and surely in direct response to Gluck's quartet, but it was cut because Raaff wanted a final aria instead for his role as Idomeneo and because Mozart realized that the text of act 3 was already too long. As to Mozart's music for "La voce" (No. 28), Gluck was again the model, especially the Oracle's pronouncement at the beginning of *Alceste*.

Why, it may be asked, did these sacrifice dramas seize the eighteenth-century imagination to the extent they did, whether on the spoken or the lyric stage? The same year that Gluck was creating his *Iphigénie en Tauride*, Goethe began writing his intensely moving play *Iphigenie auf Tauris*, after Euripides. We have seen several examples of similar coincidences between spoken and lyric dramas. On the surface, human sacrifice, or even the threat of it, would seem to be as remote from the ideals of the Enlightenment as were religious miracles.

Goethe's *Iphigenie* offers some clues as to a possible explanation. In it, Thoas is humanized and shown in an almost sympathetic light, while the self-proclaimed racial superiority of the Greeks is brought into question.[16] Moreover, Goethe's play

15. This most intense part of the opera, including the great quartet, probably stimulated the enthusiastic commentary by Johannes Brahms when he came to know the work from the first complete edition: "Look at *Idomeneo*! In general a miracle and full of freshness, because Mozart at that time was quite young and audacious! What beautiful dissonances, what harmony!" And further: "Dissonances, real dissonances, you will find used much less in Beethoven than in Mozart. Just consider *Idomeneo!*" (Richard Heuberger, *Erinnerungen an Johannes Brahms: Tagebuchnotizien aus den Jahren 1875–97*, ed. K. Hoffmann [Tutzing, 1971], p. 93; cited after Imogen Fellinger, "Brahms's View of Mozart," in *Brahms: Biographical, Documentary, and Analytical Studies*, ed. Robert Pascall [Cambridge, 1983], pp. 54–56).

16. W. Daniel Wilson (*Humanität und Kreuzzugsideologie um 1780: Die "Türkenoper" im 18. Jahrhundert und das Rettungsmotiv in Wielands "Oberon," Lessings "Nathan" und Goethes "Iphigenie"* [New York, 1984], p. 111) argues that Goethe derived his figure of the magnanimous tyrant Thoas not from any earlier version of the Iphigenia subject, but from the tradition of Turkish rescue operas. Thus he forges a link between sacrifice dramas and Mozart's next opera, *Die Entführung aus dem Serail*.

provides a bridge to philosophical and theological issues hotly debated during the Enlightenment, in which it was asked whether man was bound to obey seemingly senseless divine commands. The sacrifice of Isaac demanded by God of Abraham occupied the foreground of such debates, but the parallel sacrifices required by the gods of pagan antiquity were never far removed. One way out of the dilemma, adopted by Immanuel Kant among others, was to question whether God actually ordered Abraham to kill his son at all.[17] There must be some fault in the transmission of the legend, argued Kant, some corruption that had crept in over the centuries. In other words, and in short: blame the priests. Voltaire had trod this same path before Kant and had made explicit his horror of murder committed on ostensibly religious grounds, which he decried as the most heinous of all crimes in plays such as *Oedipe* (1718) and *Oreste* (1750).[18] Grimm, Voltaire's disciple in this as in so many other matters, put his finger precisely on what it was about sacrifice drama that fascinated, and at the same time repulsed, enlightened eighteenth-century viewers: "What I want to see painted in the tragedy of Idomeneo is that dark spirit of uncertainty, of fluctuation, of sinister interpretations, of disquiet and of anguish, that torments the people and from which profits the priest."[19]

Grimm's vision represents a tenuous link between Goethe's *Iphigenie* and Mozart's *Idomeneo*. Goethe is known to have read the *Correspondance littéraire* with great interest, and one of his most astute critics does not shrink from suggesting Grimm's essay as the possible stimulation leading the playwright to choose a sacrifice theme.[20] From Grimm in person, as we have already suggested, may have come the idea of setting the Idomeneo legend to music. Whatever the source of the choice, Grimm's words should be borne in mind, especially by future producers of the opera, at the moment of the drama when Mozart writes entrance music for the priests, a lugubrious Largo in A-flat (No. 23, mm. 8–9), placing the strings in a very low position, doubled by the bassoons (which are church instruments, to be sure, like the trombones in No. 28). Compare the similar Largo in A-flat (No. 27) when Idamante makes his final entrance, robed and garlanded for his immolation at the altar and surrounded by guards and priests. Grimm's words should be borne in mind, too, as the high priest paints a horrid picture of Crete's desolation and urges King Idomeneo to carry out his sacred duty (No. 23). The ominous unison trills, repeated on various steps to the point of obsession, tell us pretty plainly what Mozart thought of this particular high priest and how we are to respond to the "holy" crime he exhorts. They also tell us how much Mozart admired the exhortation of the high priest at the beginning of Gluck's *Alceste*.

---

17. Wolfdietrich Rasch, *Goethe's "Iphigenie auf Tauris" als Drama der Autonomie* (Munich, 1979), pp. 52–53. I am indebted to my colleague W. Daniel Wilson, Professor of German, for calling attention to Rasch's eye-opening study.

18. Ibid., pp. 74, 81.

19. "C'est donc cet esprit sombre d'incertitude, de fluctuation, d'interprétations sinistres, d'inquiétude et d'angoisse qui tourmente le peuple et dont profite le prêtre, qu'il fallait me peindre dans la tragédie d'Idoménée"; Grimm, *Correspondance littéraire* 5:461.

20. Rasch, *Goethe's "Iphigenie,"* p. 84.

EXAMPLE I.IA–B.

A: *Idomeneo*, Overture

B: *Idomeneo*, Nos. 23–24

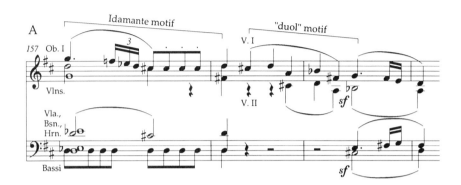

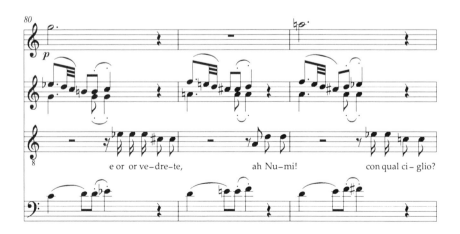

Andante

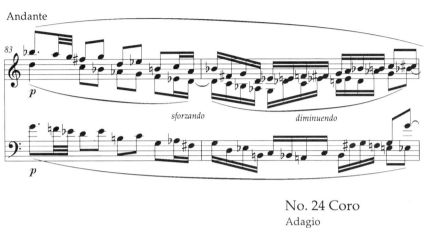

No. 24 Coro

Adagio

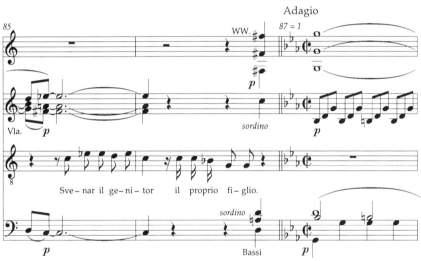

Sve – nar il ge – ni – tor   il proprio fi – glio.

2 · THE GENESIS OF *IDOMENEO*

Mozart undertook the last of his extensive tours in 1777–79. Twenty-one years old, he set out from Salzburg in September accompanied by his mother, passing by way of Munich to Mannheim, then to Paris, and back again by the same route. His aim was to secure a post that would be remunerative and worthy of his talents, or at least demanding of them. The trip turned out to be a series of personal tragedies. In Mannheim he fell under the spell of Aloysia Weber, who soon betrayed him. Alone in Paris, he endured the final suffering and death of his mother. The task of informing his father was hardly less cruel. He returned to Salzburg empty-handed and humiliated, having found no position. It has occurred to many commentators to connect the vein of deeply felt pathos in *Idomeneo* (1780–81) with the emotional coming of age forced on the composer by events. But the specific circumstances under which the work came into being remain to be explained.

On 6 November 1777, after playing in a gala concert at Mannheim, Mozart paid his respects to the elector of the Palatinate, Carl Theodor. The next day, in conversation with the elector, he offered the remark, "To write an opera here is my dearest wish."[1] Perhaps the opera would have come about directly had not an upheaval soon followed in Mannheim. Carl Theodor fell heir to the Wittelsbach succession in Bavaria during the last days of 1777. Rapid action was necessary to prevent a Habsburg coup in Munich, and the elector hurriedly left Mannheim on 1 January 1778. *Rosamunde*, the already prepared carnival opera of Wieland and Schweitzer, was canceled. By the end of 1778 the Mannheim court had moved to Munich, taking along its celebrated singers, theatrical company, and orchestra. Mozart's

Reprinted from "The Genesis of Mozart's *Idomeneo*," *Musical Quarterly* 55 (1969).

1. "mein gröster wunsch wäre hier eine opera zu schreiben"; letter of 8 November 1777 to Leopold Mozart.

wish to write an opera grew apace during his final days in Mannheim, when he wrote his father, Leopold: "Do not forget my desire to write operas. How I envy anyone who does. I could weep for chagrin when I see or hear an aria: but Italian, not German; seria, not buffa."[2] Opera fever is soon the subject again: "The writing of operas sticks fast in my head, but I prefer French to German, and Italian to both."[3] While in Paris during the spring and summer of 1778 Mozart searched for an appropriate subject. The desired commission to write a large stage work never materialized. Only two years later were his most cherished hopes fulfilled when, in the summer or early fall of 1780, the commission arrived from Carl Theodor to write the main opera for the coming carnival at Munich. It would be serious, not comic, on a very grand scale, and in the language he preferred. Moreover, it would involve the musical forces he esteemed beyond all others: the "Mannheimers," as they continued to be called.

The point of departure for the work was *Idomenée*, a *tragédie lyrique* by Antoine Danchet that had originally been set to music by André Campra and first performed at Paris in 1712. This choice is not particularly odd. Rendering older *tragédies lyriques* into Italian librettos was then common practice, and combining elements of French spectacle with Italian-style singing and music was one of the most modern currents in serious opera, indeed, had been since the proposals of Algarotti, Villeneuve, and others to this effect in the 1750s.[4] In fact, as we saw in the previous chapter, the subject of *Idomeneo* closely parallels the *Iphigénie en Aulide* after Euripides and Racine that Algarotti supplied to illustrate the point of his *Saggio sopra l'opera in musica*: a man of public responsibilities is called on by superior powers to sacrifice his own kin for the common weal. The theme has timeless appeal, and its conflicts, if well developed, cannot fail to extract a full measure of pity and terror. As Saint-Foix says of *Idomeneo*: "No other subject of classical tragedy is more beautiful, grander, or more full of pathos."[5]

In keeping with the practice of the age, the choice of subject was stipulated at the time of the commission. This much may be surmised from Mozart's letters. Precise information as to who exactly chose *Idomenée* is lacking. Carl Theodor was surrounded by a numerous company of literati who debated such matters. Surely considerable attention must have been given to so important and expensive a project as the main carnival opera. The elector, who was now also a Bavarian duke, may have had a hand himself in selecting the model, or at least in approving it. He

2. "vergessen sie meinen wunsch nicht opern zu schreiben. ich bin einen jedem neidig der eine schreibt. ich möchte ordentlich für verdruss weinen, wenn ich eine aria höre oder sehe. aber italienisch, nicht teütsch, serios, nicht Buffa"; 4 February 1778.

3. "das opera schreiben steckt mir halt starck im kopf. französisch lieber als teütsch. italienisch lieber als teutsch und französisch"; 7 February 1778.

4. See Robert Haas, "Josse de Villeneuves Brief über den Mechanismus der italienischen Oper von 1756," *Zeitschrift für Musikwissenschaft* 7 (1924): 129–63. This pamphlet has lately been attributed to Giacomo Durazzo; its authorship remains uncertain.

5. "Le sujet en est aussi beau, aussi grandiose, aussi pathétique que n'importe quel autre sujet de la tragédie antique, *Iphigénie* ou *Alceste*, par example"; Georges de Saint-Foix, *Wolfgang Amédée Mozart: Sa vie musicale et son oeuvre. Essai de biographie critique*, 3d ed. (Bruges, 1958), 3 : 221.

was second to no ruler, not even Frederick II of Prussia, in his informed cultivation of the arts and sciences. Like Frederick, his outlook was universal: he read, wrote, and spoke mainly French, the lingua franca of the time; it goes without saying that his library probably contained the entire dramatic literature of this language. Both princes maintained French theatrical troupes. Both vied in entertaining Voltaire and performing his tragedies, the most highly esteemed dramatic works of the day. In some ways Carl Theodor's Mannheim surpassed Frederick's Berlin. Nothing in Prussia rivaled the riches of the Biblioteca Palatina. Carl Theodor's "Antiquensaal," with its plaster casts of Greco-Roman statuary—so admired by the young Goethe—was one of the first of its kind in Germany. Whatever the field of endeavor (save the military), there was certain to be a close interest on the part of the elector, who in a sense became director as well as patron of his numerous projects. And to none of them did he devote more loving attention than opera, which was written mainly in Italian, the *lingua franca per musica.*

Another personality intimately connected with *Idomeneo* was the theater director Joseph-Anton von Seeau, an old Munich hand who had, in Mozart's expression, "been completely turned around by the Mannheimers" to the extent that he had "melted together with them like wax."[6] It was Seeau who negotiated the contract and oversaw the many stages of the opera's progress. Mozart, for instance, proposed cuts in the recognition scene between Idamante and Idomeneo because both performers were so poor on stage (19 December); it later turns out (27 December) that he acted not on his own, but at Seeau's instigation. The response of Leopold is revealing: "It is translated from the French according to the plan. Indeed, as the plan shows, it was desired to extend this recitative a little so that the recognition does not take place so quickly."[7] Leopold had mentioned the "plan" before: it was something he considered binding on all parties. Not only the model but also a detailed protocol of its treatment was subject to agreement with Munich. This must be deduced solely from the correspondence, because Seeau's theater papers, which should include the contract and much else pertaining to the opera, have not been found. In another instance, Mozart had to struggle with the intendant because the three trombones on stage in act 3 required an unforeseen expense.[8] Whether he won his point or not is uncertain, but in any case, his relations with Seeau were mainly happy.

Mozart himself chose his most important collaborator, the librettist Gianbattista Varesco (1735–1805) of Salzburg, a chaplain to the prince archbishop of Salzburg. All dealings with Varesco, including the original contract, passed by way of the

6. "wenn sie itzt dem graf Seeau sprechen sollten, so würden Sie ihn nicht mehr kennen, so ganz haben ihn die H: Mannheimmer umgekehrt"; 13 November 1780. "— Seeau ist von den Mannheimmern wie Wax zusamm geschmolzen"; 8 November 1780.

7. "Es ist nach dem französ: so wie der Plan es verlangte, übersetzt. ja, man sehe im Plan nach, es wurde noch verlangt man sollte dieses Recit: ein bischen verlängern, damit sie einander nicht so geschwind erkennen möchten"; 22 December 1780.

8. Letter of 10 January 1781 from Mozart to his father.

Mozarts, and at their discretion. When a German translation of the libretto came into question, Mozart again had the say, the choice falling on Johannes Andreas Schachtner, a court musician at Salzburg who had been involved earlier with Mozart's abortive Singspiel, *Zaide* (K. 344). Schachtner had the advantage of being in Salzburg when Varesco finished the final revisions of the libretto.

Similar reasons must have dictated the initial choice of the Italian poet, who later offered Mozart his *L'oca del Cairo* (K. 422). Much of the work on *Idomeneo* had been done before Mozart left Salzburg for Munich on 5 November. After completing his final revisions in early January, Varesco demanded his ducats directly, claiming he more than deserved them for having to copy out the entire text four times.[9] Some of these copies must go back as far as October, when the poet and composer probably worked together daily. Mozart did not stop altering the text and music until the first performance, on 29 January 1781. He could not have been any less imperious in person with Varesco than he was demanding of him in subsequent letters by way of Leopold. As a result, he was able to take to Munich not only a libretto that was substantially drafted—and that met with Seeau's approval—but a great deal of music as well: certainly most of the first act, plus some other arias for the singers whose voices he had gotten to know very well at Mannheim— Dorothea Spurni-Wendling (Ilia), Elisabeth Sarselli-Wendling (Electra), and Anton Raaff (Idomeneo). Completion of the entire opera required four months of work, as concentrated as any in Mozart's life. With some allowances, it is possible to assign the composition of acts 1, 2, and 3 to October, November, and December, respectively; January was occupied with such final tasks as Idomeneo's last aria, the ballet music, and the overture.

Danchet's *Idomenée* offers a natural avenue of approach to *Idomeneo*, for it is where the composer and poet began. Varesco acknowledges his indebtedness at the end of the Argument in the libretto, saying: "Consult the French tragedy, which the Italian poet imitated in a few parts, tempering the tragic to a happy ending." Comparison with Danchet reveals that the imitated "parts" are quite numerous and that in many scenes Varesco did no more than translate. *Idomeneo* begins by following scene by scene the first act of *Idomenée* (through the shipwreck of the Cretan fleet returning from Troy). The model and copy of Electra's great scene will serve as an example of the kind of transformation taking place. Electra hears that Idomeneo, father of Idamante (whom she loves), has perished; she shows no pity, no thought of anyone but herself and how this event will cross her desires, for now Idamante will be free to dispose of his own future by wedding the captive Trojan Ilia (whom he loves).

9. Letter of 4 January 1781 from Leopold Mozart to his son.

Son Père ne vit plus! Contre moi tout Conspire!
Il peut avec son Coeur disposer d'un Empire,
   Et je n'en puis douter!
Ah! d'un trouble fatal je me sens agiter,
   A mes yeux, aux yeux de la Grèce,
Une esclave Troyenne a mérité son choix!
Et moi, Fille d'un Roi Maître des autres Rois,
Je ressens pour l'ingrat une vaine tendresse!

His father no longer lives! Everything conspires against me!
He can dispose of an empire along with his heart,
   And of that I cannot doubt!
Ah, with a fateful trouble I feel agitated,
   In my eyes, in the eyes of Greece,
A Trojan slave has merited his choice!
And I, daughter of a king who is the master of other kings,
I feel tenderness for the ingrate in vain!

Estinto è Idomeneo? . . . Tutto à miei danni
Tutto congiura il Ciel. Può à suo talento
Idamante disporre
D'un Impero, e del cor, e à me non resta
Ombra di speme? A mio dispetto, ahi lassa!
Vedrò, vedrà la Grecia à suo gran scorno
Una Schiava Trojana di quel Soglio,
E del talamo à parte . . . Invano Elettra
Ami l'ingrato . . . E soffre
Una Figlia d'un Rè, che hà Rè vassali,
Che una vil Schiava aspiri al grand aquisto? . . .
O sdegno! oh smanie! oh duol! . . . più non resisto.

Idomeneo is dead? To my utter ruin
Heaven conspires. On his own
Idamante can dispose
Of a realm and a heart, and to me
Not a ray of hope remains? To my disgrace, alas,
I shall see, Greece shall see to its great shame,
A Trojan slave share that scepter
And marriage bed. In vain does
Electra love the ingrate . . . Shall
A daughter of a king, who has vassal kings,
Suffer a vile slave to aspire so high?
O disdain! o rage! o grief! I can resist no longer.

Danchet's proud and jealous woman bears a family resemblance to Racine's Phèdre. She is a consistently interesting character, even if lacking the depth possible in a spoken tragedy. (This depth must be achieved on the lyric stage by music.) Varesco accomplishes as much as Danchet, using more words to do so but not necessarily to advantage. Note that the chain of expletives in Varesco's last line has no parallel in Danchet. As a means of heightening the tension just prior to the aria, the device is not rare in Italian librettos. The extraordinary chromatic modulations that Mozart gave the orchestra and the length of the elaboration at "oh duol!" suggest that the textual addition was his, or made at his request. Electra's "Tutto nel cor vi sento Furie del crudo Averno" (No. 4) is a conventional type of rage aria, with its invocation to the Furies of Hell, its "vendetta e crudeltà." There is little here in common with the corresponding passage in Danchet, except for the recurring refrain "Fureur je m'abandonne à vous, Esclatez, servez ma vengeance" ("Fury, I abandon myself to you; explode and avenge me").

The point is a general one. Varesco throughout was able to make most use of Danchet in the narrative or conversational sections that were destined to be set as recitatives. For the arias he often had recourse to certain stock types, long familiar in Italian opera. But how uncommon is the furious intensity of Mozart's music for Electra! The stammering repetitions and hysterical leaps of the voice, the disconcerting wrenches in the harmony, the eerie twitters and roars of the orchestra conjure up not just another *infuriata*, but an offspring worthy of Agamemnon and Clytemnestra. The "madness" of Electra's reprise in darkest c minor—a seeming lapse from the d minor in which she began—is the master stroke. To be sure, the recitative has prepared us for slipping down a tone; but it is only as the stage gradually darkens for the change of scene to the coast and the c-minor chorus of shipwrecked mariners that its full import breaks upon us. The storm in Electra's breast was but a presage of greater storms to follow—of the superhuman rage of Neptune.

Idomenée began with a Prologue in which Venus pays a visit to the cave of Aeolus. The Goddess of Love is kept very busy by Danchet, who has both Idomeneo and Idamante smitten by Ilia. *Idomeneo* dispenses with this complication, and with the Prologue. By 1780, voluble deities continually in transit to and from the terrestrial realm were no longer in fashion. Danchet's several supernatural interventions have all been suppressed, with one important exception: the libretto specifies that after the vow of Idomeneo, which allows him to rescue his people from the storm, "Neptune appears above the water, calms the winds and waves, turns a menacing eye upon Idomeneo, who implores him, then disappears into the sea." The scene is separately numbered (8) and called "Pantomima." According to the autograph and several early copies of the score, it began in m. 36 of the chorus (No. 5). If well rendered and matched with the music, the pantomime could enhance considerably the dreadful situation at hand, for Idomeneo is committed to slaughter the first person he meets.

Acts 1 and 2 of *Idomenée* were combined to form act 1 of *Idomeneo*, the only major change being the deletion of the descent of Venus at the end. Varesco did some of his best work in act 1, where there is little that is not cogent and apt for music. And the benefit of Mozart's direct collaboration is apparent. Particularly praiseworthy is the recognition scene between Idamante and Idomeneo, which unfolds gradually and very movingly—a high point in Danchet from which the new opera fully profited. Mozart consented to shorten it (by twenty-one lines) only because his actors were poor: Raaff he compared to a statue, and the castrato recruited for the part of Idamante, Dal Prato, was making his first appearance on the stage.[10] In the libretto, act 1 ended with the aria for Idamante "Il padre adorato" (No. 7). What followed is termed an intermezzo and described in these terms: the seas become totally calm, the troops disembark to a march, and there is a *ballo generale*, which terminates in the singing of "Nettuno s'onori" by the joyful men and women of Crete. The text of this "ciaconna" consists of a refrain and several strophes rich in marine imagery. By specifying this as the intermezzo, the authors let the audience know that no further entertainment could be expected between the acts. Concern for dramatic continuity rarely precluded extraneous entr'actes in theaters of the time. Carl Theodor's was evidently one in which it did.

Varesco's act 2 traverses only one act (3) of Danchet and does so scene by scene, commencing with an unnecessary recapitulation of what the audience has already seen. Arguments went back and forth between Munich and Salzburg about shortening the dialogue, and Mozart, against Leopold's advice, finally did so (by twenty-nine lines). The scene is still dramatically weak. The source of the trouble is the character of Arbace, an old-fashioned confidant who has no personality and no particular raison d'être in the drama. His first lines are

Di fedeltà il Vassalo	Fidelity in a vassal
Merto non hà: virtu non è il dover	Has no merit: doing one's duty is no virtue
Ecco la vita il sangue . . .	Here is my life, my blood . . .

Here deference borders on the obsequious. Varesco's attempted aphorism is merely sententious, the immediate offer of life and blood a wretched hyperbole. Nothing has been asked of Arbace yet, not even his advice.

Arbace formed part of the "plan" because Domenico de' Panzachi, *virtuoso da camera* and an old favorite of the Bavarian court, had to be included. His part represents one of the few traces left by Munich in *Idomeneo* and, it must be admitted, is a liability to the whole. The role was drastically shortened during the course of the first performances. That it could be reduced and even deleted with scarcely any effect on the dramatic action says as much as need be said. The interesting thing about Arbace's music is that even though Panzachi was a good actor and

10. "NB: er war noch nie auf keinen theater — und Raaff ist eine statue —"; 8 November 1780.

singer, Mozart could not rise above the level of the commonplace in setting his lines. Responding only to the truly dramatic situations in the libretto, which were abundant, he proved unable to bring to life an extremely long scene the entire point of which may be summed up in one sentence of Arbace's advice to Idomeneo: "Send your son away from this fatal shore" ("Eloignés votre fils de ce fatal rivage," in the words of Danchet). The audience need only be told that Idomeneo, attempting to save Idamante, has decided to have his son escort Electra back to Greece, hoping that some friendly god will take them under his protection and prevail over Neptune. Act 2 could then begin with the truly interesting scene between Ilia and Idomeneo, or with the replacement Scena con Rondo (K. 490) for Idamante (No. 10b) that Mozart added for the Viennese performance in 1786.

The monologue that follows is the centerpiece of the tragedy. Having perceived from Ilia's tender music (rather than from her words) that she loves Idamante, Idomeneo becomes fully aware of the situation: "Quot victimae in una!" We are at the very heart of the quandary, and it is the same as in the Iphigenia legend. If Idamante must perish to save Crete, two others will die from sorrow, Idomeneo and now Ilia as well. The ground has been well prepared for the heroic showpiece of the opera. Varesco acquitted himself ably, bringing forth a shipwreck metaphor in the best Italian tradition and using expressions more direct than was his wont:

Fuor del Mar hò un Mare in seno,	Outside the sea, I have a sea within me,
Che del primo è più funesto,	Which is still more deadly,
E Nettuno ancora in questo	And Neptune in this sea
Mai non cessa minacciar.	Never ceases threatening.
Fiero Nume! dimmi almeno:	Proud God! Tell me at least,
Se al naufragio è si vicino	If shipwreck is so near
Il mio cor, qual rio destino	For my heart, what cruel fate
Or gli vieta il naufragar?	Now prevents it from being shipwrecked?

The standard of comparison here is Metastasio. A well-known example in *Artaserse* (1730) shows where the Caesarean poet's inimitable facility lay:

Vo solcando un mar crudele	I go plowing a cruel sea
Senza vele,	Without a sail
E senza sarte:	And without rigging:
Freme l'onda, il ciel s'imbruna,	The waves boil, the sky darkens,
Cresce il vento, e manca l'arte;	The wind increases, and I lack skill;
E il voler della fortuna	And the will of fortune
Son costretto a seguitar.	Am I constrained to follow.
Infelice! in questo stato	Unhappy! in this state
Son da tutti abandonato:	Am I abandoned by all:
Meco sola è l'innocenza,	With me is only my innocence,
Che mi porta a naufragar.	Which is carrying me toward shipwreck.

When Mozart clothes Idomeneo's brave words in the vocal heroics of coloratura, he is also a party to the conventions of opera seria. But how far his opera has departed from those conventions! After singing his *aria di bravura*, Idomeneo (Raaff, the "star" of the opera) remains on stage to provide a link with the next scene, which involves Electra.[11]

Continuity of scenes is a keystone of the work. It is effected in many ways—by manipulation of stage action, by musical reminiscences, by direct fusion of one piece with another. Electra's scene provides an example of all three. Idomeneo assures Electra that she will indeed sail for Greece with Idamante while the orchestra sounds another version of the motif often heard throughout the opera and in such a way as to become identified with Idamante and love (cf. Ex. 1.1A–B). Softened by the verbal (and musical) image of her companion-to-be, Electra sings "Idol mio," in which the motif appears again in the second section. Just as she is about to conclude, the winds (withheld from the aria) sound the embarkation march from a distance, whereupon Electra comments on its melodious strains and leaves the stage. The march continues and gradually increases in volume to suggest an approaching multitude. Mozart has forged these links by his musical treatment. Varesco's contribution is an aria text of surpassing obscurity:

Idol mio! se ritroso	My idol! if reluctantly
Altra Amante à me ti rendi	Another lover gives you to me,
Non m'offende	I am not offended.
Rigoroso	Rigorous,
Più m'alletta austero Amor.	Austere love entices me more.
Scaccierà vicino ardore	A close ardor will chase
Dal tuo sen l'ardor lontano:	From your breast a distant one;
Più la mano	More can the hand
Può d'Amore	Give of Love
S'è vicina l'amante cor.	If the loving heart is close.

Here one turns to Danchet, not in search of a model, but to find some clarification of what Electra can possibly mean:

Que mes plaisirs sont doux, non rien ne les égale.
Je pars avec l'objet dont je me sens charmer
Si je puis l'éloigner des yeux de ma rivale,
Les miens pourront se faire aimer.

(Act 3, Scene 5)

My pleasures are sweet and unequaled.
I leave with the object that has charmed me.
If I can get him away from the eyes of my rival,
Mine can make themselves loved.

11. No. 12a. When Mozart later revised the scene he reduced the coloratura in "Fuor del mar" and achieved continuity by other means: Idomeneo leaves the stage while the orchestral ritornello at the end of the aria makes a transition directly into Electra's recitative (No. 12b).

T A B L E I.

Key Scheme of *Idomeneo*, Act 2

	Royal apartments						Port of Sidon, with buildings along the shore			
No.	10a	10b	11	12	13	14	15	16	17	18
Key	C	B♭ →	E♭	D →	G →	C	E --→	F	c	d

Act 2, like act 1, is divided in half scenically. In act 1 the first half (Nos. 1–4) takes place in the apartments of Ilia, then opens up to the seashore for the storm chorus (No. 5) and the rest of the act. Mozart covered over the division with his music by having the end of Electra's first aria lead into this chorus. Act 2 has a similar progression of interior scenes (probably played on a shortened stage), opening up to the exterior, in this case the port of Sidon. Mozart once again minimizes the scenic change with his music, here by planning the break to come in the middle of a sequence of dominant-to-tonic patterning between numbers (indicated in Table 1 by arrows).

Originally, as the autograph shows, Mozart planned No. 15 in C. Then he changed his mind and wrote the chorus "Placido è il mar, andiamo" in the rarefied key of E. But this was not enough to interrupt the overall tonal thrust toward F that had been gathering since Idomeneo's great heroic aria in D (No. 12). The chorus, an ineffably beautiful *siciliana*, sounds like a welcome detour in the rigorous chain of resolutions, and it makes possible a subtler tonal relationship with what follows, one that functions like a deceptive cadence. The scenographer's art contributed greatly to the success of the opera in such a moment as the first glimpse of the port. Although nothing survives from Lorenzo Quaglio's original stage designs for *Idomeneo*, at least nothing that can be surely assigned to this opera, there are many port scenes by his peers and contemporaries from which to choose. One of the more evocative (Fig. 2) is by Gaspare Galliari, a member, like Quaglio, of a whole clan of stage designers. In it he depicts a port and bark of ancient times through a frame of classical columns.[12]

Neptune, goaded beyond measure by human subterfuge, finally rises to the occasion. Mozart's sixteen-measure orchestral storm may seem too slight to accomplish the peripeteia, but remember its accomplices: the wave machine, thunder drum, and reflector lamps to make lightning. Entering with a shriek on its diminished seventh chord, the chorus informs us at once that this disturbance is going

12. On the Galliaris, see Mercedes Viale Ferrero, *La scenografia del '700 e i fratelli Galliari* (Turin, 1963). There is a stage design by Quaglio in which one sees a port through a Gothic frame; it is reproduced in Daniel Heartz, "The Genesis of Mozart's *Idomeneo*," *Musical Quarterly* 55 (1969), pl. 3. For an illustrated exploration of various stage designs in the neoclassical style, see Heartz, "Idomeneus Rex," *Mozart-Jahrbuch 1973/74*, pp. 7–20.

FIGURE 2

G. Galliari: Port with antique bark

to make the previous one seem tame by comparison. The storm increases in fury, and a sea monster appears, accompanied by the hair-raising substitution of b-flat minor for an expected c minor. The flesh creeps at this new sign that "the time is out of joint." Three times, in a sequence of descending seconds, the people cry out for the person guilty of provoking Neptune's wrath to reveal himself; their wail is echoed and amplified by the massed winds. At this almost unbearably tense juncture, Idomeneo steps forward and names himself. The effect is electrifying. (Note how Mozart links Idomeneo's recitative with the preceding chorus by continuing the descending bass line so that the moment of revelation becomes a harmonic resolution.) He alone is guilty, and only he should be punished; if Neptune insists on an innocent victim, then, says Idomeneo, addressing the deity directly: "You are an unjust god! You may not have him!" Danchet concluded by having Idomeneo offer himself in lieu of another victim. The blasphemy uttered by Mozart's Idomeneo is a legacy of the Enlightenment, and particularly of Voltaire.

The people, understanding little or nothing of their king's defiance, must nevertheless suffer its consequences. The storm continues, says the libretto, and the people take flight, expressing their terror in dramatic pantomime while singing the chorus ("Corriamo, fuggiamo"), so that "the whole formed an analogous action, closing the act with the accustomed Divertimento." Terror-stricken by the violence of the scene, the audience hardly needed this reminder that there would be no further "entertainment" until act 3. One spectator at the rehearsal of act 2 reported to Leopold that the storm choruses "were so forceful that they would turn anyone ice cold, even in the greatest summer heat."[13]

How can we explain the almost revolutionary fervor of Mozart's storm music? Scarcely intimated before in his art and, for lack of an occasion, rarely to be called on again, it is quite peculiar to *Idomeneo*. According to the "plan," there was to be an aria, or rather a cavatina, between the two choruses. Mozart, once arrived in Munich, changed his mind. After working with the *maître de ballet*, Claude Legrand, and Quaglio, he saw the impossibility of a set piece here and required instead a dramatic recitative, supported by plenty of orchestral fireworks: "In this scene, which will be the finest in the opera on account of the stage action just agreed upon with Legrand, there will be so much noise and confusion that an aria would cut a poor figure—and besides, is the thunder going to stop so that Raaff can sing an aria?"[14] In other words, the headlong dramatic tempo must prevail over all.

The source of Mozart's insight is clearly enough the brilliant staging of his collaborators. We need not question the splendid reputations earned by the designer and ballet director during their many years of working together at Mannheim. The incomparable fire of the music with which Mozart responded offers testimony enough. He did not miss the opportunity that working with first-rate scenic artists offered, any more than he missed the opportunity to profit from the finest orchestra he would ever know. The most orchestrally conceived of his operas, *Idomeneo* is also the richest in crowd scenes and grand stage pictures. What is more, the opera does not fail to profit from the theatrical stirrings of the 1770s, which made Mannheim a center of Sturm und Drang. Only a year separates the first performances of Mozart's *Idomeneo* and Schiller's *Die Räuber*, two works with more in common than mere temporal coincidence on Carl Theodor's stages.

13. "Dass der Chor im zweyten Acte beym Sturme so stark wäre, dass er Jedem, auch in der grössten Sommerhitze, eiskalt machen müsste"; 25 December 1780.
14. "Nun — in der letzten scene im 2:ten Ackt hat Idomeneo zwischen den Chören eine Aria oder vielmehr art von Cavatina — hier wird es besser seyn — ein blosses Recitativ zu machen, darunter die Instrumenten gut arbeiten können — denn, in dieser scene die | : wegen der action und den Gruppen, wie wir sie kürzlich mit le grand verabredet haben : | die schönste der ganzen opera seyn wird, wird ein solcher lärm und Confusion auf dem theater seyn, dass eine aria eine schlechte figur auf diesem Platze machen würde — und überdiess ist das donnerWetter — und das wird wohl wegen der Aria von H: Raaf nicht aufhören? — und der Effect; eines Recitativs, zwischen den Chören ist ungleich besser"; 15 November 1780.

Act 3 is astonishing in several respects. The miracle is that it has not just matched but even surpassed the first two acts in richness and power. (Of how many concluding acts of other operas can this be said?) As for the libretto, it takes a surprising turn with regard to Danchet's *Idoménée*. Varesco gives no hint of what really happened when he says that the ending was changed to a "lieto fine." Whereas *Idomeneo* had followed *Idoménée* almost step by step for its first two acts, it now begins to make radical departures. Ilia's opening scene still retains some connection, as does the succeeding love duet with Idamante. At this point in Danchet, Idamante, after a scene with Idomeneo, goes out and slays the monster. Idomeneo considers this a sign that Neptune is no longer angry. Mozart and Varesco introduce this scene later, making the slaying of Neptune's fearsome envoy a sacrilege that hastens the tragedy to its conclusion—but not before their great temple scene, which contains a march and chorus of priests, a high priest's threatening speech, a reconciliation between Idamante and Idomeneo, and the heroic attempt of Ilia to substitute herself for Idamante as the sacrificial victim. None of these episodes appears in *Idoménée*. Danchet has no crowd scene "in the great square in front of the palace," and no oracle that resolves the conflict by announcing Neptune's decree. The closest Danchet comes to producing an oracular pronouncement is to bring Nemesis on stage in his last act to give the message that the gods are still unsatisfied and will exact their toll—which they quickly proceed to do. Idamante is slain by his father, and the gods are appeased. Ilia never speaks of sacrifice. All she can say to Idamante as he is put to the sword is "Ah, flee, dear lover" ("Ah, fuyez, cher Amant"). Only after his death does she say, "It is up to me alone to die" ("C'est à moi seule de mourir"), having urged Idomeneo not to kill himself with the observation, "To punish him, let him live" ("Pour le punir laissez le vivre").

The additions of Mozart and Varesco to act 3 are a crowd scene before the palace, a high priest's monologue, a chorus of mourning, a temple scene with march, an expiatory chorus of priests, a reconciliation scene, a heroic substitution, and an oracular pronouncement.

To seek a single work that deploys all these dramatic opportunities, we need go no further than *Alceste*, by Calzabigi and Gluck—a parallel that musical reminiscences such as those in the high priest's monologue, the F-major march, and the Oracle's speech help to confirm. But these resemblances pale in significance when compared with the massive grafting to which the libretto was subjected. Mozart must have wanted to demonstrate what he could do with some of the stage situations so effectively treated by the older master. He had just returned from witnessing Gluck's triumph at the Paris Opéra, and both *Iphigénie*s were well known to him. The ballet music to *Idomeneo* would profit from this acquaintance. Yet what Mozart chose to emulate was less the composer than the austere dramatist—Gluck the tyrant, with his ruthless demands on singers and musicians and his control over physical conditions in the theater, who opened the way for stage works of great scope and gravity. By creating an operatic climate of unprecedented earnestness, he helped make *Idomeneo* possible.

The libretto differed from Danchet at an early date, as may be seen in Mozart's written demands for changes in act 3. These were a second quartet, concluding the act (that is, a *licenza*), to be replaced by a final aria for Idomeneo (15 November ff.); the Oracle's speech to be shortened (29 November ff.); a second duet between Ilia and Idamante, "Deh soffri in pace ò Cara," to be deleted because, coming just prior to the Oracle, it would render the action "flat and cold" and require the other actors to stand around too long (13 November); the recitative of Arbace preceding his aria lengthened by a few lines at Panzachi's request, with precise indications of how to do it (5 December). In addition, Mozart required certain changes in the stage directions (3 January). Arbace's scene was immediately followed by another in which Arbace was to arrive on stage, prompting the aside "a blessing that he can stay away altogether."[15] Adjustments were also required in the directions for scene 8, imparting the incidental information that it was Mozart's afterthought to add the F-major march. All these changes indicate that before Mozart left Salzburg, act 3 was planned in the form we now know it. But so thorough a reworking of Danchet's libretto surely occupied much thought and time. Correspondence (now lost) passed with Munich prior to Mozart's arrival there, as is known from references made by Leopold. Whether the court had suggested certain features of act 3 or merely ratified them after submission of the "plan," there can be little doubt that here, as throughout its conception, the decisive force shaping the work was Mozart.

The last act cost Mozart more effort than he had anticipated, as evidenced by the amount of sketching he did in the autograph while writing out the great quartet. It is with some surprise that he relates of act 3, "By itself this act cost more effort than an entire opera, for there is almost no scene in it that is not of the greatest interest."[16] He now realized by experience why Gluck, unlike most composers, took months rather than weeks to conceive one of his major works. The staggering task continued into January as he (again like Gluck) undertook to compose his own ballet music. He gives the best reason why the final ballet should be performed: "because it is not just an extraneous ballet, but an integral part of the opera, . . . which makes the task grateful to me, for thus is the music by one master."[17]

Assembling the entire opera occupied the latter part of January. Leopold and

15. " — wie zum beyspiell scena VI. nach dem Arbace seiner Aria steht. *Idomeneo, Arbace Etc:* wie kann dieser gleich wieder da seyn? — — zum Glück dass er ganz wegbleiben kann"; 3 January 1781.

16. "— der allein kostet mehr Mühe als eine ganze opera — denn es ist fast keine scene darinn die nicht äusserst interessant wäre"; 3 January 1781.

17. "und habe alsdann — weil kein extra Ballet, sondern nur ein zur Opera gehöriges Divertissement ist, auch die Ehre die Musick dazu zu machen. — mir ist es aber sehr lieb, denn so ist doch die Musick von einem Meister"; 30 December 1780.

Nannerl arrived in Munich two days before the dress rehearsal on 27 January, Wolfgang's twenty-fifth birthday. Their presence deprives us of a report describing the final alterations prior to the premiere on 29 January. In the last letter written to Salzburg, Mozart announces major changes in act 3, "the rehearsal of which had gone splendidly, with the result that people found it far surpassed the first two acts, but the text is far too long, and consequently the music as well, as I have always maintained."[18] The last aria for Idamante, "Nò, la morte io non pavento" (No. 27a), dismissed as "clumsy where it stood in any case," was to be cut, together with Idomeneo's last aria.

Hardly a letter during the preceding two months had passed between Mozart and his father without discussion of the text of the final aria, which went through three entirely different phases, each furnishing material for a lengthy study in itself.[19] But now all the trouble and work done so far is cheerfully dismissed: "One must make a virtue of necessity." An equally lengthy saga comes to an end at the same time: "The Oracle's speech is still far too long—I shortened it—Varesco need know nothing of all this, for everything will be printed as he wrote it."[20] Mozart had constantly requested brevity of Varesco, and most urgently for the Oracle, as when he remarked: "If the Ghost in *Hamlet* were not so long-winded, he would be more effective."[21]

Shakespeare, the god of Sturm und Drang theater, loomed large to the Mozart of *Idomeneo*. His tragedies were in the repertory of Marchand's company (Mannheim and Munich) and of Schikaneder's (which performed in Salzburg in the fall of 1780).[22] Hamlet, as played by the great actor Friedrich Schröder, was one of the memorable events of the Munich season of 1780–81. Something of the famed realism of English theater seems to have influenced Mozart when he demands, concerning his Oracle: "The audience must believe it is real."[23] No better motto could be found for the peculiar and serious dramaturgy behind *Idomeneo*.

18. "— die Probe mit dem dritten Ackt ist vortrefflich ausgefallen. man hat gefunden dass er die 2 Erstern Ackte noch um viel übertrifft. — Nur ist die Poesie darinn gar zu lang, und folglich die Musick auch | : welches ich immer gesagt habe : | deswegen bleibt die aria vom Idamante, Nò, la morte io non pavento, weg, — welche ohnediess ungeschickt da ist — worüber aber die leute die sie in Musick gehört haben, darüber seüfzen — und die letze von Raaff auch — worüber man noch mehr seüfzt — allein — man muss aus der Noth eine tugend machen"; 18 January 1781.
19. Daniel Heartz, "Raaff's Last Aria: A Mozartian Idyll in the Spirit of Hasse," *Musical Quarterly* 60 (1974): 517–43.
20. "— der orackel spruch ist auch noch viel zu lange — ich habe es abgekürzt — der varesco braucht von diesem allem nichts zu wissen, den gedruckt wird alles wie er es geschrieben"; 18 January 1781.
21. "Wäre im Hamlet die Rede des Geistes nicht so lang, sie würde von besserer Wirkung seyn"; 29 November 1780.
22. See Georges de Saint-Foix, "Le théâtre à Salzbourg en 1779–1780," *Revue de musicologie* 16 (1935): 193–204; and Paul Legband, *Münchener Bühne und Litteratur im achtzehnten Jahrhundert*, Oberbayerisches Archiv für vaterländische Geschichte, vol. 51 (Munich, 1904). See also Chapter 15, note 1.
23. The context of this remark deserves attention, for it shows how intently Mozart weighed the effect every musical gesture would have in the theater. "Stellen Sie das Theater vor, die Stimme muss schreckbar seyn — sie muss eindringen — man muss glauben es sey wirklich so — wie kann sie das bewirken, wenn die Rede zu lang ist" ("Imagine the theater before your eyes, the Voice must be terrifying, it must penetrate; people must believe that it is real. How can this work if the speech is too long"); 29 November 1780.

The libretto had yet to be published when Mozart wrote his last letter, on 18 January. Final copy had gone to press by 3 January and represents the stage the opera had reached by the end of December (Libretto 1). The Italian text, with facing German translation, was corrected in proof at Munich. Varesco did nothing more except write Count Seeau begging him to make sure that no typographical errors remained; but many escaped detection, as the printed copies show. Nevertheless, as Mozart promised, the text was printed in the form in which Varesco left it. What Mozart did not say is that another edition of the libretto was planned or already under way (Libretto 2). This edition, corresponding with the version given at the first performance, not with that of early January, consisted of the Italian text only and had more printing errors; yet the final revisions and deletions mentioned in Mozart's letter are present, as well as many others, with changes particularly numerous in act 3.

In the end, the Oracle sang a version that matches none of the three in Mozart's autograph. The words do match the version in an early copy of act 3 that corresponds to the letter of the revised libretto and in which the accompaniment is for woodwinds and not trombones (No. 28b). Libretto 2 shows that Electra had to be content with a new obbligato recitative in place of her last aria, a revision that could have been anticipated from Mozart's remark concerning the dramatic difficulties the aria caused: "Odd that everyone should hurry off stage just so that Madame Electra can be alone"[24]—another excellent but unnecessary piece deleted for the good of the whole (so we might paraphrase Mozart's several comments on his own surgery). The drive to shorten act 3 even reached into the choruses "O voto tremendo" (No. 24) and "Accogli, ò Rè del Mar" (No. 26), which suffered reduction from three-part (ABA) to one-part form (A). We indicated these cuts in the Neue Mozart-Ausgabe by VI-DE marks, while recommending against observing them in its Foreword. Aside from the great musical losses they would entail, there are dramaturgical reasons for not making the cuts. Act 3 requires three sets: a royal garden (Nos. 18–22); a grand square adorned with statues in front of the palace, seen laterally (Nos. 23–24); and a view of the exterior of the magnificent temple of Neptune, with a vast atrium surrounding it, through which the seashore is discovered in the distance (Nos. 25–30).[25] The second set changes too quickly if No. 24 is drastically cut; and as for No. 26, Idomeneo's prayer to Neptune, it is the raison d'être of the third set.

By deleting three arias in act 3, Mozart brought the work ever closer to the ideals of *tragédie lyrique*. It was finally decided that Idomeneo was to take leave of his

24. "— es kömmt mir so einfältig vor dass diese geschwind wegzukommen eilen — nur um Mad:^me Elettra allein zu lassen —"; 3 January 1781.

25. Lorenzo Quaglio's watercolor of an interior of a temple to Neptune, with statue of the god, preserved in the Theater Museum, Munich, has often been claimed to be related to the original production of *Idomeneo*. If the set specified by the libretto was used, obviously it cannot be. Audiences expected the printed libretto to be accurate in such matters because the libretto served, among other purposes, as a memento of the production.

throne with an elaborate orchestral recitative. This speech is one of the most felici-
tous in the poem. It is, moreover, a final legacy of Danchet's *Idoménée*. What could
be more simple and touching than for Idomeneo to abdicate by asking his people
to accept Idamante as "another himself"?

Danchet, *Idoménée*: Act 5, Scene 3

Peuples, pour la dernière fois,
    Venez obéir à ma voix.
Je cède ma Couronne, et c'est un fils que j'aime
    Qui vous dispensera des loix.
Je me borne à régner par un autre moi-même.

People, for the last time,
    Come and obey my command.
I cede my crown to a beloved son
    Who will henceforth rule you.
I reign now only through another myself.

Varesco, *Idomeneo*: Act 3, Scene 11

Popoli, à voi l'ultima lege impone
Idomeneo, qual Rè. Pace v'annunzio.
Compiuto è il Sacrifizio, e sciolto il voto. . . .
Eccovi un altro Rè, un altro Me stesso.
A Idamante mio Figlio, al caro Figlio
Cedo il Soglio di Creta, e tutto insieme
Il Sovrano poter.

People, receive the last command from
Idomeneo, as king. I announce peace.
The sacrifice is done, the oath annulled. . . .
Here is another king, another myself.
To Idamante my son, my dear son,
I cede the scepter of Crete, and with it
Sovereign power.

Varesco, furthermore, is able to sustain an elevated tone to the final lines, where he
no longer has Danchet to guide him:

Eccovi la Real Sposa. Mirate
In questa bella Coppia un don del Cielo
Serbato à voi. Quanto or sperar vi lice!
Oh Creta fortunata; oh me felice!

Here is the royal spouse. Behold
In this couple a gift of heaven
Saved for you. How much there is to hope for!
Oh, fortunate Crete; happy me!

Here, for once, the nobility of the verbal expression approaches that of the music. Not surprisingly, Mozart surpassed even himself in setting the speech, preparing it with a solemn eight-measure ritornello that seems to epitomize the sublime seriousness of the entire opera. The moment is a dénouement in a purely musical as well as dramatic sense; Mozart at last provides a framework and a resolution for the "Idamante motif." He must have realized, as he carefully revised and further refined the orchestration at the end of the passage, that the opera could have no more fitting conclusion than Idomeneo's last recitative. The final directions of the libretto are: "Here follows the coronation of Idamante, which is done in pantomime, and the chorus, which is sung during the coronation and the ballet."

The genesis of *Idomeneo* is as complex and as mysterious as that of any great masterpiece. It cannot be reduced to simplistic explanations involving Gluck, or any other master. Mozart's own words, always the best guide, tell us how much he was himself in *Idomeneo*, and how much the opera is in a sense a law unto itself. No more revealing declaration exists to show the work in process of being born than that written shortly after Mozart's arrival in Munich. It concerns Ilia's second aria:

I have a request of the Abbé. The aria of Ilia in the second scene of act 2 I should like changed a little for what I require. "Se il Padre perdei in te lo ritrovo" could not be better. What comes next will always seem to me unnatural in an aria: an *a parte*. This is fine in dialogue, where one quickly utters an aside. But in an aria, where the words must be repeated, it makes a bad effect. And even did it not, what I want here is a verse—retaining the beginning if necessary, for that is charming—a verse that is entirely natural and flowing, one with which I need not be too bound by the words but free to write along quite at my ease. Because we have made an agreement here that the aria will be an Andantino with four concertante winds, namely flute, oboe, horn, and bassoon. And please may I receive it as soon as possible.[26]

26. "Ich habe nun eine Bitte an H: Abbate; — die Aria der Ilia im zweyten Ackt und zweyten Scene möchte ich für was ich sie Brauche ein wenig verändert haben — se il Padre perdei in te lo ritrovo; diese stropfe könnte nicht besser seyn — Nun aber kömmts was mir immer NB: in einer Aria, unatürlich

With the usual lightning flash of his genius, Mozart sees how to accomplish several things at once: purge the text of dramatic ineptitudes; develop Ilia's character beyond that previously encountered by giving her an *aria d'affetto* in E-flat, the vehicle of tender passion in which for decades composers of Italian opera had vied to surpass one another (especially Hasse, Traetta, and Christian Bach); satisfy local conditions by combining four excellent orchestral soloists (one of them being Friedrich Ramm, a special friend for whom the Oboe Quartet [K. 370] was shortly to be written). Mozart, in what he composed for Dorothea Wendling and the solo winds, more than satisfied local conditions. He exploited his Mannheimers to the full.

This lesson applies to the work as a whole; we have yet to take into account the full extent of the donnée. *Idomeneo* is Mozart's Mannheim opera. That is to say, it is the beneficiary and culmination of many years of superb productions under Carl Theodor. A great actress and singer like Dorothea Wendling had been inspiring the best in composers since the *Sofonisba* of Traetta (1762) and *Ifigenia* of Majo (1764). Others called on by Carl Theodor included Jommelli, Piccinni, and Salieri—the foremost in the field. What Christian Bach and Holzbauer wrote for Mannheim in the 1770s is of particular relevance to *Idomeneo*, a subject in need of exploring. Suffice it to say here that Mannheim opera was characterized by vocal, orchestral, and choreographic virtuosity in the service of stage realism, Sturm und Drang intensity, and a concept of grandeur in tune with the Greek Revival. In sum, the ingredients were as distinct from those of Calzabigi and Gluck as from those of Metastasio and Hasse.

Theatrical and orchestral brilliance stimulated one of Mozart's first impressions on rejoining his old Mannheim friends in Munich. Corneille's *Essex* was played, along with "ein Magnifiques Ballet—das theater war ganz Illuminirt," as Mozart wrote in his first letter back to Salzburg, using the Frenchified German so typical of the time. The overture was a recent work of Christian Cannabich, orchestra leader and a friend Mozart revered. It surprised Mozart, being unlike Cannabich's earlier music. "You would have been as pleased and as moved by it as I was," he writes to Leopold. "Come soon then to hear and admire the orchestra."[27] Many critics around 1780 wrote with wonderment about the Mannheimers; they have

---

schien — nemlich das *à parte reden*. im Dialogue sind diese Sächen ganz Natürlich — Man sagte geschwind ein paar Worte auf die Seite — aber in einer aria — wo man die wörter wiederhollen muss — macht es üble Wirkung — und wenn auch dieses nicht wäre, so wünschte ich mir da eine Aria — der anfang kann bleiben wenn er ihm taugt, denn der ist Charmant — eine ganz Natürlich fortfliessende Aria — wo ich nicht so sehr an die Worte gebunden, nur so ganz leicht fortschreiben kann, denn wir haben uns verabredet hier eine aria Andantino mit 4 Concertirenden Blas-Instrumenten anzubringen, nemlich auf eine flaute, eine oboe, ein Horn, und ein Fagott. — und bitte, dass ich sie so bald als möglich bekomme. —"; 8 November 1780.

27. "es wurde auf dem Churfl: Hoftheater Esex aufgeführt — und ein Magnifiques Ballet. das theater war ganz Illuminirt; den Anfang machte eine Ouverture vom Cannabich, die ich, weil sie von den

often been quoted, but one remark in particular deserves repeating for its suggestive mode of expression: "No orchestra in the world has ever surpassed the Mannheim band. Its forte is thunder, its crescendo a cataract, its diminuendo a crystal stream murmuring as it evanesces in the distance, its piano a vernal breath. The wind instruments are all so employed as they should be: they elevate and carry, or fill and animate the storm raised by the violins."[28] Dynamic range, effectiveness of the contrasts, finesse of winds and strings—these are the qualities that most impressed contemporaries. And the pages of the *Idomeneo* score repeatedly betray what Mozart made of them. Chiaroscuro is the principle at the lowest level and at the highest. The storm choruses take on their full color only in contrast with "Placido è il mar."

Idomeneo sprang from a specific tradition and far outstripped it. The happy auspices under which it was created brought forth from Mozart a work so demanding that it could hardly be performed elsewhere. Even the Mannheim-Munich forces were probably not ready for its boldness. "Magnificent," "expressive," "novel," "powerful," and "strange," its first auditors called it, with the dominating impression certainly the last. For all but a few the profundities of this *opera eroica* were too deep. In the decade Mozart had left to live, it had already become a work dispossessed. This is perhaps one of the reasons why he loved it especially among all his works. Had not the performance of both *Alceste* and *Iphigénie en Tauride* occupied Vienna during the following fall season, he might have succeeded in his wish to stage a German version of *Idomeneo* recast so as to become even more Gluckian, and with the part of Idomeneo rewritten for the bass Fischer.[29] At the least, this would have meant deleting Arbace and converting Idamante to a tenor part, which Mozart later did for the performance he arranged in the spring of 1786.

---

lezten ist, nicht gekannt. — — — Ich versichere Sie, wenn sie selbe gehört hätten — Sie würden ihnen so sehr gefallen, und gerührt haben, wie mich! — und wenn Sie es nicht schon vorher gewüst hätten, gewis nicht geglaubt haben dass sie von Cannabich ist — kommen Sie doch bald und hören sie — bewundern sie das Orchestre"; 8 November 1780.

28. "Kein Orchester der Welt hat es je in der *Ausführung* dem Manheimer zuvorgethan. Seine Forte ist ein Donner, sein Crescendo ein Catarakt, sein Diminuendo — ein in die Ferne hin plätschernder Krystallfluss, sein Piano ein Frühlingshauch. Die blasenden Instrumente sind alle so angebracht, wie sie angebracht seyn sollen: sie heben und tragen, oder füllen und beseelen den Sturm der Geigen"; Christian Friedrich Daniel Schubart, *Ideen zu einer Ästhetik der Tonkunst*, ed. Ludwig Schubart (Vienna, 1806), p. 130. For further critical comments on the Mannheim orchestra, see Adam Carse, *The Orchestra in the XVIIIth Century* (Cambridge, 1940), pp. 56–59, 98.

29. "der die Iphigenie in das teutsche übersezt hat [Alxinger], ist ein vortreflicher Poet, und dem hätte ich recht gerne meine Oper von München zum übersezen gegeben — die Rolle des Idomenè hätte ich ganz geändert — und für den fischer im Bass geschrieben — und andere Mehrere veränderungen vorgenommen, und sie mehr auf französische art eingerichtet. — die Bernaskoni, Adamberger und fischer hätten mit grösten vergnügen gesungen" ("The man who translated *Iphigénie* into German is a superb poet, and I would have gladly given him my Munich opera to translate. The role of Idomeneo I would have changed entirely, and written it as a bass part for Fischer, making several other changes that would orient the part more along French lines. Bernasconi, Adamberger, and Fischer would have taken the greatest pleasure in singing it"); 12 September 1781.

Perhaps the arias would have been cut further as well, though it is difficult to see exactly where.

Of the seven master operas by Mozart, only *Idomeneo* allows a detailed picture of its genesis. That we know more about its birth pangs than any of the others owes to the peculiar epistolary circumstances of Mozart's dealing with his librettist through Leopold. What can be learned here applies to all that follows.

3 · MOZART'S TRAGIC MUSE

Mozart was "the most universal of musical geniuses," wrote Roger Sessions in reviewing Alfred Einstein's *Mozart: His Character, His Work* upon its appearance in 1945. Sessions was responding to Einstein's chapter 6, which bears the simple title "Universality." Einstein argued that Mozart's universality was more than just his supranationality, his ability to command any national style. As Mozart himself put it: "I can imitate and assimilate all kinds and styles of composition."[1] Rather, his universality resided, according to Einstein, in that he was equally supreme as a vocal composer and as an instrumental composer. Here we propose to underscore another side of his universality by showing that he was equally great in the tragic as in the comic. Some of Mozart's contemporaries perceived his uniqueness in just this area. Christian Gottfried Körner (1756–1831) wrote to his friend Friedrich Schiller in 1794 that "Mozart was perhaps the only one who could be equally great in the comic as in the tragic."[2] In this view the tragic comes first with Mozart, as indeed it did in terms of chronology, but he could also excel in the comic, and that seemed rare in the last years of the eighteenth century, a time so largely preoccupied with tragedy—witness Schiller himself. Mozart's devotion throughout his short life to the tragic possibilities of serious opera needs reaffirmation in these days of psychobiographies that would trivialize his life and works.[3]

Revised and expanded from *Studies in Music from the University of Western Ontario* 7 (1982).

1. "ich kann so ziemlich, wie sie wissen, alle art und styl vom Compositions annehmen und nachahmen"; letter of 7 February 1778 written by Mozart in Mannheim to his father in Salzburg.

2. "Mozart war vielleicht der einzige, der ebenso gross im Komischen, als im Tragischen sein konnte"; cited in the preliminary inscription to the article of Constantin Floros, "Stilebenen und Stilsynthese in den Opern Mozarts," *Hamburger Jahrbuch für Musikwissenschaft* 5 (1981): 155–68.

3. Wolfgang Hildesheimer's *Mozart* (Frankfurt, 1977) has been taken to task especially for its failure to do justice to the world of opera seria. Peter Branscombe wrote in the *Times Literary Supplement* for

Mozart grew up in the grand tradition of Italian serious opera. He cut his compositional teeth setting isolated scenes from the dramas of Pietro Metastasio, the leading poet of opera seria from the 1720s on. As his musical models he took the greatest composers of Italian opera seria. Competence in setting a seria aria served at the time as proof that the science of composition had been mastered. Thus, when the Mozart children were taken to be exhibited in London, Paris, and The Hague, a grand tour that lasted from 1763 to late 1766, Wolfgang wrote as many as fifteen arias, according to the testimony of Leopold.[4] Only a few survive.

The earliest, dated 1765, is on a text from Metastasio's *Ezio*, "Va, dal furor portata" (K. 21) (Ex. 3.1). Note its abb' phrase structure, which is archetypical of the time. Fury is the dominant mood. Mozart conveys it with a commanding march rhythm and a defiant unison rise through the triad. The falling tritone in answer is particularly effective in conveying fury by compressing into two beats what had taken four in the first bar.[5] This rhythmic snap will still suffice the mature Mozart when he wishes to convey anger, for instance in the parody of a rage aria that Bartolo sings in *Figaro* ("La vendetta") or his setting of the word *audace* in the count's angry aria in the same opera ("Vedrò, mentr'io sospiro"). March rhythms in 4/4 time were obviously expected in rage arias.

While the nine-year-old Mozart was not able to sustain the lofty, almost arrogant beginning of "Va, dal furor portata," nor was he able to write quite correctly, even with considerable help from Leopold, he knew how to conjure an appropriate seria style for this text. Such striking musical ideas were essential to capture Metastasio's high-flown rhetoric, and were indeed the essence of the seria style. More within young Mozart's powers, as far as sustaining a piece from beginning to end, was an *aria d'affetto*, or love song, such as Mandane's first aria in Metastasio's *Artaserse*, "Conservati fedele," for which Mozart chose 2/4 time, Andante grazioso, and the

---

26 May 1978 (p. 590): "The field of opera seria is one that finds Hildesheimer at his least convincing, whether in his claims that the genre dies with Mozart, or that Mozart's own early examples can be written off." Marita McClymonds, reviewing the English translation by Marion Faber (London, 1982) in *The Eighteenth Century: A Current Bibliography*, n.s. 8 (1988), pt. 4, pp. 277–78, wrote: "Most unfortunate of all are Hildesheimer's comments on Mozart's opera seria, a genre he neither understands nor likes. . . . His inability to interpret Mozart's opera seria characters extends to the serious characters in the comic operas." Stanley Sadie, reviewing the English translation in the *Musical Times* 124 (1983): 616, wrote: "Hildesheimer's dismissal of it, indeed, reflects his long-outdated attitude to the form—and this crops up again in his attack on *opera seria* and its librettos by the criteria of two centuries on (p. 143), an attack that discloses a serious want of understanding of Mozart's own modes of thought." And lastly, Michael Tanner, writing in the *Times Literary Supplement* of 7 October 1983 (p. 1074), ends his scathing review of the English translation by remarking how Hildesheimer, in seeking to discredit Mozart's letters and other accounts of his behavior, has turned the composer into the great unknowable. "That means we can only expect from this book illumination of the works; and sadly I didn't find any. When he is dealing with the operas, where he might be expected to be at his best, he has nothing insightful to say. His remarks on *Idomeneo*, for instance, don't begin to compare with David Cairns's wonderful essay in his book *Responses*. . . . About *Don Giovanni* he is both simple-minded and vulgar."

4. Cited by Stefan Kunze in *Arien, Szenen, Ensembles und Chöre mit Orchester*, Neue Mozart-Ausgabe, ser. 2, work group 7, vol. 1 (Kassel, 1967), p. ix.

5. Imagine how much more leisurely it would sound if the descent in the second bar were three even quarters, or dotted quarter note, eighth note, quarter note.

EXAMPLE 3.1. Aria from Metastasio's *Ezio*, K. 21

key of A major (K. 23). Already evident is his later preference for this key when it came to amorous outpourings, such as love duets.

Young Mozart's familiarity with opera seria was demonstrated not only by arias written in the styles appropriate to the text; he was also asked to improvise the same at the harpsichord. Daines Barrington gave a report to the Royal Society concerning the boy's prowess in this regard, relative to Mozart's sojourn in London during 1765:

> Happening to know that little Mozart was much taken notice of by Manzoli, the famous singer, who came over to England in 1764, I said to the boy, that I should be glad to hear an exemplary *Love Song*, such as his friend Manzoli might choose in an opera. The boy on this (who continued to sit at his harpsichord) looked back with much archness, and immediately began five or six lines of a jargon recitative proper to introduce a love song. He then played a symphony which might correspond with an air composed to the single word, *Affetto*. It had a first and second part, which, together with the symphonies, was of the length that opera songs generally last; if this extemporary composition was not amazingly capital, yet it was really above mediocrity, and shewed most extraordinary readiness of invention. Finding that he was in humour, and as it were inspired, I then desired him to compose a *Song of Rage*, such as might be proper for the opera stage. The boy again looked back with much archness, and began five or six lines of a jargon recitative proper to precede a *Song of Anger*. This lasted also about the same time with the *Song of Love*; and in the middle of it, he had worked himself up to such a pitch, that he beat his harpsichord like a person possessed, rising sometimes in his chair. The word he pitched upon for this second extemporary composition was, *Perfido*.[6]

Giovanni Manzuoli was a castrato widely acclaimed for his powerful soprano voice and one of many great singers who had a profound effect on Mozart. For him Mozart later created the title role of *Ascanio in Alba* (Milan, 1771). Composers of Italian opera, especially of opera seria, were expected to tailor their music to the individual voice, an aesthetic to which Mozart subscribed wholeheartedly, and even reiterated on several occasions.[7] Besides encountering Manzuoli in London, Mozart also came under the sway of the composer of opera seria whose music, more than that of any other master, provided him inspiration: Johann Christian Bach.

The youngest son of Johann Sebastian Bach was born in 1735. Unlike the rest of his family, he went to Italy (in 1754), becoming a Catholic, an organist in Milan Cathedral, and most importantly, a composer of opera seria. He made his debut setting Metastasio's *Artaserse* for Turin in 1760 (this classic libretto was often assigned to composers who had earned their first *scrittura*, or commission). Like Handel a half-century earlier, having won his laurels in Italy he went to London as a composer of Italian opera (in 1762).

Mozart and his revered friend followed similar paths to a considerable extent. A *scrittura* for Mozart's first opera seria, *Mitridate, Re di Ponto* (K. 87), took the young composer to Habsburg-dominated Milan in 1770. There followed for Milan the wedding serenata *Ascanio in Alba* (K. 111) in 1771 and the serious opera *Lucio Silla* (K. 135) for the Carnival of 1772/73. Bach's fame as a composer of opera seria

---

6. Deutsch, *Dokumente*, p. 89.
7. See Heartz, "Raaff's Last Aria."

MOZART.

Engraved for the Encyclopædia Londinensis 1817.

FIGURE 3

Chapman: Portrait of Mozart

was such that he was called to the court of Mannheim to set Metastasio's *Temistocle* in 1772, and two years later the same *Lucio Silla* (by Giovanni de Gamerra) that Mozart had set.[8] In 1780–81 Mozart fulfilled a commission from the same court—which had meanwhile moved from Mannheim to Munich, as we have seen—by writing *Idomeneo* (K. 366–67). The two composers revived their warm friendship when they met for a final time in 1778 at Paris, where Bach was preparing to execute a commission from the Opéra with his *Amadis de Gaule* (1779). Mozart also hoped to write an opera for Paris, but these hopes were dashed. Bach died in 1781, an event mourned by Mozart as a great loss to the musical world.

After *Idomeneo*, Mozart did not readily have an opportunity to write another serious opera. Emperor Joseph II ruled in Vienna and he was opposed to the genre, mainly because of its high cost. Mozart tried repeatedly to get *Idomeneo* staged in Vienna, but he had to settle for a quasi-private performance of it in the palace theater of Prince Auersperg during Lent 1786.[9] Even so, the occasion provided him with an opportunity to return to the high style of opera seria in two additional numbers he composed, and they are the main focus of this essay.

Mozart's final legacy to the genre was a setting of Metastasio's *La clemenza di Tito*, radically adapted by another poet, to celebrate the Prague coronation of Joseph II's successor, Leopold II, who was not opposed to opera seria and who proceeded to reinstate it in Vienna. Franz Niemetschek, in his biography of Mozart published at Prague in 1798, was justly proud of Mozart's *La clemenza di Tito*, ranking it even higher than *Don Giovanni*, also written for Prague.[10] By a curious coincidence, the two Prague operas were chosen to represent the composer in an engraved portrait by John Chapman for the *London Encyclopedia* in 1817 (Fig. 3). The choice was not too surprising because these two Mozart operas had the most international success during the early nineteenth century. Chapman's portrait testifies to Mozart's mastery of both comic and tragic styles, not only by the choice of the two operas, but also by the combination of the lyre, representing tragedy, with the satyr's mask, representing comedy.

Niemetschek was also one of the first to recognize the greatness of *Idomeneo*. He wrote of it: "In Munich . . . Mozart created the exalted work, the opera *Idomeneo*, in which reigns a richness of ideas and a warmth of feeling such as could have been expected only from the youthful fire of an artist like Mozart."[11] Mozart's genius as a dramatic composer he summarized as "a certain ability to seize exactly the char-

8. The librettos of both operas Bach set for Mannheim were adapted for local conditions by the resident court poet, Mattia Verazi. This was the normal practice of the time.

9. Margret Dietrich, "'Wiener Fassungen' des *Idomeneo*," *Mozart-Jahrbuch 1973/74*, pp. 56–76. The weight of the evidence marshaled by Dietrich concerning performances in the theater of the Auersperg Palace suggests that the *Idomeneo* there in March 1786 was actually staged, and not just given in a concert version.

10. Franz Niemetschek, *Leben des k. k. Kapellmeisters Wolfgang Gottlieb Mozart* (Prague, 1798), p. 47; the biography is published in a translation by Helen Mautner as *Life of Mozart* (London, 1956).

11. "In München . . . schuf Mozart das erhabene Werk, die Oper *Idomeneo*; worinn eine Gedankenfülle, eine Wärme der Empfindung herrscht, die sich nur von Jugendkraft eines Tonkünstlers wie Mozart erwarten liess"; ibid., p. 21.

acter of each person, situation, and feeling."[12] Then Niemetschek made a statement that goes to the heart of the greatness of Mozart's seven mature operas—their individuality:

> Each of his compositions receives a certain individual tint which is confirmed even by the choice of key. Connoisseurs of his works require no particular examples, since all operas of his composition have this property in a high degree, but the most beautiful example of this is the totality of *La clemenza di Tito*. How entirely different is it with ordinary compositions. Their melodies are usually so neutral that they would do equally well for a mass as for an opera buffa.[13]

Mozart himself had something to say on the subject of appropriateness to a serious or comic genre. Just after *Idomeneo*, but before getting to work on his comic opera for Vienna, *Die Entführung aus dem Serail*, he received some advice from his father in a letter (now lost) to the effect that, if you want to insure success, write in a popular vein and keep your music light and lively. To this point Mozart answered from Vienna on 16 June 1781, humoring his father by saying, perhaps with tongue in cheek, that opera buffa should have much that is playful and comic and little that is learned, while opera seria required just the opposite.[14] He could not help it, he added, if the public wished to have comic music in a serious opera. Did he in fact yield on this point and put some comic music in *Idomeneo*?[15] Some moments in the opera do sound distinctly more lightweight than the prevailing tone of exalted seriousness. Let us consider why this is so, and why Mozart allowed such moments.

Act 1 of *Idomeneo* ends with what is called in the libretto an intermezzo, comprising the march of disembarkation (No. 8) and the dance of welcome and celebration, terminating with the great choral-orchestral chaconne praising Neptune, "Nettuno s'onori" (No. 9). Claude Legrand, the choreographer of the original production, was responsible for staging this vast tableau deploying all the theater's forces at once. The heritage of *tragédie lyrique*, not that of opera seria, becomes paramount here. Mozart set the text as a great five-section rondeau supported by the three pillars of the chaconne proper, the refrain "Nettuno s'onori." He began the piece in a fashion that is recognizably related to some of Jean-Philippe

---

12. "Einen gewissen seinen Sinn, den Character jeder Person, Lage und Empfindung aufs genaueste treffen"; ibid., p. 47.

13. "Daher hat jede seiner Kompositionen einen bestimmten eigenthümlichen Charakter, den selbst die Wahl der Tonart nicht verläugnet. Kenner seiner Werke bedürfen keiner besondern Beyspiele, da alle Opern von seiner Komposition diese Eigenschaft im hohen Grade an sich haben; aber das schönste Muster davon ist die ganze *Clemenza di Tito*. —Wie ganz anders bey dem gewöhnlichen Kompositionen! Es sind grösstentheils Gesänge von so unbestimmten Charakter, dass sie eben so gut zu einer Messe, als *Opera buffa* taugen"; ibid., p. 47.

14. For his exact words, see Chapter 4, note 13.

15. Floros ("Stilebenen und Stilsynthese," p. 156) poses this same question. He answers it by saying that, whereas Mozart uses many seria elements in his comic operas, one would seek in vain for comic elements in his serious operas.

Rameau's great act-ending chaconnes. The movement of the chaconne is a moderate 3/4, according to Meude-Monpas in his *Dictionnaire de musique* of 1787. Mozart's only tempo marking is *Ciaccona*, but of course that told all to contemporary practitioners. He does not employ a ground bass; Jean-Jacques Rousseau in his *Dictionnaire de musique* of 1767 declared that composers had almost totally liberated themselves from this constraint in their chaconnes. Mozart does observe the strict four-plus-four-bar phrase structure and the beginning on the second beat of the bar that Rousseau mentions. The first episode does not depart from the main movement and is sung by four soloists from the chorus to a text describing how Neptune tamed his watery realm with his great trident. For the second episode Varesco switches to a more jocular mood, as a dolphin disports with marine divinities. A few of Varesco's short lines will suffice to convey the tone:

Su conca d'oro,	On his golden conch shell,
Regio decoro	Neptune embodies
Spira Nettuno.	Royal dignity.
Scherza Portuno	Portunus plays,
Ancor bambino	Still a boy,
Col suo delfino.	With his dolphin,
Con Anfitrite;	With Amphitrite;
Or noi di Dite	He now has made us
Fè trionfar.	Triumph over Pluto.[16]

Mozart ignored "regal dignity" and took his affective cue from "Scherza." He chose an Allegretto in 2/4 time and the key of the subdominant, G major. Two solo sopranos sing the words to a rising melody, lightly ornamented; the first violins double the upper voice, a solo bassoon doubles the second, while the cellos and basses provide a pizzicato support and the second violins fill in with constant sixteenth-note motion (Ex. 3.2).

By Italian standards, music of so light a character was out of place in serious opera. The composer-theorist Francesco Galeazzi specifies that "il Tempo ordinario" (i.e., common time, 4/4) is the most appropriate for expressing "grand, magnificent, and majestic things" ("cose grandi, magnifiche e maestose"), while triple meter (3/4) "is best for expressing familiar and small things" ("La Tripla è ottima per esprimer cose familiari, e triviali").[17] "Even smaller and more paltry" is the character created by 2/4 ("la Dupla fa un carattere ancora più picciolo, e meschino"), and 6/8 is only used for "comic and ridiculous expressions, for pastorals, dances, and the like" ("La Sestupla serve soltanto all'espressioni buffe, ridicole, alle

---

16. Varesco, a Jesuit-educated priest well versed in the classics, constructed this text from certain descriptive passages in the *Iliad* and the *Aeneid*. See Kurt Kramer, "Antike und christliches Mittelalter in Varescos *Idomeneo*, dem Libretto zu Mozarts gleichnamiger Oper," *Mitteilungen der Internationalen Stiftung Mozarteum* 28 (1980): 1–15.

17. Francesco Galeazzi, *Elementi teoretico-pratici di musica* (Rome, 1791–1796), 2:294–95.

EXAMPLE 3.2. *Idomeneo*, No. 9

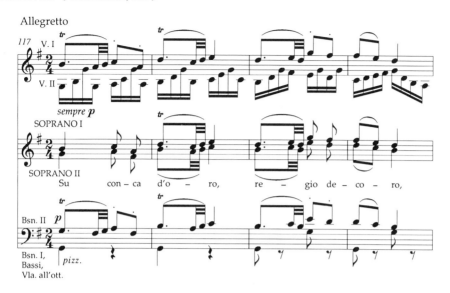

pastorali, a balli, e simile"). The low mission of 2/4 time (and of 6/8 time) accords with what Galeazzi offers on the key of G major, which he calls "innocent, simple, cold, indifferent, and of little effect" ("è un Tono innocente, semplice, freddo, indifferente, e di poco effetto"). Mozart's Allegretto episode stands indicted, at least by Galeazzi.

The Allegretto episode in G does not get any more serious as it continues. Evidently writing in great haste, Mozart arrives at the melodic idea that is going to dominate and conclude the piece only after the modulation to the dominant. This idea is first presented as a figure in the first violins at the words "col suo delfino" (mm. 129–30), where it is a countermelody to the cadences made by the two solo voices. When the tonic is restored, the voices twice sing the same countermelody in thirds and fourths. They do so in leaping up the tonic triad, leaving open fourths here and there, most notably at the top, on the accented first beat (Ex. 3.3). On repetition, the first violins supply a third to go with the fourth of the two voices, making a six-four chord with them. This kind of writing comes close to what used

EXAMPLE 3.3. *Idomeneo*, No. 9

to be known in popular parlance as "harmonizing." It is very far away from what was expected in opera seria or, for that matter, in *tragédie lyrique*. What it does approximate is Austrian or Bavarian yodeling.

Did Mozart miscalculate in allowing this episode to come so close to country music? If he had written it for one of the great Italian opera houses, it might have been received as such and deemed inappropriate. For the jewel-like Cuvilliés Theater in rococo style—the residence theater of the elector Palatine at Munich—a brilliant choreographic spectacle to accompany this marine idyll was of first importance, and surely it allowed some latitude as to musical style. With the divertissement that ended act 1 we are in one of the most decorative parts of the work, equivalent to the grand ballet at the end. Mozart has provided good dance music, with a certain amount of local savor; more was probably not expected or desired for this part of the opera.

Another stylistic "lapse" in the original score comes in a more crucial place, and that is the love duet near the beginning of act 3 (No. 20a). Idamante, the young hero, is about to go off seeking his death in order to save the people of Crete. His beloved Ilia, who up to this point has refused to confess her love for him, breaks through her reserve and declares: "I love you, I adore you, and if you wish to die, you cannot do so before grief has killed me" ("t'amo, t'adoro, e se morir tu vuoi, pria, che m'uccida il duol morir non puoi"). Mozart sets these words, ending the recitative before the love duet, to an elaborate orchestral accompaniment, Larghetto, with the violins in thirds softly playing their staccato triplets, the cellos and basses lightly providing the fundament, and only the violas sounding a sustained line (a viola role that Mozart particularly loved). We show the passage as it occurs in Mozart's autograph (Fig. 4). Ilia (in soprano clef) sings her words to an independent melodic line of great beauty, beginning with falling thirds over the harmonic sequence v/ii–ii | V–I | IV in A. The tonic is reached another way, as the bass descends by step on the last beat of the third bar, then the music rises into the tonic six-four chord via a diminished chord on the word *duol* and a crescendo to forte. "Morir non puoi," sung unaccompanied, provides the recitative cadence, followed by a passage on the dominant, "Un poco più andante" (crossed out), which is at once transition and the beginning of the love duet. Mozart wrote the bass part especially large throughout his autograph so that the continuo cellist, old Innozenz Danzi, could read it from the desk on the harpsichord at which the composer presided.

Idamante sings first in the original love duet, and is answered by Ilia:

ID.	S'io non moro a questi accenti	If I do not die at these words
	Non è ver, che amor uccida	It is not true that love kills,
	Che la gioia opprima un cor.	That joy oppresses a heart.
IL.	Non più duol, non più lamenti;	No more of suffering and laments;
	Io ti son costante e fida:	I am constant and faithful to you:
	Tu sei il solo mio tesor.	You alone are my treasure.
ID.	Tu sarai . . .	You shall be . . .

IL.	Qual tu mi vuoi.	What you will of me.
ID.	La mia sposa . . .	My spouse . . .
IL.	Lo sposo mio sarai tu,	You will become my spouse,
ID.	Lo dica amor.	Love proclaims it.
IL., ID.	Ah il gioir sorpassa in noi	Ah, joy now surpasses in us
	Il sofferto affanno rio:	The old griefs suffered:
	Tutto vince il nostro ardor.	All is vanquished by our love.

Mozart decided on a two-tempo piece, which keeps the Poco più Andante in 4/4 up until the last three lines, when he switches to Allegretto in 3/8. The first part maintains the exalted tone of Ilia's breakthrough in the preceding Larghetto and even enhances it. Particularly effective is Ilia's rejoinder, in which *duol* and *lamenti* are rendered by passing from A major to a minor. (The composer has two options when the text says "no more grief"—either to paint the grief or to convey its absence. Mozart chose the first.)

The touch of a minor makes a lovely springboard to C major for Ilia's "Io ti son costante e fida." Mozart could trust his Ilia, the veteran soprano Dorothea Wend-

FIGURE 4

Autograph page from *Idomeneo*, act 3, scene 2

ling, much more than he could trust his Idamante, the young and inexperienced castrato Vincenzo dal Prato. Thus it comes as no surprise that she is given modulatory and chromatic passages to sing, while his part is mainly diatonic. Mozart must have had a particular fondness for the duet's passage from A major to a minor, to C major, and back to A major via the minor, because when composing the opera's overture, last of all, he put the same modulation at its center (mm. 49–61). Those who study and master the original duet will be rewarded, then, by hearing what sounds like an image of Ilia's constancy and faithfulness already in the overture.

The moment in Italian love duets for which everyone waits expectantly—the two high voices will sing together for the first time!—is at hand after the lovers enter closer and closer together with their rejoinders. Mozart prepares for the expected bliss by sounding the most important melodic motif in the opera, the "Idamante motif," with the first and second violins in octaves and calling attention to it with a crescendo to forte (Ex. 3.4). This motif of a conjunct fall down a slurred fourth or fifth, the first tone being dotted and the last repeated in one or more afterbeats, has been recurring ever since the end of the overture (see Ex. 1.1) and Ilia's "Padre, germani, addio!" (No. 1, mm. 31–47 and 82–98), where it refers to Idamante and Ilia's hidden love for him.[18] There it was softly intoned by cellos and basses like a partially veiled secret. Now it has come out into the open, as it were, high in the orchestra and marked *fp*. What could be more appropriate? The "tu" it accompanies refers to Idamante. The prolonged chord, V_3^4 of V, is one that Mozart will put to very good use in the concluding Allegretto. Here it further enhances the expectancy of hearing both voices together, which Mozart saves for Love's pronouncement, "lo dica amor," sung three times, like an incantation, the last preceded by a chromatic rise in thirds for violins, violas, and oboes, forte. The stage is set, with the pause on the dominant, for the concluding Allegretto in 3/8, celebrating such a moment of joy.

The Allegretto begins as the violins propose a little trilled figure in thirds (which is answered by the bassoons), then accompany the voice with light off-beat figures (Ex. 3.5). Mozart could as well have written it in 6/8, for all the 3/8 bars are paired and the dancelike quality is evident. It comes perilously close to a little waltz song or Ländler. Mozart forswears painting the griefs of "il sofferto affanno rio," or rather he does so with a light touch on repeating the line with a rising chromatic appoggiatura in thirds on *sofferto*. The billing and cooing in thirds turn the lovers into Papageno and Papagena, when, given the dire straits they are in, they should be mustering the seriousness and strength of Tamino and Pamina before the trials. Carried away with the *gioir* of the text, Mozart has seemingly violated his own

---

18. The dramatic use of recurring motives, called by some scholars "functional recollection," was pioneered by composers working for the Opéra-comique in Paris, particularly Grétry. See David Charlton, *Grétry and the Growth of Opéra-Comique* (Cambridge, 1986); the index has an entry under "functional recollection." See also Daniel Heartz, "Tonality and Motif in *Idomeneo*," *Musical Times* 115 (1974): 382–86.

EXAMPLE 3.4. *Idomeneo*, No. 20a

EXAMPLE 3.5. *Idomeneo*, No. 20a

EXAMPLE 3.5, *continued*

fan - no ri - o, il sof - fer - to af - fan - no ri - - o:

strictures against "playfulness" in serious opera.[19] He may also have had in mind the need to spare Dal Prato as much as possible in the love duet so that he could bring maximum energy and concentration to bear on the following piece, the great quartet, the most challenging of all the music for the role of Idamante.[20]

The question remains whether Mozart has violated the tone appropriate to opera seria with so lightweight a piece as this Allegretto. He sets the last line imitatively at first, which lends a hint of the "learned" at least, but without lessening the dance character. A nicely placed chromatic rise (mm. 69–78) of the voices in thirds, duplicating the orchestral rise just before the Allegretto, allows him to do a little more justice to the words of the penultimate line and repeat the imitative setting of the last line. He closes the piece with a little coda made of the chromatically rising seconds, descending in sequence against the rising bass line. This idea struck Mozart's fancy to such an extent that he used it almost verbatim in his next opera, *Die Entführung*, to close Belmonte's rondo "Wenn der Freude Thränen fliessen" (No. 16; Ex. 3.6A–B). Both texts have joy in common, which would help to explain the musical recurrence, but what seems fitting in his Viennese comedy skirts the limits of what can appear in an Italian serious opera without disturbing the tragic tone of the whole.

Mozart saw fit to replace the love duet with another (No. 20B) for the revival of *Idomeneo* at Vienna in 1786. He procured a new text, perhaps from Lorenzo da Ponte, but used the same key of A major and many of the musical materials in the original duet. This is one of the rare cases in his works of a complete recomposi-

19. It is true that Mozart allowed an equally lightweight piece in 6/8 in *La clemenza di Tito*, the duettino "Deh prendi un dolce amplesso" (No. 3), but it is sung in praise of friendship by Sesto and Annio and thus need not be so serious as a duet between the tragic hero and heroine.

20. For a consideration of this piece and the revisions made in it during composition, see Daniel Heartz, "The Great Quartet in Mozart's *Idomeneo*," *Music Forum* 5 (1980): 233–56.

EXAMPLE 3.6A–B.

A: *Idomeneo*, No. 20a

B: *Entführung*, No. 15

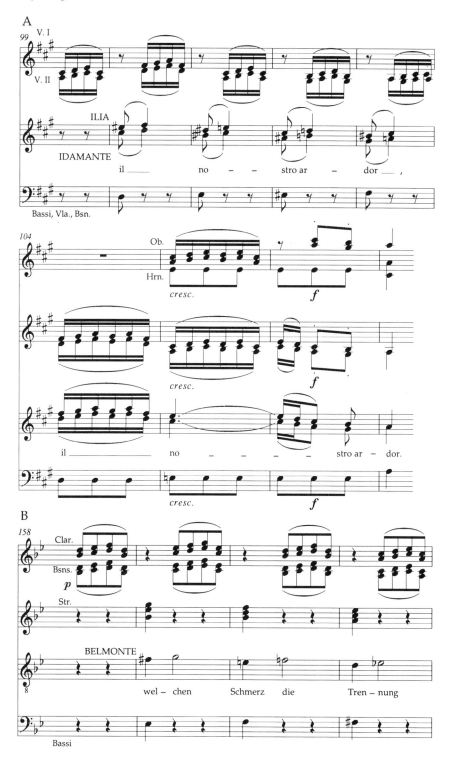

EXAMPLE 3.6B, *continued*

tion. He was not forced to replace the old duet; he could have adjusted it to take advantage of the fine tenor voice he had for Idamante in Vienna, just as he did in the case of the terzetto (No. 16) and the great quartet (No. 21). Indeed, it can be sung by a tenor an octave lower with fair results, even without adjustments.[21] By insisting on a totally new text, Mozart went to the heart of the matter that had led him astray in the first place. In the new text the emphasis is not on joy but on the mystery and wonder of love:

IL.	Spiegarti non poss'io	I cannot explain to you
	Quanto il mio cor t'adora;	How much my heart loves you;
	Ma il cor tacendo ancora	But the heart, even remaining silent,
	Potrà spiegarlo appien.	Can explain it fully.
ID.	Voci dell'idol mio	Words of my beloved,
	Ah che in udirvi io sento	Ah, in hearing them I feel
	D'insolito contento	An uncommon contentment
	Tutto inondarmi il sen.	Completely filling my breast.
IL.	Vita dell'alma mia,	Life of my soul,
ID.	Delizia del mio cor,	Delight of my heart,
IL., ID.	Non sa piacer che sia,	He knows not what is pleasure
	Non sa che sia diletto	And what is delight
	Chi non provò nel petto	Who has not felt in his breast
	Si fortunato amor.	Such a fortunate love.

Mozart chooses Larghetto in 4/4, a choice that is already significant. He uses the same lead-in from the Munich duet and an initial theme that uses the same melodic fall 5–3/4, harmonized similarly. But the new melody is simpler, less decorated with ornamental figures. At "cor tacendo ancora," which corresponds to the modu-

21. As demonstrated in the recording of Colin Davis, who inadvertently chose the wrong love duet for his tenor Idamante.

lation to the dominant, Mozart introduces the same V_3^4 chord he used before and the "Idamante motif" in the violins. The orchestra thus helps in explaining what Ilia's silent heart wishes to convey. A new, more elaborate figuration in the orchestra introduces Idamante in person: constant sixteenth notes in the second violins against a dotted rhythm in the firsts, an independent idea for the violas doubled an octave above by sustained oboes (Ex. 3.7). Against this music of great dignity Idamante enters the texture with a long held note on the first syllable of "Voci dell'idol mio," achieving the noble and elevated tone one expects to hear when a young hero contemplates his beloved.

There is a parallel dramatic situation, entailing musical parallels as well, in Mozart's earlier *Lucio Silla*, in the tomb scene at the end of act 1 when the hero, Cecilio, recognizes his beloved Giunia. There Mozart modulates to E-flat, nearly always a grave and expressive key in his operas (Ex. 3.8). He slows the tempo from Allegro assai to Andante, setting a stream of sixteenth-note motion going in the second violins against dotted figures beginning on the second beat in the first violins, imitated two beats later by the violas. The ultimate beneficiary of this "noble lover contemplates beloved" complex is Don Ottavio in the great sextet of *Don Giovanni*.[22]

Whereas the original love duet for Ilia and Idamante began earnestly and frittered away its intensity in an Allegretto in waltz time, the new duet begins even more in earnest and gains intensity up to its last bar. After Idamante makes his cadence on the tonic, Ilia replies with a short endearment, which he answers in kind. The sublime moment in which they join their voices together must be approaching, but if listeners are expecting no more than the chains of thirds and sixths heard in most Italian love duets, and in the original Munich duet, they are bound for disappointment. Mozart gives Idamante an expressive chromatic line, to which Ilia responds with a contrapuntal line of her own. The harmony is rich and subtle (Ex. 3.9). Note how the composer has layered on long, melodic sighs in the first violins, imitated by the seconds, against the most sustained line of all in the violas. The sustained viola line should in fact tell the careful listener where this passage comes from. If not, then the harmonic sequence cannot fail to. Mozart has made the core of his new duet out of the wondrous outpouring of Ilia in the Larghetto preceding the duet (see Fig. 4), a strategy betrayed by the identity of tempo (Larghetto 4/4) throughout the new duet.

His recomposition has everything that was in the original duet plus much more. It too has a passage in canonic imitation, at the beautiful line "non sa piacer che sia."[23] It even has a melisma for both singers alternately, against which the other

22. See Ex. 11.3 below.
23. Musically, this identical phrase appears in Mozart's setting of Metastasio's *Il re pastore*, a serenata he composed for Salzburg in 1775. Tamiri sings it in the aria "Se tu di me fa dono" (No. 11) to the words "perchè la colpa è mia." This aria, which is also in the key of A, offers another foretaste of *Idomeneo* in the conjunct falling fourths, with first note dotted and marked *fp* in mm. 25–27, 61–63, and 109–11. The aria is a simple rondo in one tempo.

EXAMPLE 3.7. *Idomeneo*, No. 20b

EXAMPLE 3.8. *Lucio Silla*, Act I, Scene 7, Recitative

EXAMPLE 3.9. *Idomeneo*, No. 20b

sustains a pedal on *diletto*. For the sweet-sounding chromatic rise in parallel thirds in the first duet, where Ilia and Idamante seem to be about as mature as the innocent-looking adolescents in Boucher's pastoral idylls, Mozart substitutes a unison chromatic rise in all the strings, with crescendo, lending an accent of force and physicality to this love scene, an accent that is anything but sweet, and certainly not juvenile.[24] He has, in sum, given the lovers music commensurate with the rest

24. See Ex. 12.1 below.

of their roles. It becomes credible that characters such as Ilia and Idamante in the recomposed duet have the maturity and heroic stamina to die for each other.

Critical voices have been raised from time to time at the views expressed here, saying in effect that Mozart could not possibly have found his way back to the *Idomeneo* style five years later, while in the midst of composing *Le nozze di Figaro*. We hope to have shown that he went out of his way to ground the second love duet in some of the most expressive music of his original score. What is true of the duet is equally true of the other added number, a new Scena con Rondo for Idamante (No. 10b), replacing the scene and aria for Arbace (No. 10a) at the beginning of act 2. Thus with a single stroke Mozart eliminated the weakest number in his Munich score and strengthened a main character who was in need of more forceful delineation. By giving the young hero an act-opening aria he increased the weight of the role, making him a more worthy partner for Ilia, who opens the other two acts with arias. He also, with the new Idamante aria in B-flat, provided a tonal and dramatic motivation for the mollifying of Ilia evident in her following aria in E-flat, "Se il padre perdei" (No. 11). Mozart entered the Scena con Rondo (K. 490) into his thematic catalog after the new duet (K. 489), and there is reason to believe they were composed in this order, very close together (both are dated 10 March 1786). The initial theme of the rondo, not surprisingly, resembles the initial theme of the duet.

The part of Arbace, counselor to Idomeneo, was created for one of the oldest singers of the Munich troupe in 1781, Domenico de' Panzachi, and for him Mozart had written correspondingly old-fashioned music. Most of the arias in *Idomeneo* are in the newer binary form, which is equivalent to sonata form without development, wherein the second stanza of the text is relegated to the second key area. But Arbace had opened act 2 with an aria in the older ternary form, cultivated by Mozart mainly in his Milanese operas of the early 1770s. He received another aria of this type in act 3, "Da colà ne fatti è scritto" (No. 22). Ternary form involves the use of binary form plus a contrasting middle section before the reprise; the second stanza is saved for this middle section, which meant in effect a good deal more text repetition in stretching the first stanza over both first and second key areas. These differences are summarized in Table 2 (pertaining to a major-mode aria or ensemble). Other examples of ternary aria forms in *Idomeneo* are "No, la morte" (No. 27a) for Idamante and the title role's "Torna la pace" (No. 30a). Both these pieces have middle sections contrasting in tempo and meter with the main sections—and both were cut before the premiere at Munich.

The new aria for Idamante allowed Mozart to introduce one of the latest fashions in arias into his score, the two-tempo rondo. He had written one for Belmonte in *Die Entführung*, but this is his first in one of his Italian operas. In form this type consists of an initial section in slow or moderate tempo, often of an elegiac nature, which is repeated after contrast, followed by a faster and more showy section for the second stanza, a section also repeated after contrast in most examples: i.e.,

TABLE 2.
Aria Forms

	Ternary					Binary			
Stanza	1	1	2	1	1	1	2	1	2
Music	A	B	C	A	B	A	B	A	B
Harmony	I	V	(vi)	I	I	I	V	I	I

A x A / B y B. As in Belmonte's rondo, the faster theme is related to the slower one in K. 490 so that, even with thematic transformation, the impression given is one of coming back over and over again to the same main idea, as in an instrumental rondo. Certain other characteristics belong to this aria type. The melodies very often take on gavotte characteristics, and concertante instruments are frequently added to increase the virtuosity and provide a foil for the solo voice.[25] This is the case with K. 490, which has an elaborate part for solo violin in concertante dialogue with Idamante—a treatment that seems only just, because in the next number Ilia is presented in concertante dialogue with four solo winds.

Mozart began his original act 2 with a dialogue between Arbace and Idomeneo in simple recitative (the correct eighteenth-century term for recitative accompanied by only the continuo instruments—harpsichord and solo cello). It begins in B-flat and proceeds to C, the key of the aria "Se il tuo duol" (No. 10a). Because the key of C was perhaps a little too strident to give Mozart enough affective color for setting the text of "Non temer, amato bene," sung to Ilia with many touching and tender verbal expressions, he chose instead the more delicate key of B-flat,[26] which also had the advantage of being associated with Idamante throughout the opera. Not only does he enter act 1, scene 2, with a chord on B-flat and sing his first aria, "Non ho colpa" (No. 2), in the same key (which is adumbrated already in the second section of Ilia's "Padre, germani" when she dotes on his image—thus there is a symbiotic relationship between them in tonal terms even before he appears in

---

25. Vitellia's rondo in *La clemenza di Tito*, "Non più di fiori" (No. 23), with concertante basset horn is perhaps the outstanding example. Fiordiligi's rondo in *Così fan tutte*, "Per pietà, ben mio" (No. 25), offers a lot of concertante writing for the winds.

26. Galeazzi says of B-flat, "It is a tender key, soft, sweet, effeminate, apt for expressing transports of love, charms, and graces" ("B♭ è un Tono tenero, molle, dolce, effeminato, atto ad esprimer trasporti d'amore, vezzi, e grazie"). These attributes are further strengthened when clarinets in B-flat are used, as in No. 10b. The key of C allowed only clarinets of the military type, pitched in C and very much more strident than clarinets in A, B-flat, or B natural (which Mozart requires for the two pieces in E, Nos. 15 and 19). Galeazzi emphasizes the brightness of C and contrasts it with its parallel minor, c. "C is a grandiose key, military, apt for expounding great events, serious, majestic, and noisy. Its minor is a tragic key, apt for expressing calamities, the deaths of heroes, and great actions, but sorrowful, funereal, and lugubrious" ("C'è un Tono grandioso, militare, atto ad esporre grandi avvenimenti, serio, maestoso, e di strepito. Il suo minore è un Tono Tragico, e atto ad esprimere grandi disavventure, morti di Eroi, ed azioni grandi, ma luttuose, funeste, e lugubri"); Galeazzi, *Elementi teoretico-pratici di musica*, pp. 293–94.

person), but he also enters the scene with his father (act 1, scene 10) to the same chord, and likewise act 3, scene 2.

Yet Mozart was not prepared to give up altogether an emphasis on the key of C at the beginning of act 2. Possibly he felt the need for it as a forecast and a balancing of the occurrence of this key toward the end of the act. The march for the embarkation (No. 14) is in C, and so in his original plan was the following sea idyll for chorus, "Placido è il mar" (No. 15)—before he changed his mind and substituted the rarefied and unexpected domain of four sharps, E major. Losing the concentration of C that the Arbace aria had given him at the beginning of act 2, Mozart made up for it by insisting on C in the Scena between Ilia and Idamante preceding the latter's rondo, an elaborate, orchestrally accompanied recitative (the proper eighteenth-century term for which was obbligato recitative; Ex. 3.10).

An angry Ilia complains about what she imagines to be a romance between Electra and Idamante, and she renounces him. Mozart reverts instinctively to the kind of musical contrast between rising triad and falling tritone that he invoked in his very early rage aria (see Ex. 3.1). Idamante deflects the expected cadence on C in bar 19 by entering to an Adagio in A-flat, with the falling conjunct fourth in the violins providing yet another transformation of "his" motive. (This entrance in A-flat is a wonderful stroke, because it sets up Idamante's final entrance in the opera as a whole [act 3, scene 9], in the funereal key of A-flat, Largo.) After some intervening dialogue between the lovers Mozart brings the music around to the key of g minor, that of Ilia's first aria, as Idamante sings the tender words "You were my first love and will be my last" (Ex. 3.11).[27] How fitting that he then concludes in B-flat at "l'ultimo sarai": once again the symbiotic relationship between them is made explicit.

Note also that the harmonic sequence is the same to which Ilia will finally declare her love at the beginning of act 3, to the words "t'amo, t'adoro" (Fig. 4). The foreshadowing is made even more memorable by having Idamante sing a falling third appoggiatura on *amore*. What follows is a tonal disjunction. Heroic D major, the keynote of the entire work, arrives out of nowhere, forte and Allegro assai, as Idamante says: "Let death come, I shall await it intrepidly." Now it is the young hero's tragic fate that is in question, and Mozart unerringly finds his way back to the music of the recognition scene between father and son in act 1. The climb up the triad of D, then the same on g minor, followed by another tonal disjunction, the soft arrival of the dominant seventh of E-flat—all this has been heard before, in act 1 (Ex. 3.12). With this music and its return we are at the very core of the

27. If these words are indeed by Da Ponte, he had a source of inspiration for them in Metastasio, whose original *La clemenza di Tito* includes this beautiful aria for Servilia in act 1, scene 7:

> Amo te solo
> te solo amai;
> tu fosti il primo
> tu pur sarai
> l'ultimo oggetto
> che adorerò.

EXAMPLE 3.10. *Idomeneo*, No. 10b

EXAMPLE 3.10, *continued*

tragedy. Mozart tells us as much, moreover, by drawing on it for the sweeps up to high D in his overture (mm. 23–27 and 115–20). No, Mozart's memory of *Idomeneo* and his instinct for musical tragedy were not weakened by the interval of five years, even though he was immersed in the creation of a sparkling comedy. He was, in fact, never deserted by his tragic muse.

EXAMPLE 3.11. *Idomeneo*, No. 10b

Ven– ga la mor–te, in – tre–pi–da l'at–ten– do,

EXAMPLE 3.12. *Idomeneo*, Act I, Scene 10, Recitative

IDAMANTE
è il pa – dre mi – o!

IDOMENEO *(da sè)*
(Spie – ta – tis – si – mi De – i!)

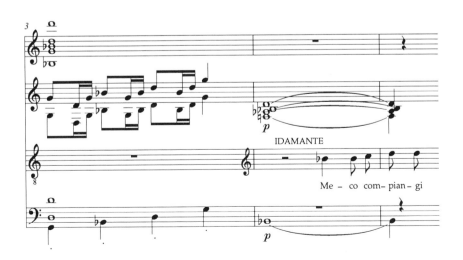

IDAMANTE
Me – co com– pian– gi

4 · COMING OF AGE IN VIENNA:
DIE ENTFÜHRUNG AUS
DEM SERAIL

by Thomas Bauman

The young Mozart who arrived at Vienna in the entourage of Archbishop Colloredo in March 1781 was not the same Mozart who witnessed the triumph of his first great Viennese opera, *Die Entführung aus dem Serail*, sixteen months later. Changes on all fronts challenged him, especially those that came in the wake of his dismissal from the archbishop's service and his betrothal to Constanze Weber, two events that placed greater strains than ever before on his relationship with his father.

Mozart's concern during his first months in the imperial capital was to establish a fruitful musical relationship with the Viennese. Performances of his music enjoyed much success, he was befriended by influential nobles such as the countess Thun, and the court took immediate notice of him with a request for a new German opera for the National Singspiel. Barely a month into his stay, he was already thinking of returning for the Lenten season in 1782: "It is up to you alone," he told Leopold, "not the archbishop—for if he won't allow it, I'll go anyway."[1] The city acted as a catalyst in emboldening Mozart to distance himself from Colloredo, little esteemed in Vienna and a sour employer who looked on Mozart's attempts to win recognition there as acts of insubordination. Mozart went so far as to propose that Leopold and Nannerl move to Vienna as well, in effect loosing the last of the ties binding him to his provincial birthplace.

With a combination of ingenuousness and cunning (to which he resorted on other occasions as well), Mozart prepared his father through his letters for his eventual dismissal from Colloredo's service. But when it finally came that May, Leopold's reaction was much more strongly negative than Mozart had anticipated. The young man defended his actions repeatedly to Leopold by turning the entire

---

1. "nur auf sie kömmt es an, nicht auf den Erzbischof — denn will er es nicht erlauben, so gehe ich doch, es ist mein unglück nicht, gewis nicht!"; letter of 28 April 1781.

affair into a point of honor. And when Leopold censured rather than seconded his motives, Mozart was stung: "I must confess to you that in not a single feature of your letter do I recognize my father!—A father, perhaps, but not the best, most loving one, concerned for his own honor and that of his children."[2]

High-minded protestations of wounded honor, however deeply felt, were not the only issue. Mozart's letters also reveal the break's deeper, traumatic effects on his self-esteem. What had galled him most in his confrontation with the archbishop was Colloredo's having called him a *Fex* (cretin), a vilification he repeated to Leopold on several occasions. For many months Mozart continued to sustain the deepest resentment against both Colloredo and Count Arco, who had done the honors in ejecting him from his employer's presence. Mozart described Arco's actions bluntly on 13 June: "He threw me out the door and gave me a kick in the rear. Now, in plain German that means that Salzburg isn't for me anymore, excepting only the opportunity of giving the count a kick in the rear in return, even if it should happen in the open street."[3] In his next letter, Mozart asked Leopold to take custody of a walking stick he had left at Salzburg,

> and carry it at the ready whenever possible. Who knows whether by your hand it can take revenge on Arco on behalf of its former master—of course, only accidentally or by chance, you understand. That hungry ass will not escape my palpable discourse, even if it takes twenty years—for to see him and to put my foot to his rear are assuredly one and the same.[4]

Four days later the form of retaliation had accrued interest: "He can expect without fail a foot in the rear from me, and a box or two on the ear for good measure. For when someone insults me, I must have my revenge; and if I do no more than he did to me, it is only retribution and no punishment."[5] A deep spiritual gulf separates the young man who wrote these words from the artist who shaped the high-minded conclusion of *The Abduction from the Seraglio* a year later.

2. "Ich muss ihnen gestehen, dass ich aus keinen einzigen Zuge ihres briefes, meinen vatter erkenne! — wohl einen vatter, aber nicht, den Besten, liebvollsten, den für seine eigene und für die Ehre seiner kinder besorgten vatter"; 19 May 1781.

3. "da schmeist er mich zur thüre hinaus, und giebt mir einen tritt im hintern. — Nun, das heisst auf teutsch, dass Salzburg nicht mehr für mich ist; ausgenommen mit guter gelegenheit dem H. grafen wieder ingleichen einen tritt im arsch zu geben, und sollte es auf öfentlicher gasse geschehen"; 13 June 1781.

4. "mithin bitte ich sie den stock mir zu liebe zu behalten. — man braucht hier stöcke, aber wozu? — zum spatzieren gehen, und dazu ist Jedes stöckchen gut; also stützen sie sich darauf anstatt meiner; und tragen sie ihn wenn es möglich beständig — wer weis ob er nicht durch ihre hand beym Arco seinen vormaligen herrn rächen kann. — doch das versteht sich accidentaliter oder zufälligerweise; — Mein handgreiflicher Discours bleibt dem hungrigen Esel nicht aus, und sollt es in zwanzig Jahren seyn. — denn, ihn sehen, und meinen fuss in seinem Arsch, ist gewis eins"; 16 June 1781.

5. "— zum schlusse aber muss ich ihm doch schriftlich versichern dass er gewis von mir einen fuss im arsch, und noch ein paar ohrfeigen zu gewarten hat; — denn, wenn mich einer beleidigt, so muß ich mich rächen; und thue ich nicht mehr als er mir angethan, so ist es nur wiedervergeltung und keine strafe nicht"; 20 June 1781.

"Salzburg isn't for me anymore." Sooner than expected, Mozart had cast his lot with the imperial city, and almost at once an anxiety to identify with Vienna and please Viennese ears took hold of him. "Ich kenne die Nation" ("I know the nation"), he claimed on 19 September, and by 3 November he was talking about "wir Wiener" ("we Viennese"). Further, Mozart foresaw right away that his reputation as a composer in Vienna would depend heavily on the opera sought from him by the court. The greatest corps of singers on any German stage were to perform it at the Burgtheater, Vienna's elite playhouse, physically as well as administratively an extension of the imperial court. The theater's elegant façade, dwarfed by the Imperial Riding School, was captured in an engraving of 1783 by Carl Schütz (Fig. 5).

Although only a child when he wrote his first opera for the Viennese (*La finta semplice*, composed at the age of twelve), Mozart no doubt retained memories of the cabals among Vienna's composers and singers, mainly Italian, that ultimately prevented its performance. The situation was more favorable in 1781. There was no Italian company of singers, only a wing of the National Theater devoted to opera in German. Eventually the charge of providing Mozart with a libretto had befallen the director of the German opera, or National Singspiel—Gottlieb Stephanie the Younger, a mediocre actor, competent playwright, and versatile adapter of texts for the German operatic stage. Ties of friendship bound Stephanie to the Mozarts from their earlier visits to Vienna, and despite a reputation for underhandedness he remained a warm supporter of Wolfgang's.

Mozart had only one serious rival among local composers for the German company—Ignaz Umlauf, who had set the enterprise's inaugural opera, *Die Bergknappen* (1778), and who served under Antonio Salieri as its musical director. Salieri himself had provided a lone opera in German for the National Singspiel, *Der Rauchfangkehrer*, which was given its premiere on 30 April 1781, shortly after Mozart's arrival in Vienna. It enjoyed a more than respectable total of thirteen performances before being dropped from the repertory with the appearance of *The Abduction* in July 1782. After completing the opera—possibly at the behest of the emperor—Salieri took no further interest in the German company.

In the summer of 1781 Stephanie had just finished adapting a libretto for Umlauf, *Das Irrlicht*, and when confronted with the task of providing Mozart with a text as well he turned to the same source—the Leipzig businessman Christoph Friedrich Bretzner, perhaps the most popular writer of German opera texts of the day. There is no evidence that Mozart had anything at all to do with the selection of the text, Bretzner's most recent libretto, *Belmont und Constanze, oder Die Entführung aus dem Serail*, performed earlier that year at Berlin with music by Johann André. Stephanie hoped that the festivities in honor of the projected visit in mid-September by the Russian grand duke Paul Petrovich and his wife, the duchess of Württemberg, would offer an advantageous occasion for him to set his friend Mozart's talents before the court. Mozart began composing hurriedly but then learned in late August that the visit had been delayed until the end of the year and in addition that

FIGURE 5

Schütz: The Michaelerplatz,
Vienna, in 1783; at right, the
Burgtheater

the court had decided to mark it with revivals of Gluck's *Iphigénie en Tauride* and *Alceste*. In the end, *The Abduction* had to wait until mid-July 1782, almost a year after its inception, to achieve its premiere with the National Singspiel. No other Mozart opera had such a lengthy gestation.

Without the delays occasioned by the Russian visitors and other factors, we would probably have in *The Abduction* today a much slighter work. Stephanie was a busy man at the time the project was hatched, and it is difficult to imagine that under such a pressing deadline he would have undertaken the significant poetic changes in Bretzner's libretto that Mozart eventually exacted from him. The more leisurely pace of composition gave Mozart an opportunity not only to create a more substantial opera, but also to write three important letters to his father in late September and early October—offering us a rare glimpse into his aesthetic of dramatic music at the time. These letters are so often quoted in the literature that we need only summarize them here.

Prior to the first, dated 26 September 1781, Mozart had sent Leopold excerpts of the overture and the numbers in act 1. In the letter, he describes the changes he and Stephanie had undertaken. The changes were motivated as much by concern for the singers of the roles involved—Johann Valentin Adamberger (Belmonte) and Ludwig Fischer (Osmin)—as by any dramatic need to develop these characters. Mozart describes an aria for each man ("Solche hergelauf'ne Laffen" for Fischer and "O wie ängstlich" for Adamberger) at a level of detail scarcely encountered elsewhere in his letters. When he mentions the various "Turkish" pieces he had completed so far—the overture, first Janissary chorus, and the drinking duet in act 2—he invariably makes mention of Viennese partiality for this style, a partiality that had received recent gratification at the Burgtheater with a revival of Gluck's *Die unvermuthete Zusammenkunft, oder Die Pilgrime von Mekka* (originally *La rencontre imprévue*).

From the same letter we also learn of Mozart's need to work quickly once he had set about an operatic project in earnest. In the next, written on 6 October, Mozart describes not only his continued impatience over Stephanie's slow labors on needed changes, but also the speed with which he had composed the first numbers:

> Now I shall soon lose patience, for I can compose nothing further for the opera.
> Granted that in the meantime I am writing other things, still, the passion is there,
> and for what would otherwise take me two weeks I would now need only four days.
> I composed the aria in A for Adamberger, the one for Cavalieri in B-flat, and the
> trio all in a single day—and wrote them out in another one and a half.[6]

6. "Nun verliere ich aber bald die gedult, dass ich nichts weiter ander opera schreiben kann. — ich schreibe freylich unterdessen andere sachen — Jedoch — die Passion ist einmal da — und zu was ich sonsten 14 Täge bräuchte würde nun 4 täge brauchen. — ich habe die aria ex A vom adamberger, die von der Cavallieri ex B, und das Terzett in einem Tage Componirt — und in anderthalb tägen geschrieben"; 6 October 1781.

In a letter (now lost) that Mozart received shortly thereafter, Leopold included some remarks criticizing the poetic texts of the excerpts his son had sent him. Mozart replied on 13 October with a measured defense of both Stephanie and Bretzner, but it is worth noting that in so doing he does not resort to even a hint of patriotic sensibilities about German opera (which he uttered freely at other times, for example on the demise of the National Singspiel). It was opera in the broadest sense that engaged him when, in the throes of creativity, he turned for a moment to aesthetic contemplation of his art. Indeed, there is more than a tinge of exasperation at the insularity of the two poets. Even good German librettists such as these, Mozart seems to imply, had a shaky sense of how to write for music. In Constanze's first aria he had had to change Bretzner's ungainly expression "doch im Hui" ("but in an instant") to "doch wie schnell" ("but how quickly"): "I don't know what our German poets are thinking about," he wrote to Leopold. "Even if they don't understand the theater as far as opera's demands are concerned, they at least ought not to have people speak as if pigs stood before them—'Hui, sow!'"[7]

Mozart's famous, seemingly counter-Gluckian dictum, "In an opera the poetry must at all costs be the obedient daughter of the music," was written in the context of this aria. Narrowly construed, the statement is about the relationship of poetic texts to the music that clothes them, not about the priority of music as the engine of dramatic power. Mozart points to the universal popularity of Italian comic operas despite their wretched librettos not to illustrate the irrelevancy of a well-planned drama to success in the genre, but rather to plead for an even better kind of opera in which the plot is skillfully worked out. He had already praised Bretzner's libretto and Stephanie's plays for their soundness of construction. What these men had yet to learn, in Mozart's view, was how to shed their poetic rules and achieve fluency and consistency in writing verses that helped rather than hampered the composer. Mozart even goes so far as to disparage the use of rhyme in musical verses: it is not heard in performance, to begin with, and it can lead the poet to words and images that hamstring the composer.

But the composer's control over the shape and tone of an opera was not absolute. Mozart's *Abduction* letters reveal the sway held by the leading singers in the National Singspiel troupe. Constanze's first aria was "sacrificed somewhat to the flexible throat of Mad:selle Cavalieri"; Belmonte's A-major aria in act 1, a personal favorite of Mozart's, was "written entirely for Adamberger's voice"; and the role of Osmin was expanded not for dramatic purposes but to take advantage of Ludwig Fischer's high standing with the Viennese public. If Mozart's comments in these letters are taken as his operatic aesthetic, it is an aesthetic that one cannot possibly

7. "das *hui* — habe ich in *schnell* verändert also: *doch wie schnell schwand meine freude* etc: ich weis nicht was sich unsere teutsche dichter denken; — wenn sie schon das theater nicht verstehen, was die opern anbelangt — so sollen sie doch wenigstens die leute nicht reden lassen, als wenn schweine vor ihnen stünden. — hui Sau; — "; 26 September 1781.

divorce from the practical realities of the first cast and first audience for which Mozart composed an opera.

In these letters Mozart deals almost exclusively with the first act, the least problematic of the three and the one left almost exactly as Bretzner had originally conceived it.[8] Bretzner's exposition, in fact, had worked perfectly to establish the main characters, which in the case of the National Singspiel meant the main singers: Adamberger, Cavalieri, and Fischer. As in *Idomeneo*, the first, expository act ends in the opera's keynote with trumpets and drums: "The conclusion will make quite a bit of noise—and that's really everything the close of an act should be. The more noise, the better; the shorter, the better—so that people don't grow too cool to clap."[9]

Later on, Mozart abandoned the three-act scheme found in both *Idomeneo* and *The Abduction* in favor of two- or four-act plans. The central pole around which these later dramas turn, an extensive finale of complication at the midpoint of the action, is missing in both earlier operas as well. *Idomeneo* belonged to a genre in which the finale had yet to gain currency. While in comic opera the Italians, and more lately the French, had made significant strides in developing multisectional, dramatically kinetic internal finales, German opera had only just begun similar explorations. For a composer like Mozart, then, finding a suitable means of bringing act 2 of *The Abduction* to a close posed some difficulty. When Bretzner had written *Belmont und Constanze* in 1780, he was as yet unpracticed in Italian ways. Although he did move far beyond northern norms in planning the abduction scene itself in the style of an opera buffa finale (even including a pantomime episode), he failed to put it where any competent Italian librettist would have placed it in a three-act plan—at the end of the second act. Instead he put it where logical plot development in a spoken drama suggested it be placed—in the middle of the third act. Mozart at first wanted this episode moved back to the end of act 2 (letter of 26 September), but that would wholly eviscerate act 3, and as his previous opera, *Idomeneo*, illustrates, Mozart was very far from regarding the last act as a throwaway. So he persuaded Stephanie to break the abduction scene down into prose and three arias, and to develop the quartet-finale we have today out of one of Bretzner's episodes in act 2.

As Mozart's later comic operas demonstrate, ensembles were essential to the creation of musical continuity in his art. In *The Abduction*, however, despite his and Stephanie's best efforts, dramatic weight could not be shifted onto such num-

---

8. Mozart asked for only two alterations from Stephanie — to change the brief opening monologue for Belmonte into a little aria, so the play might begin with music rather than speaking, and to refashion his first encounter with Osmin from dialogue to duet.

9. "und der schluss wird recht viel lärmen machen — und das ist Ja alles was zu seinem schluss von einem Ackt gehört — Je mehr lärmen, Je besser; — Je kürzer, Je besser — damit die leute zum klatschen nicht kalt werden. — "; 26 September 1781. By *schluss* Mozart refers to the final Allegro assai section in cut time, not to the entire trio, although in point of fact next to the Janissary chorus it is the shortest number in the first act.

bers to a sufficient degree. Bretzner had developed his plot well—too well, in fact. What the Viennese adapters of his drama were able to contrive here and there in the plan simply could not be sustained across entire acts, especially inasmuch as one of the principals, Pasha Selim, does not sing at all, and the chief dramatic event—the abduction—takes place with minimal musical aid. As a result, *The Abduction* remained, musically speaking, more a drama of character than one of situation. An early-nineteenth-century Viennese analyst of the opera fittingly chose to proceed through it character by character, rather than number by number as nearly all modern commentators do.[10] For the opera's first audiences as well, one suspects, it was the uniqueness and psychological depth of the individual portraits, set against a noisy background of "Turkish" music, that made the opera the one great success of the National Singspiel enterprise.

The idea that the music of an opera ought to strive for a distinctive voice, that it should somehow convey the character of the principal personages or conflicts, was not new to Vienna. In 1768, Joseph von Sonnenfels had invoked the term *characteristic* in celebrating Gluck's music to *Alceste*: "In my opinion I should like to call Gluck's style of composition the *characteristic* style, and to wish greatly that it might find as many followers among composers as it has won admirers among music lovers whose sensibility has not been spoilt by the sybaritic harmony of Italian music."[11] At the time he was working on *The Abduction*, Mozart uttered a damning opinion of the music to Umlauf's new opera, *Das Irrlicht*, for precisely the same reasons:

> He wrote it in one year; but you must not believe that it is good just because (between you and me) he spent an entire year on it. This opera (still between us) I should have taken for the work of fourteen or fifteen days. Especially since the man must have learned so many operas *by heart*! And then all he had to do was write them down—and that's surely the way he wrote it. Just listen to it![12]

10. This review, "*Die Entführung aus dem Serail*: Ein deutsches Singspiel in 3 Aufzügen," signed simply "F. Ungarese," first appeared in the *Zeitung für Theater, Musik und Poesie* 3 (1808): 361–65 on the occasion of a revival of Mozart's opera at Vienna. It was plagiarized virtually in toto in Georg Nikolaus von Nissen's *Biographie W. A. Mozarts*, ed. Constanze von Nissen (Leipzig, 1828), Anhang, pp. 77–85.

11. "Nach meiner Weise möchte ich die Setzart Glucks, die *charakteristische* nennen, und wohl sehr wünschen, daß sie unter den Tonkünstlern so viele Nachfolger fände, als sie sich unter den Liebhabern der Musik, deren Gefühl durch die sybaritische Harmonie der italiänischen Tonkunst nicht verwöhnt ist, Bewunderer erworben hat"; Joseph von Sonnenfels, *Briefe über die wienerische Schaubühne aus dem Französischen übersetzt* (Vienna, 1768), pp. 47–48.

12. "der umlauf muss auch mit seiner fertigen opera warten — die er in einem Jahre geschrieben hat; — sie dürfen aber nicht glauben, dass sie deswegen gut ist | : unter uns gesagt : | weil er ein ganzes Jahr dazu gebraucht hat — diese opera | : aber unter uns : | hätte ich immer für eine Arbeit von 14 bis 15 täge gehalten. — besonders da der Mann so vielle opern muss *auswendig* gelernt haben! — und da hat er sich Ja nichts als niedersetzen dürfen — und — er hat es gewis so gemacht — man hört es Ja!"; 6 October 1781. Ironically, the dilettante Zinzendorf passed a similar judgment on *The Abduction* after a performance on 30 July 1782: "opera dont la musique est pillée de differentes autres [auteurs?]" (Deutsch, *Dokumente*, p. 180).

Within the gallery of musical characterizations in *The Abduction*, Osmin has, perhaps not unjustly, loomed as the capital figure. So magnetic a personality has, inevitably, attracted attention to the opera's comic genius and away from the serious pole represented by the lovers. Without slighting the importance of Osmin as a watershed in Mozart's art, we shall turn our attention here to the serious pair of lovers, Belmonte and Constanze. It is with them that two major issues touching the opera can be addressed: the relationship of serious and comic style in Vienna at the time, and Mozart's involvement with refashioning Bretzner's dénouement.

During Mozart's first months in Vienna, he professed to have a fairly clear idea of how the Viennese distinguished comic and serious styles in opera:

> Do you think, then, that I would compose an opéra-comique in the same way as an opera seria? However little playfulness there should be in an opera seria, and however much of the learned and reasonable, just so little of the learned must there be in an opera buffa, and so much more of the playful and comic.
>
> I can't help it if in an opera seria people wish to have comic music as well; here, however, one distinguishes very clearly in this matter.[13]

Yet Mozart failed to follow his own advice when he set about composing *The Abduction* six weeks later. He had no doubt witnessed by then the mixture of serious and comic that characterized offerings at the Burgtheater during that period. Comedies, as one might expect, loomed large, in both the spoken and sung repertories. Yet the tragic muse was by no means out of fashion at Vienna during the 1780s, nor were pieces of mixed genre (Table 3). It is true that Joseph II harbored a well-known antipathy toward opera seria as boring, unnatural, and above all expensive, but he was easily persuaded to honor his Russian guests at the end of 1781 with new productions of Gluck's *Iphigénie en Tauride* (translated into German) and *Alceste* (done in the original Italian version). Indeed, their restrained, dignified style—"characteristic" rather than "sybaritic," to use Sonnenfels's terms—proved so popular that the court decided to revive *Orfeo ed Euridice* as well.

For the less expensive spoken stage, Joseph went to great lengths to secure the greatest tragic actors in Germany, such as Friedrich Ludwig Schröder and Johann Brockmann. In a memorandum to the directors of the theater issued on 8 February 1782, he ordered that a prize be offered for "the best and most faithful translations into Alexandrines of the foremost and finest authors, namely Corneille, Racine,

13. "— glauben sie denn ich werde eine Opera Comique auch so schreiben wie eine opera Seria? — so wenig tändelndes in einer opera seria seyn soll, und so viel gelehrtes und vernünftiges, so wenig gelehrtes muss in einer opera Buffa seyn, und um desto mehr tändelndes und lustiges.

"dass man in einer opera Seria auch kommische Mussick haben will, dafür kann ich nicht; — hier unterscheidet man aber in dieser sache sehr gut"; 16 June 1781. It is symptomatic of Mozart's cosmopolitanism, as well as of the stylistic eclecticism of *The Abduction*, that he uses French, Italian, and German designations for comic opera interchangeably in this passage ("Opera Comique," "opera Buffa," "kommische Mussick").

and Voltaire."[14] The tragedies actually performed by the National Theater were not of the French classical sort Joseph hoped to foster, but comprised original German works, several Austrian ones, and a large number of translations and adaptations from the English (including *Hamlet, King Lear, Richard the Third*, and *Romeo and Juliet*). The offerings also made room for serious genres such as the *drame* (called simply "Schauspiel" in German), the melodrama, and the dramatic ballet.

In assessing the imperial stage a few years later, Johann Pezzl remarked of local taste, "In general it seems that the German public has a greater appetite for variety than its neighbors."[15] A list of the most popular pieces at the Burgtheater during Mozart's first year in Vienna illustrates this point (Table 4). Noteworthy in this list is the popularity of opera relative to spoken works, a nearly universal state of affairs on German stages that mixed spoken and sung repertories. Also typical of the best German stages is the variety of types and styles: serious, sentimental, and comic works mixing Italian, French, and German traditions. For a young and ambitious composer, Vienna offered a perfect venue in which to attempt a work that drew on all of these.

The Colloredo episode had faded as Mozart began work on *The Abduction*, but soon another crisis arose to occupy its place. In early May 1781 Mozart had rented quarters from the Webers, and by midsummer Viennese gossip about his disporting with the three daughters had gotten back to Leopold, who ever since Mozart's infatuation with Aloysia Weber at Mannheim in 1778 had regarded the family with a mixture of suspicion and contempt. Mozart parried the reports Leopold had received with assurances that for him marriage represented a positive evil. Six months later he was writing precisely the opposite. Marriage was now exactly what he needed, and the only sane head in the Weber household, Constanze, was his chosen one. He made her out a martyr and asked his father's blessing on the match, "that I might rescue this poor one."

Not a single letter from Leopold to Mozart is preserved from this or any of his subsequent years in Vienna, but Wolfgang's responses leave no doubt that Leopold's earlier displeasure at his son's dismissal from Colloredo's service was but a mild prelude to his icy anger over the liaison with Constanze Weber. And although pressures from several quarters were urging an early marriage on Mozart—not the

14. The prize offered was not inconsiderable—fifty ducats and the receipts from the third performance: "dass man demjenigen 50 Ducaten samt der 3ten Einnahme übergeben wolle, welcher von den hier benannten französischen Trauerspielen von den ersten und besten Autoren nämlich von Corneille, Racine und Voltaire die beste und getreueste Übersetzung in alexandrinischen Versen einschicken wird"; *Joseph II als Theaterdirektor: Ungedruckte Briefe und Aktenstücke aus den Kinderjahren des Burgtheaters*, ed. Rudolf Payer von Thurn (Vienna, 1920), p. 28.

15. "Und überhaupt scheint das deutsche Publikum mehr Hunger nach Mannigfaltigkeit zu haben, als seine Nachbarn"; Johann Pezzl, *Skizze von Wien: Ein Kultur- und Sittenbild aus der josefinischen Zeit*, ed. Gustav Gugitz and Anton Schlossar (Graz, 1923). Pezzl observes that the British even after two hundred years have not tired of repeating Shakespeare's plays, nor have the French for nearly one hundred fifty years with the works of Corneille, Racine, and Molière. What can the Germans offer? They don't have enough good plays to fill even fourteen evenings.

least of them the notoriety the relationship gained among Viennese gossips—he waited until after the triumphant premiere of *The Abduction* had made his fortune with the Viennese secure to ask Leopold directly for his permission to marry Constanze.

After Mozart's announcement in December of his intention to wed, only scattered references—with a minimum of detail—indicate resumption of work on *The Abduction*. We find in the letters of early 1782 scarcely a trace of the earlier shoptalk

T A B L E 3.
National Theater and National Singspiel Performances
in the Burgtheater, January 1781–July 1782

Spoken Categories	Number of Performances	Musical Categories	Number of Performances
Comedies	273	Operas	153
Tragedies	62	Melodramas	4
Drames	44	Ballets	14

Source: Franz Hadamowsky, *Die Wiener Hoftheater (Staatstheater) 1776–1966, Teil 1: 1776–1810* (Vienna, 1966).

T A B L E 4.
Most Frequently Performed Works
at the Viennese National Theater, January 1781–July 1782

Title	Author-Composer	Original Category	Times Performed
Die eingebildeten Philosophen	Bertati-Paisiello	opera buffa	18
Der Rauchfangkehrer	Auenbrugger-Salieri	komische Oper	13
Iphigenie auf Tauris	Guillard-Gluck	tragédie lyrique	11
Das öffentliche Geheimniss	Gozzi	fiaba [fable]	11
Die unvermuthete Zusammenkunft	Dancourt-Gluck	opéra-comique	10
Zemire und Azor	Marmontel-Grétry	opéra-ballet	9
Alceste	Calzabigi-Gluck	tragedia per musica	7
Das Irrlicht	Bretzner-Umlauf	komische Oper	7
Die pücefarbnen Schuhe	Stephanie-Umlauf	komische Oper	7
Wahrheit ist gut Ding	Schletter	Lustspiel	7
Das Loch in der Thüre	Stephanie the Younger	Lustspiel	7
Monsieur Fips	Stephanie the Younger	Lustspiel	7
Die heimliche Heyrath	George Colman	comedy	7

Source: Franz Hadamowsky, *Die Wiener Hoftheater (Staatstheater) 1776–1966, Teil 1: 1776–1810* (Vienna, 1966).

that might illuminate such matters as the decision to add Cavalieri's controversial *aria di bravura* "Martern aller Arten" at the heart of the drama, to create a new finale for act 2, and to substitute a new dénouement at the end of act 3.

These changes demanded much more than a simple extension of the tone set in act 1. Belmonte, it is true, was already fully and completely drawn in his two arias, and the fact that one or the other of his further solo numbers in acts 2 and 3 is almost always omitted suggests how little they contribute to filling out his character. Constanze was another matter. Her first aria in act 1 (No. 6, "Ach, ich liebte") establishes her voice more clearly than her emotional nature, as Mozart himself half admitted in describing it as an "Italian bravura aria" written for Cavalieri's "flexible throat." Like many numbers in the opera, it follows a slow-fast pattern, but here the first part of the text, initially set to the rather short-breathed principal theme of the Adagio, comes back in the midst of the turmoil of the Allegro, minimizing its potential for emotional depth ("Ah, I loved, was so happy, and did not know love's pain!").

In her two demanding arias sung back to back in act 2 (Nos. 10 and 11), Constanze comes into clearer focus, and in stronger colors. The sorrow (*Kummer*) present only in the text of her earlier aria informs every feature of both "Traurigkeit" itself, one of the high points in Mozart's life-long association with the profound pathos of g minor, and the obbligato recitative Mozart had Stephanie write as preparation for it. With this recitative a new tone enters the opera: for the first time we hear unmistakable accents of Mozart's seria style. The recitative's drooping pairs of slurred seconds become the chief ingredient of the aria that follows. Here Mozart achieves marvels of flexibility in phrasing, and he also enriches the orchestra's role considerably, especially in his writing for the winds (including two basset horns). Scarcely has the glow of this portrait of deepest sorrow subsided when "Martern aller Arten," in a burst of C major, reveals to Selim's astonishment—and ours—an unsuspected dimension to Constanze's personality.[16] The pasha's words on Constanze's exit offer a clue to what Mozart and Stephanie may have meant to convey with this controversial aria, bearing in mind that the entire episode—prose and poetry—was added expressly to accommodate this final tour de force for Cavalieri:

> "Is this a dream? Where has she suddenly gotten the courage to behave so toward me? Does she perhaps hope to escape from me? Ha! That I shall guard against! (He starts to leave.) But that can't be it, for then she would dissemble, try to lull me to sleep. —Yes! It is despair!"

After a well-earned rest, Constanze will need every bit of this bravura born of despair in her next two musical numbers, both of them ensembles that focus on

---

16. The point touched on briefly here is developed further in my study *W. A. Mozart: "Die Entführung aus dem Serail"* (Cambridge, 1987), pp. 77–85.

Catarina Cavalieri   *Valent: Adamberger*

FIGURE 6

The first Constanze and Belmonte

her relationship with Belmonte. To judge from contemporary profiles in silhouette of the two original singers, she cut a figure at least as imposing as his (Fig. 6).

The first of these ensembles represents the most substantial expenditure of poetic energy that Mozart demanded from Stephanie—the new quartet-finale for act 2. Stephanie took a passing prose episode in Bretzner's version, in which jealous suspicions about the women's behavior during their captivity momentarily seize Belmonte and Pedrillo, and expanded it into a miniature drama of doubt, protestation, regret, and forgiveness. Like more extensive finales, this one involves both serious and comic characters, and in consequence the resolution of the conflict demanded a mixture of light and shade (Blonde's box on the ear in reply to Pedrillo and Constanze's dignified incomprehension in the face of Belmonte's jealous doubts) as yet unheard of in the opera. The admixture makes possible the amalgamation of the sublime and humane heard in the glorious Andantino, "Wenn unsrer Ehre wegen"—a transfigured recomposition of "Placido è il mar" in *Idomeneo*, hearing which we catch a first intimation of the hymnic humanism that pervades *The Magic Flute*.

Ehre (honor) is the byword of the lovers' moral, and so too of Mozart's fluctuating world during his first year in Vienna. On 16 May 1781 he had summed up his goals in Vienna in a letter to Leopold: "Honor, fame, and money" ("Ehre, Ruhm und Geld"). Under Count Arco's foot, however, the first of these suffered a stinging blow that engendered the dark thoughts of revenge discussed earlier. This state of mind remained with Mozart even after he had begun work on *The Abduction*. A week into the new project he related to Leopold a story that was all the talk in Vienna, where it was known as "die tyroller geschichte" ("the Tyrolean story"). An acquaintance from Mozart's Munich days, a nobleman named Wiedmer, had organized a theatrical company, which he had taken to Innsbruck. A certain Baron Buffa insulted Wiedmer there on a public street, and to such a degree that the impresario answered him with a blow to the head. Wiedmer was arrested, taken to the local house of correction, and beaten so severely that he remained bedridden for three weeks. Mozart, who seldom retailed such stories in his letters to Leopold,[17] took a keen interest in the poor man's cause:

> If I were Wiedmer, I would demand the following satisfaction from the emperor. He [Buffa] would have to be given fifty [blows] in the same location, and I would have to be present—and then he would have to give me 6,000 ducats. And if I could not attain this satisfaction, then I would not want any, but rather on the next available occasion I would stick my dagger through his heart.[18]

Over the next eight months this unhappy obsession with revenge, born of his own experiences, was somehow exorcised. Perhaps he was able to externalize it in his opera through the classical dramatic avenue of making vice laughable, that is, by way of the very incarnation of rage, Osmin. Yet *Ehre* lies beyond the surly old overseer's sphere. It belongs rather to Belmonte and to Pasha Selim, and nowhere more clearly than in their grand confrontation after the failure of the abduction attempt in act 3.

Bretzner had conceived this final scene as follows. Brought before the pasha, Belmonte and Constanze vie for the privilege of dying for the other's sake. Selim assures them with icy sarcasm that they will both have their wish. He is almost moved by their rapturous duet on the prospects of expiring in each other's arms, but the arrival of Pedrillo and Blonde rekindles his anger, and he orders all four strangled. As the sentence is about to be carried out, Constanze utters Belmonte's name. Astonished, Selim quickly discovers that Belmonte is his own son, left in a Spanish monastery when only four years old. Over Osmin's protestations, all four are freed in a scene of tearful reunion.

17. Less than a year earlier, however, in the postscript to a letter of 30 December 1780, Mozart passed on the rumor (false, as it turned out) about how the great castrato Marchesi had been forced to take poison at Naples by henchmen of a rival for the affections of the duchess. Like the letter under discussion here, this one also contains Mozart's thoughts on how he, were he in the same situation, would try to extract a Mosaic eye for an eye: "but since [Marchesi] was an Italian coward, he died *alone* and let his murderers live in peace and quiet. I would at the very least (in my room!) have taken a couple of them into the next world with me, if it were really a question of having to die" ("weil er aber ein Welscher hasenfuss war, so starb er *allein* — und liess seine herr Mörder in Ruhe und frieden leben — ich hätte wenigstens | : — in meinem Zimmer! : | ein paar mit mir in die andere Welt genommen, wenn es schon gestorben hätte seyn müssen").

18. "— wenn ich *Wiedmer* wäre, ich würde von kayser folgende Satisfaction ver = langen. — er müste auf den Nämlichen Platz 50 aushalten, und ich müsste dabey seyn — und dann müsste er mir erst noch 6000 duckatten geben. — und könnte ich diese Satisfaction nicht erlangen, so wollte ich gar keine, sondern stechte ihn mit der nächsten, besten gelegenheit den degen durch das herz"; 8 August 1781.

Stephanie and Mozart decided to make several changes in this plan. At the moment of confrontation, the pasha discovers not his long-lost son, but the son of his worst enemy, the man who brought about his ruin and forced him to leave Spain. Initially, Selim determines to deal with Belmonte just as the young man's father had dealt with Selim. He and Osmin leave to contemplate appropriate tortures for the hapless pair, who in turn are left alone onstage to sing the new recitative and duet that Stephanie and Mozart created for them (No. 20). When Selim returns, he has mastered his thirst for revenge; in a final act of austere magnanimity he forgives and releases the lovers.

Johann Schink, who witnessed the premiere of *The Abduction from the Seraglio*, complained that the substituted scene, though nobler than Bretzner's, was also "incomparably more unnatural."[19] By his own admission, Schink was evaluating the work mainly as a spoken drama, and from this perspective the charge carries some merit, particularly since Selim's ruminations remain his private affair, carried on offstage. The lovers and what they sing dominate the scene, not Selim and what he speaks. This primacy of the serious pair's final emotional development in the opera would have been impossible had Bretzner's duet been retained. Indeed, Schink's complaint notwithstanding, what Stephanie asks Belmonte and Constanze to sing to each other alone onstage is psychologically much more "natural" than what Bretzner's lovers sing in the presence of the pasha. Bretzner sketches two lovers sinking into their grave smiling and embracing, anticipating the joy and bliss of wandering Elysium's peaceful fields hand in hand. Stephanie presents the Belmonte we have been seeing throughout the opera: a mixture of anxiety and ardor in act 1, passionate and yet weakened by jealous fears in act 2. Now, at the crux of the drama, Belmonte torments himself with the realization that he has brought about Constanze's destruction. She, however, uses the inner strength she had shown us in act 2 to calm his troubled soul with a higher vision: he is to die for her sake—should she not also die with him? Their only aim, they realize, was to live for each other; for one to live without the other would be endless pain. And so they welcome their common fate.

The principal virtue of Stephanie's text lies in the fact that what was the point of departure for Bretzner's duet has been made the psychological goal achieved by Belmonte and Constanze only in the closing section of their recitative and duet. This must have been Mozart's doing. He had already taken an active role in asking for every other change or addition made to the opera's poetic texts,[20] and the se-

---

19. Johann Friedrich Schink, "*Die Entführung aus dem Serail*: Komische Oper in drei Aufzügen, von Brezner, die Musik von Mozart," in *Dramaturgische Fragmente* (Graz, 1782), 4:1002. Schink adds that this sort of gesture is still common coin in Vienna, although out of fashion nearly everywhere else. The entire review is reprinted in Deutsch, *Dokumente*, pp. 185–86.

20. In a letter of 26 September 1781 to Leopold, Mozart relates how he and Stephanie wrote Osmin's aria, "Solche hergelauf'ne Laffen": "— die aria hab ich dem H: Stephani ganz angegeben; — und die hauptsache der Musick davon war schon fertig, ehe Stephani ein Wort davon wuste." Dent (*Mozart's Operas*, p. 73) translates as follows: "I have given Herr Stephanie the aria complete, and most of the music was ready before he knew a word about it." So translated, the passage seems to imply that Mozart

Plan of No. 20, Recitative and Duet in *Die Entführung*

	Recitative	Andante (3/4)		Allegro (C)		
lines:	1–12	13–24	13–24	25–30	31–35	31–35
sections:		A$_1$	A$_2$	B	C$_1$	C$_2$
keys:	F (E♭) →	B♭ F (B♭)	E♭ F →	B♭		
			(V)			

quence of affects that Stephanie's text provides here fits precisely the musical structure Mozart employed in the recitative and duet (Table 5).

The recitative explores the dominant and subdominant by way of preparation for the main tonality of B-flat. This arrives with the Andante, patterned like a cavatina but without recapitulation or tonal closure in the tonic. The first half moves to the dominant, as one would expect; the second, however, skirts the tonic and settles instead into E-flat, followed by a broad preparatory passage on F. Reasserting B-flat is the task of the concluding Allegro, especially in the characteristic enhanced repetition of the cadenzalike setting of the final stanza (C$_1$ C$_2$). Stephanie's text is tailored precisely to this scheme. Belmonte's anguish and Constanze's calm resolve fall into the two main tonalities of the recitative. The same emotions (and tonalities) mark the Andante. It is only in the closing Allegro that the lovers' resolve to face death together is at last anchored in the tonic. Belmonte and Constanze finish this duet a matured, calmly heroic pair and thus, by the canons of opera seria, worthy objects of the clemency Selim bestows on them.

Mozart lavished the opera's noblest music on this recitative and duet. It bears a strong kinship not only with the seria features heard earlier in *The Abduction*, but also with motifs explored in Mozart's greatest achievement in serious opera, *Idomeneo*. The opening recitative complements the equally beautiful obbligato recitative preceding Constanze's g-minor aria, "Traurigkeit." Both move at a dignified Adagio pace and open with a bare sixth suggestive at once of the agitation proper to such numbers in serious opera. Perhaps most striking is Mozart's use of the same

---

handed Stephanie his music for the aria, and the poet then concocted a text to put under it as best he could. Emily Anderson (*The Letters of Mozart and His Family*, rev. ed. [London, 1985], pp. 768–69), with characteristic freedom, comes much closer to its more probable meaning with a different interpretation: "I have explained to Stephanie the words I require for the aria—indeed I had finished composing most of the music for it before Stephanie knew anything whatever about it." Both translations take liberties with Mozart's verb *angeben*. Especially when accompanied by *ganz*, *angegeben* is best rendered as "specified." A careful, if not entirely elegant, translation ought to read: "I have given Stephanie complete specifications for the aria—and the substance of the music for it was already finished before Stephanie knew a word about it." On this reading, and taking the order of the two clauses into account, the letter implies that Mozart first provided Stephanie with a detailed outline of the text—its content, its stanzaic structure, and probably its metric characteristics as well—and then proceeded to finish (that is, write down) the music while Stephanie set about writing a text to Mozart's specifications.

rising four-bar chromatic bass line in each, linking Belmonte's "Pein" with Constanze's "Leiden" (Ex. 4.1A–B). Both these passages point toward the same elemental tonality: d minor, Mozart's key of death. The deceptive cadence that evades this goal in Ex. 4.1A introduces Constanze's resolute, calming presence in response to

EXAMPLE 4.1A–B.

A: *Entführung*, No. 20, Recitative

B: *Entführung*, No. 10

Belmonte's pained self-reproach. In the passage following this example, the plunging seventh outlined by the violins at the start of the recitative disappears, and sustained chords in the strings move to the ethereal comfort that an entire century of opera had invested in E-flat major. "Engelsseele!" sings Belmonte in response to his beloved, his plunging figure now softened momentarily in Constanze's key of superlunary consolation.

A similar pattern recurs in the Andante. Momentarily, Belmonte gathers courage, and a heroic strain from seria traditions links him to the young protagonist of *Idomeneo*. "Meinetwegen," Belmonte's incipit, recalls note for note Idamante's act 1 cry: "Non ho colpa!" (Ex. 4.2A–B).[21] But then he relapses. In the continuation of this passage, a hint of the b-flat minor heard at the end of the recitative reasserts itself as Belmonte picks his way toward a hesitant dominant over an agitated tremolo in the strings. Again Constanze dispenses calm; an anticipatory A-flat in the first violins smooths the way into the rich harmonic terrain of D-flat and the sinking chromaticism that follows (Ex. 4.3). Not only is the chromatic language another echo of *Idomeneo*, but the specific harmonic relationship between Belmonte and Constanze had seen use in the original version of the A-major duet for Idamante and Ilia (No. 20a, "S'io non moro a questi accenti"): Idamante's opening statement moves tentatively onto the dominant, Ilia's reply ("No more sorrow, no more laments!") redirects things to flat III (C major) by way of the parallel tonic minor.[22] Stephanie gave Mozart much more room to maneuver than had Varesco, and precisely by departing from Bretzner so as to give the two lovers contrasting sentiments. After her consolatory turn to D-flat, Constanze takes up Belmonte's agitation figure, with which he had reproached himself, and gives it a firmer pur-

21. The texts, of course, mean precisely opposite things: "Because of me [you are to die]," sings Belmonte; "I am guiltless!" Idamante protests. But the purpose of the lapidarian seria gesture common to both is to convey conviction in the singer's mind of the truth of what he sings. The contrast, if one is needed, ought to be drawn between Belmonte's assertive statement here and the mixture of hope and fear that informs both of his act 1 arias.

22. See pp. 47–49 for the complete text of the duet and a discussion of Mozart's fondness for this progression.

EXAMPLE 4.2A–B.

A: *Entführung*, No. 20, Duet

B: *Idomeneo*, No. 2

EXAMPLE 4.3. *Entführung*, No. 20, Duet

pose—to drive home her determination to die with him, capped by a definitive arrival in the dominant.

The clarinets emerge with a sweet anticipation of the lovers' joining together in thirds, at the same time recalling the tender figure with which the orchestra had helped Constanze plead her case to Pasha Selim in "Martern aller Arten" (Ex. 4.4A–B).[23] When the lovers at last accelerate into the duet's final Allegro, another reminiscence of *Idomeneo* appears. "Ich will alles gerne leiden" ("I will suffer everything gladly"), the lovers sing in a triumphant dissipation of the anguish that had beset Belmonte at the beginning of the recitative (Ex. 4.5A). Mozart had availed himself of the same stable motif to anticipate the words "Soggiorno amoroso" in Ilia's aria "Se il padre perdei" in *Idomeneo* (Ex. 4.5B).

Mozart's operas, we are beginning to perceive, speak to each other in uncanny ways, each reacting to and building on its predecessors. At times they also seem to resonate with Mozart's own life experiences. The mood of the recitative and duet for Belmonte and Constanze, for instance, offers a close artistic analogue to the composer's own situation at the time it was composed. The number must have been conceived and written very late in the compositional process. The text in the original printed libretto was apparently thrown together in some haste; an entire stanza in the opening recitative is missing, and elsewhere it does not agree with Mozart's autograph in several particulars. From Mozart's letters we can deduce that the duet was probably written between 7 May 1782, when he played the completed second act of the opera for Countess Thun, and 30 May, when he played her the third act and had already begun correcting parts for the first rehearsal, set for a few days later.

These were difficult times. Leopold had not softened in his attitude toward Wolfgang's prospective bride. Constanze's mother and her guardian, Thorwaldt, had been making life miserable for the young couple. At the end of April, Mozart and Constanze had suffered a falling out occasioned by his jealous reaction to her allowing a young dandy to measure her calves during a game of forfeits. Now, however, they were fully committed to marrying as soon as practicable, especially since Vienna was beginning to regard them as already married. Each was estranged from his or her lone surviving parent—Constanze was in fact soon to leave her mother and take lodgings with the baroness von Waldstätten.

The parallel with the young couple onstage might not have been as striking had Mozart retained both the duet and the dénouement of Bretzner's version, where the lovers sing their blissful acceptance of the fate awaiting them in front of the man who turns out to be Belmonte's own father. Instead, Mozart and Stephanie cleared the stage of everyone but the two beleaguered lovers, that Belmonte and

23. In his memorandum of 8 February 1782, Joseph II had taken steps to engage two virtuosos of the instrument, the Stadler brothers Anton and Johann, as clarinetists in the National Singspiel's orchestra. Mozart took full advantage of their talents, particularly in the penultimate numbers of each act—all three for the serious lovers, and all three in B-flat. See Payer von Thurn, *Joseph II als Theaterdirektor*, p. 30.

EXAMPLE 4.4A–B.

A: *Entführung*, No. 20, Duet

B: *Entführung*, No. 11

EXAMPLE 4.5A–B.

A: *Entführung*, No. 20, Duet

B: *Idomeneo*, No. 11

Constanze might come to grips with their difficult situation and arrive at a common resolve alone.

The Mozart who composed this duet had suffered much in the year leading up to its creation, as had the lovers it portrays. But there is another, even deeper parallel: he had also embarked on a journey that had taken him beyond obsession with revenge on those who had wronged him a year earlier. And yet the power this emotion holds had not been forgotten. Instead, it was channeled into Osmin. This consummate musical personality among all of Mozart's operatic creations to date was drawn, we suggest, not by a simple observer of human nature, but by a participant in all its guises. At the same time, Osmin, unlike his creator, cannot free himself of its toils, and in the end even the frame of the vaudeville breaks down under his remorseless hunger for revenge. Spiritually, Osmin remains exactly who he was at the beginning of the opera, a fact fittingly captured in the return of his a-minor tirade, "Erst geköpft, dann gehangen." In the aftermath of this final storm, the lovers turn from their earlier conventional expressions of gratitude to the real moral of the story: "Nothing is as hateful as revenge."

In Carl Maria von Weber's opinion, with *The Abduction from the Seraglio* Mozart's artistic powers came of age.[24] If so, this fact appears most clearly in the composer's ability to identify not simply with his main characters, but with each of the personalities that shape the opera's course. Like all Mozart's operas, *The Abduction* was a child of circumstance, beholden to the conditions under which it was created for its virtues as much as for its shortcomings. Those circumstances should not exclude the parallel emotional coming of age Mozart experienced in his first sixteen months in Vienna. At the midpoint of this period, on 23 October 1781, he wrote the last of his letters to his cousin Maria Anna Thekla Mozart. Unlike the notorious earlier "Bäsle" letters, it is serious and circumspect, without so much as a trace of off-color juvenilia. One passage in particular can be seen in retrospect as a summation of Mozart's first, turbulent months in the imperial capital: "In the meantime, as you probably know, many important things have happened to me, which have given me not a little to think about, and much vexation, sorrow, and care."[25]

---

24. *Sämtliche Schriften von Carl Maria von Weber*, ed. Georg Kaiser (Berlin, 1908), p. 303. Weber published his discussion of *The Abduction* in conjunction with a production of the opera under his direction mounted by the Dresden Royal Court Theater in June 1818. An English translation of Weber's article appears in Carl Maria von Weber, *Writings on Music*, trans. Martin Cooper, ed. John Warrack (Cambridge, 1981), pp. 264–65.

25. "Es sind unterdessen, wie sie wohl wissen werden, vielle wichtige sachen mit mir vorgegangen, wobey ich nicht wenig zu denken, und vielle verdrüsslichkeiten, ärgernüss, kummer und Sorge hatte."

5 · THE POET AS STAGE DIRECTOR: METASTASIO, GOLDONI, AND DA PONTE

D omenico Guardasoni, we are told, staged the first production of *Don Giovanni*.[1] He was co-manager of the Nostitz Theater at Prague, along with Pasquale Bondini, when the opera had its premiere there on 29 October 1787. The claim on behalf of Guardasoni is contradicted by what Da Ponte says in his memoirs about his Prague sojourn (he arrived at the latest on 8 October): "I spent eight days there directing the actors who were to create it."[2] Da Ponte had to hurry back to Vienna because another premiere was impending at the Burgtheater, where his official duties lay. He made his quick trip to Prague precisely in order to stage *Don Giovanni* and put any finishing touches needed on its libretto. The purpose of this essay is to confirm that, under normal conditions, the poet—not the manager, the composer, or anyone else—was expected to direct stage movement.[3]

Pietro Metastasio began writing poetry at an early age. By the time he was fourteen he had written a tragedy in verse, *Giustino* (Rome, 1712). His stage works intended for musical setting began with the serenata *Angelica e Medoro* (Naples, 1720) to celebrate the birthday of the Habsburg emperor, Charles VI. He wrote his first opera seria, *Didone abbandonata*, for the Carnival season of 1724 in Naples, a city then under Austrian rule. By 1730 he had written six more full-length librettos for serious operas on commission from the theaters of Naples, Rome, and Venice. His triumphal conquest of Italian stages led to his appointment as imperial poet to the Viennese court in 1730, in succession to Apostolo Zeno. Metastasio's relation-

---

1. *Mozart's "Don Giovanni" in Prague*, Divadelní ústav [Theater Institute], no. 334 (Prague, 1987).
2. See note 20 below for the original Italian text.
3. Winton Dean, writing about a late seventeenth-century context, says that the role of stage director was regularly assumed by the librettist; see his review of William C. Holmes, *"La Statira" by Pietro Ottoboni and Alessandro Scarlatti* (New York, 1983), in *Music and Letters* 66 (1985): 165. See also Winton Dean and John Merrill Knapp, *Handel's Operas, 1704–1726* (Oxford, 1987), p. 23.

ships to the stage are documented repeatedly in his much-admired letters, which are brimming with ideas about stagecraft.[4]

During his earlier years the poet entered into the practical matters of staging with gusto. His letter of 11 January 1732 from Vienna to his Roman friend the singer Marianna Bulgarelli shows that he controlled not only stage movement but the placement of such stage properties as thrones and chairs:

> I have thought much about sending you a sheet of stage directions [*foglio di direzione*] concerning my *Demetrio*, but examining the opera, it seems to me a thing so lacking in intricacy that I should wrong us both by seeking to instruct you. The sole scene that is a little complicated as to where the characters are located is the scene by the port in the first act, when the queen is about to choose [a husband] and encounters Alceste [act 1, scene 8]. In this scene the throne ought to stand, as usual, on the right; and beside it there should be four seats or cushions "alla barbara," that is to say, two on each side; these serve for the grandees of the realm. Two other similar seats ought to be situated facing the throne, on the side of the second harpsichord [i.e., on the right, facing the stage] but as close to the orchestra as possible. And near these there are three more similar seats for Fenicio, Olinto, and Alceste. Thus the seats in all should number nine, six for the grandees and three for the personages cited. Those for the former can be attached by twos for more convenience; but the musicians ought to have each his own [i.e., the supposed shepherd Alceste et al.]. If you observe the layout I gave you, which can be understood still better from the drawing I am enclosing [it does not survive], you will find that all the rest goes well.

Having begun his paragraph by saying that no instructions were necessary, and ending it by implying no more would be forthcoming, Metastasio proceeds to provide further counsel:

> The other scene that is not easy to act is that of the chairs in act 2 between Cleonice and Alceste; they ought to sit down after the line "Io gelo e tremo. —Io mi consolo e spero" [act 2, scene 12; the libretto indicates "siede"]. Alceste should get up after the line: "So che non m'ami, e lo conosco assai"; and Cleonice does the same at the line: "Deh non partir ancor!" They both return to sitting at the line: "Non condannarmi ancor. M'ascolta e siedi." Cleonice commences to weep at the line: "Va: cediamo al destin"; and when she arrives at the words "Anima mia" she should be unable to say more that is not interspersed with tears, and with this interruption and suffering the recitative should end. Alceste gets up from his seat and kneels at the line: "Perdono, anima bella, oh Dio, perdono!" and then both get up at the lines: "Sorgi, parti, s'è vero —Ch'ami la mia virtù." This is the disposition I observed, and I saw bears weeping. You do the same.

4. Metastasio's correspondence is found in *Tutte le opere di Pietro Metastasio*, ed. Bruno Brunelli, 5 vols. (Milan, 1943–54). Volume 3 contains his letters, in chronological order. The translation here, and throughout this essay, is our own, unless otherwise indicated. Useful for the period flavor of the English translation is Charles Burney's *Memoirs of the Life and Writings of the Abate Metastasio in Which Are Incorporated Translations of His Principal Letters*, 3 vols. (London, 1796; facsimile reprint: New York, 1971). Burney omits passages without indication.

As in French classical tragedy, Metastasio's main model, the stage picture in his operas was minimal. It consisted almost entirely of human beings confronting each other in the throes of strong emotions. All the more important in the restrained style of acting that he approved was that every movement, such as standing, sitting, or kneeling, should be in precisely the right place. And the goal was very much the same with Metastasio in Vienna as Voltaire in Paris: to make the audience weep.

Not long after his first letter on staging *Demetrio* to his friend in Rome, Metastasio sent a second, dated 19 January 1732. Meanwhile he had heard from her how a new Roman production of *Didone abbandonata* had failed. Reacting to the bad news he worries that the same fate will befall *Demetrio*, "which is precarious to attempt, because it depends more on acting than on surprising decorations." In this same letter he enclosed several practical remarks on the sets required by *Issipile*, advice that shows him taking a leading role in the design of his operas:

> The second decor for the first act, which returns as the first of the second act, and must of necessity be the same, should represent a grove of practicable trees since more than one person must hide there. In the second decor of the second act the military tents are located only on the first harpsichord part of the stage and not elsewhere. In the last decor of the third act you should know that the principal ship comes far forward, so that it is as close to the side of the first harpsichord as possible, and that it be made easy for two people to converse on the stern. The rest is clear enough from the enclosed sheet [which does not survive].

Metastasio was not loath to instruct composers, as well as scene designers and actors. He wrote a famous letter in 1749 to Johann Adolph Hasse, Capellmeister at Dresden and generally regarded as the greatest master of Italian opera at the time, in which he spells out how Hasse should set *Attilio Regolo*, down to the specifics of which speeches were to be set in simple recitative and which warranted a more elaborate setting with orchestral accompaniment. In other words, he wished to exert the kind of total control over all aspects of opera that is associated with much later figures, such as Wagner. In answer to another theater poet, Giovanni Claudio Pasquini, who wanted help with staging *Demofoonte* at Dresden, he wrote a letter on 10 February 1748 describing the staging plan he employed in Vienna. Burney omitted this letter, which diagrams the location of the characters throughout the opera (Table 6).

Once again, striking is the simplicity with which the poet regulated his dramas, the skill with which, for instance, he builds the climax in act 3 by gradually increasing the number of characters from the solo scene of Creusa (scene 8) until the *scena ultima*. In conclusion he wrote:

> This is the manner in which I ordered the characters' places in the imperial theater. Sometimes, by necessity of the drama, the more exalted character is on the left, but that does not produce the slightest inconvenience. In the first place, the right side is not the most honorable with all nations; and then, even if it were, it takes only one step forward to make a character on the left more distinguished.

TABLE 6.
Metastasio's Staging Plan for *Demofoonte*

Atto Primo

Destra		Sinistra
	Scena I.	
Matusio		Dircea
	Sc. II.	
Dircea		Timante
	Sc. III.	
Adrasto	Demofoonte	Timante
	Sc. IV.	
	Timante	
	Sc. V.	
Creusa		Cherinto
	Sc. VI.	
Creusa	Timante	Cherinto
	Sc. VII.	
Creusa		Cherinto
	Sc. VIII.	
	Cherinto *solo*	
	Sc. IX.	
Dircea		Matusio
	Sc. X.	
Timante		Dircea
	Sc. XI.	
Timante	Dircea	Matusio
	Sc. XII.	
Timante Adrasto Dircea		Matusio
	Sc. XIII.	
Timante		Matusio

Atto Secondo

Destra		Sinistra
	Scena I.	
Demofoonte		Creusa
	Sc. II.	
Demofoonte		Timante
	Sc. III.	
	Demofoonte *solo*	
	Sc. IV.	
Timante		Matusio
	Sc. V.	
Dircea		Timante
	Sc. VI.	
Creusa		Dircea
	Sc. VII.	
Creusa		Cherinto

Sc. VIII.

Creusa *sola*

Sc. IX.

Dircea   Timante

Sc. X.

Demofoonte   Dircea   Timante

Demofoonte, per l'aria, può
passare in mezzo.

Sc. XI.

Dircea   Timante

Atto Terzo

Scena I.

Timante   Adrasto

Sc. II.

Timante   Cherinto

Sc. III.

Timante   Matusio

Sc. IV.

Timante *solo*

Sc. V.

Dircea   Timante   Adrasto   Olinto

Demofoonte   Creusa

Sc. VI.

Dircea   Creusa   Demofoonte   Adrasto

Sc. VII.

Dircea   Creusa

Sc. VIII.

Creusa *sola*

Sc. IX.

Timante   Cherinto

Sc. X.

Dircea   Timante   Cherinto

Matusio   Adrasto

Sc. XI.

Dircea   Timante   Demofoonte   Cherinto

Matusio   Adrasto

Sc. ultima

Demofoonte

Timante   Cherinto

Dircea   Creusa

Matusio   Adrasto

Squabbles persisted at Dresden over precedence, because the prima donna playing the part of Dircea, "an undiscovered Princess," believed that she outranked Creusa, who was a queen. The author had to write more letters to settle the matter once and for all: Creusa outranked Dircea. In other words, the drama came first, even before the singers' hierarchical prerogatives. Thus did the poet prevail as director, even when he was not present.

In 1749, just after Metastasio passed his fiftieth year, he was given an assistant director in the person of Giovannambrogio Migliavacca, a young poet from Milan who was in the service of the court of Dresden. As might be expected when a young director replaced a veteran, the singers, or at least one of them, saw an opportunity to rebel. Exerting his rights to call rehearsals and direct them, Migliavacca ran into trouble with the primo uomo, Caffarelli. Metastasio tells the story in a letter to the princess Belmonte, quoted here in Burney's translation:

> To this young author, the managers of this theater have confided, not only the set-tling the books of the words [in this case Zeno's *Merope* for Jommelli et al.], but the arrangements of the stage. I know not whether it proceeded from rivalry of talents, or personal beauty, but the poet and the singer, from the beginning, have been upon the *qui vive*, and treated each other with sneers and sarcasms. At length, Migliavacca (the poet) issued out orders for a rehearsal of the opera that was preparing. All the performers obeyed the summons, except Caffarelli; whose absence was occasioned either by a mutinous spirit, or an innate aversion to every species of obedience.[5]

The great soprano appeared only at the end of the rehearsal, and questioned why there should be any rehearsal at all. One thing led to another, all amusingly re-counted by Metastasio, until the poet and singer were at swords' points, the latter yielding his sword only on the entreaties of the prima donna, La Tesi. Migliavacca survived several further tours of duty in Vienna as poet and stage director. Meta-stasio, after 1750, apparently confined his stage directing to dilettante performances at court, and not without complaints about how much of a burden these imposed on him. Thus he wrote about *Il re pastore* at Schönbrunn that he was obliged to remain in the cold and empty theater during the rehearsal; and of the premiere of *L'eroe cinese* he wrote: "I am worn out; the whole weight of the business fell on my shoulders."[6]

Goldoni began his long theatrical career at Feltre around 1730, when he was twenty-three, writing comic intermezzi for a few amateur singers.[7] He was licensed in Venetian jurisprudence in 1734, and at the same time he wrote several more

---

5. Burney, *Memoirs of the Life and Writings of the Abate Metastasio* 1 : 271.
6. Ibid., 2 : 5, 21.
7. *Tutte le opere di Carlo Goldoni*, ed. Giuseppe Ortolani, 14 vols. (Milan, 1935–56). Volume 1 con-tains the prose autobiographies in Italian, written as prefaces for the seventeen-volume Pasquali edition of Goldoni's stage works. In French, published originally as *Mémoires de M. Goldoni pour servir à l'histoire de sa vie et à celle de son théâtre* (Paris, 1787).

intermezzi for Giuseppe Imer and his troupe of comedians in the San Samuele Theater, which was owned by Michele Grimani. In the preface to volume 12 of the Pasquali edition of his works, written in 1772, Goldoni calls these little pieces "only comic sketches, and yet susceptible to all the most comic and original characters; they could serve me as trials and exercise until the day when I could treat them at more length and depth in full-scale comedies."[8] Goldoni gained the confidence of both Imer and Grimani with such works, and the latter asked him to adjust Zeno's *Griselda* for Vivaldi; the result was satisfactory to all, and staged in the San Samuele in May 1735. Two years later, after several successes with the Imer troupe, Grimani asked Goldoni to take over the direction of both his theaters, the San Samuele and Venice's main opera house, the San Giovanni Grisostomo. In the fall of 1737 and following Carnival season, Goldoni staged a brilliant operatic season, with productions based on librettos by Zeno and Metastasio (adjusted for the occasion, of course) set by Porpora, Hasse, Latilla, and Giai. The singers included the renowned castrato Carlo Scalzi. Goldoni took more than usual care with the ballets, stage settings, and costumes—witness the unusual naming of the artists responsible on all four printed librettos: "Balli di Gaetano Grossatesta, Scene di Antonio Joli modenese, Vestiario di Nadal Canciani." Goldoni remained director until 1741 and wrote several librettos for serious operas himself, including two in collaboration with Galuppi, *Gustavo Primo Re di Svezia* (San Samuele, Ascension 1740) and *Oronte Re de' Sciti* (San Giovanni Grisostomo, Carnival 1740/41). Of the latter he recalls in the preface to Pasquali's volume 16: "The painter, who had to create the settings, was the excellent Jolli, who wished to do himself honor with some magnificent scenery, for which I gave him occasion, and he succeeded admirably."[9]

Goldoni's beginnings as a writer of spoken comedies were sporadic and beset with difficulties. Only gradually did he persuade actors to give up their improvisatory routines and accept his "comedy of character," in which the roles were increasingly written out and had to be committed to memory. The key work, according to Goldoni himself, was *Momolo cortesan* (1738), for the Imer troupe. Normally, a director like Imer—a *capo comico*, that is—would assign the roles to his players and otherwise function as stage director. In Goldoni's play *Il teatro comico* (1750), for instance, it is the *capo comico* who instructs a novice actress how to position herself on stage and how to coordinate speech with gestures. But Imer apparently shared some of the directing duties with Goldoni, who became an indispensable adjunct to his company. Of *Momolo cortesan* Goldoni says in his *Mémoires* (finished in 1784), "J'avais bien concerté les acteurs" ("I coordinated the actors well"). Of his *Don Giovanni Tenorio* (1736) he says, "Je fis distribuer les rôles sans faire la lecture de la

---

8. "Gl' Intermezzi non sieno che Commedie abbozzate, sono però suscettibili di tutti i Caratteri più comici e più originali, e che ciò potea servirmi di prova e di esercizio, per trattarli un giorno a più distesamente e più a fondo nelle grandi commedie"; Goldoni, *Tutte le opere* 1:709.

9. "Il Pittore, che dovea far lo scenario, era il bravissimo Jolli, il quale desiderando di farsi onore con delle scene magnifiche, io gliene ho data l'occasione, ed egli è riuscito mirabilmente"; ibid., p. 741.

pièce" ("I had the roles distributed without a reading of the play"). By the time Goldoni was invited to Rome in 1758–59 he was so famous he went not only as playwright but also as the director of a troupe of comedians in the Tordinona Theater.

Goldoni was responsible for a new dramaturgy in the full-length comic operas he wrote for Venice beginning in 1748. He gives himself no credit for this in his *Mémoires* (his life as told in the Pasquali prefaces was taken only as far as 1743, so they are not relevant). But it was mainly to Goldoni that we owe the creation of a libretto type best called *dramma giocoso*; to him also is due the epochal creation of the buffo finale.[10]

In 1748 Goldoni returned to Venice after five years in Tuscany spent mainly do-ing legal work. The theater became his full-time occupation from this point on. He carried his "reform" of the spoken stage to its term, writing innumerable plays on the widest variety of subjects, many of them contemporary and filled with local color. During the six years following his return he wrote some twenty librettos. In one of his most important prefaces to a libretto, the *dramma giocoso De gustibus non est disputandum* (Venice, 1754), he explained how he had sought to find a median way between the nobility of serious opera and the ridiculousness of comic opera. *Dramma giocoso* had gradually become his most usual designation for this median way, which combined characters designated as *parti serie* with others called *parti buffe*. With this mixed genre he sought to succeed with a wider public and accom-modate the many demands inherent in opera. He questions whether he has succeeded:

> The outcome depends greatly on the music, even more on the actors, and often also on the decorations. The populace decide the outcome in an instant; if the opera fails, the book is bad. If it is a little serious, it's poor because it doesn't bring laughs; if it's too ridiculous, it's poor because it lacks nobility. I wished to please universally in this genre of composition, as I have in others, but in six years [1748–54], during which necessity and my obligations have forced me to write such works, I have seen no libretto from elsewhere that succeeded or could instruct me. Despairing thus of writing better and of obtaining either praise or pity, I resolved to give up such a disgusting exercise, which was rendered all the worse by the labors it entailed as to the burden of directing in the theater.[11]

10. Daniel Heartz, "*Vis comica*: Goldoni, Galuppi, and *L'arcadia in Brenta* (Venice, 1749)," in *Venezia e il melodramma nel settecento*, ed. Maria Teresa Muraro (Florence, 1981), 2:33–69; and Daniel Heartz, "The Creation of the Buffo Finale in Italian Opera," *Proceedings of the Royal Musical Association* 104 (1977/78): 67–77. For more on the *dramma giocoso*, see Chapter 11.

11. "L'esito dipende talora dalla musica, per lo più dagli Attori, e sovente ancora dalle decorazione. Il Popolo decide a seconda dell'esito; se l'Opera è a terra, il libro è pessimo. Se è un poco serio, è cattivo perché non fa ridere; se è troppo ridicolo, è cattivo perché non vi è nobiltà. Volea pure imparare il modo di contentare l'Universale anche in questo genere di composizioni, ma in sei anni che la necessità e gli impieghi mi costringono a doverne fare, non ho veduto alcun libro straniero che abbia avuto fortuna e che potesse insegnarmi. Disperando dunque de poter far meglio e di ottenere né lode, né compatimento, avea risoluto di tralasciare un esercizio sì disgustoso, reso anche peggiore dalle fatiche che porta seco l'impegno della direzione al Teatro"; Goldoni, *Tutte le opere* 11:103.

There is no reason to doubt Goldoni's word on the last claim. In addition to writing play after play, libretto after libretto, he was responsible for directing their performance onstage.

Goldoni did not give up writing librettos, of course. In fact, he went on to write many more *drammi giocosi*, including some of his finest. Like Metastasio, he occasionally complained about the burden on the poet of having to direct, but he did it. Ortolani annotates Goldoni's complaint by saying that "apparently Goldoni and his composer collaborated in the stage direction."[12] This seems unlikely in the absence of any positive evidence, and also because the composer (in this case, Giuseppe Scarlatti) had his hands full preparing and directing (from the harpsichord) the musical side of the performance.

Goldoni admired the librettos of Metastasio as the best of their kind ever written. His comparison of Metastasio's qualities with those of his predecessor Zeno remains the most astute criticism written on the subject. Yet his reverence for the graceful works of the Roman poet did not prevent Goldoni from helping himself liberally to borrowed aria texts, or even from doing a takeoff on one of the most celebrated passages in *Didone abbandonata* (in *Il teatro comico*). What worried many literary lights around 1770 was that no one had appeared who could carry on opera seria at the high level of inspiration and finesse attained by Metastasio. In his preface (1772) to *Don Giovanni Tenorio*, dedicating the work to his former patron, Michele Grimani, Goldoni laments the inadequacies of his own and other poets' librettos for serious opera (*drammi per musica*):

> The destiny of lyric stages all over Italy is doomed at present. They lack serious dramas, since the most suave Metastasio has ceased writing. Many who have tried after him have been valorous and learned. But the ear accustomed to those sweet verses, those tender thoughts, to that brilliant mode of staging of the distinguished poet, has still not found anyone worthy of equaling him.[13]

Lorenzo Da Ponte was thirty before he tried writing a play (a translation at Gorizia in 1779), but he had already written many verses and was, according to his own testimony, a devoted student of the great Italian poets.[14] He passed a kind of apprenticeship as an opera poet assisting Caterino Mazzolà at Dresden in 1781, where one of his projects was translating Philippe Quinault's *Atys et Cybèle* from French into Italian. Mazzolà recommended him to Salieri in Vienna, where he settled in late 1781 or early 1782. He caught the attention of Metastasio with his

12. Ibid., p. 1271*n*3.

13. "Fatale in oggi è il destino per tutta Italia de' Musicali Teatri. Mancano i Drammi dacché ha cessato di scriver il soavissimo Metastasio. Molti provati dopo di lui si sono valorosi e dotti. Ma l'orecchio avvezzato a que' dolci versi, a que' gentili pensieri, a quel brillante mode di sceneggiare dell'egregio Poeta, non ha trovato ancora chi vaglia ad uguagliarlo"; ibid., 9:213. *Sceneggiare* means both "to dramatize" and "to stage."

14. Lorenzo Da Ponte, *Memorie*, ed. G. Gambarin and F. Nicolini (Bari, 1918), 1:73.

favola Filemone e Bauci, but the aged poet died shortly after their meeting in the spring of 1782. Joseph II decided to recruit an Italian buffo troupe for Vienna shortly thereafter, and he had need of an Italian poet to adjust their librettos and see them through the press. The choice fell on Da Ponte, who is particularly informative in his memoirs about the part of his duties that concerned correcting librettos. Da Ponte stresses anything that had to do with his standing as a man of letters, while underplaying almost everything that had to do with his activities as a man of the theater. He says little about the Italian singers in the Burgtheater for whom he worked, and does not even mention the most eminent among them, the primo buffo Francesco Benucci, by name. This circumstance can be understood as a part of the same ego-enhancing efforts that made Da Ponte suppress the facts about how the Don Juan story was chosen for Mozart, who was offered Bertati's *Don Giovanni* by Guardasoni on behalf of the Prague theater management in early 1787.[15] Naturally, one would expect Da Ponte to cover up his indebtedness to Bertati, and he does.

Da Ponte was hypersensitive to the charge that he based his librettos mainly on other librettos and plays. What he says about a surprise visit to his successor Bertati actually tells us a lot about his own working methods:

> When I told him that I had something to communicate to him, he found himself obliged to have me enter the room, which he did, but with some reluctance. He offered me a chair in the middle of the room: I sat down, without any malice, near the table where I judged by appearances he customarily wrote. Seeing me seated, he took the desk chair, and began dexterously closing a quantity of notepads and books that encumbered the table. Yet I was quick enough to see what the books in great part were: a tome of French comedies, a dictionary, a rhymer, and Corticelli's grammar all stood to the right of the signor poet; those that he had on the left I was not able to see. I then believed I understood the reason why he was not pleased to have me enter.[16]

Here Da Ponte taunts Bertati for the same thing that Giambattista Casti taunted Da Ponte. When Da Ponte turned Goldoni's fine French comedy *Le bourru bienfaisant* into an Italian libretto for Martín y Soler, *Il burbero di buon core*, which was given its premiere in the Burgtheater on 4 January 1786, Casti praised it, while adding so many *buts* that the compliment became a censure: "But in essence, he [Casti] would say, it's no more than a translation; we must wait and see how the

15. See Chapter 9.
16. "Quando gli dissi ch' avea qualche cosa da comunicargli, trovassi obbligato di farmi entrar nella stanza, il che fece però con qualche renitenza. Mi offrì una sedia nel mezzo della camera: io m'assisi, senza alcuna malizia, presso alla tavola, dove giudicai dall'apparenze ch'ei fosse solito a scrivere. Vedendo me assiso, s'assise anch'egli sul seggiolone e si mise destramente a chiudere una quantità di scartafacci e di libri, che ingombravano quella tavola. Ebbi tuttavia l'agio di vedere in gran parte che libri erano. Una toma di commedie francesi, un dizionario, un rimario e la grammatica del Corticelli stavano tutti alla destra del signor poeta: quelli, che aveva alla sinistra, non ho potuto vedere che cosa fossero. Credei allora d'intendere la ragione per cui gli dispiaceva di lasciarmi entrare"; Da Ponte, *Memorie* 1: 169–70.

affair would go with an original work."[17] Four months later, after weeks of arduous rehearsals, *Le nozze di Figaro* received its premiere on the same stage (1 May 1786). Casti remained true to form:

> To the disgust of the count [Rosenberg], of Casti, and of a hundred devils, the work generally pleased, and was held by the sovereign and by true connoisseurs to be something sublime, almost divine. The libretto was also found beautiful and my most chaste commentator was the first to point out its beauties. But what were these beauties? To be sure, it's only a translation of the comedy by Beaumarchais, but there are some fine verses and some good arias, for example these most light lines:
>
> > Non più andrai, farfallone amoroso
> > notte e giorno d'intorno girando.[18]

Out of the maelstrom of finishing and staging *Figaro* in the spring of 1786, Da Ponte made a poem, "The State of the Theater Poet," which he inscribed to Casti—not without some irony, since Casti sought his post. We reproduce the original text along with a literal translation.

Epistola	Epistle
Gentil Casti, ho stabilito	Gentle Casti, I have decided
Di mandarvi un memoriale;	To send you a memorandum;
Fate voi che sia esaudito:	See to it that it is heeded:
Che sebben ei non sia tale	Because even if it is not such
Da potersi dare in mani	As can be given in hand
A un prettissimo toscano	To a Tuscan archpriest or
Ad un uom a udire avvezzo,	To a man accustomed to listening
E a far versi d'altro prezzo,	And to making verses at another price,
Pur, se voi lo leggerete	Still, if you read it
Al Signor che già sapete,	To the Signor [Rosenberg?] you already know,
Basterà, mel dice il core,	Twill suffice, my heart tells me,
A disporlo a mio favore,	To dispose him in my favor
Ed a rendermi propizio	And render me propitious
Un Signor di tal giudizio.	To a man of such judgment.
Ecco il caso; state attento,	Here's the case; pay attention,
Perchè serio è l'argomento	Because the argument is serious
Qui si tratta di danaro;	And a question of money;
Che a dì nostri è così raro	Which is such a rare thing these days
E, la pare un'eresia	That it appears to be a heresy
Di danar per poesia.	To pay it for poetry.

17. "Ma, in fondo—diceva egli—non è che una traduzione. . . . Bisogna vedere com'andrà la faccenda in un' opera originale"; ibid., p. 107.

18. "Ad onto dal conte, di Casti e di cento diavolo, piacque generalmente, e fu dal sovrano e da' veri intendenti come cosa sublime e quasi divina tenuta. Anche il libretto si trovò bello; e il mio castissimo comentatore fu il primo a farne rimarcar le bellezze. Ma quali erano queste bellezze? —E vero che non è che una traduzione della commedia di Beaumarchais; ma vi sono de' bei versi e qualche bella aria. Ecco, per esempio, due versi leggiadrissimi: . . ."; ibid., pp. 120–21.

Voi sapete, e tutti il sanno,	You know, and everyone knows,
Che trascorso è già il terz' anno,	That three years have already passed
Da ch'io faccio, o bene, o male,	Since I, for better or worse,
Il poeta teatrale;	Have been the theater poet;
Ch'è un mestiero certamente	Which is a profession certainly
De' piu duri, de' piu tangheri,	Among the hardest and most loutish,
E che Giobbe il paziente	And which would make the patient Job
Potria fare uscir d'gangheri.	Go beside himself with rage.
Contenta in prima conviene	It requires satisfying at first
Il maestro di cappella,	The maestro di cappella,
A cui sempre in capo viene	To whose head there always comes
Una, od altra bagatella:	One trifle or another:
Qui cangiar vuol metro o rima,	Here changing the meter or rhyme,
E porre *A* dove *U* v'è prima,	And putting *A* where *U* stood before,
Là d'un verso gli fa d'uopo,	There sacrificing a verse,
Quel ch'è innanzi or vorria dopo;	Transposing the order of things;
Peggio poi, se a svegliar l'estro	Worse still, to awaken the fire
De lo stitico maestro	Of the constipated maestro
Tu dei metter, come s'usa,	You have to put, according to custom,
Specialmente ne la chiusa,	Especially in the closing,
Or il canta degli angelli,	Now the song of the angels,
Or il corseo de' ruscelli,	Now the coursing of brooks,
Or il batter de' martelli	Now the beating of hammers,
E il dindin de' campanelli	And the dingdong of bells,
E la rota, e il tamburino,	And the wheel, and the tambourine,
E la macina, e il mulino,	And the millstone, and the mill,
E la rana, e la cicala,	And the frog, and the cicada,
E il pian pian, e il cresci, e cala.	And the soft, the swelling, and fall.
Quando poscia egli è contento	When at last he is content
Ti rimangon mille impicci,	You still have a thousand troubles
Dei combattere con cento	To fight over with a hundred
Teste piene di capricci:	Heads full of caprices:
S'anco i primi son discreti	If the first singers are discreet
Co' maestri, e co' poeti,	With composers, and with poets,
V'è il terz'uom, la quarta buffa,	There's the third man, and fourth woman,
Che risvegli la baruffa,	Who reawaken the fray,
Chi la parte vuol migliore,	One wants a better part,
Perchè egli è secondo attore,	Because he is second actor,
Chi vuol l'aria di bravura,	Another wants a bravura aria,
Perchè là fa più figura;	So he can cut a better figure,
Chi non vuol queste parole,	One doesn't want these words,
Chi la musica non vuole,	Another doesn't want this music,
Questa ha il pezzo de'sorbetti,	This lady has the sherbet piece,
Quei non entra ne' terzetti;	That one doesn't enter in trios;
Ed in mezzo il tafferuglio,	And in the middle of the brawl,
Il disordine, il miscuglio	The disorder, the cacophony,
Pria che vada in scena l'opera,	Before the opera can be staged,
Se prudenza non adopera,	If prudence is not used,

Il poeta, ed io lo scuso,	The poet, and I excuse him,
Rompe agli altri, o rotto ha il muso.	Breaks with the others, or destroys his muse.
Viene alfin la prima recita,	There comes at last the first performance,
Giusto Ciel, che crepacuore!	Good Heavens, what heartbreak!
Chi mal canta, chi mal recita,	The one sings badly, the other recites poorly,
Chi ha la tosse, o il raffreddore,	This one has a cough, the other a cold,
E nel Publico, che giudica	And the public, which judges
Sol da quel che sente, e vede,	Only by what it hears and sees,
Solo il vate si pregiudica,	Blames only the bard,
Una bestia ei sol si crede.	Believing he must be a beast.
Per tal vita, o saggio Casti,	For such a life, o wise Casti,
Ho una spezie di salario,	I have a kind of salary,
E procuro che mi basti	And procure what I need
Al bisogno necessario,	For my bare necessities,
Ma sia caso, o fallo sia	But in case of failure,
Di cattiva economia,	Or bad economic conditions,
Quando giunge l'anno nuovo	When the new year comes
Più tre soldi io non mi trovo,	I'll have no more than three cents
E finisce a un'ora stessa	And both the candle and the Mass
La candela co la messa.	Will finish at the same time.

Da Ponte included this in the *Extract* from his memoirs published in 1819, appending a note saying, "The remainder of this letter will be found in my life," but the epistle to Casti appears only in the second edition of the memoirs (1829). The reason he excluded it in the first edition may lie in his decision to paraphrase a passage from it in prose. Thus, when he is describing how he wrote *Una cosa rara* after a Spanish play for the Spanish composer Martín y Soler, he says:

> Scarcely were the parts distributed when the fire broke out. This one had too much recitative, the other not enough; for one the aria was too low pitched, for the other too high; these did not get into any ensembles, others had too many; this one was sacrificed to the prima donna, another to the first, second, third, and fourth comic singer. A general conflagration! [19]

During the summer of 1787 Da Ponte was laboring simultaneously on *Don Giovanni* for Mozart, *L'arbore di Diana* for Martín y Soler, and *Axur, Re d'Ormus* for Salieri. He says he dashed off the plan for *L'arbore di Diana* in half an hour, yet he regarded it as the best of his librettos. Its premiere, on 1 October 1787 in the Burgtheater, was given to honor Emperor Joseph's eldest niece, Maria Teresa, who was then passing through Vienna on her way from Florence to Dresden, where she was to marry the heir of Saxony. The plan was for Prague to honor her with the first

19. "Appena si distribuiron le parti, che parve scatenato l'inferno. Chi aveva troppi recitativi, chi non n'aveva abbastanza; per uno l'aria era troppo bassa, per un altro tropp'alta; questi non entrava ne' pezzi concertati, quegli ne dovea cantar troppi; chi era sacrificato alla prima donna, chi al primo, al secondo, al terzo ed al quarto buffo: il foco era generale"; ibid., p. 125.

performance of *Don Giovanni* on 14 October, and Da Ponte was dispatched to Prague to direct the singers accordingly. An even more important event brought him hurrying back to Vienna, the impending marriage of the emperor's eldest nephew and designated heir to the throne, Francis, which was to be celebrated with Salieri's *Axur*. This is the context, then, of Da Ponte's statement, quoted briefly to begin this essay, and given here at greater length:

> Only the first performance of this opera [*L'arbore di Diana*] had been given when I was obliged to leave for Prague for the opening of Mozart's *Don Giovanni* on the occasion of the arrival of the princess of Tuscany in that city. I spent eight days there directing the actors who were to create it; but before it appeared on the stage, I had to hurry back to Vienna, because of the fiery letter I received from Salieri, in which he informed me, truly or not, that *Axur* had to be ready at once for the nuptials of Prince Francis, and that the emperor had ordered him to call me home. Returning to Vienna I traveled day and night.[20]

In the event, *Don Giovanni* was not ready for the Prague visit of Maria Teresa, and the nuptials of her brother Francis were deferred until early January 1788. Da Ponte says that Guardasoni paid him fifty sequins for his services in Prague. This can be believed, but the letter he said Mozart wrote him from Prague, quoted in the *Extract*, has long been recognized for the forgery that it is:

> Our opera of *Don Giovanni* was represented last night to a most brilliant audience. The princess of Tuscany, with all her company, was present. The success of our piece was as complete as we could desire. Guardasoni came this morning, almost enraptured with joy, into my room. Long live Mozart, long live Da Ponte, said he: as long as they shall exist, no manager shall know distress. Adieu! my dear friend. Prepare another opera for your friend Mozart.[21]

Prepare another opera for Mozart Da Ponte eventually did, *Così fan tutte*, but it had nothing to do with the success of *Don Giovanni*, which in fact was not well received when it was produced in Vienna. Not content with forging a letter of

20. "Non s'era fatta che la prima rappresentazione di questo spettacolo, quando fui obbligato di partire per Praga, dove doveasi rappresentar per la prima volta il *Don Giovanni* di Mozzart, per l'arrivo della principessa di Toscana in quella città. Mi vi fermai otto giorni per dirigere gli attori, che doveano rappresentarlo; ma, prima che andasse in scena, fu obbligato di tornar a Vienna, per una lettera di foco che ricevei dal Salieri, in cui, fosse vero o no, informavami che l'*Assur* doveva rappresentarsi immediatamente per le nozze di Francesco, e che l'imperatore gli aveva ordinato di richiamarmi. Tornai adunque a Vienna, viaggiando dì e notte"; ibid., p. 133.

21. *An Extract from the Life of Lorenzo Da Ponte, with the history of several dramas written by him, and among others, Il Figaro, Il Don Giovanni & La Scuola degli Amanti set to music by Mozart* (New York, 1819), p. 19. In the *Memorie*, Da Ponte quotes only the middle of what is present in the *Extract* and says that Guardasoni sent him this in a letter: "Evviva Da Ponte, evviva Mozzart. Tutti gli impresari, tutti i virtuosi devono benedirli. Finché essi vivranno, non si saprà mai che sia miseria teatrale" (1:134). Gabarin and Nicolini annotate the supposed letter from Mozart to Da Ponte in the *Extract* from secondary Italian sources and call it apocryphal (2:283).

praise from Mozart, Da Ponte follows it with another from Salieri, purportedly written from Paris and bearing the opinion of none other than Beaumarchais:

> I gave a copy of your *Figaro* to Monsieur de Beaumarchais, who desired me to thank you kindly for your attention. I met him a few days after, and demanded his opinion. "I admired," said he, "the art of the Italian poet, in contracting so many Colpi di Scena in so short a time, without the one destroying the other. Had I altered thus a comedy of another author, I would not hesitate a moment to call it my own work."[22]

Incidentally, we note in connection with Salieri's visit to Paris in 1787 that it was Beaumarchais who supervised the rehearsals of their *Tarare* (from which Da Ponte derived *Axur*) at the Opéra.[23] Thus Beaumarchais may be added to our list of poets who served as stage directors in operatic productions.

At some point before he was dismissed from his post as theater poet in the spring of 1791, Da Ponte wrote an undated memorandum entitled "Ordine necessarissimo in una direzione teatrale," a copy of which survives in the Viennese archives.[24] Its contents are translated in their entirety in the Appendix to this chapter. Here it suffices to call attention to the passages in which Da Ponte spelled out the poet's reponsibilities with regard to coaching the actors. It is the duty of the poet, he says, "to instruct the actors in the truth of the action and of the expression." The music director assigns the roles to the singers, but not without consulting the poet. Furthermore, the singers "must execute the music as ordered by the maestro, and remain faithful to the action and expression that will be prescribed by the poet."

The theoretical underpinnings of the tradition demonstrated in practice throughout this chapter were provided by Francesco Algarotti's *Saggio sopra l'opera in musica* (1755). Algarotti spelled out the poet's specific duties and urged his overall control of the entire mechanism. We quote him in an anonymous English translation of 1768:

> It is therefore the poet's duty, as chief engineer of the undertaking, to give directions to the dancers, the machinists, the painters; nay down even to those who are entrusted with the care of the wardrobe and dressing the performers. The poet is to carry in his mind a comprehensive view of the *whole* of the drama; because those parts which are not the productions of his pen ought to flow from the dictates of his actuating judgment, which is to give being and movement to the whole.[25]

22. Da Ponte, *Extract*, p. 25. Italian version does not exist.

23. Thomas E. Crow, *Painters and Public Life in Eighteenth-Century Paris* (New Haven, Conn., 1985), p. 226. Noteworthy too was that the Comédie Française and the Comédie Italienne allowed playwrights the last word about casting; see Xavier de Courville, *Luigi Riccoboni, dit Lélio* (Paris, 1943–58), 2 : 283.

24. This memo is printed in the original Italian in Otto Michtner, *Das alte Burgtheater als Opernbühne: Von der Einführung des deutschen Singspiels (1778) bis zum Tode Kaiser Leopolds II (1792)* (Vienna, 1970), pp. 439–40.

25. Oliver Strunk, *Source Readings in Music History* (New York, 1950), pp. 657–58.

The eighteenth century knew no simple term that embraced the creative range exercised by the modern stage director. Yet it is clear from Algarotti's sweeping charge to the poet that the concept had already arrived, even if the term had not.

APPENDIX

Lorenzo Da Ponte to the Directors of the Court Theater. Rules Most Necessary to the Theater Direction

1. The poet's duties are to read the book before the parts are distributed; to correct all the errors in it of whatever kind; to propose the subject should other parts be needed; to change the arias that, in the judgment of the music director, do not suit the voice of the singer; to enrich the score with good ensembles if there is need of them; to abbreviate scenes that are too long; to instruct the actors in the truth of the action and of the expression; and to look after the first and last rehearsals for the sake of an opportune harmony and facility of execution.

2. The *maestro di capella* is obligated to examine the score before it is given to the copyist, so as not to lose time and money on useless copying; as it often happens that a score is refused because its music is trivial or bad when heard at the first rehearsal, he should order a special [musical] rehearsal if he does not believe sufficiently in the probability of a good effect; moreover, he should distribute the roles with impartiality according to the character and ability of each singer, and not without consultation of the poet and the assent of the director; he should take part in the first and last rehearsals of all operas; he should adjust errors in the score and compose all the recitatives that were changed or augmented by the poet and assist in the introduction of those pieces which, together with the poet, were judged of utility to the work.

3. No singer is allowed to say "I will or will not sing in this opera," but must always accept whatever part is assigned by the poet, the maestro, and the director, and will not even be permitted to appeal for dispensation. In the adjusted arias the singer must depend absolutely on the maestro, the poet, and the director and may not ask the poet to make new changes or to introduce something that pleases him more. He must execute the music as ordered by the maestro and remain faithful to the action and expression that will be prescribed by the poet. He must sing every evening that the direction ordains. In case of real sickness the direction may not reduce in any way his usual stipend; but for imagined or feigned illnesses, recognized as such by an honest doctor, he will be condemned to a suspension of wages until he reappears on the stage. He must take part in all rehearsals, and always at the hour announced by the messenger. He will accept the form, genre, and quality of costume fixed by the direction; he may never be responsible for the ornamenta-

tion or the character of what he wears, which are fixed by the poet, the tailor, and the director. He may not arbitrarily omit any piece from the opera, but must demand permission from the maestro, and from the poet, who will not concede him the omission without just reasons, not wishing ever to defraud the paying public out of a performance of all the music heard on opening night. If it is proven by certain evidence that a singer committed some offense so as to cause harm, including harming his own health, he may, after being warned, upon renewed offense, be denied his accustomed pay by the direction. But this point is so delicate it will always be examined and decided by the incorruptible justice of the director.

6 · FROM BEAUMARCHAIS TO DA PONTE: THE METAMORPHOSIS OF *FIGARO*

Pierre-Augustin Caron de Beaumarchais, born the son of a Parisian watch-maker in 1732, worked his way upward in society by marrying a widow with property. By 1760 he was harp teacher to the unmarried daughters of Louis XV. The path of his long climb to prominence was strewn with litigations and brilliantly written polemic pamphlets. In March 1774 he traveled to London as a secret agent under the false name Ronac in order to squelch a pamphlet attacking Madame Du Barry, the king's mistress. With the aid of a large bribe he succeeded in buying off the pamphlet's author and burning the manuscript along with three thousand copies already printed. When he returned to Versailles he found, instead of the hoped-for reward, a mortally ill king. Louis XV died on 10 May 1774, with the succession passing to his nineteen-year-old grandson, the dauphin, and his Austrian bride, Marie Antoinette, who was only eighteen. Beaumarchais schemed to ingratiate himself with the new rulers along lines all too plainly related to the Du Barry episode.

Under the guise of defending the honor of Marie Antoinette and her mother, the empress Maria Theresa, Beaumarchais made a secret trip to Vienna in the summer of 1774 (once again under the name Ronac), supposedly in pursuit of the last copy of a scurrilous pamphlet and its publisher. On the way he staged a wounding attack on himself near Nuremberg, ascribed it to said publisher, rescued the pamphlet, then hastened on to Vienna, where, admitted to see the empress almost at once, he presented her with the pamphlet. Her chancellor of state, Prince Kaunitz, had the good sense to see through his cock-and-bull story and to suspect that Beaumarchais himself was the pamphlet's author. Beaumarchais was clapped into

Revised and expanded from *San Francisco Opera Magazine: Le nozze di Figaro* (Fall 1986).

prison and interrogated by Joseph von Sonnenfels (who was also a playwright).[1] Word soon came from the first minister in Paris to release him. Did Beaumarchais know so much that the French royal family feared him?

Beaumarchais, then, was in ill repute with the rulers in Vienna long before the question arose of tolerating his outrageously cheeky play *La folle journée, ou Le mariage de Figaro*—as this episode makes clear. Maria Theresa had died in 1780, but Chancellor Kaunitz remained all-powerful, alongside her son, Joseph II. Their reaction to a proposed play by the Parisian adventurer and scandalmonger of 1774 can well be imagined. Yet the way to acceptance was paved by the Viennese success of the first Figaro play by Beaumarchais, *Le barbier de Séville*, German versions of which played in the Burgtheater from 1776 to 1783.[2] As adapted in an Italian libretto by Petrosellini and set to delightful music by Paisiello, *Il barbiere di Siviglia* enjoyed some seventy performances in the same theater between 1783 and 1788. The Viennese public was naturally curious to follow the fortunes of Figaro and the other characters further.

In January 1785, Joseph instructed his censor that a German translation of the second play planned for production in the Kärntnerthor Theater should be banned unless expurgated of its more offensive passages. Nevertheless, he permitted the unexpurgated version to be printed at once, and even made jesting reference in a letter to one of the play's touchy issues, "le droit du Seigneur," a lord's right to deflower any virgin on his domain (the "right" was in fact a fabrication of Beaumarchais).[3] Da Ponte told a tale in his memoirs, written over three decades later, about how Mozart and he surprised the emperor with a secretly written Figaro opera in the spring of 1785. Mozart's Czech friend and early biographer, Niemetschek, told what sounds like the unvarnished truth: "Emperor Joseph determined Mozart to seek fame on the Italian operatic stage with this play, after it had been suitably altered to serve as a libretto."[4]

Mozart composed most of the music for *Figaro* in the fall of 1785. The opera was no secret. By late October, the emperor's chamberlain and deputy theater director, Count Rosenberg, was pressing the composer to finish his score, as Mozart at that time wrote to his father. A premiere was originally planned for the early months of 1786, but other premieres intervened and *Le nozze di Figaro* was not revealed to the public until the first of May. The emperor made it a practice to attend rehear-

1. Alfred Ritter von Arneth, *Beaumarchais und Sonnenfels* (Vienna, 1868), reproduces the entire interrogation. In his memoirs, Beaumarchais plays the innocent injured party, as might be expected. For a recent study of him, see René Pomeau, *Beaumarchais, ou la bizarre destinée* (Paris, 1987).

2. Hadamowsky, *Das Wiener Hoftheater (Staatstheater) 1776–1966, Teil 1: 1776–1810* (Vienna, 1966), No. 118.

3. Payer von Thurn, *Joseph II als Theaterdirektor*, pp. 69–70. The correspondence at one point concerned giving permission to Luisa Laschi to marry the tenor Domenico Mombelli. Joseph wrote Count Rosenberg from Prague on 29 September 1786: "Le mariage de Mombelli avec la Laschi peut s'exécuter sans attendre mon retour, et je vous cede à ce sujet le droit du Seigneur" ("The marriage of Laschi and Mombelli may take place without awaiting my return, and in this matter I cede to you the *droit du Seigneur*").

4. "Mozart ward vom Kaiser Joseph dazu bestimmt, diesem Lustspiele, nachdem es in ein Singspiele umgegossen ward, auch auf dem italienischen Operntheater durch sein Musik Celebrität zu verschaffen"; Niemetschek, *Leben des k. k. Kapellmeisters Mozart*, p. 25.

sals, which the new opera, being the longest and most complicated one ever staged in the Burgtheater, required in great numbers. Despite a noisy cabal against Mozart and Da Ponte, the first two performances won over the public, and by the third the emperor had to prohibit the encoring of any pieces other than solo numbers. He was aware of having sponsored the creation of an epochal work and took pride in it. A clever critic in the *Realzeitung* pointed up the history of the Figaro saga in Vienna during 1785–86 by beginning his review, "Nowadays what is not allowed to be spoken is sung"; his astute readers would have recognized this as a paraphrase of a line spoken by Figaro at the beginning of *Le barbier de Séville*.[5] The reviewer also said that opinions were divided at the first performance, "which is understandable, since the work is so difficult it did not go as well as it might have, but after repeated performances one would have to admit either to being a part of the cabal or to tastelessness in maintaining any view other than that Mozart's music was a masterpiece of art."[6]

What offended authorities in *Le mariage de Figaro* by Beaumarchais was mainly Figaro's great political speech in the last act, an attack on the establishment that took in rulers, magistrates, censors, and prisons, all of which had brought Figaro to grief; and in this regard, the character Figaro was but a thin disguise for the playwright himself. Beaumarchais had wrapped this diatribe within a denunciation of women, Figaro's imagined deception at the hands of his bride becoming the capper to his woes. Da Ponte preserved only the wrapping and turned Figaro's self-pitying rantings into a catalog of feminine wiles, probably working closely with Mozart, who usually knew what kind of text he needed for the musical effect he had already conceived. All the emphasis placed by the operatic Figaro on women's faithlessness ran the risk of offending Viennese canons of morality, which were much stricter than those of Paris, at least on the public stage.

The countess was given a complex character by Beaumarchais. She is very adept at feminine wiles, as we know from our encounter with her as Rosina in the first play, but is also generous and forgiving, which she remains in the second play. (For the sake of simplicity we adopt the Italian name forms throughout.) As the young Rosina, she was not insensitive to the lure of the sensual. It is thus only consistent with her character that, even as Countess Almaviva, she should be moved to some degree by the amorous attentions of her young page, especially since she has been neglected and betrayed by her husband. She retains a typically Gallic independence of mind (the Spanish setting used by Beaumarchais fooled no one). While her subtly drawn portrait was bound to please the Parisians, it was not one that could be exhibited in Vienna without being cleaned up. Two paeans to conjugal love,

5. Act I, scene 2: "Aujourd'hui ce que ne vaut pas la peine d'être dit, on le chante." The reviewer transformed "what is not worth being said" into "what is not allowed to be spoken": "Was in unseren Zeiten nicht erlaubt ist gesagt zu werden, wird gesungen." The review is quoted at length in Michtner, *Das alte Burgtheater*, pp. 208–9; and in Deutsch, *Dokumente*, pp. 243–44.

6. "Und folglich waren mit Ende des Stückes die Meinungen geteilt. Überdies hat es seine Richtigkeit, dass die erste Aufführung, weil die Komposition sehr schwer ist, nicht am besten von statten ging. Jetzt aber nach wiederholten Vorstellungen würde man sich offenbar entweder zur Kabale oder Geschmacklosigkeit bekennen, wenn man eine andere Meinung behaupten wollte, als dass die Musik des Hern Mozart ein Meisterstück der Kunst sei"; ibid.

"Porgi, amor" at the beginning of the operatic second act and "Dove sono" in act 3, sufficed to achieve the transformation of the countess into a model wife, a nearly saintly tower of constancy. (The relationship of these two pieces to other music by Mozart is explored at the end of this chapter.)

Young Count Almaviva is a complex personality, too. In the first play, what inflamed his desires for the eighteen-year-old Rosina was not her beauty or her noble soul, but her unavailability. Winning her over obstacles did wonders for his self-esteem, but not much for his long-term commitment to her. In the second play, he says he loves his wife, the countess, "but three years together makes marriage so respectable!" Even though the countess is still very young, her husband seeks the titillation of new challenges. Being much concerned with propriety and appearances, he is not about to go the libertine route of another Spanish grandee, Don Giovanni; yet he has more than a little of the Don Juan complex in him.

"A quasi-novel genre of spectacle" is what Da Ponte calls *Le nozze di Figaro* in his preface to the original printed libretto. He also says, "I have not simply translated this excellent comedy, but rather made an imitation, or better put, an extract." (See the Appendix to this chapter for the complete preface text.) The number of roles in the play was cut from sixteen to eleven (still requiring at least nine singing voices, two or three more than normal), and "many most charming scenes" had to be cut, laments Da Ponte, who goes on to apologize with this understatement: "In spite of all . . . study, diligence, and care taken by the composer and by me to be brief, the opera will still not be the shortest one ever put on in our theater." It was in fact much longer than the average opera. Mozart listed it in his catalog of works as thirty-four numbers, but about four of these were abandoned or perhaps never set to music. Even so, the opera is so long that it is almost never given without a few numbers being cut. Primarily responsible for its inordinate length were the intricacies of the five-act play by Beaumarchais, the longest comedy that Parisian theatergoers had ever witnessed. "We hope that excuse enough will be found," says Da Ponte, "in the variety of threads with which the action of this drama is woven, the vastness and greatness of the same, and the multiplicity of musical numbers that had to be made, in order . . . to express step by step with diverse colors the diverse passions that rival each other, and to carry out our desire of offering a quasi-novel genre of spectacle to a public of such refined taste and such just understanding."

The richness of the play is evident especially in Beaumarchais's deft characterization of the accessory figures. Take the case of Marcellina. She is only mentioned in the first play, as Rosina's governess. In the second play she has a small but crucial role and undergoes considerable character development. From the bitter and faded beauty who first arrives at the château with Doctor Bartolo, by the end she has turned into a wise and sympathetic matriarch.[7] We see her throughout mainly in

7. Wye J. Allanbrook, "Pro Marcellina: The Shape of 'Figaro' Act IV," *Music and Letters* 63 (1982): 69–84.

interaction with Susanna, first as a rival pretender to Figaro's hand in marriage, later as a doting mother to Figaro and his bride-to-be, and finally as a staunch defender of women in general, and Susanna in particular, against the silly vituperations of Figaro. As Marcellina grows in human qualities, so does Susanna, who at first is almost as shrill as her future mother-in-law. Susanna's sharp tongue in the initial encounter finds these choice expressions for Marcellina: *pédante* (turned by Da Ponte into *vecchia pedante*), *vielle sibyle* (*Sybilla decrepita*), *femme savante* (*dottoressa arrogante*). As Marcellina makes her exit in the play, Susanna says: "Just because she has studied a little and tormented the youth of my mistress, she thinks she can run things here in the château." Da Ponte manages to shorten even this, and he sharpens the point about Marcellina's studies by having her drop into a few words of French, at which Susanna exclaims, "Che lingua!"

Bartolo remains the same old curmudgeon who delighted us in *Le barbier de Séville*; indeed, it belongs to his character that he cannot change with the times. In the first play he inveighs against everything that might be called social or scientific progress: freedom of thought, the theory of gravity, electricity, religious toleration, inoculation, quinine, the *Encyclopédie*, and, finally, modern dramas. We learn early what kind of medical doctor he is—a menace to man and beast alike, as Figaro says. Much of the malicious wit with which he is drawn by Beaumarchais has to be sacrificed in the opera's text, but Mozart makes up for it in a single stroke with the doctor's one aria, "La vendetta," a consummate portrait of pomposity mingled with stupidity. Don Basilio, Rosina's singing teacher, while not as stupid as Bartolo, is even more corrupt and malevolent. His weapons are calumny, behind a person's back, or, face to face, innuendo. "One is wicked," he tells Susanna in the play, just before Cherubino is discovered hiding in the armchair, "because one sees things clearly."

Da Ponte says in his preface that he had to omit one whole act of the play. More accurately, he combined the trial (act 3) with the double engagement (from act 4) to make his third act, while moving the solo scenes for Barbarina and Marcellina to the beginning of his fourth and last act. Some loose ends remained untied in the opera's libretto after all this cutting and splicing. Da Ponte does not explain how Susanna got the purse of money with which to buy Figaro's freedom from his promissory note obliging him to marry Marcellina, a boon that Beaumarchais spelled out as coming from a characteristic act of generosity on the part of the countess. An advantage of treating a play that was so popular and well known becomes obvious here: the libretto could cut many corners and still remain intelligible. Similarly, the play, with all its richness of detail and allusion, could serve as a kind of subtext or commentary on the compressed action of the opera.

Beaumarchais also availed himself of a preface—a very long one—when the definitive edition of *Le mariage de Figaro* was printed early in 1785.[8] He defended

---

8. It is reprinted in Augustin Caron de Beaumarchais, *Théâtre: "Le barbier de Séville." "Le mariage de Figaro." "La mère coupable,"* ed. René Pomeau (Paris, 1965), pp. 108–34. See also Hans Ludwig Scheel,

himself against the charges of having written a grossly immoral play by turning the tables on his critics and showing how every major character had a moral lesson to teach the public. He protested a little too much about the innocence of the countess, particularly since he had already mentioned in the same preface his plans for a third play in the cycle, *La mère coupable* (the guilty mother being the countess, after she has had a child by Cherubino). Perhaps he felt justified claiming her innocence, because in successive versions of *Le mariage de Figaro* he toned down some of the more suggestive passages pertaining to the countess, so that in the final version she is merely ambiguous. On the subject of Cherubino he asks: "Is it the person of the page or the conscience of the count that torments the latter every time I condemn them to meet?" He answers the question in a very moral fashion. "Even the man of absolute power, once he has embarked on a wicked course of action, can be tripped up by the least important being, by the person who most fears getting in his way." He reveals Marcellina's youthful sin of indiscretion, the one that thirty years earlier led to the birth of Figaro, he says, not to debase her or the female gender, but to point out the really guilty person, her vile and irresponsible seducer, Bartolo. Beaumarchais was a feminist, one of the first. He condemns all vile seducers of women, and most especially the count, who is the worst because of his very great temporal powers. The whole play focuses ultimately on teaching the count a lesson he will not forget, just after teaching another of the same kind to Figaro.

The metaphor of instruction looms large in the Figaro cycle. At the end of the first play, the count, after throwing off his cloak and revealing the magnificent costume of a Spanish grandee, makes a very mean remark about teaching old Bartolo a lesson. No! replies his bride-to-be, the young Rosina: her overflowing heart has no room for vengeance (already a sign of trouble ahead for this pair). Figaro would teach the count to dance to his tunes in "Se vuol ballare, Signor Contino," and to end the same act Figaro gives Cherubino superb instruction on the military life ahead of him in "Non più andrai, farfallone amoroso." The lessons do not stop there.

Beaumarchais took infinite pains with details of staging and costuming in his plays. He devised an exact prescription for every character's costume, which was printed along with the dramatis personae at the beginning. The count, for example, is instructed to appear in Spanish court costume but with hunting boots in the first two acts, after which he dons an even more gala costume. Beaumarchais turned to one of the leading Parisian artists and illustrators, Jacques-Philippe-Joseph de Saint-Quentin, to procure suitable vignettes with which to adorn the first edition of *La folle journée*, brought out in early 1785 at Kehl, across the French border from Strasbourg. Born in 1738, Saint-Quentin was a pupil of Boucher and won the first prize from the Royal Academy of Painting in 1762 (ten years after Fragonard, an-

"*Le mariage de Figaro* von Beaumarchais und das Libretto der *Nozze di Figaro* von Lorenzo da Ponte," *Musikforschung* 28 (1975): 156–72.

other of Boucher's pupils). His drawings, one for each of the five acts of the play, were engraved for publication by various artists. They help to recreate the atmosphere of the first production in 1784, and they are still suggestive as to staging. We reproduce all five from the excellently preserved copy of the first edition, now rare, in Harvard College Library; in the absence of any iconographic evidence concerning the first production of the opera, these engravings are invaluable.

The choice for act 1 fell on the chair scene (Fig. 7). A dashing young count lifts the robe from the chair to reveal Cherubino. He wears the specified hunting boots that reach mid-calf and the costume of a Spanish grandee. Spanish court dress, which remained about two hundred years behind the times (with obvious symbolic implications for political fashions as well), was very like Elizabethan male finery: neck ruff, plumed hat, puffed trunk hose, tights, sash, and cape. Susanna, raising her hands in shocked horror at the discovery, wears a low-cut gown and headgear as prescribed by the playwright. Basilio, expressing shocked delight at the situation, is clad as a cleric in dark garb. Cherubino looks like a miniature version of the count. The style of the room is plain and almost without adornment, as befits an antechamber. An elegant Louis XV chair in the foreground lends a counteraccent to all the gesticulations.

The boudoir of the countess in act 2 has decorations above the bed and the dressing room door, from which Susanna emerges to the surprise of both the count and his wife (Fig. 8). Susanna has lost her headgear here, but in another illustration showing Mademoiselle Contat (who created the role) at the identical spot in act 2, scene 17, she wears a hat.[9] The guitar with which Susanna accompanied Cherubino's Romance sung to the countess (the *canzonetta*, No. 11 in the opera) rests on the chair in the right foreground, and the open window reminds us of how the page escaped. More clearly visible here is the sash around the count's waist. The time would seem to be close to midday because of the lighting.

Act 3 is illustrated by the trial scene, depicted in a magnificent room with ornate columns (Fig. 9). The shadows have lengthened, corresponding to the mid- to late-afternoon time. Count Almaviva, more splendidly dressed than ever, presides from the raised dais. Figaro, in plebeian costume of breeches, weskit, kerchief, and sash, has a loose hair bag that anticipates the revolutionary caps that will be worn by the sans-culottes a few years later. He confronts Doctor Bartolo across the room in one of the funniest scenes of the play as they argue over the wording of his promise to marry Marcellina, who stands to the left of Bartolo. A stuttering magistrate adds to the hilarity.

For act 4, Beaumarchais calls for a gallery illuminated by candelabra and *lustres*. Saint-Quentin does not show these, nor does he otherwise account for the source of his light (Fig. 10). The dancing has begun in the background, while the count places a bridal hat and veil on Susanna, who is showing even more décolletage.

9. In Howard C. Rice, Jr., *Thomas Jefferson's Paris* (Princeton, N.J., 1976), Fig. 101.

7 The Chair scene

FIGURES 7–11

Saint-Quentin: Five vignettes from
Le mariage de Figaro

8 The Closet scene

The countess sits behind them, apparently intent on the words of the duet sung by two maidens with flowers in their hair. They sing the praises of the count for delivering the young bride into the hands of her husband "chaste and pure." Figaro looks on with Marcellina behind him. The room makes a potent statement about the triumph of the neoclassical style in Paris. Aguas-Frescas outside Seville would not have been nearly so advanced or up-to-date.

9 The Trial scene

Evening has come, and the action moves to a spot in the garden under the chest-nut trees (turned into pines by Da Ponte) where there are two small pavilions (Fig. 11). Saint-Quentin (and Beaumarchais?) had no real choice here except to depict the dénouement—the moment of truth when the count recognizes in the person kneeling before him his wife disguised as Susanna. Figaro kneels next to her. To the count's left are Marcellina and the real Susanna, flanked by Antonio

10 The Ball scene

and, behind him, Bartolo. The magistrate and the many other characters of *Le mariage de Figaro* crowd around to witness the final lesson of "la folle journée."

The role of the countess in the opera shows the most divergence from its counterpart in the play. Of great moment was the decision by Mozart and Da Ponte to withhold her from act 1 (where she appears for an instant in the play to plead for Cherubino) so as to introduce her at the beginning of act 2 with a soliloquy,

11 The Dénouement

"Porgi, amor, qualche ristoro." This fervent and ever-so-moving plea to love had its parallels in Italian opera, notably in the solo scene for the young Rosina in Paisiello's *Barbiere*.[10] As we shall see, it had resonances as well with another type of music in Mozart's vast oeuvre, as did her soliloquy in act 3, "Dove sono i bei

10. As argued in Chapter 8.

EXAMPLE 6.1A–B.

A: *Figaro*, Sketch for No. 20

B: *Figaro*, No. 20

EXAMPLE 6.2. Mass in C
(Coronation Mass), K. 317,
Agnus Dei

momenti," for which there is also no model in the play. The troubles Mozart took
to conquer the seemingly simple melody of "Dove sono" are apparent in a surviving melodic sketch, given here just above the final version (Ex. 6.1A–B). It is possible that Da Ponte's words are lacking in the sketch because he was not even asked
to supply them until Mozart got the melody the way he wanted it. In the sketch,
Mozart seems to be fighting against the obvious: the natural inclination to rise
from the third to the fifth degree, after having risen from the first to the third. The
result is a too-great emphasis on the tone E. Did Mozart resist his final solution at
first out of a realization that he had already written something very similar to it, a

EXAMPLE 6.3. Missa solemnis,
K. 337, Agnus Dei

Andante sostenuto

rise through the third to the fifth with instrumental linkings between the vocal utterances in his "Coronation" Mass of 1779 (K. 317; Ex. 6.2)? The sacred context in which he first conceived this idea cannot help but color our conception of the countess and of the seriousness of her plight. What is true of "Dove sono" is no less true of "Porgi, amor," the opening melodic motif of which may be found set by Mozart to sacred words many times over.[11] One particular example, in his last complete mass, the Missa solemnis in C of 1780 (K. 337), even sets the motif in E-flat, as a refreshing oasis of relief coming after the brightness of C major, and accompanied by prominent solo winds (Ex. 6.3). It is no wonder, then, that both soliloquies of the countess exude an aura of fervor that is close to prayer: both melodic incipits had been used by Mozart for real prayers.

APPENDIX

Le nozze di Figaro
Da Ponte's Preface to the Italian Libretto[12]

Il tempo prescritto dall'uso alle drammatiche rappresentazioni, un certo dato numero di personaggi comunemente praticato nelle medesime; ed alcune altre prudenti viste, e convenienze dovute ai costumi, al loco, e agli spettatori, furono le cagioni per cui non ho fatto una traduzione di quella eccelente comedia, ma una imitazione piuttosto, o vogliamo dire un estratto.

Per questo sono stato costretto a ridurre a undici attori i sedici che la compongono, due de' quali si possono eseguire da uno stesso soggetto, e ad ommettere,

11. Examples in which Mozart began with a rise from 5 to 8 over tonic harmony followed by a 4–3 melodic sigh over dominant harmony include the following: "Sancta Maria ora pro nobis" in Litaniae Laurentanae BVM, K. 109, of 1771; "Dona nobis pacem" in the Missa brevis, K. 194, of 1774; and the opening Kyrie of the Missa brevis, K. 275, of 1777.
12. Our Italian text comes from the original libretto in the Library of Congress. The citation of it in Deutsch, *Dokumente*, p. 239, drops one entire line of text, an error not rectified in the *Addenda and Corrigenda* that came out in 1978.

oltre un intiero atto di quella, molte graziosissime scene, e molti bei motti, e saletti ond'è sparsa, in loco di che ho dovuto sostituire canzonette, arie, cori ed altri pensieri, e parole di musica suscettibili, cose che dalla sola poesia, e non mai dalla prosa si somministrano. Ad onta però di tutto lo studio, e di tutta la diligenza e cura avuta dal maestro di capella, e da me per esser brevi, l'opera non sarà delle più corte che si sieno esposte sul nostro teatro, al che speriamo che basti di scusa la varietà delle file onde è tessuta l'azione di questo dramma, la vastità e grandezza del medesimo, la moltiplicità de' pezzi musicali, che si son dovuti fare, per non tener di soverchio oziosi gli attori, per scemare la noia e monotonia dei lunghi recitativi, per esprimere tratto tratto con diversi colori le diverse passioni che vi campeggiano, e il desiderio nostro particolarmente di offerire un quasi nuovo genere di spettacolo ad un pubblico di gusto sì raffinato, e di sì giudizio intendimento.

Il Poeta

The time prescribed by usage in music dramas, a certain number of characters practiced in the same, and other prudent considerations and expediencies arising from the customs, the place, and the spectators were the reasons why I have not simply translated this excellent comedy, but rather made an imitation, or better put, an extract.

For this reason I was forced to reduce sixteen actors to eleven, two of which can be played by the same person, and to omit, besides an entire act, many most graceful scenes and many bons mots and pungent witticisms with which the play is strewn, in place of which I had to substitute canzonette, arias, choruses, and other inventions, and words susceptible to music, things provided only by poetry, never by prose. In spite of all this study, diligence, and care taken by the composer and by me to be brief, the opera will still not be the shortest one ever put on in our theater, for which we hope that excuse enough will be found in the variety of threads with which the action of this drama is woven, the vastness and greatness of the same, and the multiplicity of musical numbers that had to be made, in order not to allow excessive idleness to the actors, and to avoid the annoyance and monotony of long recitatives, and to express step by step with diverse colors the diverse passions that rival each other, and to carry out our desire of offering a quasi-novel genre of spectacle to a public of such refined taste and such just understanding.

The Poet

7 · SETTING THE STAGE FOR *FIGARO*

The Burgtheater in Vienna during the decade up to 1786 operated under the close personal supervision of Emperor Joseph II. Bitten by the ambition to become his own theater director, he founded the so-called Nationaltheater in 1776.[1] In so doing he shattered the relationship between the two imperial theaters, which had hitherto seen a wide variety of spectacles including Italian opera, French plays and opéras-comiques, full-length pantomime ballets (a Viennese specialty), and dramas and musical comedies in German. The theatrical variety of which Vienna had boasted changed in an instant when Joseph dismissed the entire Burgtheater company: singers, dancers, orchestra members, and everyone else necessary to the functioning of an opera house. In their stead he installed the German company of players and their orchestra who had previously occupied the Kärntnerthor Theater. Patriots expected great things to come of the prominence to be given thenceforth to plays in German, but they were bound to be disappointed. Looking back at the winter of 1776–77 and the havoc wrought by the emperor on Vienna's long-nourished theatrical traditions, we are apt to reflect on the darker side of absolute monarchy and its caprices. There were more starving artists than usual on the streets of Vienna that winter.

In 1778 Joseph added a Singspiel wing to the German players, who had previously been restricted by their talents to quite modest musical offerings. Ignaz Umlauf's *Die Bergknappen* inaugurated this phase, which lasted until 1783. The great majority of lyric offerings during these years were opéras-comiques in German translation, just as a very large part of the spoken repertory was made up of French plays in translation. Vienna preferred Grétry to its local composers. A lack

Reprinted from *Musical Times* 127 (1986).

1. Franz Hadamowsky, *Die Josefinische Theaterreform und das Spieljahr 1776/77 des Burgtheaters: Eine Dokumentation*, Quellen zur Theatergeschichte, vol. 2 (Vienna, 1978).

of truly gifted poets and composers beset the Nationaltheater from its inception, but all its strivings were crowned with one supreme final accomplishment, *Die Entführung aus dem Serail* (1782). Even it was not enough to rescue the notion of an all-German theater. By 1783 Joseph tacitly admitted this fact by recruiting an Italian company of *buffoni* through the offices of his ambassador to Venice, Count Giacomo Durazzo, who, ironically, had been the theater director in Vienna when Joseph was a young man, and the architect of such operatic triumphs as Gluck's *Orfeo ed Euridice* in 1762 and Traetta's *Ifigenia in Tauride* in 1763. The new Italian buffo company was installed in the Burgtheater in April 1783, alongside the German company, with whom they were to alternate. Antonio Salieri, long in imperial service, became their music director, and the newly arrived Lorenzo Da Ponte was given the task of adjusting their librettos as needed. The primo buffo was Francesco Benucci, the prima buffa Nancy Storace. Others included Stefano Mandini (baritone), Michael Kelly (tenor), and Francesco Bussani (bass).

Not everyone around the emperor approved his latest move, which was in fact a step back toward the way things had been before his 1776 reform. Joseph von Sonnenfels, author, critic, and one of the most enlightened of the emperor's advisors, made an impassioned plea that the work of the German troupe not be sacrificed on account of the Italians—this in the preface, dated 1784, to a set of critical reports that first came out in 1768, *Briefe über die wienerische Schaubühne*. The public, unswayed by appeals to patriotism, decided in favor of the Italians. As Friedrich Nicolai observed in the fourth volume of his *Beschreibung einer Reise* (1784): "Vienna again has an Italian buffo company, which plays half the days in the so-called Nationaltheater, and more than divides the applause with the German players."

The most telling account of the Burgtheater and its public in the 1780s is that of Johann Pezzl in his *Skizze von Wien*, published in installments from 1786 to 1790. Pezzl was a former monk, born in Bavaria in 1756, who became one of the leading proponents of Joseph's social and political reforms. Because the theatrical reform of 1776 could be regarded as part of the wider reform movement, in that new plays using the vernacular language familiar to most Viennese were deemed the most expeditious way of enlightening the public, Pezzl, one imagines, would speak only in praise of the German theater. Quite the contrary—he takes a position that is hardly complimentary to it:

> At first everyone went eagerly and squeezed in to see the new *Schauspiel*. After a few years the house was again poor. Finally we were restricted for a while to nothing but the Nationaltheater. Soon people yawned at this eternal sameness, and the emperor, knowing the restless curiosity of his Viennese subjects, again gave them (in the year 1783) an Italian opera, or better, comic opera, and it is still the reigning form. This beautiful monster, as it has been called by Schubart (who is still lingering in a prison, put there by his prince), has become the favorite of the more refined public.

Next Pezzl lists the comic operas given in the Burgtheater between 1783 and 1786 that gained the most approbation, in ascending order of popularity: *Il barbiere di*

Franciscus Benucci   *Anna Storace*

FIGURE 12

The first Figaro and Susanna

Siviglia (Petrosellini-Paisiello); *Fra i due litiganti il terzo gode* (Lorenzi-Sarti); *La grotta di Trofonio* (Casti-Salieri); *Il Rè Teodoro in Venezia* (Casti-Paisiello); and *Una cosa rara: Bellezza ed onestà* (Da Ponte–Martín y Soler). Pezzl wrote and published this installment of his *Skizze* in 1787, one year after *Figaro*, which was not enough of a popular success even to rate mention. He says in addition:

> The singers at the opera are select and well paid. Mandini and Benucci are the most accomplished *buffo* actors one can see. The chief idol in this comic Pantheon, up to the present, was La Storace, of Italian descent, but born in London. She earned over 1,000 ducats yearly. To tell the truth, she sang very well, but her figure was not advantageous: a thick little head, without any feminine charm, with the exception of a pair of large and nearly expressionless eyes. Storace returned just recently to London.

Pezzl concluded this topic by saying that German opera was being given too, mostly in the Kärntnerthor Theater, but since it received less support than the Italian opera in the Burgtheater it made do with lesser singers and was generally inferior. Thus the relationship of the two theaters had revolved around to nearly the same state it had been in before 1776.

The first opera but one by the new buffo troupe in Vienna was a revival of Salieri's *La scuola degli gelosi*, on a text of Mazzolà and Bertati. It had been making the rounds in Italy for several years since its premiere as a Carnival opera at the San Moisè in Venice in 1778, and it was the last opera that Storace had sung in Italy, also in Venice, before she came to open in it in Vienna. Salieri and Da Ponte revised the work so as to put the singers in the best possible light, principally Storace and Benucci (Fig. 12), who carried the day for this production and were to do so for most of its successors. Zinzendorf noted in his diary for 22 April 1783:

"*La scuola de' gelosi.* Mlle Storace the Englishwoman, a pretty, voluptuous figure, beautiful neck, and good as a Bohemian girl. . . . The buffo Benucci very good, Bussani the lover, less so. The audience was greatly pleased." And again on 9 May: "I went to hear the opera *La scuola de' gelosi* and was enchanted. The English-woman sang like an angel and the buffo is admirable."[2] The success of the opera was reported as far away as Berlin, with reservations about the acting, but not the singing of Storace; high praise for Benucci ("the best ever seen here with regard to the naturalness of his acting"); and a dismissal of the rest as unworthy of mention.[3] The emperor was traveling during May and June. He wrote to Count Rosenberg on 2 June 1783 that since Benucci pleased the public, they should try to retain him until the following Easter, then sign him for a further year's contract, and likewise with Storace; as for the others, the best were to be retained if Benucci and Storace stayed, but if not, they were all to be dismissed. The fate of Vienna's buffo troupe hung on the wishes of its two principal singers—or more precisely, on the avail-ability of Benucci. As Joseph wrote on 19 June 1783 to Rosenberg: "As for the opera buffa, since Benucci cannot stay, it is not worthwhile keeping the others. . . . It is opportune to distribute the roles of the *Barber of Seville*, in order to take advantage of Benucci while he is still present."[4] Joseph held Paisiello in high esteem and was intent on staging *Il barbiere di Siviglia*, written the previous autumn for the court of St. Petersburg, while he still had the forces to do so. It was by imperial com-mand, then, that the immortal figures of Beaumarchais's Figaro cycle first trod the Burgtheater stage.

Mozart watched the debut of the buffo troupe and reported to his father by letter (7 May 1783) that it greatly pleased the public and that the buffo, Benucci, was particularly good. His very next words concern the hundreds of librettos he had been poring over, finding hardly a single one that satisfied him—and even then much would have to be changed here and there, and if a poet were willing to do that, he could perhaps as easily make a whole new book, which is always preferable in any case. This train of thought leads him to mention a certain Abate Da Ponte, who was madly busy with all the revisions he had to make for the theater, and who was obligated to make an entirely new libretto for Salieri, which would not be ready before two months, but then, says Mozart, he had promised to make *him* one. "Who knows now if he will be able to keep his word, or willing to!" An unkind remark about crafty Italians leads him back to Salieri: "If he is in league with Salieri, I'll never get a thing out of him—and I'm dying to show what I could

2. "La scuola de'gelosi. Mlle Storace, l'inglesina, jolie figure voluptueuse, belle gorge, bien en bohémienne. . . . Le buffo Vennuci [Benucci] très bon, amoroso Bussani moins. L'auditoire fort con-tent. . . . Je fus entendre l'opera La scuola de'gelosi et en fus enchanté. L'inglesina chanta comme une ange, le buffo est admirable"; Michtner, *Das alte Burgtheater*, p. 150.
3. "Die erste Sängerin singt vortrefflich, dagegen ist ihre Gestikulation unausstehlich. Der Buffo wird in Ansehung des natürlichen Spiels für den Besten gehalten, den man hier sah. Die übrigen sind nicht der Rede wert"; *Litteratur- und Theaterzeitung*, quoted in ibid., p. 151.
4. "Quant à l'opera buffa dèsque Bennuci ne peut point rester, il ne vaut pas la peine de garder les autres. . . . Il sera tems de distribuer tout de suite les roles du Barbiere de Seville, afin d'en tirer encore parti pendant la presence de Benucci"; Payer von Thurn, *Joseph II als Theaterdirektor*, p. 33.

do in an Italian opera."[5] More than a hint of self-delusion emerges here. How could the imperial theater poet be anything but "in league" with the theater's music director? He would soon lose his job were he not.

Da Ponte was indeed busy with his revisions. Viennese versions of Cimarosa's *L'italiana in Londra*, Sarti's *Fra i due litiganti*, and Anfossi's *Il curioso indiscreto* followed in quick succession after Salieri's opera. Zinzendorf commented on each in his diary. Mozart inserted his foot in the door, as it were, by writing substitute arias for Aloysia Lange and Valentin Adamberger, the first two German singers to perform alongside the Italians, in Anfossi's opera. Mozart implies in a letter to his father (21 June 1783) that these arias were commissioned; yet the strenuous efforts by Salieri, under orders from the theater director, Count Rosenberg, to dissuade Adamberger from singing K. 420, also reported by Mozart (2 July 1783), would suggest the contrary.

The Viennese premiere of Paisiello's *Il barbiere di Siviglia* took place on 13 August 1783. Joseph reported the next day in glowing terms on the troupe's acting, which exceeded his expectations: "As for their acting, they acquitted themselves even better than was hoped, above all Benucci, who in certain moments copied and all but became Schröder [principal tragic actor of the German troupe]. La Storace sang an *aria cantabile* very well."[6] The lyric number in question was probably Rosina's cavatina "Giusto ciel!" which closed act 1. As to the acting of La Storace, Joseph complained of some coarseness, lapsing from French into Italian for the term *sguaiatezza*. *Il barbiere* held the stage of the Burgtheater for five consecutive seasons. In several senses it paved the way for an operatic version of the second play in the Figaro cycle, which first became known to the world at large during 1784.

Paisiello himself returned in triumph to Vienna in 1784. He had been fêted there when he passed through in 1776 on his way to Russia with a special performance of his opera *La molinara*. On his return he was heaped with new honors. Joseph asked him to write an original work for the buffo troupe. A new libretto was prepared expressly for him, not by Da Ponte, who was considered too inexperienced still, but by his archrival, the Abate Casti. Thus emerged *Il Rè Teodoro in Venezia*, fashioned from an episode of Voltaire's *Candide*. The 1783–84 season had languished for lack of successful productions, not because of the operas, but because of the absence of Benucci, who honored his commitments to Rome. When he returned in May 1784, even the mediocre scores caught the public's imagination.

---

5. Letter of 7 May 1783: "der Buffo ist besonders gut. er heist Benuci . . . wir haben hier einen gewissen abate da Ponte als Poeten. — dieser hat nunmehro mit der Correctur im theater rasend zu thun. — muss *per obligo* ein ganz Neues büchel für dem Salieri machen. — das wird vor 2 Monathen nicht fertig werden. — dann hat er mir ein Neues zu machen versprochen; — wer weis nun ob er dann auch sein Wort halten kann — oder will! — sie wissen wohl die Herrn Italiener sind ins gesicht sehr artig! — genug, wir kennen sie! — ist er mit Salieri verstanden, so bekomme ich mein lebtage keins — und ich möchte gar zu gerne mich auch in einer Welschen opera zeigen."

6. "Ils s'en sont tirés pour l'action en verité au dela de l'esperance, surtout Benucci qui dans des certains moments a copié et presque frisé Schröder. La Storacci à tres bien chanté un air cantabile"; Payer von Thurn, *Joseph II als Theaterdirektor*, p. 35.

EXAMPLE 7.1A–B.

A: Paisiello, *Il Rè Teodoro a Venezia*, No. 2

B: *Figaro*, No. 4

Zinzendorf summed up the situation in three words with respect to a 1790 revival of *Il Rè Teodoro*: "Benucci anima tout."[7] Of the premiere on 23 August 1784 he reported that there were many beautiful pieces but the opera was long and the public did not enjoy it. He cited in particular the piece sung by Mandini in the title role: "The aria 'Io re sono' scarcely pleased me."[8] Can it be coincidence that Mozart chose the same general tempo, meter, key, and head-motif for Bartolo's revenge aria "La vendetta" in *Le nozze di Figaro* (Ex. 7.1A–B)? Mozart had friendly relations with the Neapolitan master, as is evident in his letter to his father of 9–17 June 1784: "I am fetching Paisiello in my carriage, as I want him to hear both my pupil and my compositions."[9] Beginning a bass aria with identical music (but then going on to write an entirely different piece, as his text demanded) may have been Mozart's way of expressing friendly emulation, as only one composer can emulate another.

Salieri cannot help but have been overshadowed by the presence of Paisiello in Vienna, but he had the good fortune to be called to Paris in 1784 and again in 1786–87 as an opera composer in lieu of his now aged mentor, Gluck. Joseph was instrumental here, too. He remained in close touch with his sister Marie Antoinette, queen of France, and they corresponded about theatrical matters, among many other things. Back in Vienna in late 1784, Salieri set Da Ponte's original libretto, the long-deferred work mentioned by Mozart in May 1783, *Un ricco d'un giorno*.

7. "Benucci animated all"; Michtner, *Das alte Burgtheater*, p. 394.

8. "L'air Io re sono ne me plut guère. . . . Bref il y a beaucoup de beaux morceaux, mais l'opéra est long et le public ne l'a pas gouté"; ibid., p. 393n26. For a list of incipits in some arias in *Il Rè Teodoro* and an attempt to compare them with Mozart, see Wolfgang Ruf, *Die Rezeption von Mozarts "Le nozze di Figaro" bei den Zeitgenossen* (Wiesbaden, 1977), p. 63.

9. "ich werde den Paesello mit dem Wagen abhollen, um ihm meine Composition und meine schüllerin hören zu lassen"; 12 June 1784. Michael Kelly, in his *Reminiscences* (London, 1826), 1:234–35, comments on the friendly meeting of the two; and Rochlitz, in his "Anekdoten" in *Allgemeine musikalische Zeitung 1* (1798/99): col. 115, says he heard Mozart speak favorably of Paisiello, whose works he knew very well ("So habe ich ihn z. B. sehr vortheilhaft von Paisiello, dessen Arbeiten ihm sehr wohl bekannt waren, sprechen hören").

The opera was a total failure, leading Salieri to swear he would never work with Da Ponte again. Yet Da Ponte retained the confidence of the emperor and remained theater poet—which meant that he could look to other collaborators. Mozart's hour was approaching. Salieri's preoccupations with Paris, his failed Viennese collaboration with Da Ponte—these conditions were combining to prepare the coming to pass of a miracle.[10]

The small theater next to the palace that witnessed this miracle was plain, almost homely, during the 1780s, in keeping with Joseph's vaunted severity and simplicity. An Austrian engraver, J. E. Mansfeld, rendered the stage and audience in a partial view for Joseph Richter's *Bildergalerie weltlicher Misbräuche* (1785; Fig. 13): four tiers of boxes without adornment continue directly onto the apron of the stage, under an undecorated proscenium arch. The boxes are also documented on a contemporary engraving showing the plan of the ground floor and the first level above it (Fig. 14). These documents should be studied together, for they confirm each other, though they do not reflect the many phases the theater went through in its long history.[11] There were only a few loges on the left side on the ground floor. At the level above, the choicest of all, box number 2 was rented to Prince Esterházy;[12] directly across on the right side was the loge of the director, Count Rosenberg, adjoining the imperial double loge, whence Emperor Joseph watched the productions of his companies and where he customarily sat at concerts, as when a fortepiano was played on the stage.[13] In the "Parterre noble" Mansfeld shows many ladies, seated on benches, as well as gentlemen. The variety of costume depicted suggests a diversity of social class and a certain informality. On stage, the actress in wide pannier and feathered headdress gesticulating to her male partner is preaching a sermon to her husband.[14] It is a pity the artist set so little store by depicting the members of the orchestra. From the plan of the ground floor we can see that the entrance to the orchestra space in front of the stage was on the left. In Mansfeld's

10. Johannes Brahms spoke of the opera using this very term: "Each number in Mozart's *Figaro* is for me a miracle; it is simply incomprehensible how anybody was able to create something of such an absolute perfection, never has anything like this been made, and not even by Beethoven" (*Billroth und Brahms in Briefwechsel*, ed. O. Gottlieb-Billroth [Berlin, 1935], p. 315; cited in Fellinger, "Brahms's View of Mozart," pp. 54–55.

11. On the evolution of the theater, see Daniel Heartz, "Nicolas Jadot and the Building of the Burgtheater," *Musical Quarterly* 68 (1982): 1–31.

12. Otto G. Schindler, "Das Publikum des Burgtheaters in der josephinischen Ära," in *Das Burgtheater und sein Publikum*, ed. Margret Dietrich (Vienna, 1976), p. 61.

13. According to Mozart, in a letter of 24–28 March 1781: "ich hätte kein Concert, sondern | : weil der kayser in der Proscen loge ist : | ganz allein | : die gräfin thun hätte mir ihr schönes steiner-Pianforte darzu gegeben : | Preludirt, eine fuge — und dann die variationen je suis lindor gespiellt" ("I would have played all alone—not a concerto, because the emperor sits in the proscenium box and Countess Thun would have loaned me her beautiful Stein pianoforte, but rather a prelude, fugue, and then the variations on 'Je suis Lindor'"). Mozart's "Lindor" variations (K. 354) are written on the stage tune sung by the count as a serenade to Rosine in *Le barbier de Séville* by Beaumarchais, and thus constitute an early evidence of Mozart's fascination with the Figaro cycle.

14. Joseph Richter, *Bildergalerie weltlicher Misbräuche: Ein Gegenstück zur Bildergalerie katholischer und klösterlicher Misbräuche, von Pater Hilarion, Exkuzuzinern. Mit Kupfern und anpassenden Vignetten* (Frankfurt and Leipzig [actually published in Vienna], 1785), pp. 257–58, gives a detailed explanation of the plate, which is the illustration for his chapter 19, "Uiber öffentliche Schauspiele."

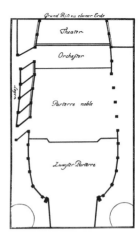

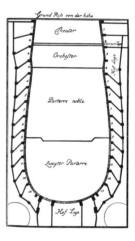

FIGURE 13

Mansfeld: Stage of the Burgtheater
in 1785

FIGURE 14

Floorplan of the Burgtheater in the
1780s

vignette we observe the prompter's box and the sparsely decorated flats to the side of the Viennese stage that first welcomed Figaro.

Beaumarchais conceived *Le mariage de Figaro* at the same time as *Le barbier de Séville*, as his preface to the first play makes clear. Many thematic strands, besides the obvious continuity of plot and characters, tie the two plays together. *Figaro* depends on its audience's full knowledge of the happenings in the previous play; hence it forgoes a proper dramatic exposition. The advantages to writing a Figaro opera in sequence to Paisiello's *Barbiere* were obvious: everyone knew and loved these characters. But the drawbacks were enormous, too. The second play, unlike the first, created a scandal when public performance was finally allowed by Louis XVI in 1784. What was shocking in Paris was hardly likely to pass the censors in Vienna, who had long been eviscerating relatively innocent plays and opéras-comiques from Paris.

Le mariage de Figaro was so shocking that it offended not only conservatives but every faction in the spectrum of French politics, including the radical left. Beaumarchais was attacked by the anti-royalist critic Brissot, for example, who railed against the play, calling it

> a scandalous farce where, behind an appearance of defending morality, morality itself is held up to ridicule; where, behind an appearance of defending great truths, they are debased by the despicable interlocutor who voices them; where the aim seems to have been parodying the great writers of the century, but putting their language in the mouth of a rake's valet, and of encouraging oppression while leading people to laugh at their own degradation . . . and lending to the entire nation, by heinous imposture, this character of insouciance and triviality found only in the capital.[15]

A *succès de scandale* it may have been, but a success even so, especially with the ladies. According to Mrs. Thrale, a member of Dr. Johnson's circle who visited Paris in September 1784, women had favorite lines from the play engraved on their fans and pocket-handkerchiefs, as London women had done at the time of Gay's *Beggar's Opera*. Although London stages were used to indecencies that would not then have been allowed by Parisian censors, Mrs. Thrale was shocked, as she related in her travel diary:

> [The Parisians] are all wild for love of a new comedy written by Mons. de Beaumarchais, and called "Le Mariage de Figaro", full of such wit as we were fond of in the reign of Charles the Second, indecent merriment, and gross immorality; mixed, however, with much acrimonious satire, as if Sir George Etherege and Johnny Gay had clubbed their powers of ingenuity at once to divert and corrupt their auditors.[16]

Mrs. Thrale understood better than most students today the obscene implications of the proverb cited by Bazile, with which act 1 of the play ends: "tant va la cruche à l'eau, qu'à la fin."[17] The object of this remark was little Fanchette (Barbarina), but also, by extension, her cousin Suzanne.

The play spread quickly and widely by innumerable editions and translations. A production was proposed by Schikaneder's German troupe in the Kärntnerthor Theater in early 1785. The emperor expressed his concern at the prospect. His letter of 31 January 1785 to Count Pergen, chief of police and the official responsible for censorship, warned that the play would have to be either greatly revised or banned altogether because it contained so much that was offensive. The difference between Joseph and his Habsburg predecessors and successors is that they would have banned it outright without qualification.

---

15. Crow, *Painters and Public Life in Eighteenth-Century Paris*, p. 226.

16. Hester Lynch Piozzi, *Observations and Reflections Made in the Course of a Journey Through France, Italy, and Germany*, ed. Herbert Barrows (Ann Arbor, Mich., 1967), p. 12.

17. "The pitcher that goes to the well too often breaks"—but Figaro interpolates instead "gets filled."

8 · CONSTRUCTING *LE NOZZE DI FIGARO*

Lorenzo Da Ponte is our main witness as to how he and Mozart put together their three operas. Yet his memoirs, first published in 1823, mystify the topic more than they illuminate it. Some additional light is shed by an earlier publication entitled *An Extract from the Life of Lorenzo Da Ponte, with the history of several dramas written by him, and among others, Il Figaro, Il Don Giovanni & La Scuola degli Amanti set to music by Mozart* (New York, 1819).[1] Whoever translated this from Da Ponte's original Italian worked from a text different in many details from what was published four years later as the *Memorie*.[2] The well-known passage about how the poet must rack his brains in order to invent situations for the buffo finales reads as follows in the *Extract*:

This Finale in Italian comic operas, though strictly connected with the other parts of the drama, is a kind of little comedy by itself: it requires a distinct plot, and should be particularly interesting: in this part are chiefly displayed the genius of a musical composer, and the power of the singers; and for this is reserved the most striking effect of the drama.

Recitativo is entirely excluded from this division of the piece. The whole of it is sung, and it must contain every species of melody. The adagio, the allegro, the andante, the cantabile, the armonioso, the strepitoso, the arcistrepitoso, with which last every act commonly ends. It is a theatrical rule, that in the course of the Finale, all the singers, however numerous they may be, must make their appearance in solos,

Reprinted from *Journal of the Royal Musical Association* 112 (1987).

1. I am indebted to John Stone of London for calling my attention to this early form of a part of the memoirs, which remains unknown to the specialist literature on Mozart. His annotated edition of the *Extract* is eagerly awaited.

2. Da Ponte's memoirs have undergone many modern editions and translations. To be preferred is the annotated critical edition of the *Memorie* by G. Gambarin and F. Nicolini (Bari, 1918), in the series Scrittori d'Italia.

duets, trios, quartetos etc. etc. And this rule the poet is under the absolute necessity of observing, whatever difficulties and absurdities it may occasion; and though all the critics, with Aristotle at their head exclaim against it, I must observe here that the real Aristotles of a dramatic poet* are in general, not only the composer of the music, but also the first buffo, the prima donna and not very seldom the 2d 3d and 4th buffoon of the company.

(pp. 5–6)

Da Ponte changed this passage in his memoirs by adding more about the "chiusa" or "stretta" that closes the finale, by exaggerating the procession of singers that had to appear—"tutti i cantanti, se fosser trecento, a uno, a due, a tre, a sei, a sessanta, per cantarvi de' soli, de' duetti, de' terzetti, de' sestetti, de' sessantetti"—and, what is more instructive still, by deleting the last clause (beginning "I must observe"). The asterisk on "dramatic poet" sent the reader to a footnote, which read: "I have described the fate of the poor dramatic poet in a letter to Casti, the perusal of which, I flatter myself will afford some entertainment to my Italian reader, it will be found at the end of this pamphlet."[3] Da Ponte probably deleted the final clause because it came too close to a famous passage in the memoirs of Goldoni, describing his first encounter with the "rules" of libretto writing, delivered in the form of this admonition from a friend: "The Dramma per musica, which is in itself an imperfect composition, has been subjected to the use of rules, contrary, it is true, to those of Aristotle, of Horace, and of all those who have written about poetics, but necessary in order to serve music, actors, and composers."[4]

Da Ponte was willing to credit Goldoni in the *Extract* for some "very pretty" comic librettos. He had a kind word also for the genial author of *Le bourru bienfaisant*: "I made use accordingly of the excellent play of Goldoni entitled Il Burburo di buon core." But he removed these references to his illustrious Venetian predecessor in the memoirs. It is possible that the unfavorable comparisons of Da Ponte's memoirs with the more stylish memoirs of Goldoni were at work already in the early 1820s,[5] souring Da Ponte to the point of being unwilling to give Goldoni any credit at all. He was unhappy as well about sharing any of his renown with singers; the "first buffo," named ahead even of the prima donna, can mean in this Viennese context none other than Benucci.

Francesco Benucci was the greatest basso buffo of his generation. He was the mainstay of the Italian troupe in the Burgtheater from their arrival in 1783 throughout the decade that followed. Besides the role of Figaro, he created the first Viennese Leporello (1788) and the first Guglielmo in *Così fan tutte* (1790). He was a particular favorite of Emperor Joseph II, as well as of the Viennese public, both

---

3. For the Epistle to Casti, with translation, see pp. 99–101.

4. "Il Dramma per musica, ch'è per se stesso un componimento imperfetto, è stato suggettato dall' uso delle regole, contrarie, egli è vero, a quelle di Aristotele, di Orazio e di tutti quelli che hanno scritto della Poetica, ma necessarie per servire alla Musica, agli Attori e ai Compositori"; Goldoni, *Tutte le opere* 1 : 688. In the *Mémoires* (*Tutte le opere* 1 : 258) Goldoni adds to his list: "Il faut consulter le peintre-décorateur" ("It is necessary to consult the painter-decorator").

5. Sheila Hodges, *Lorenzo Da Ponte: The Life and Times of Mozart's Librettist* (London, 1985), p. 201.

for his acting and for his singing. If a single resource had to be named as the strength that emboldened Mozart to conceive of writing an opera on the scandalous *Figaro* play, we suggest that it was Benucci. His name was not deemed worthy of mention in Da Ponte's memoirs, as we have seen, yet it occurs very often in the correspondence between the emperor and his theater director, Count Rosenberg. Just a few months after the premiere of *Figaro* on 1 May 1786, when it was a question of rehiring Nancy Storace, the first Susanna, Joseph wrote to Rosenberg: "As to La Storace, if we can keep her, which I would hope, it would be necessary to engage her securely for the year 1788 . . . but never to the detriment of Benucci, because this man is worth more than two Storaces."[6] Da Ponte's name does not occur in this particular correspondence, from which it might be inferred that he too stood on a lower rung than Benucci, as viewed by the powers that ran the Burgtheater.

Joseph II framed his objections to the Figaro play in a letter to Count Pergen of 31 January 1785, taking care to point out that the censor, if he did not ban the play outright, would have to see that it was cleaned up.

> I understand that the well-known comedy *Le mariage de Figaro* has been proposed in a German translation for the Kärntnerthor Theater. Since this play contains much that is offensive as I understand it, the censor will either reject it altogether or have such changes made in it that will allow him to take responsibility for its performance and the impression it makes on the public.[7]

Da Ponte echoes the banning in his memoirs, but not the emperor's suggestion of redeeming the play through revisions: "The emperor had shortly before forbidden the company of the German theater to perform this comedy, which he said was written too liberally for a proper audience."[8] In the *Extract* he writes:

> There was an obstacle which first appeared insurmountable—the emperor had a few days before forbidden its performance in Vienna. I resolved nevertheless, to write the drama secretly, and wait for a good opportunity to have it performed in Vienna, or in some other city. In the course of two months the opera was completed in all its parts; and as fortune would have it, the person we feared [Salieri], a great rival of Mozart, and who had the chief direction of the theatre, was then absent from the

6. "Quant à la Storace, si on ne peult la conserver, ce que je desirerois, il faudra au moins l'engager bien surement pour l'anée 1788 . . . mais jamais au detriment de Benucci, puisque cet homme vaut plus que deux Storaces"; Payer von Thurn, *Joseph II als Theaterdirektor*, p. 70; letter of 29 September 1786.

7. "Ich vernehme, dass die bekannte Komedie *le Mariage de Figaro* in einer deutschen Übersetzung für das Kärntnerthortheater angetragen seyn solle; da nun dieses Stück viel Anstössiges enthält; so verstehe ich mich, dass der Censor solches entweder ganz verwerfen, oder doch solche Veränderungen darinn veranlassen werde, dass er für die Vorstellung dieser Piece und den Eindruck, den sie machen dürfte, haften werde könnten"; ibid., p. 60.

8. "Vietato aveva pochi di prima l'Imperadore alla compagnia del teatro tedesco di rappresentare quella comedia, che scritta era, diceva egli, troppo liberamente per un costumato uditorio"; Da Ponte, *Memorie*, p. 110.

city. I seized the opportunity to offer Figaro to the sovereign in person; informing his majesty that Mozart had composed the music.

(pp. 13–14)

Taken literally, Da Ponte's "few days" after the emperor's ban would mean that work began on the opera as early as February 1785. The two months in question (shortened to six weeks in the memoirs) are unlikely to have come before the summer of 1785 even so, or at least no earlier than the departure from Vienna in April of Leopold Mozart, who was in ignorance of the project until early autumn. As to Salieri's absence from the city, Da Ponte has confused 1785 with 1786; Salieri was in Vienna throughout 1785 and left for Paris in the spring of 1786.[9]

By October 1785 at the latest the opera was accepted for production in the Burgtheater. In a letter of 11 November 1785 to his daughter, Leopold Mozart says that he had a letter from Wolfgang dated 2 November describing how he was overwhelmed with work on *Le nozze di Figaro*. With a long acquaintance with his son's working habits, and the trials over *Idomeneo* and *Die Entführung aus dem Serail* still fresh in his memory, Leopold worries most about the text and the time-consuming negotiations that would have to take place before it suited the composer exactly:

> He begs forgiveness because he is up to his ears since he must finish the opera
> *Le nozze di Figaro*. . . . I know the play; it is a very intricate work, and the translation from the French will surely require much revision in order to become an opera, if it is to have the effect an opera should have. God grant that the action comes off; about the music I have no doubt. That will cost him much running back and forth, and arguing, until he gets the libretto so arranged as he wishes for his purpose. And then he will always put things off and lose valuable time, according to his lovely habit; now he must go at it seriously because he is being driven by Count Rosenberg.[10]

Da Ponte painted Count Rosenberg as an enemy who tried to stop the opera, not as the theater manager of exemplary loyalty to the emperor who drove Mozart to finish his score. Contradictions accumulate, and it finally becomes difficult to accept Da Ponte's main claim, that he won the day for the new opera in a personal interview with the emperor. The *Extract* parallels the memoirs at this point: "You know very well, said the Emperor, that Mozart, who is certainly great in instrumental music, has never composed more than one drama, and that not good for

9. Ignaz von Mosel, *Ueber das Leben und die Werke des Anton Salieri, k. k. Hofkapellmeisters* (Vienna, 1827), p. 93.

10. "Er bittet um Verzeihung, weil er über Hals und Kopf die opera, *le Nozze di Figaro*, fertig machen muss. . . . — ich kenne die piece, es ist ein sehr mühsammes Stück, und die Übersetzung aus dem franz: hat sicher zu einer opera frey müssen umgeandert werden, wenns für eine opera wirkung thun soll. Gott gebe, dass es in der action ausfallt; an der Musik zweifle ich nicht. das wird ihm eben vieles Lauffen und disputieren kosten, bis er das Buch so eingerichtet bekommt, wie ers zu seiner Absicht zu haben wünschet: — und er wird immer daran geschoben, und sich hipsch Zeit gelassen haben, nach seiner schönen Gewohnheit, nun muss er auf einmahl mit Ernst daran, weil er vom Gr: Rosenberg getrieben wird"; letter of 11 November 1785.

much. And had it not been for your majesty's protection, replied I, I should never have written more than one drama in Vienna" (p. 14). Da Ponte, newly arrived in the Habsburg dominions, might have been aware only of *Die Entführung* among Mozart's earlier operas, but it is not possible to believe that Joseph's knowledge was so limited; his words about Mozart having written only one opera were put in his mouth so as to set up Da Ponte's clever response above.

> But that Marriage of Figaro, returned he, I have forbidden to be performed in the national theatre: you ought to have known that. Sir, answered I, as I had to write an opera, and not a comedy, I have been able to omit certain scenes, and shorten others, and I have carefully expunged whatever might offend the decency of a theatre over which your majesty presides. If that is the case, replied he, I rely on your opinion for the goodness of the music, and on your prudence for the choice of the characters: you may immediately give the parts to the copyist.
>
> (ibid.)

(The translator has done poorly here in rendering "della vostra prudenza quanto al costume"—meaning theatrical propriety, as in Da Ponte's phrase quoted above, "per un costumato uditorio.")

If we believe Da Ponte, the emperor capitulated with the speed of a *commedia dell'arte* clown. Rare will be the reader so credulous as this. By suggesting in the first place that the play be revised to make it more respectable, Joseph had from the beginning shown more interest in it than Da Ponte let on. And although the planned production in the Kärntnerthor Theater was abandoned, Joseph allowed the German translation of the play to be printed as it stood, uncut, something unthinkable even a few years earlier, when Maria Theresa was alive. What Da Ponte, many years later, claimed credit for initiating—the revision, cutting, and cleaning up of the play—is similar to what Joseph told Pergen would have to be done in January 1785. We suggest that, contrary to Da Ponte's version, the emperor was in on the "secret" from the beginning.

At this point in his tale Da Ponte brings in Mozart. In the *Extract*, the composer is made to seem an eavesdropper waiting in the shadows for his cue:

> I instantly brought Mozart into the imperial presence, to perform some pieces of his music; and the emperor was most agreeably surprised. I need not add, that this proceeding was by no means gratifying to the other composers, nor to the manager, Count Rosemberg [*sic*] who hated both Mozart and myself. We had to make head against a host of intriguers, both before and after the representation of the piece.
>
> (pp. 14–15)

This account must have struck Da Ponte as somewhat brisk, or lacking in plausibility, because he padded it with several further details between 1819 and 1823. In the memoirs he runs to Mozart to give him the good news, only to find an imperial courier already at hand with a note bidding the composer to bring his score to the palace instantly. Mozart obeys the royal command and plays diverse pieces, "which pleased the emperor marvellously and, without any exaggeration, astounded him." There follows a digression on the emperor's exquisite musical taste—all this material is added to the version found in the *Extract*.

The new opera was being talked about openly by late 1785, and not only in Vienna. In far-distant Paris, the German composer Joseph Martin Kraus knew what was going on; in a letter to his sister dated 26 December 1785 he wrote about Mozart: "He is working on his Figaro, an opera in 4 acts, about which I rejoice."[11] The pressure on Mozart by Count Rosenberg to finish the score in November points to an original plan to stage the opera after Christmas, during the Carnival season. But the premiere was deferred until after Easter in the event. One reason for the delay may have been the absence of Luisa Laschi, who created the role of the countess; she had been given leave to sing at Naples during Carnival.[12] Martín y Soler's successful setting of Da Ponte's *Il burburo di buon core* occupied Storace, Benucci, and the other singers of the Italian troupe during January and February 1786; and Benucci, Mandini, and Storace also had to learn Salieri's *Prima la musica, e poi le parole* for the special entertainment in the Orangerie of Schönbrunn Palace on 7 February 1786, to which Mozart contributed music for still other singers in the play *Der Schauspieldirektor*. In addition, there was the performance during Lent of *Idomeneo* on 13 March in the palace theater of Prince Auersperg, for which Mozart had to make adjustments in the score and write two new pieces.

A long-standing project of the emperor came to fulfillment with the staging of Paisiello's *La serva padrona* in the Burgtheater late in March. Joseph had received the score from Count Cobenzl, his ambassador to the court of St. Petersburg, three years earlier, at which time he put in a standing order for the scores of Paisiello's operas as they appeared—but he specified only the comic, not the serious. The performance is known of only through an entry in Zinzendorf's diary, dated 26 March 1786: "à l'opéra La serva padrona, musique nouvelle de Paisiello au lieu de l'ancienne de Pergolese. Benucci et Storace jouèrent."[13] It was not until 1 May 1786, then, that *Le nozze di Figaro* was ready to be exposed to the public, after several weeks of rehearsals. The emperor attended the dress rehearsal on 29 April; Zinzendorf confirms Da Ponte's memoirs on this point.

11. "Er arbeitet nun an seinem Figaro, eine Operette in 4 Aufzügen, worauf ich mich herzlich freue"; Irmgard Leux-Henschen, *Joseph Martin Kraus in seinen Briefen* (Stockholm, 1978), p. 310; the letter is written to Kraus's sister Marianna in Frankfurt am Main.

12. Roger Fiske in his article on Nancy Storace in *The New Grove Dictionary of Music* (London, 1980), 18:182, says that the part of the countess was intended originally for Storace, on the basis of what evidence we know not. Since Storace was more experienced than Laschi, and more highly paid, it seems reasonable to believe that she had her pick of either role.

13. "To the opera La serva padrona, new music by Paisiello instead of the old setting by Pergolesi. Benucci and Storace played in it"; *Joseph II und Graf Ludwig Cobenzl: Ihr Briefwechsel*, ed. A. Beer and J. von Fiedler (Vienna, 1901), 1:370; cited in H. C. Robbins Landon, *Haydn: Chronicle and Works* (Bloomington, Ind., 1976–80), 2:413n.

Salieri provides a detailed description of how a composer approached setting a comic opera to music in those days (see the Appendix to this chapter). His teacher Florian Leopold Gassmann, imperial court composer, was called to Italy to write an opera seria (Metastasio's *Ezio*) for the Roman Carnival of 1770. In his absence, young Salieri (born in 1750) was asked by Giovan Gastone Boccherini, brother of the composer and a dancer in imperial service, to set a libretto he had written with the help of Raniero de Calzabigi. The result was *Le donne letterate* (adapted from Molière's *Les femmes savantes*), given in the Burgtheater in January 1770. Salieri says they first decided on the distribution of the roles, taking into account the abilities of the singers then in the company (and, it goes without saying, subject to the approval of the theater director). He read the libretto through, then read it again, and read the lyric verses a third time. Only then did he begin to think of the music: "Following the practice of my teacher, I decided first on the key appropriate to the character of each lyric number." After further reading of the text he began to think of some passages in terms of melody for the first time. When he returned to his task after lunch he was seized with a desire to compose the music for the *introduzione*. He sought to imagine the character and situation of the actors as if they were alive before his eyes, and suddenly he found an orchestral motion that seemed to carry and bind together the sung texts of different sections: "I transported myself to the parterre of the theater and imagined hearing my ideas performed: they seemed characteristic; I wrote them down, tried them over, and as I was satisfied, I continued further." In half an hour a sketch for the *introduzione* stood on the music desk. The same evening, working until midnight, he attacked the first finale, reading it over twice before making a tonal and rhythmic plan of the whole, "which took three hours, without a single note being written down." In four weeks' time the score was more than two-thirds complete.

Several useful points emerge from Salieri's candid observations. The finales required special attention from composers no less than from librettists (and the same applies to the finale procedure moved to the beginning of the act, i.e., the *introduzione*). Not only the finale's sequence of keys, but also their sequence of time changes required advance planning. Salieri's many successes as a theater composer surely had a lot to do with visualizing how his music would work in projecting the dramatic action across the footlights. His notion of orchestral textures and rhythms tying together separate sung passages, one of his earliest musical thoughts, represents a valuable testimony to the beginnings of this indispensable finale technique. His first musical thoughts of all, it should be emphasized, were how to stretch the available tonalities over the whole framework so as to match key and textual affect (while achieving both unity and variety, he might have added). In this vital respect, he says, he merely copied the practice of his teacher, Gassmann.

Mozart fell heir to the Viennese opera buffa tradition of Gassmann and Salieri, and there is no reason to believe he operated very differently when approaching a libretto (except that he seems to have taken more pains than any other composer with the shape of the libretto in the first place). In 1785 for him, as in 1770 for Salieri, a great French comedy provided the initial impetus. At this time the art of the finale was raised to its highest peak of poetic and dramatic perfection in the two crowning glories of the species that end acts 2 and 4 of *Le nozze di Figaro*. Choosing the key of the second finale meant choosing the keynote of the opera. There were not many possible choices, to be sure, for only three keys commonly accommodated trumpets and drums in the 1780s: C, D, and E-flat. Mozart chose D major. Since he wanted a noisy end with trumpets and drums to the opera's medial finale as well (to ensure applause, as he said in so many words about the finale to act 1 of *Die Entführung*), his choice was narrowed down to C or E-flat—the keynote would not do, for obvious reasons. He finally chose E-flat to end act 2 and, perhaps as an inspired afterthought, also to begin it. This still left C major to close acts 1 and 3 in a blaze of trumpets and timpani, while providing the needed tonal contrast with acts 2 and 4. With the distribution of his three universal keys, the scaffolding of the edifice was in place. Every subsequent choice of key had to be calculated on textual affect (and traditional musical affect too), from the one side, and relationship to the three act-ending keys from the other.

Eighteenth-century sensibilities allowed that a key could take on a quite specific personality, or, depending on how it was used, it could remain neutral. This, at least, is one way we might read Schubart's enigmatic statement on the subject: "Every key is either colored, or not colored."[14] Take the case of Mozart's use of the key E-flat in *Figaro*. It was broad enough to embrace the *strepitosissimo* racket that ends the finale of act 2; but when used to project a tender mood and colored by delicate shadings from the clarinets and other winds, it assumed the "plaintive softness" claimed for it by the historian Hawkins (1776), and also the "noble and pathetic" character attributed to it by the composer Grétry (1797).[15] By a stroke of genius (surely Mozart's idea), this potently loaded weapon of affect-laden E-flat as amorous plaint was planted at the beginning of act 2 in a solo scene for the countess, marking her first appearance—"Porgi, amor, qualche ristoro," capitalizing in text and music on a long tradition adherent to the *aria d'affetto*.

More was at stake for Mozart and Da Ponte than just a tradition of love songs in E-flat, though. They were putting themselves in competition with a solo scene for young Rosina, before she married Count Almaviva, in the opera by which more than any other *Figaro* would be measured: *Il barbiere di Siviglia* by Petrosellini and Paisiello. Exactly halfway through *Il barbiere*, at the end of act 1, part 2, Rosina, alone onstage for the only time in the opera, pours out her secret emotions; amorously attracted to Lindoro (the count in disguise), she sends her sighs up to Heaven, asking it, in its justice and in knowledge of her honest heart, to grant her

---

14. "Jeder Ton ist entweder gefärbt, oder nicht gefärbt"; Schubart, *Ideen zu einer Ästhetik der Tonkunst*, p. 377.

15. Rita Steblin, *A History of Key Characteristics in the Eighteenth and Early Nineteenth Centuries* (Ann Arbor, Mich., 1983), pp. 70, 107.

soul the peace it does not have. The poet says this very economically in a cavatina of four short, mellifluous lines:

Giusto ciel, che conoscete
Quanto il cor honesto sia,
Deh voi date all'alma mia
Quella pace che non ha.

Paisiello set this plea as a Larghetto in 2/4 and in E-flat, with lots of wind color and delicate chromatic shadings, particularly from the pair of clarinets that answer a pair of bassoons in little fluttering motions. A fourteen-bar orchestral introduction exposing the main theme precedes the vocal entry. Mozart does the same in fifteen bars, preceded by a two-bar "curtain" (because he is opening an act). Paisiello's melody sinks gracefully from the high third to the upper tonic, then pauses for a *messa di voce* on B-flat before a syncopated flurry carries the voice upward by leaps, then down to the lower tonic (Ex. 8.1). His harmonies move slowly, by the bar; his choice of a modal degree (the supertonic) for the second chord is one of his favorites, as is the very tender progression of subdominant six-four chord to tonic at the second "Quanto il cor." A more dramatic tone intrudes when, in the middle of the piece, there is a forte outburst in the orchestra on an augmented-sixth chord and Rosina responds with a "giusto ciel," carrying her voice up to high G-flat (see Ex. 8.2). The Rosina who sang this with great success in the first Viennese production of *Il barbiere* was Nancy Storace. It was in all likelihood this piece that won Storace the emperor's praise for her cantabile.

Countess Almaviva sings a more desperate plea for relief from the torments of love. Once again she takes us, the audience, into her confidence, but no one else. Only a few years older, she is a lot wiser and sadder. The young count not only neglects her but has become a philanderer as well. Her plea finishes with an ultimatum—give me back my love or let me die:

Porgi, amor, qualche ristoro
Al mio duolo, a' miei sospir:
O mi rendi il mio tesoro,
O mi lascia, almen morir!

Mozart adopts an emotional temperature closer to "Giusto ciel" than this text might suggest. The same key, meter, tempo, and rhythmic motions recur, and the similarities do not stop there. Mozart uses a *messa di voce* on B-flat, but in the more traditional position of introducing the voice part. His instrumentation is surprisingly similar, with paired clarinets responding to paired bassoons. Their whispered sighs include many of the same chromatic shadings. Does the emphasis on modal degrees (e.g., ii and vi in m. 22) not sound familiar? Also the lingering sweetness of subdominant six-four to tonic? Perhaps the syncopated rise and fall of the melody in mm. 11–13 testifies most minutely to his fascination with Paisiello's

EXAMPLE 8.1. Paisiello, *Il barbiere di Siviglia*, No. 11

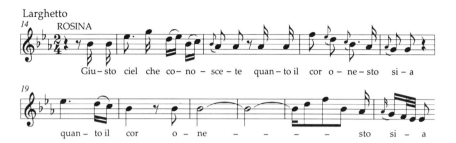

Larghetto

ROSINA

Giu – sto ciel che co – no – sce – te quan – to il cor o – ne – sto si – a

quan – to il cor o – ne – – – – sto si – a

EXAMPLE 8.2. Paisiello, *Il barbiere di Siviglia*, No. 11

ROSINA

Giu – sto ciel, giu – sto ciel

cavatina. To project the last word, *morir*, Mozart takes the voice up to a prolonged A-flat—a moment of greater intensity, and appropriately so, than Paisiello's momentary high G-flat. Mozart's minor-ninth appoggiatura on G-flat in the first bassoon (m. 38) is a personal touch that will recur in several of his late works. Every musical gesture counts to the full in Mozart's terse construction, and nothing could be altered or omitted. By comparison, Paisiello's cavatina is somewhat loose-jointed and discursive, though not inferior in sensuous appeal.

Mozart seems to have planted a few musical links between the characters in *Il barbiere* and their reappearance in *Le nozze di Figaro*. It would not take the most astute listener to catch a resemblance between what Figaro sings in the duetto (No. 6) of *Il barbiere*, when telling the count that his shop is only four steps away (Ex. 8.3), with the vigorous dactyls he sings at the end of "Se vuol ballare," now in defiance of the same count (Ex. 8.4). The melody is also made to introduce him in act 2, scene 1, when he sings it to "la la la la la la la la la la," lending it the force of a "signature tune" with a life of its own. In the text of *Il barbiere*, Figaro is described from the outset by the count as "grotesco e comico" and "grosso e grasso," whereas Figaro recognizes the count under his disguise by "quel aria nobile." Paisiello conveys Figaro's earthy and rather doltish qualities from the very first words he sings, a song he is making up (none too expertly) in praise of wine; it begins with a thud on the downbeat and uses the combination of 6/8 time and G major in a singsong way that will characterize Mozart's peasants (see Ex. 8.5). It is Figaro, of course, who leads on the peasants in act 1 of *Le nozze* so that they can sing their little chorus of praise to the count for abolishing the *jus primae noctis* (Ex. 8.6). Both airs project the same simple-minded rusticity, aided by the same flat-footed beginning without upbeat and the stepwise movement of the tunes from the tonic up to

EXAMPLE 8.3. Paisiello, *Il barbiere di Siviglia*, No. 6

La mia bot – te – ga è a quat – tro pas – si

EXAMPLE 8.4. *Figaro*, No. 3

tut – te le mac – chi – ne ro – ve – scie – rò

EXAMPLE 8.5. Paisiello, *Il barbiere di Siviglia*, No. 2

f Dia – mo al – la no – ja il ban – do

EXAMPLE 8.6. *Figaro*, No. 8

f Gio – va – ni lie – te

EXAMPLE 8.7. *Figaro*, No. 15

Si – gno – ri di fuo – ri son già i suo – na – to – ri

the fifth, as in many folksongs. G major conveys an equally rustic, down-to-earth quality when Figaro breaks into the finale of act 2 in *Le nozze*, which had just reached a big cadence on B-flat, and without any transition we hear the pipers who have come to start the nuptial festivities (Ex. 8.7). That tune could have been placed in Figaro's mouth in the previous opera by Paisiello without seeming out of place, but it comes from elsewhere, being an old vaudeville tune from Paris that had been known in Vienna for at least thirty years, ever since Gluck arranged it in *Le Chinois poli en France* (Ex. 8.8).[16]

Did Mozart know he was quoting a vaudeville of many years earlier? What appears most likely is that this simple but catchy little air had entered the reper-

16. Bruce Alan Brown, "Christoph Willibald Gluck and Opéra-Comique in Vienna, 1754–1764," Ph.D. diss., University of California, Berkeley, 1986, pp. 345–46.

EXAMPLE 8.8. Gluck, *Le Chinois poli en France*, Vaudeville

tory of dances played by Viennese tavern fiddlers and the like—in other words, had survived the intervening decades between 1756 and 1786 as a popular tune. If this theory is correct, Mozart not only knew that he was quoting but also made a most canny musical choice by which to convey to his audience the arrival of the rustic pipers.

The most comic role in Paisiello's *Barbiere* belonged not to Figaro but to old Doctor Bartolo, played in Vienna by Benucci. Some of the sardonic wit of the duped Bartolo in the earlier opera seems to have passed into Benucci's part as Figaro, who himself comes to believe he has been duped in the last act of *Le nozze*. The final aria for Figaro/Benucci accordingly became a bitter recitation of women's failings. Here Da Ponte faced a case of major surgery. Beaumarchais had made Figaro's great monologue in act 5 the high point of the play. Recounting the pica-resque details of his life, Figaro takes the opportunity to denounce aristocratic privilege in no uncertain terms, along with rulers, prisons, censors, and a few other choice targets (accounting in large part for what Joseph II found "offensive" in the play). His denunciation of women is only the framing prelude and coda of this famous tirade, which begins: "O femme! femme! femme! créature faible et décevante!" and ends with another threefold invocation: "Suzon, Suzon, Suzon! que tu me donnes de tourments!" Da Ponte used the latter as the climax of the recitative leading into the aria "Oh Susanna, Susanna, quanto pena mi costi!"

For his catalog of invectives he relied more on older Italian models. Mozart, we suggest, profited from Benucci's acting and singing of Bartolo's scornful aria in E-flat, in which he taunts Rosina (Ex. 8.9). It debases all the amorous-noble-pathetic content of E-flat, replacing it with their opposites. The rhythmic pattern Paisiello uses is one of his preferred ones for an eight-syllable line, the accent patterns of the words permitting. To set Figaro's hard words, Mozart chooses the same key, meter, and tempo: E-flat in common time, moderato. Moreover, he confines Figaro at first to rocking thirds, back and forth, then the same a step higher (after an intervening line), which comes quite close to what Benucci had sung as the irate Bartolo (Ex. 8.10). Bartolo goes on to mock Rosina, quoting her fib about sending some sweets to Figaro's daughter (when she was, of course, sending a message to the count), a grim moment which Paisiello captures by repeating the same short motif over and over, driving home his point (Ex. 8.11). Mozart does something with similar effect when he makes Figaro intone his monotonous litany of feminine wiles (Ex. 8.12). Buffo patter like this brings Figaro right down to the level of Bartolo. He is indeed his father's son in this, his lowest moment, and there is a delicious irony in the family resemblance.

Benucci's famous "Non più andrai" to end act 1 of *Figaro* betrays, in its turn, a few hints of inspiration from the previous Figaro opera. The rhythmic pattern with which it begins has just been described as one of Paisiello's favorites for lines accented on the third and penultimate syllables (cf. Ex. 8.9). Mozart does not wait until the end of act 1 to press this rhythm on us; it is present from the opening of the first number, the duettino in G, and it is associated with Figaro. The orchestra sounds it as he measures off a space for his nuptial bed with Susanna in the anteroom between the bedchambers of the count and countess. It has the same upbeat in dotted rhythm as Ex. 8.9 and "Non più andrai," giving it strong forward motion and a marchlike vigor. Figaro joins the treble line on the strongest accent, the penultimate quarter note, his vocal leaps sounding gruff and coarse in comparison with the smooth secondary idea sung by Susanna, as she tries to get Figaro to look at her and admire her hat. The reason is partly that Susanna's line is conjunct and nicely ornamented with melodic turns and a little closing sigh. More subtly, it is that Mozart has made a metric displacement, starting the line on the third beat, in the manner of a gavotte.[17] When the third and first beats vie for the metric accent,

---

17. Our reading of the duettino No. 1 parallels to some extent that of Wye Jamison Allanbrook, *Rhythmic Gesture in Mozart: "Le nozze di Figaro" and "Don Giovanni"* (Chicago, 1983), pp. 75–77, but does not stem from it.

EXAMPLE 8.9. Paisiello, *Il barbiere di Siviglia*, No. 9

EXAMPLE 8.10. *Figaro*, No. 26

EXAMPLE 8.11. Paisiello, *Il barbiere di Siviglia*, No. 9

EXAMPLE 8.12. *Figaro*, No. 26

the result is an ambiguity and delicacy that are also projected as dramatic qualities defining Susanna.

Susanna completes the phrase with another and more melodically expansive passage in gavotte rhythm, covering the territory from the high tonic to the low as she repeats the words "sembra fatto in ver per me." (Here Mozart is quoting himself, whether he knows it or not. The very same cadential phrase occurs in the *Ouverture* [mm. 68–70 and 72–74] to his ballet *Les petits riens*, composed in Paris during the summer of 1778.) Susanna becomes a little more *mondaine* with that confidently tossed off cadential phrase, which seems to say that she is in control here. And indeed she is. Every reader will know how the duettino comes out in the end: Susanna makes Figaro sing her tune to her rhythm while complimenting her on her hat. With this little drama in music, which almost needs no text, Mozart has succeeded in foreshadowing the entire opera in the first number. By the end of act 4 Figaro will have been taught a lesson by Susanna, and learned to sing her tune for good, we hope, with regard to matters of mutual trust and respect.

The conflict of march and gavotte, of military masculinity contrasted with the feminine grace of one of the most *galant* court dances, can be seen further in connection with "Non più andrai." Figaro's grand lesson to Cherubino on military life represented as bold a solution to ending act 1 as "Porgi, amor" did to beginning act 2. Beaumarchais had allowed his first act to wind down with a proverbial and off-color joke, as we saw at the end of Chapter 7. The architects of *Le nozze* aimed much higher. "Non più andrai" arrives with a sense of inevitability not simply because Mozart planted its rhythm in the opening number but, more importantly, because it has been set up as a tonal goal, both in short-range terms, being preceded by the twice-sung peasants' chorus in G (which serves as dominant preparation), and in long-range terms that reach back to the initial duettino in G. Da Ponte was particularly proud of "Non più andrai," and justifiably so. He quoted it in both the *Extract* and the *Memorie* as an example of how far his verses went beyond a few seminal ideas from the play to make for some of the most important numbers in the opera. It diminishes none of his accomplishment to call attention to a long tradition of such arias painting the sights and sounds of war in Italian librettos.[18] Nor does it take away any of his luster to note that once again the idea must have come from Mozart, whose scheme of things made an aria like this in C major a musical necessity. The composer's requirements determined such large-scale decisions as how to begin and end the big segments of the opera.

Cherubino as amorous butterfly, flitting from one lady to another, disturbing their repose, is a charming image that Da Ponte embroidered on a single line addressed by Figaro to the young man: "Dame! tu ne rôderas plus tout le jour au quartier des femmes." Mozart sets it to the rhythm noted above, which he makes even more pointed by additional dotted figures to accommodate the ten-syllable lines. After the cadence at "Adoncino d'amor" ("little Adonis of love"), the strings sound a new figure on the dominant, with trilled turns that bring a coquettish flutter to the melody. Figaro continues, describing the beautiful plumes adorning the page's light and elegant coiffure. At this modish image, Mozart switches to gavotte rhythm, just as he did for the finery of Susanna's headgear. The violins insist on the melodic turns the second time around by repeating them ever so daintily, and with a little chromatic inflection that increases the *galant* affect. What a portrait of adolescent foppery! What a showpiece for the great Benucci! The account of the opera by Michael Kelly, who created the roles of Basilio and Don Curzio, singles out Benucci's performance of this aria as winning Mozart's praises:

> I remember at the first rehearsal of the full band, Mozart was on stage . . . giving the time of the music to the orchestra. Figaro's song, "Non più andrai, farfalone amoroso" Benucci gave out with the greatest animation and power of voice. I was standing close to Mozart, who, sotto voce, was repeating, Bravo! Bravo! Benucci; and when Benucci came to the fine passage, "Cherubino alla vittoria, alla gloria militar,"

18. For a Venetian example of 1749, see Heartz, "*Vis comica*," p. 37.

which he gave out with Stentorian lungs, the effect was electricity itself, for the whole of the performers on stage, and those in the orchestra, as if actuated by one feeling of delight, vociferated Bravo! Bravo! Maestro. Viva, viva, grand Mozart.[19]

Perhaps the time has come, after two hundred years, when we can give a little credit to Mozart's singers for inspiring such a triumph of the operatic art. A little credit for the triumphant effect of "Non più andrai" belongs to Paisiello as well.

Act 1, part 1, of *Il barbiere* (equivalent to act 1 of *Figaro*) is constructed with a clever use of dominant-to-tonic patterning within and between the numbers (Table 7). The strophic serenade in B-flat stops the cycle, and sets up the refreshing arrival of the climactic duet in G for Figaro and the count.[20] The count's serenade, "Saper bramate, il mio nome," is generally agreed to have been the model for Cherubino's serenade "Voi che sapete," which is also in B-flat.[21] Unlike "Voi che sapete," "Saper bramate" never modulates, and since it is in slow tempo (Lento amoroso) it makes for a long static block of B-flat harmony, providing maximum contrast with the following number, a sparkling Allegro presto in G.

The Allegro presto begins without instrumental introduction. There is an element of surprise in this, as in the choice of key. The count starts impetuously, assuring Figaro that he will bring enough gold with which to batter the fortress where Rosina is imprisoned (see Ex. 8.13). G major seems so right, so welcome, partly because it was the first tonal resolution following the *introduzione*. There is thus the sense of completing the tonal span proposed by the beginning of the act, following the intervening stops along the circle of fifths.

If we grant Paisiello the success of his tonal strategy, we must admit that Mozart did something similar in relating his outer numbers. "Non più andrai" comes as both a local and a long-distance resolution, which helps explain why it is at once so satisfying and so electrifying. It begins without a proper ritornello too, and with the same universal melody type chosen by Paisiello: 5-3, 4-2; 4-2, 3-1. Mozart does nothing to disguise his admiration for Paisiello's applause-inducing duet, and even includes the same vocal cadence as in Ex. 8.13 to end his second section in the dominant (Ex. 8.14).

Mozart's admiration for Paisiello's popular opera may have extended even to the playing off of a flat key against a sharp key—specifically, B-flat against G—as

19. Kelly, *Reminiscences* 1:255–56.

20. Sabine Henze-Döhring analyzes the music and dramatic action of act 1, part 1, in *Opera seria, Opera buffa und Mozarts "Don Giovanni": Zur Gattungsconvergenz in der italienischen Oper des 18. Jahrhunderts* (Laaber, 1986), pp. 104–10. She shows that Paisiello matches music with stage action here in a manner that before this time had been found only in finales.

21. Dent, *Mozart's Operas*, pp. 108–9. Speaking of Paisiello, Dent says: "The influence of his music on *Figaro* is apparent mainly in *Voi che sapete*, which was very probably intended as an improvement on the serenade of Count Almaviva at the beginning of *Il barbiere di Siviglia*." Dent argued (p. 112) that "the supreme moment of the opera is the sextet in act III." It is odd that he did not note its technique of passing short motifs from voice to voice in a rising sequence adumbrated in the quintet No. 14 of *Il barbiere*. One scholar who has pursued links between Paisiello and Mozart further is Frits Noske, in *The Signifier and the Signified: Studies in the Operas of Mozart and Verdi* (The Hague, 1977), p. 26. Noske also effectively contradicts Abert by showing that the second finale of *Figaro* ranks equally with the first (pp. 16–17).

TABLE 7.
Key Scheme of *Il barbiere di Siviglia*, Act 1, Part 1

Overture	1	2	3	4	5	6
	Intro.	Scena e Duetto	Aria	Duetto	Cavatina	Duetto
C	D	↗G D A D g [G]	↗C	↗F	↗B♭	G

shown by the pairing of these two keys in successive numbers and within the two finales of *Le nozze di Figaro* (Table 8). The pairings occur in every act. At the end of act 1, the terzetto (No. 7) and the repeated peasants' chorus (No. 8) mirror the G–B-flat tonalities of the opening with B-flat–G. This might be considered a mere happenstance if Mozart did not develop a very similar plan for act 4. In act 2, following "Porgi, amor" in E-flat, come "Voi che sapete" in B-flat and then Susanna's dressing aria in G (which was replaced by an aria less difficult to act out on-stage in the 1789 Viennese revival, but retaining the key of G). We have already seen how G arrives as a surprise in the finale of act 2. Note that the B-flat–G pairs occur after E-flat not only in this finale but also in the sequences of Nos. 6–8, Nos. 10–12, and one last time in the finale of act 4—another indication of how schematic Mozart was in laying out the whole opera in regard to tonalities. Act 3 ends in C, with considerable flavor of a minor for the Spanish dancing, thus helping to tie the act together because of the a minor with which the duet between Susanna and the count begins (No. 16). The parallel with act 1 pertains not only to C as ending key but also to how it is arrived at via the chorus of peasant girls in G, and before that to the letter duet in B-flat. Act 4 may have originally begun with the arias in G and B-flat for Marcellina and Basilio, if, as has been surmised, the little cavatina for

EXAMPLE 8.13. Paisiello, *Il barbiere di Siviglia*, No. 6

EXAMPLE 8.14. *Figaro*, No. 9

TABLE 8.

Key Scheme of *Le nozze di Figaro*

Overture	Act 1 1	2	3	4	5	6	7	8	9
D	G	B♭	F	D	A	E♭	B♭	G	C

Act 2 10	11	12	13	14	15	(Finale)				
E♭	B♭	G	C	G	E♭	B♭	G	C	F	B♭	E♭

Act 3 16	17	18	19	20	21	22
a/A	D	F	C	B♭	G	C a C

Act 4 23	24	25	26	27	28	(Finale)		
f	G	B♭	E♭	F	D	G	E♭	B♭	G	D

Barbarina was an afterthought.[22] One last surprise arrival of G directly after B-flat is reserved for the second finale, as the count bursts in with his men ("Gente, gente, all'armi!"), surprising Figaro embracing the countess—or so he thinks. From the peaceful music of forgiveness that follows, the opera can back into the final tonic D like a plagal cadence, a long-breathed "amen," as it were. Comparisons would not be out of place with the subdominant emphasis Mozart liked to give "Dona nobis pacem" in some of his masses. It probably pleased his sense of long-term symmetry that the "folle journée" ended with the scampering motions of the overture ("Corriam tutti"), mirroring the relationship of the overture to Nos. 1 and 2.

Le nozze di Figaro was twice as long as *Il barbiere di Siviglia*, which made for problems. Yet it could scarcely be otherwise, for *Le mariage de Figaro* was more than twice the length of *Le barbier de Séville*, far more complicated by plots and subplots, and had three times the number of characters. The biggest problem occurs in the last act of the opera, where "it is obvious that the arias for Basilio and Marcellina in Act IV are very much in the way and contribute nothing to the drama; and they come far too late to illustrate the characters of the singers—we were left in no doubt about those in Act I."[23] The relationship of the two following

22. Alan Tyson, "*Le Nozze di Figaro*: Lessons from the Autograph Score," *Musical Times* 122 (1981): 459; reprinted in *Mozart: Studies of the Autograph Scores* (Cambridge, Mass., 1987), p. 120.
23. Dent, *Mozart's Operas*, p. 110. For the best argument that can be made against Dent, see Allanbrook, "Pro Marcellina."

EXAMPLE 8.15. *Figaro*, Sketch

for early version of No. 27

Non tar – dar a – ma – to be – ne   vie – ni   vo – la al se – no   mi – o

EXAMPLE 8.16. *Figaro*, Sketch

for early version of No. 27

giu – sto ciel!   per – ché mai tar – di?

arias for Figaro and Susanna, which are both essential to the drama, gave Mozart trouble. He first sketched the garden aria (No. 27) as a rondo in cut time and in the key of E-flat to a text that began "Non tardar amato bene vieni vola al seno mio" (Ex. 8.15). Evidently he intended to produce a big rondo of the fashionable two-tempo variety, but he broke off his setting in m. 36, just after the theme of the opening slow part made its customary return. Susanna is disguised as the countess, so it is not unreasonable that she should put on airs and sing something such as Rosina herself might. In fact, the declamatory outburst in mm. 12–14 on the words "Giusto ciel! perchè mai tardi?" taking the voice up to G-flat over a dissonant chord with sforzato, is close to what the young Rosina did sing in the middle of Paisiello's "Giusto ciel" (Ex. 8.16; cf. Ex. 8.2 above). Storace would have noticed the resemblance, since it was she who had to produce the high G-flat in both pieces. Was it this parallel that made Mozart abandon "Non tardar amato bene"? Or was it general disenchantment with a piece of music that laid on the pathos with such heavy brushstrokes? The choice of E-flat was of course appropriate for pathos, but since it followed Figaro's E-flat aria (or preceded it at one stage, still reflected in the autograph), the result was an anomaly: two successive arias in the same key.

The roles of the countess and of Susanna are treated equally in *Le nozze*; it is inappropriate to speak of either as the prima donna, although the noble rank of the former normally would have conferred the distinction on her.[24] Storace had been in Vienna longer than Laschi and had sung more leading roles. From her point of view, it is easier to understand why she wanted a big dramatic rondo to sing when masquerading as the countess. She may in fact have demanded one, believing that parity of the two roles was at stake. Laschi had sung one in the middle of act 3,

---

24. Stefan Kunze (*Mozarts Opern* [Stuttgart, 1984], p. 245) maintains that Rosina was not noble by birth, that the count's one unconventional deed was to marry a "Bürgermädchen." Beaumarchais intended otherwise; in act 4, scene 8, of *Le barbier de Séville*, the count says of his future wife: "Mademoiselle est noble et belle." The two soprano parts for Rosina and Susanna in *Figaro* were so equal as to be exchangeable in the ensembles, a question explored by Alan Tyson in his article "Some Problems in the Text of *Le nozze di Figaro*: Did Mozart Have a Hand in Them?" *Journal of the Royal Musical Society* 112 (1987): 99–131; reprinted in *Mozart: Studies of the Autograph Scores*, pp. 290–327.

and it was the most serious piece in the whole opera, "Dove sono i bei momenti," a piece with which Mozart took infinite pains, as his melodic sketches show. Originally he inscribed it, twice, with the title "Rondo," and it is just as proud an exemplar of the two-tempo rondo in form and style as Donna Anna's "Non mi dir," Fiordiligi's "Per pietà bell' idol mio," or Vitellia's "Non più di fiori." Mozart scratched out, or someone scratched out, the proper appellation *Rondo* on "Dove sono" in the autograph and replaced it, twice, with *Aria*. When Storace lost her rondo in act 4, it was easier to keep peace in the family if Laschi's rondo were at least not called a rondo. It is just possible that "Non tardar amato bene" was only a feint by Mozart until he brought Storace around to singing what he wanted her to sing all along. This would explain its impossible key of E-flat. To the everlasting credit of Nancy Storace, she settled finally for "Deh vieni non tardar" in F, a marvel of subtle understatement in comparison with "Non tardar," and all the more effective because of it. "Deh vieni" completes Susanna's portrait in the opera so deftly that we barely notice that its theme derives from the cadential phrase of her first vocal utterance. "Sembra fatto in ver per me," indeed!

Nancy Storace was open to musical variety to an extent that belies her Italian training. On English stages she was called on to sing very simple songs as well as arias and for this reason, perhaps, was more inclined to accept the seeming simplicity of "Deh vieni non tardar." With her mother, brother Stephen, and the rest of her entourage, La Storace left Vienna to return to London in early 1787. Four years later the painter Samuel De Wilde captured her playing the part of Euphrosyne in the *Mask of Comus* by Thomas Arne (1738) (see Frontispiece). She is depicted singing the simple syllabic ballad in act 3 that begins:

> The wanton God, that pierces Hearts,
> Dips in Gall his pointed Darts,
> But the Nymph disdains to pine,
> Who bath's the Wound in rosy wine.

To enhance the bacchanalian sentiment she raises a glass of rosy wine herself. Her hair and costume are garlanded with flowers (roses?), and the artist surrounds her head with light by opening up the foliage behind her so as to create a kind of halo. Short and plumpish she may have been, as contemporaries claimed, but she exuded charm nonetheless, as this picture shows. Glimpsing it we can almost believe the tales told about how she held in thrall an emperor (Joseph II) and a future monarch (the Prince of Wales).

The problem of the two rondos and parity between Susanna and the countess remained when the opera was revived in 1789. Fiordiligi/La Ferrarese sang Susanna, and since she was not willing to settle for "Deh vieni non tardar," Mozart substituted a huge concertante rondo in two tempi, "Al desio di chi t'adora." But the key stayed the same, F, providing another hint that Mozart never could have intended E-flat as a viable solution. Caterina Cavalieri, who had created the role of Constanze in *Die Entführung*, took over the role of the countess. She reacted to the

FIGURE 15

Transition passage added to "Dove sono"

enhancement of Susanna's part as might be expected. There are additions to "Dove sono" in a London manuscript, which Alan Tyson assigns to this 1789 revival (Fig. 15).[25] They transformed the piece from its perfect original state to a more showy

25. See Tyson, "Some Problems in the Text of *Le nozze di Figaro*," pp. 126–28; reprinted in *Mozart: Studies of the Autograph Scores*, pp. 321–23.

one, with a transition between the slow and fast themes very similar to the transition in Sesto's rondo "Deh per questo istante solo." We have long wondered how the motif from the beginning of the *Figaro* overture wandered into Sesto's rondo, at the beginning of the transition to the fast theme (mm. 38–41; see Ex. 18.1). Now it appears there was an intermediate link two years earlier in the revised and extended "Dove sono" of 1789, for which none other can be responsible than Mozart.

A P P E N D I X

Salieri kept a record of his life and professional career. He turned over these papers to Ignaz von Mosel, who translated them from Italian into German and used them as the basis for his publication Ueber das Leben und die Werke des Anton Salieri, k.k. Hofkapellmeisters *(Vienna, 1827). The following account occurs on pp. 30–32.*

Mein Meister Gassmann wurde zu jener Zeit nach Rom berufen, um dort eine tragische Oper für den Carneval (1770) zu schreiben. Ich blieb in Wien zurück, um unter dem Vice-Kapellmeister Ferandini die Proben zu Leiten. Gaston Boccherini, ein Tänzer des Wiener Operntheaters, der die Dichtkunst leidenschaftlich liebte, hatte unter Beihülfe des Herrn von Calzabigi . . . eine komische italienische Oper, unter den Titel: Le donne letterate, geschrieben, die er dem Kapellmeister Gassmann bestimmte. Calzabigi rieth ihm, sie lieber mir anzuvertrauen, der, ein Anfänger in der Composition, wie er in der Dichtkunst, sich leichter mit ihm einverstehen würde. Boccherini kam daher eines Morgens zu mir, und fragte mich nach der ersten Begrüssung, ohne weitere Einleitung: Wollten Sie wohl ein von mir verfasstes komisches Operngedicht in Musik setzen? Ich antwortete unbefangen: Warum nicht? Und nun erzählte er mir ganz aufrichtig, welche Absicht er damit gehabt, und wie Calzabigi ihm gerathen habe. Aha! dachte ich, man hält dich also schon fähig, Opern zu componieren! Nur Muth! Wir wollen die Gelegenheit nicht ungenutzt vorüber gehen lassen! —Ich bat daher den Dichter mit grosser Ungeduld, mir den Stoff seiner Oper mitzutheilen und das Gedicht selbst vorzulegen. Beides geschah; und nachdem wir die Rollen nach der Fähigkeit der damaligen Sängergesellschaft vertheilt hatten, sagte Boccherini: Ich verlasse Sie nun, machen Sie indessen Ihre Bemerkungen, und wenn Sie hier und da einige Veränderungen in Rücksicht auf die musikalische Wirkung verlangen, wollen wir sie, wenn ich wiederkomme, gemeinschaftlich vornehmen. Als ich allein war, sperrte ich mich ein, und mit entflammten Wangen—wie ich auch späterhin pflegte, so oft ich eine Arbeit mit Lust und Liebe unternahm—durchlas ich das Gedicht von Neuem, fand es für die Musik allerdings günstig, und, nachdem ich die Gesangstücke ein drittes Mal gelesen, bestimmte ich für's Erste, wie ich von meinem Meister gesehen hatte, die dem Character eines jeden Gesangstückes entsprechende Tonart. Das es bald Mittag war, und ich folglich nicht hoffen durfte, noch vor der Mahlzeit die Composition anfangen zu können, benützte ich die bis dahin noch übrige Stunde, das Gedicht nochmals durchzublättern. Schon begann ich bei einigen Stellen auf die Melodie zu denken, als Madame Gassmann (denn mein Meister war damals schon verheirathet) mich zur Tafel rufen liess. So lang dieselbe wahrte, kam mir mein Operngedicht nicht aus dem Kopfe, und ich habe mich nachher nie mehr erinnern können, was ich an seinem Mittag gegessen hatte. Nach der Tafel machte ich . . . mein MittagsSchläfchen . . . [then he takes a walk].

So bald ich mich allein sah, befiel mich ein unwiderstehliches Verlangen, die Introduction der Oper in Musik zu setzen. Ich suchte mir daher den Character und die Situation der Personen recht lebhaft vor Augen zu stellen, und plötzlich fand ich eine Bewegung des Orchesters, die mir den, dem Texte nach zerstückten Gesang des Tonstückes angemessen zu tragen und zu verbinden schien. Ich versetzte mich nun im Geiste in das Parterre, hörte meine Ideen ausführen; sie schienen mir characteristisch; ich schrieb sie auf, prüfte sie nochmal, und da ich damit zufrieden war, fuhr ich weiter fort. So stand in einer halben Stunde der Entwurf der Introduction auf dem Notenblatte. Wer war vergnügter als ich! Es war sechs Uhr Abends und dunkel geworden; ich liess mir Licht bringen. Vor zwölf Uhr, beschloss ich, gehst du heute nicht zu Bette; die Phantasie ist entflammt, diese Feuer soll benüzt werden. Ich lese das erste Finale, das, was die Worte betrifft, beinahe eben so anfing, wie die Introduction; ich lese es noch einmal, mache mir einen dem Ganzen angemessenen Plan der Tact- und Ton-Arten wozu ich drei Stunden verwendete, ohne noch eine Note geschrieben zu haben. Ich fühlte mich müde, und die Wangen brannten mir; ich ging daher in meinem Zimmer einige Mal auf und ab, bald zog es mich wieder an das Schreibpult, wo ich den Entwurf begann, und als die Mitternacht kam, schon so weit damit vorgerückt war, dass ich mich hochvergnügt zur Ruhe begab.

Mein Kopf war den ganzen Tag zu voll von Musik und Poesie gewesen, als dass ich nicht auch davon hätte träumen sollen. In der That hörte ich im Traume eine seltsame Harmonie, aber so sehr aus der Ferne, und so verworren, dass ich mehr Qual als Vergnügen empfand und endlich darüber aufwachte. Es war vier Uhr Morgens. . . . Kurz, nachdem ich meine Arbeit mit demselben Eifer fortgesetzt hatte, sah ich binnen vier Wochen zwei gute Drittheile der Oper in Partitur gesetzt und instrumentiert.

9 · *DON GIOVANNI*: CONCEPTION AND CREATION

Prague witnessed a production of *Le nozze di Figaro* in the new Nostitz Theater in December 1786, only six months after its premiere in Vienna. The opera orchestra of the theater invited Mozart to visit Prague in early 1787, and he accepted. Traveling with his wife Constanze, he left Vienna on Monday, 8 January, and arrived three days later. A newspaper article welcomed him and expressed the wish that he would play in a concert during his stay. They lodged in the town palace of old Count Thun, for whom Mozart had written the Linz Symphony (K. 425) in 1783, and were overwhelmed by invitations from the local gentry. In a letter of 15 January to his friend Jacquin in Vienna, Mozart tells of being taken by Count Canal to one of the Carnival balls, where "I saw with complete satisfaction how all these people, so inwardly pleased, jumped about to the music of *Figaro*—transformed into genuine contredanses and teutsche. For nothing is talked about but *Figaro*! Nothing played, blown, sung, or whistled but *Figaro*: no opera is so well attended as *Figaro* and always *Figaro*! Certainly a great honor for me."[1]

On 19 January, Mozart gave an academy in the theater at which the magnificent new Symphony in D (K. 504), subsequently named the Prague Symphony, received its premiere. He obliged the public further by improvising three fantasies at the piano, the last on "Non più andrai" from *Figaro*, an aria that was evidently Prague's favorite, and that would return in a different guise in the opera he was to

1. "— ich sah aber mit ganzem Vergnügen zu, wie alle diese leute auf die Musick meines figaro, in lauter Contretänze und teutsche verwandelt, so innig vergnügt herumsprangen; — denn hier wird von nichts gesprochen als vom — figaro; nichts gespielt, geblasen, gesungen und gepfiffen als — figaro: keine Opera besucht — als figaro und Ewig figaro; gewiss grosse Ehre für mich"; letter of 15 January 1787. One tune that needed little or no transformation to become a contredanse was "Non più andrai." As such it was used by Mozart in the first of the five contredanses for small orchestra, K. 609, of 1791. A manuscript of the Prague Carnival dances arranged from *Figaro* exists in the form of a keyboard score made by Nepomuk Kanka; for a page from it, see Paul Nettl, *Mozart in Böhmen* (Prague, 1938), plate facing p. 92, which shows a "Deutsch" made from the Andante in 6/8, "Pace, pace" in the second finale, beginning in m. 275.

write next. Before returning to Vienna on 8 February, he completed a set of six "Teutsche Tänze" (K. 509) to enliven Prague's Carnival balls still more. The giddy days and nights in Prague during Carnival season, the balls in which his music, as contredanses and "teutsche," animated all, left their mark on Mozart. Out of such experiences the ballroom scene in *Don Giovanni* was born.

Mozart had ample opportunity to study the theatrical troupe at Prague. He led a performance of his *Figaro* there on 22 January 1787. On this occasion he could observe the effect of the singers and orchestra in the Nostitz Theater (later called the Tyl Theater). A Prague critic boasted a month earlier that connoisseurs who had seen *Figaro* in Vienna greatly preferred the Prague production, "probably because the winds have so much to do throughout the whole piece, and the Bohemians were decisively superior in wind playing."[2] The concert at which the Prague Symphony received its premiere provided another spur to Mozart's musical imagination. In particular, the play of light and shade in that work's slow introduction, of somber d minor against brilliant D major, brought Mozart one more step toward the monumental act of musical imagination it required to conceive *Don Giovanni*. The management of the Nostitz Theater, the partners Pasquale Bondini and Domenico Guardasoni, did their part, offering Mozart the coveted *scrittura* commissioning a new opera—and more. Da Ponte let slip in an early version of a part of his memoirs that Guardasoni went so far as to offer Mozart Bertati's *Don Giovanni*. In the final version of his memoirs, though, he suppressed this inconvenient piece of information, and claimed instead that he himself suggested the Don Juan legend to Mozart.

A performance of *Don Giovanni* at London in early 1819 was the distant cause that forced Da Ponte to publish a portion of his unfinished memoirs, translated from Italian into English and entitled *Extract from the Life of Lorenzo Da Ponte* (New York, 1819). An anonymous critic writing in the *Edinburgh Review* had assessed the London performance as a triumph for Mozart without so much as mentioning Da Ponte by name. Yet the typography of the *Extract*'s title page (Fig. 16) tells us where Da Ponte thought he stood relative to Mozart. He lashed back furiously, claiming that dramatic poets rank high in the creation of an opera, even when they take up a subject as hackneyed as the Don Juan legend. "A poet deserves to be esteemed no less because he labors on a well-known theme." Then he revealed the embarrassing fact later suppressed in the memoirs: "Why did Mozart refuse to set to music the *Don Giovanni* (of evil memory) by Bertati, and offered to him by one Guardasoni . . . manager of the Italian theatre of Prague?"[3] Da Ponte contin-

2. Report in the *Prager Oberpostamtszeitung*, 12 December 1786: "Kenner, die diese Oper in Wien gesehen haben, wollen behaupten, dass sie hier weit besser ausfalle; und sehr wahrscheinlich, weil die blasenden Instrumenten, worinn die Böhmen bekanntlich entschiedene Meister sind, in dem ganzen Stück viel zu thun haben"; in Deutsch, *Dokumente*, p. 246.

3. After the name of the manager, Da Ponte inserts between parentheses: "non adhibeo testes dormientes" ("I do not call sleeping witnesses"). John Stone, in his annotated edition of the *Extract*, kindly supplied to me in typescript, provided this translation from the Latin, which he calls "an almost incomprehensible aside, but perhaps some tenuous philological pun on the name Guardasoni."

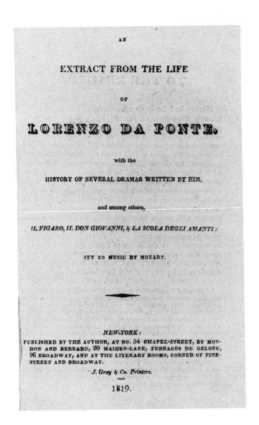

FIGURE 16

Title page of Da Ponte's *Extract*

ued with two more questions. "Why did he [Mozart] insist upon having a book written by Da Ponte on the same subject, *and not by any other dramatist*? Shall I tell you why?" (Da Ponte's emphasis).

Having set up his answer so elaborately, Da Ponte next delivers himself of an artistic credo that is the main point of the *Extract*, and not quite like anything that was eventually published in the memoirs:

> Because Mozart knew very well that the success of an opera depends, FIRST OF ALL, ON THE POET: that without a good poem an *entertainment cannot be perfectly dramatic*, just as a picture cannot be good without possessing the merit of invention, design, and a just proportion of the parts: that a composer, who is, in regard to a drama, what a painter is in regard to the colours, can never do that without effect, unless ex-cited and animated by the words of a poet, whose province is to choose a subject sus-ceptible of variety, incident, movement, and action; to prepare, to suspend, to bring about the catastrophe; to exhibit characters interesting, comic, well supported, and calculated for stage effect; to write his recitativo short, but substantial, his airs vari-ous, new, and well situated; in fine his verses easy, harmonious, and almost singing of themselves, without all which requisites, the notes of the most sublime and scien-tific composer will not be felt by the heart, the passions remaining tranquil, and un-moved, their effect will be transient, and the best of his airs, after a short time, will be heard with no more attention or pleasure, than a trio or a sonata. Whether these qualifications are, or are not to be found in my operas, is not for me to decide.

(pp. 17–18)

Anyone familiar with Da Ponte and other librettists would have to concede him that his operas, at least those for Mozart, do possess the literary and dramatic qualities he describes. An impartial critic would also, unlike Da Ponte, have to admit finding the same qualities in his most illustrious predecessors, notably Goldoni and Metastasio.

The Italian opera troupe at Prague was small. Bondini's wife, Caterina, had sung Susanna in *Figaro* and would create the first Zerlina in *Don Giovanni*. Donna Anna was created by Teresa Saporiti, Donna Elvira by Caterina Micelli. The young Luigi Bassi sang the title role, and his sidekick-servant Leporello was created by Felice Ponziani. The tenor Antonio Baglioni sang Don Ottavio. In fact, he was a direct link with the *Don Giovanni* of Bertati and Gazzaniga, first staged on 5 February 1787 in the San Moisè Theater at Venice, a production in which he had sung the title role.[4] If a copy of Bertati's libretto got into Guardasoni's hands by way of Baglioni, it was presumably after the singer finished the Carnival season at Venice, from which it would follow that Guardasoni offered the work to Mozart no earlier than the late spring or early summer, perhaps in writing or perhaps during a trip to Vienna. The bass Giuseppe Lolli doubled the roles of Masetto and the Commendatore. Seven singers taking eight parts had to suffice the new opera. (How did they manage to stage *Figaro* with so few singers?)

The Prague company gave seasons at Dresden and Leipzig as well. It was typical for such small Italian companies to be itinerant. Typical as well was the choice of the Don Juan subject, with its inherently popular appeal, by itinerant Italian companies. Bertati's *Don Giovanni* in Venice was preceded by another little work of the impresario's dilemma type in which a singer complains that Don Juan dramas lacked verisimilitude and broke the rules, to which the impresario answers:

Ma credete voi forse	Perhaps you believe
Che si badi alle regole?	In following the rules?
Si bada a quel che piace; e spesse volte	Pleasure and profit are what matter.
Si fanno più danari	More money is made
Con delle strampalate	With foolishness
Di quello che non cose	Than with things
Studiate, regolate, e giudiziose.[5]	Studied, regular, or judicious.

This should be enough to show that Da Ponte was not the only Italian poet who could be pithy and funny at the same time. Bertati had his moments.

Don Juan shows enjoyed a long vogue in Italian popular theater. Goethe testified to the level they had reached by 1787, when he witnessed a Don Juan opera in

---

4. *Don Giovanni, o sia Il convitato di pietra, dramma giocoso*, was preceded by *Capriccio drammatico*, also by Bertati and a pasticcio as to the music. For their complete texts and commentary, see Stefan Kunze, *Don Giovanni vor Mozart: Die Tradition der Don-Giovanni-Opern im italienischen Buffa-Theater des 18. Jahrhunderts* (Munich, 1972). As Kunze points out (pp. 36–37), Bertati's dialogue in the *Capriccio* names the poet's resources in putting together his *Don Giovanni* as Tirso de Molina, Molière, and the Italian popular theater.

5. Ibid., p. 144.

Rome. He was amazed at the drawing power of the old potboiler among the common people: "No one could live until he saw Don Juan roasting in Hell and the Commendatore, as a blessed spirit, ascend to Heaven."[6] It remained, in other words, the morality play it had started out as in the early seventeenth century.

Goldoni inveighed against Don Juan plays in his *Mémoires*, which by coincidence also came out during the same year, 1787:

> Everyone knows the bad Spanish play that the Italians call *Il convitato di pietra*, and the French *Le festin de pierre*. I have always regarded it with horror in Italy, and I could not understand how this farce sustained itself for so long, drawing crowds of people, and giving delight to a civilized nation. The Italian actors were astonished themselves, and either by joking or by ignorance claimed that the author of the play made a pact with the devil to sustain it.[7]

Don Juan plays had, in short, descended to the level of vulgarity.

The Viennese court theater, ruled in every detail by the high-minded Joseph II, never would have chosen Don Juan for Da Ponte and Mozart. But Prague, not directly under the control of the imperial family, could go its own way, and had done so for decades in the matter of operatic productions. Prague had seen several Don Juans before 1787, most recently Vincenzo Righini's *Il convitato di pietra ossia Il dissoluto punito*, on a libretto by Nicola Porta, in 1776.[8] Vienna had seen several Don Juans as well, but not as court operas. The German troupe at the Kärntnerthor Theater had put on the *Comödie Das steinerne Gastmahl* in 1760, Gluck his pantomime ballet *Don Juan, ou Le festin de pierre* in 1761. Righini brought his *Convitato di pietra* to the Kärntnerthor in the summer of 1777. Even closer to the time of Mozart and Da Ponte was *Don Juan, oder Der steinerne Gaste*, in the suburban theater of Karl Marinelli in 1783. Associations with suburban theaters—that is, with popular theater—would be enough by themselves to discredit the Don Juan subject in the eyes of the emperor and the officials of the court theater, and this attitude

6. "So erlebte ich in Rom, dass eine Oper, *Don Juan* (nicht der *Mozartische*), vier Wochen, alle Abende gegeben wurde, wodurch die Stadt so erregt ward, dass die letzten Krämers-Familien, mit Kind und Kegel in Parterre und Logen hauseten, und Niemand leben konnte, der den Don Juan nicht hatte in der Hölle braten, und der Gouverneur, als seligen Geist, nicht hatte gen Himmel fahren sehen"; *Der Briefwechsel zwischen Goethe und Zelter* 1 : 417; cited in Kunze, *Mozarts Opern* (Stuttgart, 1984), p. 328.

7. "Tout le monde connaît cette mauvaise pièce espagnole, que les Italiens appellent *Il Convitato di Pietra*, et les Français *le Festin de Pierre*. Je l'ai toujours regardée, en Italie, avec horreur, et je ne pouvais concevoir comment cette farce avait pu se soutenir pendant si longtemps, attirer le monde en foule, et faire les délices d'un pays policé. Les comédiens italiens en étaient étonnés eux-mêmes, et soit par plaisanterie, soit par ignorance, quelques-uns disaient que l'auteur du Festin de Pierre avait contracté un engagement avec le diable pour le soutenir"; *Mémoires de M. Goldoni pour servir à l'histoire de sa vie et à celle de son théâtre* (Paris, 1787), ed. Paul de Roux, in the series Le temps retrouvé (Paris, 1965), p. 163. Goldoni's play *Don Giovanni Tenorio* (1735) was an important source of ideas and verbal expressions for both Bertati and Da Ponte. On the latter's relationship to the play, see Dent, *Mozart's Operas*, pp. 123–25.

8. Tomislav Volek, "Prague Operatic Traditions and Mozart's *Don Giovanni*," in *Mozart's "Don Giovanni" in Prague*, published by the Theater Institute (Divadelní ústav), Prague, to mark the opera's bicentennial. The earliest Don Juan opera Volek discusses is *La pravita castigata*, a "rappresentazione morale per musica" put on in Count Sporck's theater in 1730 (pp. 23–27).

may help explain why, when Mozart's *Don Giovanni* was brought to the Viennese Burgtheater after the first production in Prague, it failed.

Emperor Joseph II had no surviving children from his two early marriages in the 1760s, and he made it known that he would not marry again. The succession was to devolve on his death to his brother Leopold, who ruled Tuscany as grand duke. Leopold had several children, so the future of the house of Habsburg-Lorraine appeared secure. The eldest son and daughter were the object of special attention by their uncle Joseph: Francis, named after his grandfather Francis of Lorraine, was brought to Vienna to be tutored; Maria Teresa, named after her empress grandmother, was carefully raised so as to undertake a marriage of state, which came to pass at the same time as Mozart's *Don Giovanni*. She was affianced to Prince Anthony of Saxony, and as she made her royal progress from Florence to Dresden in the fall of 1787 new theatrical works were the order of the day. Her arrival in Vienna was marked by a performance at the court theater of the new opera by Da Ponte and Martín y Soler, *L'arbore di Diana*, a *dramma giocoso* in two acts that had its premiere on 1 October; it was described on the title page of the libretto as "per l'arrivo di sua altezza reale, Maria Teresa, arciduchessa d'Austria, sposa del serenissimo principe Antonio di Sassonia."

Not to be outdone, the directors of the Prague theater determined to give their new opera its premiere on the day the royal party was due to arrive in Prague, 14 October. They had a libretto printed in Vienna reflecting this event, using the identical formula as on the title page of *L'arbore di Diana*, a formula they must have gotten from the Viennese court (Fig. 17, *left*). As in Righini's Prague opera of a decade earlier, "Il dissoluto punito" figures in the title (in fact becomes the main title), unlike in Bertati's *Don Giovanni*, where it does not figure at all. But Mozart usually refers to the opera simply as *Don Giovanni* (in his list of works he uses both titles). Libretto 1, as we shall call it, is seriously flawed with every possible kind of typographical error. Yet it must come straight from Da Ponte, even to the spelling of the composer's name, "Mozzart," a spelling Da Ponte still maintained as late as his memoirs. Most mysterious is the omission of the second half of the first act. Alfred Einstein speculated that this early libretto was printed to get the approval of the imperial censors.[9] Tomislav Volek, while not dismissing the censor theory, suggested that the incomplete libretto was printed as a commercial speculation by the Prague directors in hopes of getting some money in subsidy out of the Viennese court.[10] Neither these scholars nor any other Mozart specialist has explained how the imperial censorship worked under Joseph II.

The censorship law of 1781 required that theatrical works for public performance anywhere in the hereditary crown lands be submitted to the censors in Vienna before being printed, but it seems to have applied mainly to plays, not operas.[11] At

9. Alfred Einstein, "Das erste Libretto des 'Don Giovanni,'" *Acta musicologica* 9 (1937): 149–50.
10. Volek, "Prague Operatic Traditions," p. 55.
11. The law of 1781 and the emperor's preliminary draft of it are printed side by side in Appendix 2 of Herman Gnau, *Die Zensur unter Joseph II* (Strassburg, 1911), pp. 253–58.

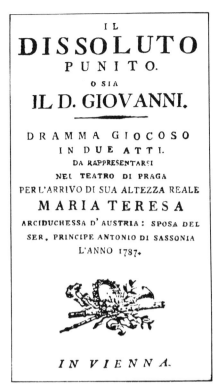

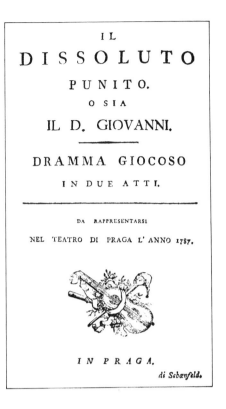

FIGURE 17

The earliest librettos for

Don Giovanni (1787)

first works had to be submitted in manuscript to receive the imprimatur; then in May 1786, the emperor ruled that they could also be submitted to the censors already printed, which made it more difficult to suppress a work should the censors disapprove it. In one case in 1789, a play printed in twenty-three copies had to be suppressed and all copies confiscated by the police after the censors banned it.[12]

The early *Don Giovanni* libretto, poorly printed and proofread, looks very much like a hasty job concocted for submission to the censors. As for the missing second half of act 1, Da Ponte may have been wary about official reaction to the words "Viva la libertà!" uttered by Don Giovanni in welcoming the noble maskers to his house in the finale of the first act. He had reason to worry if he realized the emphasis Mozart intended to place on these words in his musical setting, and the way they would be received in Prague, where even during Mozart's lifetime "Viva la libertà!" was transferred from the ensemble of solo singers to the chorus.[13] In any case, Da Ponte withheld that portion of the opera, and the early printed libretto ends act 1 in the middle of the quartetto (No. 9). The inquiring eye of the emperor

12. Ibid., pp. 189–91.
13. Volek, "Prague Operatic Traditions," p. 66.

or one of his censors could conceivably have been duped into believing that this ensemble was an act ending, especially since the Bertati model ended its first part in a parallel spot. The first act in this duplicitous version takes up to page 23, and the second, which is nearly complete, from page 24 to page 54, a disparity in size that is not large enough to cause suspicion.

The definitive libretto (Fig. 17, *right*), printed in Prague, made no mention of the Florentine princess, Maria Teresa. She had arrived at Prague with her brother Francis on schedule, but *Don Giovanni* was not ready by 14 October. As Mozart explained in a letter, you cannot drive the singers in such a small company as this, because if one gets sick there is no replacement and the whole production is endangered.[14] On the appointed day in Prague, Emperor Joseph ordered a gala performance of *Figaro* under Mozart's direction, which of course meant further delays in rehearsing *Don Giovanni*. The princess left the next day for Dresden. Not until 29 October 1787 did the Prague public finally witness the first production of the "opera of all operas."

Bertati's *Don Giovanni* supplied Da Ponte with a framework for the first half of his act 1 and the second half of his act 2. Da Ponte followed Bertati rather closely up to the quartetto (No. 9) and the succeeding recital of the attempted rape told by Donna Anna to Don Ottavio. Bertati placed this recital at the beginning soon after the event itself and made it lead up to an aria in which Ottavio sang about his dashed hopes. A major decision by Mozart and Da Ponte moved Anna's recital several numbers forward and made it lead up to her impassioned call for revenge, "Or sai, chi l'onore" (No. 10). It is tempting to believe that, in their original thinking, this stirring aria in D major ended not only the opening block of numbers but also the first act of the opera. Possibly Mozart had ringing in his ears the act-ending heroics of "Divinités du Styx" in Gluck's *Alceste* or Pylades' "Divinités des grands âmes" in *Iphigénie en Tauride*. As for ending the first act in the keynote of the opera, Mozart had already done that in *Idomeneo* and *Die Entführung aus dem Serail*. The strongest argument in support of an original four-act plan for *Don Giovanni* is provided by the great sextet (No. 19), which in purely musical terms is as conclusive as any finale, and at one time obviously was intended to end the third act. German theatrical troupes began giving the opera in four acts as early as 1789.[15] Possibly Mozart saw the superior wisdom of continuing right on after Anna's aria when he realized that he could bring the two driving passions of the work into close confrontation: Anna's relentless quest for revenge and Giovanni's relentless quest for pleasure, as expressed in all its lurid shades in No. 11, "Fin ch'han dal vino." But Mozart destroyed this perfect confrontation when his Viennese tenor could not

14. Mozart to Jacquin, 21 October 1787: "da die truppe klein ist, so muss der Impressario immer in Sorgen leben, und seine leute so viel möglich schonen, damit er nicht, durch eine unvermuthete unpässlichkeit in die unter allen krittischen allerkrittischste laage versezt wird, gar kein Spektakl geben zu können!"

15. Christof Bitter, *Wandlungen in den Inszenierungsformen des "Don Giovanni" von 1787 bis 1928* (Regensburg, 1961), p. 73.

sing "Il mio tesoro" (No. 21) and received in compensation "Dalla sua pace," slipped in after Anna's call for revenge—that is to say, where Bertati had originally placed the aria for Ottavio.

The symmetries of the opera are many. Its first half opens with a labor complaint from Leporello, and so does the second half. The only place for an Ottavio aria is following what were presumably the original endings of acts 1 and 3. Confrontation followed by escape ends the first finale (original end of act 2) and the great sextet (original end of act 3). It might be objected that, if the curtain comes down on the sextet, how can Leporello escape? But how, indeed, do Giovanni and Leporello escape after the attempted rape of Zerlina in the ballroom scene of the first finale? We are not told. They simply take to their heels at the curtain, apparently, and so could Leporello at the end of the sextet. This is a practical problem that had to be solved as soon as companies started giving the opera in four acts.

Plot lines not borrowed by Da Ponte from Bertati could well have been suggested by Mozart. Three simultaneous dances in the ballroom scene, all presaged in the text of "Fin ch'han dal vino" (a good example of how Da Ponte used his skills to "prepare" events), obviously belong to the composer's realm of invention. Gluck's *Don Juan*, which Mozart knew well, had a parallel ballroom scene in the palace of the Don. The exchange of costumes between Leporello and Giovanni, so that the latter can woo the maidservant of Donna Elvira, has a long history in Don Juan plays. Already in Molière's *Dom Juan, ou Le festin de pierre*, the Don changes clothes with his servant, and before that in *Il convitato di pietra*, dating from around 1632 and attributed to Cicognini. Da Ponte did not invent this ploy, but he did outdo his predecessors in drawing trenchant wit from it, as when his Giovanni explains why he wished to shed his great cloak and plumed hat for Leporello's simpler raiments: "Han poco credito con gente di tal rango / Gli abiti signorali" ("Signorial attire has little credit with people of that station"). The early engraving by Medardus Thoenert depicting Bassi as Giovanni confuses the issue by showing the Don serenading in his own costume (Fig. 18).

The serenades sung in turn to Elvira and to her maidservant argue for the likelihood that the composer had a hand in developing this plot line as well. Once again a parallel is to be observed with Gluck's *Don Juan*, which also has a serenading Don.[16] Costume exchanges and serenading are the very stuff of *commedia dell'arte* improvisations, and it did not take a poet of Da Ponte's inventive skills to come up with this caper. Mozart had enough experience in the invention of pantomime skits to have suggested it himself. The closeness of the opera to its ancestors in popular theater is nowhere more apparent than in the first half of act 2.

One of the peculiarities of Libretto 1 is its use of small type to distinguish the recitatives from the set pieces. Thus at the end of Donna Elvira's entrance aria,

16. As pointed out by John Stone in "The Making of 'Don Giovanni' and Its Ethos," *Mozart-Jahrbuch 1984/85*, pp. 130–34.

Don Giovanni.
Rappres.ta d'al Signor Bassi.

Dissegn. e Intagl. Thoenert.

FIGURE 18

Thoenert: The first Don Giovanni

in costume

"Ah! chi mi dice mai" (No. 2), the next lines of Don Giovanni and Leporello are set in smaller type than that of her two quatrains of verse for the aria:

GIOVANNI: Udisti: qualche bella
    (a Leporello) Dal vago abbandonata? poverina!
    Cerchiam di consolare il suo tormento.
LEPORELLO: Così ne consolò mille, e ottocento.
GIOVANNI: Signorina!

It could have been guessed from the length of the first four lines (7, 11, 11, and 11 syllables), as well as from their lack of rhyme, that they were intended by Da Ponte to be set in recitative, not as part of the aria. Yet the situation is not totally clear, because Leporello responds with a line matching Giovanni's both in length and in end-rhyme. This is one way Da Ponte has of making Leporello appear a very clever fellow—more clever often than Giovanni himself, in fact. (Note also that Da Ponte has cannily made a plant here to "prepare" the catalog aria, No. 3.) Da Ponte could not have foreseen that Mozart would move these lines back into Elvira's aria as interjections; that they were printed in small type in the early libretto leaves no doubt that Da Ponte intended them for recitative. In the Prague libretto only one type size is used for both set numbers and recitatives, so the distinction disappears.

The use of small type in the early libretto applies not only to recitatives. Some of the rhymed verses obviously meant for musical setting are also in small type, for example Massetto's "Ho capito, signor sì" (No. 6). Mozart wrote out this aria very late, in Prague; it therefore figures (on Prague paper) in his autograph, but not in the early performance copies.[17] Did the early libretto serve, among other purposes, that of telling a potential patron how much was already composed? This explanation would fit with Volek's theory of a commercial venture launched by the Prague managers. Yet it can be pushed only so far, alas. The opening duetto of act 2, "Eh via buffone" (No. 14), also late and composed in Prague, is set in small type, but so are the texts of the following two numbers, which are disputed as to date of composition. Giovanni's aria "Metà di voi qua vadano" (No. 17) is set in large type, but Volek claims it was composed in Prague; the finale of the second act, which we know Mozart finished in Prague, is also set large.[18]

Many lessons remain to be learned from comparing the two librettos. Da Ponte completed most of the text in Vienna before leaving for Prague—of this Libretto I leaves no doubt. It contains almost all of act 2, up to just after the beginning of

17. Alan Tyson verified that "Ho capito" was written on Prague paper; see the Appendix to this chapter. On the early performance copies, see Manfred Schuler, "Mozarts 'Don Giovanni' in Donaueschingen," *Mitteilungen der Internationalen Stiftung Mozarteum* 35 (1987): 63–72.

18. Alfred Einstein, in the foreword to his edition of *Don Giovanni* (Eulenberg Edition [n.d.], No. 918), says on the basis of physical evidence that Nos. 5, 6, 14, 16, and 24 plus the overture were added to the autograph in Prague. Wolfgang Plath and Wolfgang Rehm, in their foreword to the Neue Mozart-Ausgabe edition (1968), p. viii, question his inclusion of Nos. 5 and 16. They promise a searching review of the evidence in their forthcoming "Kritische Bericht."

the Scena ultima, where it breaks off. A few telling additions were made during the rehearsals in Prague—emendations that suggested themselves, it seems, as a result of Da Ponte "directing the actors," as he says in his memoirs. Following the terzetto (No. 15), the original dialogue between Elvira and Leporello (dressed as Giovanni), as printed in Libretto 1, was shorter. Da Ponte stretched it out by adding these cruelly comic lines:

> D. ELV. Crudele! se sapeste
> Quante lagrime, e quanti
> Sospir voi mi costate!
>
> LEP. Io vita mia?
>
> D. ELV. Voi.
>
> LEP. Poverina! quanto mi dispiace!
>
> D. ELV. Mi fuggirete più?
>
> LEP. No muso bello.
>
> D. ELV. Sarete sempre mio?
>
> LEP. Sempre.
>
> D. ELV. Carissimo!
>
> LEP. Carissima! (la burla mi dà gusto)
>
> D. ELV. Mio tesoro!
>
> LEP. Mia venere!
>
> D. ELV. Son per voi tutta foco.
>
> LEP. Io tutto cenere.
>
> D. GIO. (Il birbo si riscalda.)
>
> D. ELV. E non m'ingannerete?
>
> LEP. No sicuro.
>
> D. ELV. Giuratemi.

Especially funny is what Leporello replies to Elvira's "Son per voi tutta foco" ("I'm all fire for you"): "Io tutto cenere" ("I'm all cinders"). "Io tutto cenere" has the added advantage of rhyming with his previous "Mia venere" ("My Venus"). In this new version, present in Libretto 2, and in Mozart's autograph score as a separate added leaf, Elvira has a chance to become heated by degrees. Credit its addition to the acting abilities of Caterina Micelli as Elvira and Felice Ponziani as Leporello.

The supper scene in the finale of act 2 provides a good opportunity for studying further the interactions of poet, composer, and performers. There are at least two puns on the names of members of the Prague company in this scene. Donna Anna was sung by the young Teresa Saporiti, acclaimed for her figure, and an actress who had some experience with seria roles before, having taken over castrato parts. Not by chance, then, does Giovanni sing the praises of his table with "Ah che piatto saporito!" ("What a tasty dish!"). To drive home the point, Mozart writes: "Ah che piatto saporito, saporito, saporito!" The pun can be extended from Teresa

Saporiti to include Giovanni's relishing of Donna Anna. Of a similar kind is the more involved two-language pun concerning the opera orchestra's harpsichord player, Jan Kritel Kuchar (1751–1828). He made a keyboard reduction of *Le nozze di Figaro* advertised for subscription in Vienna during June 1787, and he was making a similar reduction of *Don Giovanni* from Mozart's autograph even before the premiere.[19] *Kuchar* in Czech means "cook," or "cuoco" in Italian, which explains Leporello's insistence at the end of the supper scene (final reprise of the melody from *Figaro*!) on the words "si eccellente è il vostro cuoco," which Giovanni then repeats as "si eccellente è il cuoco mio." As arranger of Mozart's two operas, Kuchar was a "cook" in a very special sense. The repetitions of *cuoco* for emphasis correspond to those of "che piatto saporito," and they show up in the score, not the libretto. Both are present before Prague, in Libretto 1. It was thus Mozart, who had been in Prague recently and was familiar with the theater personnel there, and not Da Ponte, who supplied these puns to the libretto.

Choice of the tune by Giuseppe Sarti to enliven the supper music comes as no surprise, since Mozart had expressed his enthusiasm for Sarti to his father in the same letter of 12 June 1784 in which he mentions fetching Paisiello by carriage (see Chapter 7): "If Maestro Sarti did not have to make his departure today, he would have come with me too. Sarti is an honest, good man! I played a lot for him, also including variations on one of his arias, from which he took very great pleasure."[20]

Speaking of the supper scene, Volek mentions "an entire stratum of allusions" invented for Prague but lost in subsequent productions. Yet he chooses to ignore the possible allusions brought to the scene by the original texts of the three pieces of *Tafelmusik* played by Giovanni's band. He interprets the choice of "Come un agnello" from Sarti's *Fra i due litiganti* as a bow to old Count Thun, Mozart's longtime friend and patron, in whose private theater Sarti's opera had been performed in 1783. The melody from Martín y Soler's *Una cosa rara*, Volek says, was chosen because of Leporello's ambiguous deprecation of it to Giovanni: "Mozart needed—as prescribed by the libretto—some music of no great value."[21] But surely this is putting the cart before the horse. The libretto was in constant flux and had to respond to Mozart's music as long as he was composing. It might also be argued whether the chosen music was of "no great value" and whether Mozart would have ensconced it in his score had he believed this to be the case.

The thread that links these three pieces of supper music, and that led to their choice, we suggest, has to do with their original texts. Sarti's "Come un agnello" is sung by Mingone in demeaning his rival for the hand of Dorina: "Like a lamb going to the slaughter, you will go bleating through the city." It does not take the mentality of a cryptographer to bring the allusion to bear on Giovanni, who is on

19. Volek, "Prague Operatic Traditions," p. 77.
20. "wenn Maestro Sarti nicht heute wegreisen hätte müssen, so wäre er auch mit mir hinaus. — Sarti ist ein rechtschaffner braver Mann! — ich habe ihm sehr viel gespiellt, endlich auch Variazionen auf eine seinige Aria gemacht, woran er sehr viele freude gehabt hat"; 12 June 1784.
21. Volek, "Prague Operatic Traditions," p. 70.

the verge of going to his own slaughter. The piece from *Una cosa rara* is a jubilant section from the first-act finale, "O quanto un sì bel giubilo," celebrating the happy reunion of two rustic couples in spite of the lecherous designs of a nobleman on Lilla (who possessed the "rare thing" of the title, both beauty and virtue). She is importuned by a prince named (what else?) Don Giovanni.[22] Substitute Zerlina for Lilla and the allusion becomes clear. Giovanni's conquests have ended, and his time for "diverting himself" in whatever fashion is rapidly drawing to a close by the time the third and culminating tune recalls the text "Non più andrai farfallone amoroso / Notte e giorno d'intorno girando, / Delle belle turbando il riposo" ("No longer will you go, you amorous butterfly, alighting here and there day and night, disturbing the repose of the ladies"). It is as if the creators of both operas were wagging a finger at Giovanni through the vehicle of his house band.

In planning the supper scene as a whole, precedence surely went from the beginning to this tune from *Figaro*, the great favorite of the Prague public. It arrived like the last line of an epigram, and everything leading up to it must have been plotted backwards accordingly. In musical terms it is easily the best of the three tunes, and it arrives in one of the crucial tonalities of the opera, B-flat, coming after F, which comes directly after D, the keynote. This is the same sequence of keys as at the beginning of the opera—overture, "Notte e giorno faticar," and the duet of struggle between Anna and Giovanni. Moreover, the way Mozart connects "Come un agnello" in D to "O quanto un sì bel giubilo" in F represents an extreme reduction (to one bass note, E-natural) of the transition from D to F at the end of the overture.[23]

The tonal parallel between the beginning of the opera and the finale of act 2 could be extended by noting that both set up the eventual arrival of "tragic" d minor. Mozart had deflected the ending of the *introduzione* from an expected d minor to a surprising f minor for the death of the Commendatore (Ex. 9.1; cf. the comparable deflection in *Idomeneo*, No. 4, mm. 76–77). When the Commendatore returns as the Stone Guest, the same diminished chord to which he was mortally wounded in act 1 sounds again, but this time there is no reprieve from its resolution to d minor (Ex. 9.2). Justice is inevitably served even in terms of the large-scale tonal architecture. For the opera to work to the maximum degree, we must hear the second passage as a recurrence.

The exclamations by which Leporello identifies the sources of the tunes as *Fra i due litiganti* and *Una cosa rara* and his greeting to the tune from *Figaro* are lacking not only in Libretto 1 but also in Libretto 2. But they are present in Mozart's autograph, leading us to believe that Mozart reached his final decisions about the

22. This was pointed out in a term paper, "Don Giovanni's Banquet Music," by my former student Joshua Kosman, whom I thank.
23. The D to F progression also applies to the way Masetto's aria in F, "Ho capito" (No. 6), is connected with the previous recitative ending in D. It has been suggested, implausibly, that the aria was originally intended to be in G, then transposed down to F. See Appendix.

EXAMPLE 9.1. *Don Giovanni*, No. 1

EXAMPLE 9.2. *Don Giovanni*, No. 24

banquet music very late, during the rehearsals in Prague. Bitter suggests that the verbal additions were interpolations by Leporello/Ponziani that Mozart simply incorporated. But this gives the singer more responsibility than is credible. Arguments about a largely improvised banquet scene stem from a misunderstanding of the kind of latitude allowed when singing to a fixed orchestral score. Luigi Bassi, the first Giovanni, was quoted much later as saying: "With Guardasoni we never sang this number the same way twice. We did not keep the time very strictly, but made a joke of it, each time something new, and only taking heed of the orchestra—everything *parlando* and nearly improvised, as Mozart wished it."[24] There could well have been verbal interpolations that made the scene different at each performance, and rhythmic stretchings that lent the desired air of informality and spontaneity, while still "taking heed of the orchestra." The succession of keys and the choice of tunes in the scene were certainly not left to chance, as we have seen. Bassi's reference to Guardasoni implies that the latter took charge of the staging after Da Ponte left Prague for Vienna in the middle of the rehearsals.[25]

Instructive as to how Mozart and Da Ponte put the opera together is a comparison of the Scena ultima, or what little of it was printed in Libretto 1, with the final form in Libretto 2 (Fig. 19). In the first place, Elvira is not listed among the tutti in the earlier version, though this may be a mere oversight. In the second, the discrepancies that follow show that the end of the opera was still in a very fluid state when Libretto 1 was printed (in mid-summer?). Originally Da Ponte gave Donna Anna no solo quatrain after the first tutti; Mozart must have insisted on bringing Anna and her *pene* to the forefront here. This is not the only indication that Mozart envisaged Anna's grief as the mainspring of the entire work. Leporello's quatrain remained intact, with the tiny exception that "Più nol cercate" ("Don't search for him anymore") became simplified to "Più non cercate" ("Don't search anymore"). Eliminated were the following tutti demanded in the early libretto, "Dov'è nascosto / Parla rispondi," along with Leporello's temporizing response, "Piano che tosto/ve lo dirò." Mozart evidently wanted a quicker dramatic tempo here, a more direct plunge into Leporello's narration of the Stone Guest's arrival. This is a small but revealing lesson as to how the libretto remained unsettled until Mozart made his musical decisions.

The Scena ultima thus did not take final shape until well into the rehearsals in Prague. Surely, though, Mozart had in mind very early an idea of how he wanted to end the opera. The descending chromatic lines that have so saturated the work—and always in some connection with Giovanni himself, whether as the "dying fall" of sexual love or of death—find no more telling statement than the new and subtle one between the first and second violins, joined by the winds, on the

---

24. "Wir haben bei Guardasoni in dieser Nummer nicht in zwei Vorstellungen gesungen dasselbe, wir haben nicht so strenge gehalten Takt, sondern haben gemacht Witz, jedesmal neue und nur auf das Orchester gehalten Acht; alles parlando und beinahe improvisiert, so hat es gewollt Mozart"; Bitter, *Wandlungen in den Inszenierungsformen des "Don Giovanni,"* p. 29.

25. The librettist's function with regard to the acting on stage is examined at length in Chapter 5.

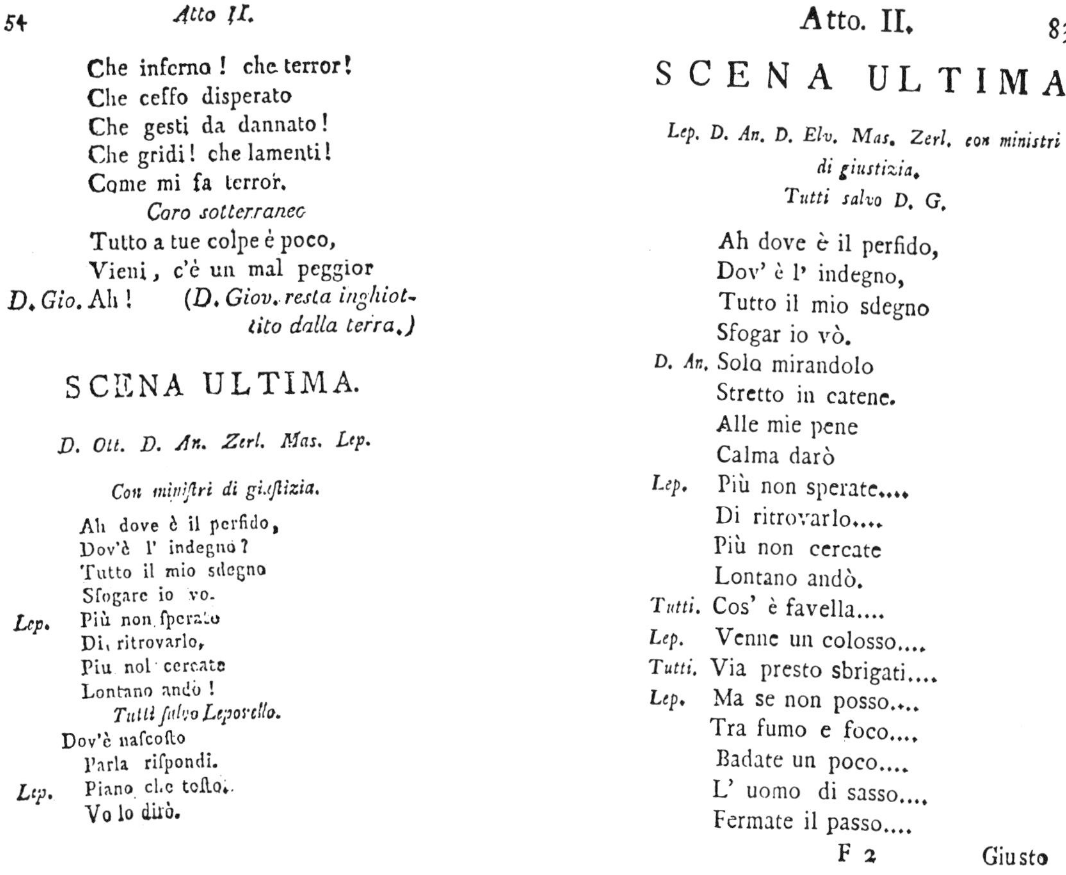

Che inferno ! che terror!
Che ceffo disperato
Che gesti da dannato!
Che gridi ! che lamenti!
Come mi fa terror.
     Coro sotterraneo
Tutto a tue colpe è poco,
Vieni , c'è un mal peggior
D. Gio. Ah !   (*D. Giov. resta inghiot-*
             tito dalla terra.)

SCENA ULTIMA.

D. Ott. D. An. Zerl. Mas. Lep.

    Con ministri di giustizia.

Ah dove è il perfido,
Dov'è l' indegno?
Tutto il mio sdegno
Sfogare io vo.
Lep. Più non sperato,
Di, ritrovarlo,
Piu nol cercate
Lontano andò !
     Tutti salvo Leporello.
Dov'è nascosto
Parla rispondi.
Lep. Piano che tosto.
Vo lo dirò.

SCENA ULTIMA.

Lep. D. An. D. Elv. Mas. Zerl. con ministri
di giustizia.
Tutti salvo D. G.

     Ah dove è il perfido,
     Dov' è l' indegno,
     Tutto il mio sdegno
     Sfogar io vò.
D. An. Solo mirandolo
     Stretto in catene.
     Alle mie pene
     Calma darò
Lep. Più non sperate....
     Di ritrovarlo....
     Più non cercate
     Lontano andò.
Tutti. Cos' è favella....
Lep. Venne un colosso....
Tutti. Via presto sbrigati....
Lep. Ma se non posso....
     Tra fumo e foco....
     Badate un poco....
     L' uomo di sasso....
     Fermate il passo....
          F 2   Giusto

FIGURE 19

Beginning of the Scena ultima in Librettos 1 and 2 of *Don Giovanni*

last page of the score (Ex. 9.3). This understated orchestral passage summarizes the whole opera, as if to say: Don Giovanni may be gone, but you will not forget him.

Low comedy plays much more of a role in *Don Giovanni* than it does in *Figaro*, a state of affairs for which Bertati in particular, and the popular nature of the subject in general, may be blamed (or praised). One of the most crucial decisions for Mozart and Da Ponte in creating a full-length opera out of Bertati's material must have been how to strike just the desired balance between the farcical and risible on the one hand, and the starkly serious and tragic on the other. Long after Da Ponte had come to America, one of his New York friends, Dr. John W. Francis, asked the poet the sort of question we should all like to ask him: how, exactly, did he work together with Mozart? Da Ponte's answer, as reported by Dr. Francis, centered on *Don Giovanni*:

The opportunities which presented themselves to me of obtaining circumstantial facts concerning Mozart from the personal knowledge of Da Ponte, were not so frequent as desireable, but the incidents which Da Ponte gave were all of a most agreeable character. His accounts strengthened the reports of the ardent, nay, almost impetuous energy and industry of Mozart; his promptness in decision, and his adventurous intellect. The story of Don Juan had indeed become familiar in a thousand ways; Mozart determined to cast the opera exclusively as serious, and had well advanced in the work. Da Ponte assured me, that he had remonstrated and urged the expediency on the great composer of the introduction of the vis comica, in order to accomplish a greater success, and prepared the rôle with Batti, batti, Là ci darem, Etc.[26]

Let us assume, for the sake of argument, that Da Ponte did say something like this to Dr. Francis and, moreover, that it approximated the truth. How does this information jibe with other evidence? That Mozart often started composing the music before he had the poem in hand can be documented several times over. That he wanted to emphasize the serious side of the old Protean tale also rings true. Indeed, he has done just this in his score, especially as compared with the lightweight music of Gazzaniga's *Don Giovanni*. The central focus of the new opera is Giovanni's downfall, presaged already in the overture, and carried out relentlessly from the slaying of the Commendatore to Giovanni's own demise after the Commendatore returns as the Stone Guest. This basic framework is tragic, and no amount of comic relief can change that. Mozart's uncertainties about cutting the Scena ultima from the Viennese production of 1788 (he eventually decided not to) confirm that his main vision of the work was a tragic one.

Yet he could never have intended "to cast the opera exclusively as serious," in the words of Dr. Francis quoting Da Ponte. For one thing, the limited vocal resources at Prague would not have allowed it, nor did the Bertati model suggest it. Still, it is quite conceivable that Da Ponte plumped for more comic relief, "to accomplish a greater success," as Dr. Francis plausibly claims; and consequently, "Da Ponte prepared the rôle with Batti, batti, Là ci darem, Etc." Presumably the title role is what is intended here, but the only role that "Batti, batti" and "Là ci darem" have in common is that of the peasant girl Zerlina, who is, truly enough, one of the three buffa characters, along with Masetto and Leporello. The altogether seria characters are of course Anna, Ottavio, and the Commendatore. Supposing Mozart did want to give the opera a more serious tincture, he could have done so by throwing Anna's clarion call for revenge, "Or sai chi l'onore," into even greater relief by having it end the first of four acts. Just possibly it was Da Ponte who argued Mozart out of giving Anna any more prominence than she possesses in the ultimate two-act conception of the opera.

26. John W. Francis, *Old New York, or, Reminiscences of the Past Sixty Years* (New York, 1865), pp. 265–66.

EXAMPLE 9.3. *Don Giovanni*, No. 24

There is another piece of evidence bearing on the overriding importance that Mozart attached to the serious side of the opera: the overture. It was written last of all, as was the custom. While he could have chosen countless other beginnings for it, he chose the somber music in d minor that accompanies the arrival of the avenging Stone Guest in the second finale. Thus he shapes our entire perception of the work. He could have followed the opening Andante, which is like a slow introduction to a great symphony (specifically, the Prague Symphony!), with an Allegro altogether buffo in style, something on the order of the overture to *Figaro* or the Allegro part of the overture to *Così fan tutte*. But he did not.

The Allegro takes as its point of departure a rising chromatic figure expressive of pain and sorrow, actually sung by the noble and long-suffering Ottavio in the great sextet. "Pena avrà de' tuoi martir," he sings to Donna Anna, and this too concerns the Commendatore, who would be pained, if he were alive, to see his daughter suffer so (Ex. 9.4). There is festal music in the overture's Molto allegro and fanfares like those in the supper scene at the beginning of the second finale, but scarcely anything that reflects the opera's comic side. The second theme, a gruff

EXAMPLE 9.4. *Don Giovanni*, No. 19

pe - na a - vrà ___ de' tuoi ___ mar - tir,

unison figure in descent, has affinities with passages at the end of the great sextet and the following aria for Leporello, and it is this figure that Mozart puts through its paces in his long and intense Development section—a feature not even present in the overture to *Figaro*.

Richard Wagner heard the Allegro of the overture to *Don Giovanni* not as comedy, but as a struggle between inexorably opposed forces.[27] What he says about the overture applies to the opera as a whole. The comedy does not begin until the curtain goes up, revealing Leporello in the flesh, while the orchestra paints him to a fault—even before he opens his mouth to complain, "Notte e giorno faticar."

APPENDIX

Masetto's Aria "Ho capito, Signor sì" (No. 6)

In the article "*Le nozze di Figaro*: Lessons from the Autograph Score" (*Musical Times* 122 [1981]: 456–61), Alan Tyson writes in his note 6: "Masetto's aria 'Ho capito', in F, is preceded by a recitative with a cadence in D—a strange relationship. It seems likely, however, that this aria was originally written in G, and later transposed down a tone for the singer's benefit. This finds support in the fact that it is the only part of the first-act score of *Don Giovanni* that is on Prague paper." Tyson makes only a slight change of wording when reprinting the article in *Mozart: Studies of the Autograph Scores* ([Cambridge, Mass., 1987], p. 338, n. 5), where "it seems likely" becomes "it is possible." Flaws are manifold in this proposal, which creates problems where none existed in the first place. "Ho capito" in G would make for two successive vocal numbers in the same key, an anomaly Mozart avoided in his operas. Masetto's highest tone in the aria is the fifth above the tonic, middle C (in F) or the D above it (in G). Neither tone is high for a bass, and indeed Mozart asked Giuseppe Lolli to sing D's throughout both of his roles (as Masetto and the Commendatore). Lolli must have had an especially good D above middle C for Mozart to make the tone so prominent at his entrance as the Commendatore. D followed by the key of F is not a "strange relationship" in this opera, as we have seen. It is one of the crucial tonal relationships that gives the work its special color.

27. Wagner's essay "De l'ouverture" appeared in installments in the eighth year of the *Revue et gazette musicale de Paris*, issues of 10 and 17 January 1841; rewritten as "Über die Ouvertüre," it was printed in Richard Wagner, *Gesammelte Schriften und Dichtungen*, ed. Wolfgang Golther (Berlin, 1913), pp. 194–206.

Also to be considered are the strong dynamic and agogic accents on the tone D, otherwise unexplained, in a harmonic context of F major (mm. 53 and 75). The unknown reasons why Mozart left writing "Ho capito" until so late cannot be adduced in "support" of a transposition theory. Yet this idea has found its way into the musical practice, and "Ho capito" may be heard sung in G on more than one of the currently available recordings.

The lesson to be learned here is that performers should refrain from grasping at ideas put forward by scholars until they have been verified. The Moberly-Raeburn reordering of act 3 in *Figaro* is in the same category as a transposed "Ho capito." Tyson marshaled evidence discrediting the reordering in his 1981 article on the *Figaro* autograph. Yet it is still commonly heard in our opera houses, for instance in the production of *Figaro* at the San Francisco Opera during the work's bicentennial, 1986.

10 · AN ICONOGRAPHY OF THE DANCES IN THE BALLROOM SCENE OF *DON GIOVANNI*

M ozart was a keen observer of the dance wherever he went. He wrote his sister from Milan on 3 March 1770, when he was fourteen, that the Carnival balls there were like those in Vienna, but more unruly: "In Vienna there is more order" ("Zu Wien mehr ordnung ist"). Indeed, Mozart was more than an observer in the ballrooms of his day: he was passionately fond of dancing, as was his whole family. His father, Leopold, rarely missed going to the Bavarian court in Munich for the Carnival balls there if he could get out of his duties as a court musician in Salzburg; and in a letter of 21 February 1775 from Munich he urged his wife not to miss the Redoute masquerade balls in Salzburg. The Mozarts belonged to a higher social rung than did the families of Haydn or Beethoven, which may help explain why we do not hear of those two composers being preoccupied with going to masquerade balls. Mozart's letter from Vienna of 22 January 1783 to his father well illustrates his mania for the dance:

> You doubtless know that it is Carnival time and there is as much dancing here as in Salzburg or Munich. Well, I should very much like to go as Harlequin (but not a soul must know it) because so many stupid fools are at the Redoute here. So I should like you to send me your Harlequin costume. But please do so very soon, for we shall not attend the Redoutes until I have it, although they are in full swing. We prefer private balls. Last week I gave a ball in my own rooms, but of course the *chapeaux* each paid two gulden. We began at six in the evening and kept on until seven. What, only an hour? Of course not. Until seven o'clock next morning.[1]

1. "sie wissen ohne zweifel dass izt fasching ist, und dass hier so gut wie in Salzburg und München getanzt wird; — und da möchte ich gerne | : aber dass es kein Mensch weis : | als Harlequin gehen — weil hier so vielle — aber lauter Eseln, auf der Redoute sind; — folglich möchte ich sie bitten mir ihr Harlequin kleid zukommen zu lassen. — aber es müsste halt recht gar bald seyn — wir gehen eher nicht auf die Redoute, obwohl sie schon im grösten schwunge ist. — uns sind die Hausbälle lieber. — vergangene Woche habe ich in meiner Wohnung einen Ball gegeben. — versteht sich aber die chapeaus haben Jeder 2 gulden bezahlt. — wir haben abends um 6 uhr angefangen und um 7 uhr aufgehört; — was nur eine Stunde? — Nein Nein — Morgens um 7 uhr."

Then, three weeks later, on 15 February 1783, he wrote his father that he was planning to gather a company of masqueraders and put on a small pantomime during the last days of Carnival. Leopold did send his Harlequin costume, and his son used it, as he reported back in his letter of 12 March:

> On Carnival Monday our company of masqueraders went to the Redoute, where we performed a pantomime that exactly filled the half-hour it was allowed. My sister-in-law [the soprano Aloysia Lange, married to the court actor and painter Joseph Lange] was Columbine. I was Harlequin, my brother-in-law [Lange] Pierrot, an old dancing master named Merk was Pantalon, and the painter Grassi was the Doctor. The invention of the pantomime and the music were both of my doing. Merk the dancing master was so kind as to coach us, and I must say we played it very skillfully. I am enclosing the program, which was distributed to the maskers by a masker dressed as a postillion. The verses, although only doggerel, could have been better; they are not mine—the actor Müller scribbled them.[2]

Mozart's music for this pantomime survives partially as a first violin part (K. 446), which has the action cued in verbally. The end of it is missing, so we do not know how the skit came out, but it may be presumed, on the basis of *commedia dell'arte* traditions, that Harlequin comes back to life, after having been killed, and gets the girl, Columbine. In other words, Mozart invented a drama in dance in which he, as the young rogue Harlequin, ends up getting his first love, Aloysia Weber. Constanze Mozart, née Weber, was at this time expecting her first child (Raimund Leopold, born 17 June 1783, died 19 August the same summer). She later told the tenor Michael Kelly that, great as Mozart's musical genius was, he was also an enthusiast in dancing, and he often said that his taste lay in that art rather than in music. She told her second husband, Georg Nissen, that Mozart was especially skilled at dancing the minuet, also that he often assumed one of the comic masks, and that he was incomparable as Pierrot as well as Harlequin. His dance teacher, she said, was Vestris (presumably Gaetano Vestris, *premier danseur* and ballet master of the Paris Opéra). She was emphatic in stating that Mozart not only danced but also invented pantomimes and ballets. Against this background we may now consider the ballroom scene that ends the first act of *Don Giovanni*.

"Una gran festa" is what Don Giovanni decides to put on for the peasants he invited to his palace, the better to seduce Zerlina—and several others as well. Da Ponte's very clever words for Giovanni's aria (No. 11) deserve close attention for they set up the ensuing plot line. Giovanni instructs Leporello to keep the wine flowing so that it goes to the head, and to prepare a great feast, this in short four-

---

2. "wir haben am fasching Montag unsere Compagnie Masquerade auf der Redoute aufgeführt. — sie bestund in einer Pantomime, welche eben die halbe stunde, da ausgesezt wird, ausfüllte. — Meine schwägerin war die Colombine, ich der Harlequin, Mein schwager der Piero, ein alter tanzmeister [Merk] der Pantalon. ein Maler (grassi) der Dottore. — die Erfindung der Pantomime, und die Muzik dazu war beydes von mir. — der Tanzmeister Merk hatte die güte uns abzurichten; und ich sag es ihnen wir spielten recht artig. — hier leg ich ihnen die ankündigung davon bey, welche eine masque als kleperPost gekleidet den masquen austheilte. — die Verse, wenn sie schon knittelverse sind, könnten besser seyn; das ist kein Product von mir. — der schauspieler Müller hat sie geschmiert."

and five-syllable lines, probably ordered specifically by Mozart to match the rhythm and melody he had in mind:

> Fin ch'han dal vino
> Calda la testa
> Una gran festa
> Fa preparar.
> Se trovi in piazza
> Qualche ragazza
> Teco ancor quella
> Cerca menar.

"And if you find some girl in the public square," Giovanni tells Leporello, "seek to bring her along also."

Let us consider again how Mozart saturated his score with expressive chromatic lines, especially descending ones such as had accompanied the death of the Commendatore. The chromatic lines turn up unexpectedly in seemingly innocent and lighthearted pieces, for example in the second part of the seduction duet between Don Giovanni and Zerlina, "La ci darem la mano" (No. 7), as the violins, commenting on "un innocente amor," seem to say with their drooping chromatics, "not innocent at all, but fatal." The aria under consideration here goes by so fast we scarcely notice at first that Mozart has slipped a descending chromatic fourth into Giovanni's vocal line as he thinks about the girl in the piazza who might become a new conquest for him. In this opera chromatic lines spell death, but also the related phenomenon of love death, or the sexual act, as is made abundantly clear in the great sextet (No. 19), and where the descending chromatic line is complemented by the rising chromatic line (see Ex. 12.2 below). But the same is true already in "Fin ch'han dal vino." Mozart points up the chromatic descent in the vocal line by doubling it in the first violins and the flute, which introduce at the same time the first sustained legato line in the piece. And before the refrain comes around for the last time, there is a chromatic line, but rising, in the bassoons and clarinets, slurred as before (mm. 107–10)—an appropriate preparation for Giovanni's last quatrain, about how he will add ten or so conquests to his list by tomorrow morning:

> Ed io frattanto,
> Dall'altro canto,
> Con questa, e quella
> Vo' amoreggiar.
> A la mia lista,
> Doman mattina,
> D'una decina
> Devi aumentar.

Giovanni's hot Latin blood seems to rise with that wickedly suggestive bassoon line rising in octaves. If the censors had only known how suggestive of the erotic Mozart's music could be, they would surely have banned it.

The central point to our purpose here is the enumeration of the dances, and how they will be danced at the "gran festa":

Senz'alcun ordine	Without any order
La danza sia,	The dancing should be,
Ch'il minuetto	Here the minuet
Chi la follia	Here the follia
Chi l'alemanna	Here the German
Farai ballar.	You will make them dance.

These instructions will be carried out later in the actual ballroom scene, with Leporello as dance master. How telling of Giovanni and the wildness of his character that the dances are to be mixed together, without any order.

Mozart himself must have conceived this idea—the same Mozart who observed that south of the Alps the balls had less *Ordnung*, less *ordine*, than those in Vienna. Certainly it was the composer rather than the poet who had to come up with a conception so dependent on an intimate knowledge of dance lore, confident that he could later execute what is forecast in this aria text. The *follia* is an old Spanish dance. Its choice accords with the Spanish setting of the opera, which otherwise has even less local color than *Figaro*, with its fandango indebted to Gluck's *Don Juan*. In terms of the poem, *follia*, meaning madness, was a perfect choice to convey Giovanni's madcap idea of an orderless ball scene, and besides this, the word fits the meter and rhyme scheme of the verse, "chi la follia" matching the line "la danza sia." The actual middle dance of the three danced in Giovanni's palace is the *contredanza*, which word would not have fit.

The minuet opens the ballroom scene, as was proper everywhere at the time. It is danced, appropriately, by Don Ottavio and Donna Anna. Just so was it necessary for one couple to begin the ball while the others watched. The partners are across from each other for most of the minuet, separated by a few yards. Only at the conclusion do they come together and touch hands, and that is all they touch. How fitting a way to characterize this altogether proper aristocratic couple! The minuet was not only the most aristocratic of dances, it was also the most demanding of skill and grace. William Hogarth has some choice things to say on the subject in his 1753 treatise *An Analysis of Beauty*:

> The minuet is allowed by the dancing masters themselves to be the perfection of all dancing. . . . The ordinary undulating motion of the body in common walking . . . is augmented in dancing into a larger quantity of *waving* by means of the minuet-step, which is so contrived as to raise the body by gentle degrees somewhat higher than ordinary, and sink it again in the same manner lower in the going on of the dance. The figure of the minuet path on the floor is also composed of serpentine lines. . . . [3]

3. William Hogarth, *The Analysis of Beauty with the Rejected Passages from the Manuscript Drafts and Autobiographical Notes*, ed. with an introduction by Joseph Burke (Oxford, 1955), pp. 156–57.

The dance is done to a moderately slow triple meter, to which the dancers must move in a kind of rhythmic counterpoint, by distributing four steps over two bars in 3/4 time, for example: ♩ ♩ ♩ ♩ ♩ ♩ ♩ . The motion described by Hogarth came about by bending the body slightly at the knees before the first beat, then rising up on point for the small steps. The feet never leave the floor.

The minuet proper, that is to say the *menuet* of the French court, scarcely changed from the beginning of the eighteenth century until the end. It epitomized the entire century as did no other dance, indeed, no other cultural artifact of any kind. Although Mozart could have chosen a more recently arrived fashionable dance as the core of his ballroom scene, for instance the polonaise, he could not have chosen a more universal symbol for the entire realm of dance than the minuet. He even chose the rhythm— ♩ ♪♪♪♪ ♩ ♩ —that had been the classic motto of this French dance ever since the early years of the eighteenth century.[4]

Antoine Watteau captured the minuet visually with a grace of expression comparable to Mozart's. In his painting known as *Les plaisirs du bal* (Fig. 20), he depicts a couple inaugurating the dancing with a minuet while the large assembly of people look on or otherwise amuse themselves. It was considered even in Watteau's day one of the most beautiful of all his paintings. The scene is laid in what appears to be a courtyard, open to nature at the back. To the right is a small band composed of an oboe, some violins, and a double bass: a two-part texture of treble and bass sufficed much eighteenth-century music made for dancing.

Just as Harlequin and Pierrot were Mozart's favorite masquerade figures, so were they Watteau's, and the painter rarely missed an opportunity to introduce them in an assemblage of fashionable people like *Les plaisirs du bal*. Harlequin assumes one of his characteristic poses, with his arms akimbo, and Pierrot in his white clown suit lets his arms hang down limply, a characteristic gesture for him. Arm movements were an important part of the minuet too.

The French dancing masters of the early eighteenth century taught a principle called "the opposition of the arms and legs," according to which the gentleman would, while moving his left leg, slightly raise his right arm.[5] Watteau's gentleman is doing just this (his lady uses her arms to manage a floor-length gown). This painting has recently been dated 1716–17.[6] In 1716 a Venetian dancing master, Gregorio Lambranzi, brought out an illustrated dance manual in Nuremberg; his last illustration shows a dancing master teaching a male dancer the opposition of the

---

4. On this point, see the air sung by the character Menuet in an early vaudeville comedy, quoted as Example 11 in Daniel Heartz, "Terpsichore at the Fair: Old and New Dance Airs in Two Vaudeville Comedies by Lesage," in *Music and Context: Essays for John M. Ward*, ed. Anne Dhu Shapiro (Cambridge, Mass., 1985), p. 296. For a general study of the music of the ballroom scene, see Hans Heinrich Eggebrecht, *Versuch über die Wiener Klassik: Die Tanzszene in Mozarts "Don Giovanni"* (Wiesbaden, 1972).

5. Wendy Hilton, *Dance of Court and Theater: The French Noble Style, 1690–1725* (Princeton, N.J., 1981), pp. 140 and 203 bottom.

6. Margaret Morgan Grasselli and Pierre Rosenberg, *Watteau 1684–1721*, Catalog of the Tercentenary Watteau Exhibition (Washington, D.C., 1984), p. 368.

legs and the arms to a dance that he spells in the French fashion, *Menuet* (Fig. 21). The accompanying melody displays the required 3/4 time and phraseology; it even has the rhythmic motto of the classic minuet at the medial cadence.[7] The concurrence of Watteau and Lambranzi reinforces the point that the minuet was an internationally understood symbol of grace and dignity—not just a French dance—throughout the eighteenth century. And that is why it is so useful to Mozart. He could count on his audience feeling the rightness of this aristocratic dance beginning the ball in Don Giovanni's palace. The minuet was equally at home in Seville and in the palaces of Prague and Vienna; hence it worked in whatever imaginative context one chose to give the opera.

The contredanse, second of the dances to be struck up in the Don's ballroom (but the first to float out the palace windows before the noble maskers enter), was a slightly more recent dance than the minuet, but within Mozart's lifetime it too became a universal favorite. It came about when French dancing masters took up

7. Gregorio Lambranzi, *Neue und curieuse theatralische Tantz-Schule* (Nuremberg, 1716), translated by Derra de Moroda and edited with a preface by Cyril W. Beaumont as *New and Curious School of Theatrical Dancing* (New York, 1966).

FIGURE 20

(*Opposite*) Watteau: *Les plaisirs du bal*

FIGURE 21

Lambranzi: *Menuet*

the English country dance and transformed it to their tastes.[8] The country dance, like its French analogue, was a group dance performed with little hopping motions (as in the branle, from which it descends), motions that distinguish it very clearly from the minuet. It was typically performed by a whole group of people, using figures such as the square, the circle, and parallel lines. Hogarth depicts the last, what the English call "longways," in his *Analysis of Beauty* (Fig. 22); the picture is thought to represent the earl of Tynley and his household. Only the earl and his lady at the left exhibit postures that are graceful enough that they represent what Hogarth calls "the line of beauty." He diagrams their related curves with the wavy lines to the extreme left at the top of the page. As we descend through society along the line of dancers, finally reaching the servants, the attitudes and postures become more boisterous and unrefined, and to diagram them Hogarth uses various sharp angles. Right under these he diagrams the serpentine floor pattern of the minuet.

8. Jean-Michel Guilcher, *La contredanse et les renouvellements de la danse française* (Paris, 1969).

The boisterousness of the country dance or contredanse also characterized its music, which at its most typical was in a moderately fast duple meter with vigorous melodic leaps. The French in their contredanses preferred squares or quadrilles and circles to the English "longways." One dance of this type, called "La Bionni" (after Bionni, choreographer of the troupe) and dating from 1761, is preserved from the Théâtre Italien in Paris (Fig. 23). Gabriel de Saint-Aubin engraved the figures of this contredanse on a long plate, together with its music and floor patterns; those

FIGURE 22
Hogarth: *Country Dance*

who bought this engraved sheet, in sum, would have all the information necessary to perform this theatrical dance at home on the occasion of a costume party. The typical masks of the Italian comedy are easily identifiable, even though they are very small in Saint-Aubin's rendering. Arlequin and Arlequine stand out by the motley that they wear, Pierrot likewise by his white suit, and also identifiable is a Pulcinella (on the right of the first pictures). The melody is in E major and 2/4 time, and it covers a wide range. Fourth and fifth intervals rocking back and forth

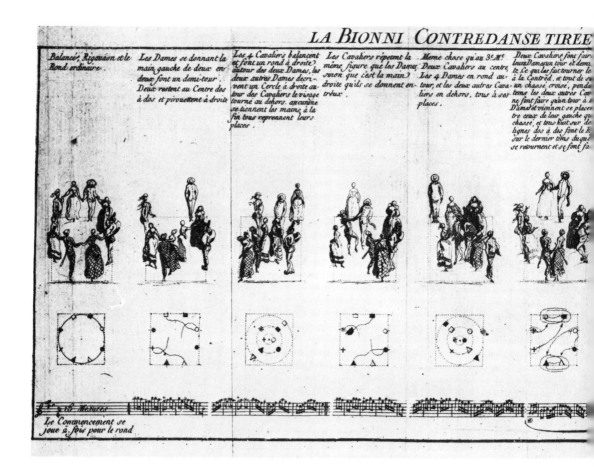

FIGURE 23

G. de Saint-Aubin: Contredanse

are characteristic of contredanse music, as in the portion of the melody beneath the eighth diagram in Figure 23 where the address "A Paris etc." begins.

There is a certain down-to-earth rusticity in that *martellato* figure that comes close to the essence of the contredanse. But if this is true of "La Bionni," it must be true as well of the music with which Mozart chooses to introduce us to Don Giovanni's servant Leporello in the opening vocal number of the opera: "Notte e giorno faticar, per chi nulla sà gradir." For Mozart's audience, the orchestral ritornello typed Leporello as a comic servant even before he opened his mouth. Mozart may well have told Da Ponte, "I'm going to use this melody to characterize Leporello on his first appearance, so give me four lines in *versi tronchi* [ending with an accented syllable], and then for the fifth line, Leporello should express the wish to be a gentleman in a line ending with a weak syllable [a category called *versi*

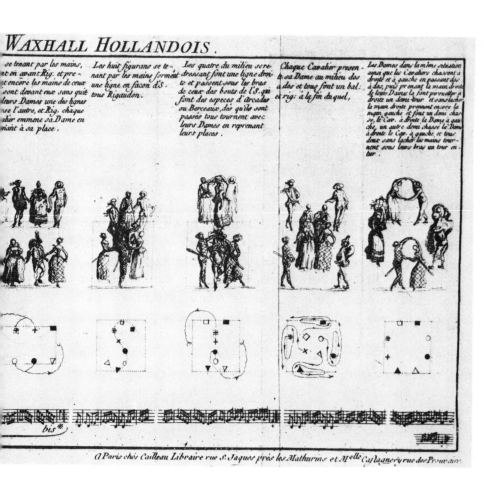

WAXHALL HOLLANDOIS.

piani]." He is known to have worked with his librettists in this way. In any case, Da Ponte obliged with "Voglio far il gentiluomo," at which point the contredanse skips give way to conjunct melodic motion, more characteristic of the minuet.

Was dancing the minuet, the true test of a gentleman, within Leporello's powers? His level, established from the outset by contredanse characteristics, was plebeian. Yet he is such a clever mimic of his master, for instance in the suave minuet strains of the Andante con moto of the catalog aria, as he describes Giovanni's wooing, that we should not be surprised if he executed the steps to go along with this music. In the ballroom scene Don Giovanni dances the "contredanza" with Zerlina, as is specified by the stage directions. A man for every social class, Don Giovanni picks a dance appropriate to Zerlina's social status. The vigor of the steps and the hopping motions allow no possibility of confusion with the minuet, danced simultaneously by Donna Anna and Don Ottavio. In musical terms, Mozart concocts a melody in 2/4 with many leaps and an initial upbeat. There are similarities here as well with "La Bionni"; cf. especially Mozart's *martellato* figure in fourths down from the high D (m. 445).

German dance or Deutscher, the third of the dances Mozart introduced into his ballroom scene, had begun to join the minuet and the contredanse in actual ballrooms as recently as the 1770s, that is to say, only a decade or so before *Don Giovanni*. According to the memoirs of Caroline Pichler, some couples in the large Redoutensaal in Vienna around 1780 performed the Deutscher, while others performed the Strassburger—a contredanse.[9] Goethe describes in *Werther* (1774) a ball where minuets, contredanses, and "deutsche tanzen oder walzen" succeed each other. The Deutscher was one of the ancestors of the waltz, and was performed by couples in close embrace to rapid triple meter.[10] It was particularly at home in the Austrian countryside and in the rural, mostly Catholic parts of southern Germany.

A south-German painter of the mid-eighteenth century, Januarius Zick, depicts such a dance in a painting that has an old peasant embracing a younger girl (Fig. 24). The minimal dance band of one violin and one bass accompanies them (the man in the background is not playing an instrument but smoking his pipe). A country tavern provides the outdoor setting and the season is spring, as is evident from the faintly discernible maypole in the right background.

In the ballroom scene of *Don Giovanni*, a proper house band of strings, horns, and oboes plays the minuet, while the contredanse gets at first only violin and double bass, until the oboes defect from the minuet and declare their allegiance to the contredanse; the Deutscher, with fast triplets to every quarter note of the minuet, is likewise played by one violin and a double bass, supported by the horns from the stage band for the minuet. Leporello, in order to divert Masetto's attention from what Don Giovanni is doing with Zerlina, forces the young peasant to dance with him. The tight embrace of the Deutscher serves a good dramatic purpose here, as Masetto is unable to free himself from Leporello's grasp, nor while whirling around the room to the fast triplets can he see very well; he therefore does not observe that Giovanni has forced Zerlina out a door. The Deutscher is also appropriate to Masetto because he is a peasant, a fairly crude fellow unafflicted with aspirations to higher estate such as beset and confuse Zerlina.

Thus we have all at once the lofty and elegant minuet, the more plebeian contredanse, and the crude and vulgar Deutscher, which Mozart renders even more vulgar by using Viennese dialect to label it "Teitsch." A century of dance history unfolds in this one scene, which he renders with the utmost realism by having the second and third stage bands tune up before beginning their respective dances.

9. Sarah Bennett Reichart, "The Influence of Eighteenth-Century Social Dance on the Viennese Classical Style," Ph.D. diss., City University of New York, 1984, p. 312.

10. Already around 1760 in Johann Sigmund Valentin Popowitsch's *Vocabula Austriaca et Styriaca*, "Walzen" is defined as a kind of "Teutschtanzen." See Reingard Witzmann, *Der Ländler in Wien: Ein Beitrag zur Entwicklungsgeschichte des Wiener Walzers bis in die Zeit des Wiener Kongresses* (Vienna, 1976), p. 58.

FIGURE 24

J. Zick: Rural couple dancing

Was this simultaneity of differing dances something that actually happened in ballrooms of the time? The succession of minuet followed by contredanse was so common during the 1780s that the practice had spread as far as the newly formed United States of America. Thus in Albany, New York, in 1782 we read that "the ball opened with a minuet, and a country dance was next called."[11] Count Fekete de Galántha wrote an *Esquisse d'un tableau vivant de Vienne en 1787* in which he names the dances in the large Redoutensaal for the Carnival balls as minuets, contredanses, and German dances.[12] Since different orchestras played in the adjacent small and large Redoutensäle, there was bound to be some audible impinging of the one on the other. The practice of multiple dance bands in the same ballroom is documented at the Carnival balls given in the theater of the Palais Royal

11. Charles Hamm, *Music in the New World* (New York, 1983), p. 68.
12. Johann Graf Fekete de Galántha, *Wien im Jahre 1787: Skizze eines lebenden Bildes von Wien, entworfen von einem Weltbürger*, trans. and ed. Victor Klarwill (Vienna, 1921), p. 93.

in Paris, first allowed by the regent in 1716. Orchestras were placed at either end of the hall, which, for the occasion, was enlarged by bringing the parterre up level with the stage.

Louis de Cahusac assures us in his article "Contredanse" in the *Encyclopédie* that different contredanses were danced simultaneously at either end of the hall. The painter Rousseau depicted the masked balls during the Carnival season of 1761 in the court theater at Bonn, where the stage and the parterre have also been made level; two separate orchestras play on either side of the stage, accompanying dancers who are performing a minuet.[13] Another pictorial source that is suggestive for the ballroom scene in *Don Giovanni* is the painting by Giuseppe Terreni of a grand gala in the courtyard of the Palazzina (1790) in Florence.[14] Two well-staffed orchestras on risers on either side of the courtyard play for a multitude of dancers (mostly couples performing the minuet) and onlookers.

Closer still to Mozart is the satire on public dance halls in Joseph Richter's *Picture Gallery of Secular Abuses* (1785). Richter, who satirized all aspects of life in Vienna, aided by pictorial vignettes engraved by Mansfeld (Fig. 25), gave this explication of the picture:

> (1) A large ballroom full of chandeliers and mirrors. The room would perhaps accommodate eight or ten couples dancing the minuet, but twice as many are dancing, with the resulting confusion that men and lady dancers no longer know how they originally paired off, consequently many a man who began the dance with a serving wench ends up with his wife, willy-nilly.
> (2) A cobbler, who knows little about bearing, and keeps himself strictly to one, two, three, four, tramples the feet of a cook, who falls powerless in the arms of her butcher.
> (3) Various men in traveling cloaks, who are there merely to obstruct the dancers' space, clap their hands and shout "einen Deutscher, einen Deutscher!" while the minuet lovers demand that the minuet continue. The band of musicians, of which each one has in front of him an emblem of his profession, a large bottle of wine, are divided like the Dutch provinces in their choice, so that half play minuets, the others strike up a Deutscher, when the already reigning confusion among the dancers reaches the highest degree.[15]

Confusion, *Verwirrung* in the original German, is the opposite of *Ordnung* or *ordine*, of which Don Giovanni wanted none in his ballroom entertainment, and for a specific purpose. Richter's troublemakers in traveling cloaks look as if they may be Don Juans too, out to find female prey in the tumult of the dance floor. Such a satire must have drawn its material from what was happening in the real

---

13. Preserved in Schloss Augustusburg, Brühl, West Germany, and reproduced as color plate 24 (catalog item no. 254) in *Kurfürst Clemens August Landesherr und Mäzen des 18. Jahrhunderts* (Brühl, 1961). The makeup of the orchestras is explored and diagramed in Reichart, "The Influence of Eighteenth-Century Social Dance," pp. 81–83.

14. Preserved in the museum Firenze Come Era, Florence, and reproduced in Luigi Squarzina, *Teatri e scenografia* (Milan, 1976), pp. 18–19.

15. Richter, *Bildergalerie weltlicher Misbräuche*, pp. 233–36.

world of Viennese ballrooms, not from fantasies. These instances unite to suggest that Mozart did not invent the idea of contrasting dances both successively and in combination with each other, simultaneously. He had observed such phenomena in the world about him.

FIGURE 25

Mansfeld: A Viennese ballroom
in 1785

11 · GOLDONI, *DON GIOVANNI*, AND THE *DRAMMA GIOCOSO*

It has long been argued whether the appellation *dramma giocoso* applied to *Don Giovanni* by Da Ponte carried any meaning. Was it just a commonplace expression indistinguishable from opera buffa? At least during one phase of operatic history, represented by Goldoni's brilliant series of Venetian librettos from the 1750s, *dramma giocoso* took on a specific complexion that forecast in an almost uncanny way some ingredients that later went into *Don Giovanni*. Even so, there is no denying that poets, including Goldoni himself, often used the term *dramma giocoso* loosely, as the rough equivalent of opera buffa.[1]

Carlo Goldoni had become Italy's leading playwright by the mid-eighteenth century. After he returned to his native Venice in 1748 he began coining a new kind of libretto for comic opera. It was he who, with the help of Venetian musicians like Galuppi, created the buffo finale, that long chain of unbroken action and music to enliven the act ending—an invention of epochal importance for all opera that followed.[2] Earlier Neapolitan comedies showed him the way to a certain extent, particularly with regard to plot and intrigue. But no librettist before him had taken so much interest in character, or in the clash of social classes on the stage. And no one had brought to the lowly task of writing comic librettos so much wit or verve. Goldoni cultivated many types of comedy, for both the spoken and lyric stage. The one that interests us here represents, along with the buffo finale, his greatest contribution to opera.

In several librettos written around 1750, Goldoni combined character types from serious opera (*parti serie*), usually a pair of noble lovers, with the ragtag of servants, peasants, and others (*parti buffi*) who populated his unalloyed comic librettos.

Revised from *Musical Times* 120 (1979).

1. Pointed out by Kunze, *Don Giovanni vor Mozart*, p. 58.
2. See Heartz, "Creation of the Buffo Finale."

Sometimes he also added roles that were halfway between the two in character (*di mezzo carattere*). His name for such an amalgam, applied fairly consistently from 1748 on, was *dramma giocoso*.[3] It summed up the ingredients quite well, inasmuch as *dramma* by itself signified at the time the grander, heroic world of opera seria, while *giocare* means to play or frolic, also to deceive or make a fool of. "A frolic with serious elements" would be one paraphrase of *dramma giocoso*.

Goldoni was quite aware of the novelty and originality of what he had created, and to leave no doubts in the minds of others, he spelled out his paternal claims in the prefaces to some of his librettos. In 1752, prefacing *I portentosi effetti della madre natura*, he wrote: "These *drammi giocosi* of mine are in demand all over Italy and are heard with delight; noble, cultivated people often attend, finding in them, joined to the melody of the singing, the pleasure of honest ridicule, the whole forming a spectacle rather more lively than usual. . . . Although serious operas are imperfect by nature and comic ones even more so, I have striven to make them less unworthy."[4] Two years later he embroidered on these ideas in the preface to *De gustibus non est disputandum*: serious opera has its faults, he says, but so does comic, especially in those authors who pay insufficient attention to plot, intrigue, and character. If the drama is a little on the serious side, it is condemned for want of levity; if it is too ridiculous, it is damned for want of nobility. Wishing to find a way to content everyone, but finding no models anywhere, he was forced to create them himself.[5] The six years from 1749 to 1754 were decisive in his reform of the comic libretto. Within this period he wrote a dozen *drammi giocosi*, of which three are somewhat known even today because Haydn later set them to music: *Il mondo della luna*, *Le pescatrici*, and *Lo speziale*.

The high point of Goldoni's long collaboration with Galuppi came in their *dramma giocoso Il filosofo di campagna* (1754). The comedy has two noble lovers, Eugenia and Rinaldo, listed in the libretto as *parti serie*. They both require high voices, as would be the case in serious opera, and singing techniques beyond the average in comic opera. Rinaldo, like Eugenia, is a soprano. Although he was played by a woman in the original production, it was not uncommon for such parts to be taken by castratos, those cynosures of opera seria; in fact, it was the rule in Rome and the Papal States, where women could not appear on the stage. Neither Rinaldo nor Eugenia participates in the concerted finales at the ends of the first and second acts; these are reserved to the five *parti buffe*. But they are compen-

3. Kunze (*Mozarts Opern*, p. 326) gives an account of Goldoni's mixing of seria with buffa parts beginning with his 1748 adaptation of the Neapolitan comedy *La maestra* by Antonio Palomba.

4. "Questi giocosi Drammi per Musica sono in oggi per tutta l'Italia desiderati, e con piacere intesi, e le persone nobili e colte v'intervengono frequentemente, trovando in essi alla melodia del canto unito il piacere dell'onesto ridicolo, il che forma un divertimento assai più allegro del solito. Spero che anche V. E. vorrà compiacersene, e troverà con che appagare il nobil genio e l'ottimo gusto di cui va adorna; poiché, quantunque i Drammi per Musica, e molto più i Drammi Buffi, opere siano di lor natura imperfette, ingegnato mi sono di render questo meno indegno di essere dalla Nobiltà compatito, e da V. E. principalmente protetto"; Goldoni, *Tutte le opere* 10:1157. The *eccellenza* who received this dedication was Signora Catterina Loredan Mocenigo.

5. The preface is quoted at length and accompanied by the original Italian text in Chapter 5.

sated in the length and earnest tone of the solo music Galuppi gives them, particularly Rinaldo, who sings an aria in act 1 about vengeance that would be quite at home in one of the composer's serious operas. An Allegro in common time, like the vast majority of serious arias, it has the requisite form (five-part da capo structure), technical demands, and orchestral elaboration. Ex. 11.1, from the middle of the piece, will convey the nature of the difficulties encountered. The kind of high, legato singing required here is not made any easier by the diminished-seventh leaps, the syncopations, and the chromatic line. In act 2 Rinaldo sings an equally formidable aria, "Perfida, figlia ingrata," which, being in c minor, sounds a very somber note within the generally comic proceedings. While the *parti buffe* were given simple strophic songs of folklike nature, or at the most short binary airs, Galuppi pulled out all the stops of his heroic style for the *parti serie*, which required great voices like those in opera seria. Goldoni's remark about the importance of singing in the *dramma giocoso* has particular relevance to these roles, for they allowed the humbler audiences and smaller theaters of comic opera to taste some of the vocal delights of the grand manner.

Two years after *Il filosofo di campagna*, Goldoni wrote *La buona figliuola* (Parma, 1756), which was destined to surpass all his other librettos in the influence it wielded. Niccolò Piccinni made the classic musical setting for Rome in 1760. Here the noble lovers (*parti serie*) are Marchesa Lucinda and Cavaliere Armidoro. Lucinda's brother, the Marchese, is in love with a girl beneath his station, Cecchina (a character derived ultimately, by way of several intermediate stages, from Richardson's Pamela)—who turns out in the end, after having gone through the opera as a gardener's assistant, to be nobly born after all. Both these parts are *di mezzo carattere*, and Cecchina's introduces a new strain into comic opera, one that is best called sentimental. The remaining four characters are pure buffo types.

Again, neither of the seria singers appears in the act finales. Their musical style would not be appropriate there in a context of simple, songlike ditties and rapid dialogue exchanges. The Marchese, a baritone, participates in the finales, as does Cecchina. Part of his *mezzo carattere* function is to be at home with both the chattering servants on the one hand and his ostentatiously pretentious sister and her lover on the other—indeed, to function as a bridge between them, as does Cecchina. The Marchese's liaison with the gardener's assistant holds Armidoro back from marrying the beautiful Marchesa; in the first aria he expresses his disdain

EXAMPLE 11.1. Galuppi, *Il filosofo di campagna*, "Taci, amor"

EXAMPLE 11.2. Piccinni, *La buona figliuola*, No. 11

MARCHESA

Fu-rie di don-na i-ra — ta   In mio soc-cor-so in-vo-co

at the thought of possibly being related to a commoner, with emphasis on the insult this would represent to his honor and glory. (Goldoni, a commoner himself, is surely poking fun at social pretension here.)

Piccinni sets the text to an Allegro spiritoso in D major, the heroic key par excellence, and gives Armidoro plenty of scope to display his *virtù* in the traditional way—coloratura runs and arpeggios to convey *gloria* and *onore*. (Hints of "Or sai, chi l'onore" to come, in *Don Giovanni*, abound here.) The aria goes up to high C and includes a substantial middle part in a contrasting tempo and meter before returning to the common time of the first part, da capo. The Marchesa is not to be outdone: she sings a rage aria in which she invokes the Furies to a vigorous motif and energetic rhythm (Ex. 11.2). Mozart's outraged women are hardly more furious than this (compare Electra, Vitellia, the Queen of the Night—and also Anna in "Fuggi, crudele, fuggi!"). Like most seria lovers, these two seem to be playing a game by assuming various traditional poses, in this case the prima donna's typical high dudgeon. They convey not so much their love for each other, which is never fulfilled, as their exalted reactions to the subject of love. The poet most responsible for creating this state of affairs was Metastasio.

With Piccinni's 1760 setting of *La buona figliuola*, most of the musical elements of the *dramma giocoso* in its specific sense were in place. The touchingly sentimental made inroads here that marked the entire next generation. Johann Adam Hiller, writing in his weekly newsletter on music, summed up Piccinni's contribution with considerable insight in 1768 as he described the mixture of seria and buffa parts in Italian comic opera:

> Now Piccinni dominates the comic stage and seems, through the great quantity of his operas, to be nearly exhausting the possibilities of innovation in that department. Not so simple melodically as Pergolesi, less comical than Galuppi and Cocchi, he seems more inclined to the naive and the tender. He has pieces as touching as we might hope to hear in a serious opera, at least in one by an Italian. Lest it should be thought that the serious opera is quite forgotten, the Italians now never fail to introduce in their comic operas a pair of serious characters who would prompt as much yawning as the others do laughter, were it not that their somewhat better style of singing attracts a modicum of attention.[6]

6. *Wöchentliche Nachrichten und Anmerkungen, die Musik betreffend* 3/8 (22 August 1768); translated by Piero Weiss in *Music in the Western World: A History in Documents*, ed. Piero Weiss and Richard Taruskin (New York, 1984), p. 282. A decade after Hiller wrote this, the poet Giovanni Battista Lorenzi claimed that he had invented something new by combining comic and serious elements in *L'infedeltà*

The categorical "never fails" is an exaggeration: many Italian operas remained entirely comic. Nevertheless, it was astute of Hiller to single out the pair of serious characters and the more demanding level of singing associated with them as the outstanding feature of newer Italian comic opera.

Mozart joined the ranks of composers working in Italian opera that same year, 1768, with his setting of the *dramma giocoso La finta semplice*. The libretto was one of Goldoni's last, dating from 1764, after he had left Venice for Paris. Revised slightly for Vienna by Marco Coltellini, it offered sparkling finales but few seria elements. Goldoni's model was Philippe Néricault Destouches's *La fausse Agnès, ou Le poète campagnard* (1734), a comedy that was well known in Italy. The role most susceptible to seria treatment was that of the leading woman, the Hungarian Baroness Rosina, who plays the feigned simpleton of the title. Mozart set her "Senti l'eco" in act 1 (No. 9) to an elaborate two-tempo aria of the *ombra* type, in E-flat with both horns and English horns. He allows her ample coloratura passages as well. In act 2 he gives her a stunningly beautiful aria in E major, "Amoretti" (No. 15)—the ancestor of Mozart's later "gentle breezes" numbers in the same key (e.g., "Zeffiretti lusinghieri" in *Idomeneo* and "Soave sia il vento" in *Così fan tutte*).

In 1774, Mozart was commissioned to set the *dramma giocoso La finta giardiniera* for Munich. In the libretto (an anonymous and clumsy offspring of *La buona figliuola* that has been attributed to Giuseppe Petrosellini), Pamela/Cecchina has become the feigned gardener Sandrina—actually the noble Violante in disguise, estranged from her lover Belfiore, who believes her dead. These are *mezzo carattere* parts. The seria lovers are Arminda and Ramiro, both sopranos, and Ramiro, correspondingly, has the most coloratura singing in the opera. Arminda establishes her credentials as a seria character with a very long rage aria in g minor, Allegro agitato, at the beginning of act 2. Yet they take part in the finales and in this respect and others are less set apart than earlier *parti serie*.

Lest the reader think that these distinctions as to type of dramatic role and vocal character are mere historical musings, it will be well at this point to quote the master himself. In a letter of 7 May 1783, Mozart informed Leopold of his plans for a new opera. *Die Entführung* had been produced the previous year, and he was now burning to show the Viennese what he could do in Italian opera. Leopold was urged to approach the Salzburg poet who had written the libretto for *Idomeneo* about writing a new comedy with seven characters.

> The most necessary thing is that the story, on the whole, be truly *comic*, and, if then it were possible, he ought to introduce *two equally good female roles*; one must be seria, the other *mezzo carattere*, but both roles must be absolutely equal *in quality*.

---

fedele, a "commedia per musica" set by Cimarosa for Naples in 1779. When Haydn set the same libretto as *La fedeltà premiata* a year later, it was styled a "dramma pastorale giocoso." See Andrew Porter, "Haydn and 'La fedeltà premiata,'" *Musical Times* 112 (1971): 331–35.

But the third female character may be entirely buffa, and so may all four male characters, if necessary. If you think that something can be done with Varesco, please discuss it with him soon.[7]

Without so much as a story line to set off his imagination, and no particular singers in mind either, as far as we know, Mozart has begun the act of creation. His first thoughts are of vocal-dramatic types, and specifically of the interaction of three kinds of female role. And where do these thoughts eventually lead? They reached fruition neither in the abortive plans of 1783–84, nor in *Figaro* of 1785–86, which does not have a truly seria part. Rather, this line of thinking is prophetic of *Don Giovanni*. The greatest seria role in all Mozart is surely Donna Anna, who is matched in a *mezzo carattere* role of equal weight and excellence, the sentimental Donna Elvira. The trio is rounded out, the spectrum of womanhood rendered complete, at least in this opera, by the crafty but sympathetic peasant girl, the buffa Zerlina.

Da Ponte stated in his memoirs, some forty years after the fact, that it was he who suggested the Don Juan legend to Mozart. The unlikelihood of this claim should have caused suspicions long ago. Mozart was always searching for a story that would be perfect for the music he wanted to write. He scoured printed librettos from numerous sources to this purpose. In the case of *Don Giovanni*, we now know that the Prague management proposed to him a libretto that had been put on at Venice just a few months earlier. He then got Da Ponte to redo it. Once the work was under way, most of the decisions as to treatment were made by Mozart, not Da Ponte. It is perfectly clear from his letters to Leopold concerning the creation of *Idomeneo* and *Die Entführung* that Mozart made his librettists do his bidding, down to the tiniest details of the prosody required by the music he had in mind.

Don Juan on the stage, spoken or lyric, was the opposite of a novelty. The Spanish playwright Tirso de Molina started the vogue in the early seventeenth century. Molière took up the subject in his *Le festin de pierre* (1665), a prose comedy that introduces the characters of Donna Elvira and a peasant couple as victims of Don Giovanni. Boucher illustrated Molière's play superbly in 1749, showing a cowering servant and defiant Don Juan at the tomb (Fig. 26). Goldoni treated the subject in an early play, *Don Giovanni Tenorio, o sia Il dissoluto* (1736); his legacy is a Donna Anna who is betrothed to Ottavio against her will. Several Italian operas on the subject appeared in the following two decades. The direct model on which

7. "ich möchte gar zu gerne mich auch in einer Welschen opera zeigen. — mithin dächte ich, wenn nicht *Varesco* wegen der Münchener opera noch böse ist — so könnte er mir ein Neues buch auf 7 Personen schreiben. — basta; sie werden am besten wissen ob das zu machen wäre; er könnte unterdessen seine gedanken hinschreiben, und in Salzburg dann wollten wir sie zusammen ausarbeiten. — das nothwendigste dabey aber ist, recht *Comisch* im ganzen. und wenn es dann möglich wäre 2 *gleich güte frauenzimmer Rollen* hinein zu bringen. — die eine müsste Seria, die andere Mezzo Carattere seyn — aber *an güte* — müssten beide Rollen ganz gleich seyn. — das dritte frauenzimmer kan aber ganz Buffa seyn, wie auch alle Männer wenn es nöthig ist. — glauben sie dass mit dem Varesco was zu machen ist, so bitte ich sie bald mit ihm darüber zu sprechen"; 7 May 1783 (Mozart's emphasis).

FIGURE 26

Boucher: Dom Juan and his
servant at the tomb

Mozart and Da Ponte worked was *Don Giovanni, o sia Il convitato di pietra: Dramma giocoso in un atto*, first performed at Carnival season in Venice, February 1787. (Da Ponte scrupulously avoids any mention of this work in his memoirs.) The poet was Giovanni Bertati, much maligned by Da Ponte as we have seen, but one of the most sought after librettists at Venice following Goldoni's departure, and the author of the excellent book to Cimarosa's *Il matrimonio segreto* (1792). Giuseppe Gazzaniga, a prolific and highly esteemed opera composer, wrote the music. It must have reached Vienna at once too, because several signs in Mozart's score indicate that he was aware of it.

Being in a single act, the Venetian opera was only half the length of its famous consequent. Even so, it provided Da Ponte with the situations, and sometimes even the language, for much of his libretto: up to scene 14 in act 1 and from the cemetery scene to the end of act 2. It also dictated the ingredient that makes the work a true *dramma giocoso* in the specific sense: two noble lovers of the seria stripe, Donna Anna and Duca Ottavio (a tenor); and it gave a relatively complete characterization of Donna Elvira. Mozart and Da Ponte improved on the model in several ways. They reduced the ladies from four to three (a Donna Ximena is deleted, or rather her role is conflated with the remaining female parts). Similarly, they reduced the servants who sang solo parts from two to one (Leporello). By cutting down on the number of roles, they eliminated all but one of the doublings in the model (Masetto and the Commendatore). Most important for the continuity and interest of the drama, they enhanced the role of Donna Anna and extended it over the whole opera. Her thirst for revenge now becomes the driving force that unites the work and propels it to the inevitable catastrophe. The original Spanish concept of retribution emerges much more clearly as a result.

It would be a mistake to underrate either Bertati or Gazzaniga just because Mozart so far surpassed them. He profited from both, and from their failings as well as their strengths. It was poor dramaturgy to have Anna disappear from the cast after the first scenes. Very impressive in Gazzaniga's score, in contrast, is the death of the Commendatore, set to expressive harmonies, including the Neapolitan sixth, in the remote key of e-flat minor. Mozart did it differently, but Gazzaniga's expert use of the Neapolitan served as a reminder—if any were needed—of a potent harmonic resource. Following the calamity there comes with lightninglike rapidity the broadest kind of farce. Leporello asks in recitative, "Who is dead, you or the old man?"—a line taken directly from Bertati. In receiving so rude a shock (like a slap in the face, in fact), we are reminded that this is no tragedy, but a comedy with seria parts woven into it. The abrupt turn also presages the levity of the final ensemble, which follows the parallel but far more protracted death of Don Giovanni. This event, a most necessary one for purging society of his seductive and destructive force, has to be celebrated at length. And so it is in both operas. Yet whereas an almost pagan hedonism overcomes the earlier work at this point, its successor remains relatively sober and ends with the moral, sung to a fugato.

In the earlier opera more weight was given to Ottavio. After Giovanni and his servant leave the stage following the death of the Commendatore, Bertati brings on Anna and Ottavio. The corpse is removed, and Ottavio attempts to comfort Anna. She relates the midnight attack to him. Then she puts off Ottavio's marriage proposals on account of her grief and exits, leaving the stage to the tenor. His solo scene concludes with an old-fashioned metaphor aria about the lover's dashed hopes of entering port safely: "Vicin sperai l'istante d'entrar felice in porto." Neither the dubious taste with which Ottavio is made to verbalize his hopes regarding Anna nor the questionable propriety of parodying Metastasio so overtly ("Sperai vicino il lido," sings the hero in *Demofoonte*) gainsays the dramatic effectiveness of the tenor's big scene. Gazzaniga responded with a spacious lyrical aria in two tempos, which was not old-fashioned in the least. Ottavio, because of this music, becomes a force, a personality to be reckoned with in the story. But his exit aria also stops the drama. Mozart and Da Ponte substituted the intensely moving duet in which Anna leads Ottavio into swearing revenge, an act that urges the drama forward. Once the moment for Ottavio's lyric outpouring was postponed, it proved no easy task to find another. The original solution was to defer his aria all the way to act 2, scene 10 ("Il mio tesoro"), but this is too late in the opera to give him much dramatic weight, and in any case, what he says is poorly motivated by the preceding action. For the Viennese revival of 1788, where the tenor was not up to singing "Il mio tesoro," Mozart substituted "Dalla sua pace," placing it in act 1, scene 14, where it is not any better motivated. Modern audiences usually hear both.

Ottavio and his peculiarities represent a legacy of the *dramma giocoso* in its specific sense. A decade earlier he would have been a soprano, not a tenor. By the 1780s tenors gradually began to replace sopranos as noble lovers even in the totally serious operas. In *Idomeneo*, for instance, the young prince Idamante was a castrato in the first production at Munich in 1781; for a performance at Vienna in 1786 Mozart adjusted and rewrote the part for tenor, also adding an elaborate concertante aria to strengthen the role and bring it up to parity with that of the heroine, Ilia, as we saw in Chapter 3. Despite these efforts, something of the recent and castrated past hangs over Idamante as a character type, one whose fate is beyond his control. It hangs as well over Don Ottavio. Not that he is effete; he is merely ineffectual. Having no decisive role in the outcome of the drama, he is made to exist solely at the whim of Anna ("on her peace depends my own"). The seria lover was in fact never much more than a peripheral figure in *dramma giocoso*, ever since Goldoni established the specific kind. He (or she) is there to display a voice type and kind of music associated with serious opera and so enhance the variety of the entertainment. The tenor's lyric aria fills this function admirably in both Gazzaniga and Mozart. Strange as it may seem, Giovanni, as well as Ottavio, was a tenor in Gazzaniga's score; there he sang a mellifluous love song that left its imprint on the terzetto in act 2 of Mozart's opera. By turning Giovanni into a baritone, Mozart was reverting to the traditional choice for a *mezzo carattere* male part, an intermediate vocal type to match his intermediary social role—at home with both low born and high born (albeit a scourge to both in the case of Giovanni).

The preternatural brilliance of what Mozart wrought for Prague in 1787 can be observed nowhere better than in the great sextet of act 2, "Sola, sola in bujo loco." Here it is a matter of throwing comic and serious into relief not in successive numbers, but within the same number. Elvira begins the piece in E-flat, singing rather simply of her hopes and fears, with well-founded misgivings about the man (the disguised Leporello, whom she takes for Giovanni) who has led her to this darkened courtyard. Leporello, on another part of the stage, is seeking the "damned door" through which to escape. The music slips several notches toward buffo style as he lapses into quick-note patter repeating "questa porta sciagurata," at which point the audience usually titters. He finds the door just as the music finds its new destination: B-flat, the dominant. But the cadence is interrupted when an augmented sixth chord moves the tonality suddenly to D, the keynote of the entire opera, and always a matter of highest dramatic significance on its various returns throughout the work. Leporello is cut off from escaping. Trumpets and drums, the instruments of high estate, softly announce the arrival of Anna and Ottavio, who are dressed in mourning. By his music alone Mozart creates in an instant the whole world of these seria lovers. It moves in majestic, long-breathed phrases, over which Ottavio pours out the noblest of love songs, pleading with Anna to relent and give up her grieving. In accompanying him the first violins sound a bar-long rising figure in dotted rhythm against the incessant sixteenth-note motion of the seconds (Ex. 11.3). (Mozart had used a very similar orchestral texture a year earlier when rewriting the love duet in *Idomeneo*, at the point where Idamante enters.)[8]

Anna cuts off Ottavio's beautifully delayed cadence. At the same time, she turns the music from D major to d minor (Ex. 11.4), a gesture that already tells us her answer is another refusal. She begins by singing a motif related to Ottavio's melody, but related more closely still to the distraught line she sang when raging over the circumstances of her father's death: "Fuggi, crudele, fuggi!" (Mozart uses the motif again when the three noble maskers approach the exterior of Giovanni's palace in the finale of act 1.) Her melodic line is no less long-breathed than Ottavio's and is supported by the same continuous orchestral texture. It grows more impassioned as she continues, the ornamental turns and wide leaps at "sola morte" becoming almost unbearably poignant. They are also very difficult to execute, requiring a perfect sostenuto in the high register and control between the registers. (Compare Ex. 11.1 above, where the same qualities of the seria style and even some of the same notes are in evidence.)

In the course of Anna's lament the music moves from d minor down to the even darker realm of c minor. At the first "il mio pianto" Mozart resorts to a half-bar of Neapolitan sixth harmony as Anna works her way up to the melodic peak note, high A-flat. Her descent is partly chromatic, increasing the pathos, which reaches

8. See Ex. 3.7.

EXAMPLE 11.3. *Don Giovanni,* No. 19

EXAMPLE 11.4. *Don Giovanni,* No. 19

its most intense level with the entire bar of Neapolitan harmony before the cadence on "può finir." (To find another example in which d minor is replaced by c minor, we have only to look at the despairing Electra's first aria in *Idomeneo.*)

Both the descending chromatic line and the Neapolitan harmony have wide import in *Don Giovanni.* The first is associated repeatedly with Giovanni and the death that he first inflicts, later suffers. When the orchestra picks up the chromatic descent after Anna's cadence and starts repeating it over and over, like an obsession, poor, deluded Donna Elvira asks, "Where is my husband?" It is as if Don Giovanni were present—which he is in spirit if not in body, as the cause of everyone's woes. Even after he is dispatched to Hell at the end, his ghost still hovers above the chromatic descents in the voices before they drop out on the last pages of the score, leaving one last chromatic descent to be played softly by the orchestra alone (see Ex. 9.3). The powerful progression from Neapolitan sixth to tonic elaborates the tonal climax of the opening duet for Anna and Ottavio, and one is tempted to hear it as the crux of her personal tragedy. From the duet it was taken over as the climax of the slow minor section of the overture. Related to this is the music for the uncanny return of the Commendatore as the Stone Guest. Here, as always, Mozart marshaled his most potent resources, deploying them to the utmost dramatic advantage.

12 · DONNA ELVIRA AND THE GREAT SEXTET

Who was Donna Elvira? How are we to take her meaning? Almost as much has been written about her as about Donna Anna. E.T.A. Hoffmann set the tone for most subsequent criticism with his fantastic tale "Don Juan" of 1813, which he republished in *Phantasiestücke in Callots Manier* (1814). As is well known, he artfully misread Mozart and Da Ponte so as to make Donna Anna the sensuous woman of the opera, secretly aflame with desire for Don Giovanni. The unfortunate corollary of this was that he made Donna Elvira into something of a caricature, not unrelated perhaps to some of the hags who appear in the *commedia dell'arte* drawings of Jacques Callot. He introduces her as the "tall, emaciated Donna Elvira, bearing visible signs of great, but faded beauty" ("die lange, hagere Donna Elvira mit sichtlichen Spuren grosser, aber verblühter Schönheit"). Da Ponte's libretto specifies only that she be young. Hoffmann's view prevailed as far as the Romantics were concerned. Baudelaire refers to "the chaste and thin Elvira" ("la chaste et maigre Elvire"), and even Richard Wagner mistook Hoffmann's fictional Anna for fact.[1] "Chaste" Elvira surely was—with respect to everyone but Don Giovanni, that is. This seems only in keeping with the passionate single-mindedness with which she pursues Giovanni throughout the opera. Dent bridled at Baudelaire's second epithet, which to him seemed "peculiarly inappropriate to anyone who has seen the opera in Germany." Yet the thinness of Elvira—Hoffmann's legacy of making her a less voluptuous specimen of womanhood than Anna—is still very much with us. In Peter Sellars's production of *Don Giovanni* staged in 1987 Elvira is described as "arriving pale and haggard from the bus station."

Revised and expanded from "'Che mi sembra di morir': Donna Elvira and the Sextet," *Musical Times* 122 (1981).

1. *Wagner Writes from Paris . . . Stories, Essays, and Articles by the Young Composer*, ed. and trans. Robert L. Jacobs and Geoffrey Skelton (London, 1973), p. 59.

Hermann Abert sets this matter aright in the long chapter he wrote on the opera in his 1924 revision of Otto Jahn's monumental biography of the composer. He disregards the Romantic tradition and interrogates afresh the words and music in the score concerning Elvira. He concludes:

> She is a passionate woman whose love for Don Giovanni is not merely a passing episode but the decisive experience of her life. She is of all the women in the opera the one who in her whole being is closest to Don Giovanni. His love has kindled in her a spark of the same consuming passion that burns in him. Her aim is therefore not to be revenged but to win back Don Giovanni's love; this is always apparent even in her fiercest outbursts of hatred. And even when she has to recognize the hopelessness of her quest she strives to save her beloved from the fatal consequences of his actions. Therefore she returns at the end neither as the pious "sister" to win his soul for Heaven, nor, like Gretchen, to bring about his "salvation," a thought far from Mozart's mind; she simply wants to save the man she loves from annihilation.[2]

Restoring Donna Elvira to the fullness of her humanity, as Mozart and Da Ponte conceived her, Abert could also reach a clearer vision of Donna Anna by way of comparison: "Donna Anna is the daughter of a distinguished nobleman, an aristocratic character, who, in contrast with Elvira, a woman completely possessed by passion, has all her feelings under control. No wonder this noble lady is deeply shocked by the death of her father, quite apart from filial affection; she feels the wounds as if they were her own."[3] Yet both Alfred Einstein and, more recently, William Mann have rejected Abert's vision of Donna Anna in favor of Hoffmann's, for which they have been soundly and justly rebuked by Julian Rushton.[4]

Donna Elvira was originally introduced onto the stage by a French playwright, the greatest of all those who cultivated the comedy of character: Molière. It will not be amiss, then, to look for further elucidation of her character in a few of the many French critics who have devoted themselves at length to Mozart's operas. Georges de Saint-Foix reaches *Don Giovanni* in the penultimate book of his magnificent five-volume study of the composer's life and works. He writes with particular fervor in defense of Elvira's aria "Ah! fuggi il traditor" (No. 8), denying the frequently heard charges that it sounds archaic and somehow like a parody of Handel:

> This aria, admirable for its passionate fury, strikes a tone markedly in contrast with the atmosphere of the preceding duet, "Là ci darem la mano." The fiery glow of the whole opera illuminates "Ah! fuggi" throughout, even unto its bit of ending coloratura—we can be certain that Mozart wrote it in a burst of enthusiasm, along with the other successful scenes from the beginning of the work. "Flee the traitor,"

2. Hermann Abert, *Mozart's "Don Giovanni,"* trans. Peter Gellhorn (London, 1976), p. 70.
3. Ibid., p. 65.
4. Julian Rushton, *W. A. Mozart: "Don Giovanni,"* Cambridge Opera Handbooks (Cambridge, 1981), p. 144 *n*21.

cries the poor woman who, here, has no accents of pity such as inspire most of her role. She cries out her misfortune as one who knows, probably better than any other—she knows that the looks as well as the lips of Don Giovanni can only deceive. Moreover, this aria prepares for the quartet to follow, a monument of musical poetry and at the same time of Elvira's dramatic psychology in which, despite her troubled being, she is able to alert Anna and Ottavio by her presence to the magisterial treachery of Giovanni. . . . The winds play no role in "Ah! fuggi," but in our opinion strings alone do not argue for a conscious archaism, not when Mozartian ardor inspires them.[5]

This last point could be made as well about Electra's aria "Idol mio," accompanied only by strings, in act 2 of *Idomeneo*. Strings alone bring a special color to a set piece precisely because they are so rarely heard without winds in Mozart's master operas.

Following the paths that Saint-Foix did so much to open, Brigitte and Jean Massin wrote another life and works of enormous scope, in which they explore "le pathétique profond d'Elvire" by imagining what was in store for her after the demise of Giovanni:

> The only person, after all, who is irremediably broken among the survivors is Elvira. Because, in a sense different from Leporello, she is the one who is closest to Don Giovanni, on account of her intransigence with regard to the present. The incoherence which makes her pass from fury to tenderness, from despair to illusion, testifies to the same refusal to construct time as does the nonstop versatility of her seducer. Simply, chased from one instant to the next by the continual pursuit, Don Giovanni denies himself any looks toward the past or the future. But Elvira demands something still more impossible; she demands that eternal stability be conferred on the one privileged instant of her past, the moment when Don Giovanni made her happy. Naturally, she was unlucky in that for her first and only amorous experience she met Don Giovanni; but it suffices to hear her sing to understand that she lacks that voluntary firmness indispensable to constructing a life, a love, a future. Is it a man she loves, or is it only a certain image of her youth that she refuses to abandon? She is still very young, as the libretto specifies, and existence may still instruct her; but in the convent where she goes to be immured, we imagine all too well the sole recourse she will choose: this poor tragic figure, thirsting for tenderness, eternally conscious of having been scoffed at, passing from indignation to powerless emotion, looking for herself in vain in the sterile mirror of memory. Unless one day, worn out, she should go searching for eternity in another moment, a prey designated in advance for new mirages.[6]

Which of the two authors could have written such a passage? Unless we are mistaken, these are the thoughts of a woman. They probe the sad fate of Elvira with utmost empathy and searing intensity.

5. Saint-Foix, *Wolfgang Amédée Mozart* 4 : 287–88.
6. Jean Massin and Brigitte Massin, *Wolfgang Amadeus Mozart* (Paris, 1970), pp. 1064–65.

By the time of the sextet, halfway through the second and last act of *Don Gio-vanni*, the opera's strands of action have been firmly laid out and all the characters have already been painted in fine detail by Mozart's music. Obviously intended to conclude what was once act 3, before four acts were combined into two, the sextet draws together in one potent and concentrated ensemble the opera's main dramatic ideas and, on a local level, concludes the episode of Elvira's deception by Leporello under the cloak of Don Giovanni. It relies for its music on several characteristic turns of phrase or rhythms that Mozart has used earlier in connection with the same personalities. Moreover, it relies heavily on the recurrent use of a single motif, the descending chromatic fourth.

To Mozart's audience the motif meant pain, suffering, and death—it could not be otherwise, since they and their forebears had for several generations heard simi-lar chromatic descents in mass settings to convey the words "Crucifixus, passus et sepultus est," corroborating their experience in the opera house on the demise of heroes and heroines (e.g., Dido). The descending fourth with chromatic steps is present as a bass from the first notes of the Andante of the overture to *Don Giovanni*, which is of course modeled on the music to which Anna's father, the Commendatore—slain by Giovanni at the outset, to the accompaniment of many chromatic "dying falls" in the orchestra—makes his entrance as a statue in the finale of act 2. The balancing of chromatic falls with chromatic rises is employed by Mozart very suggestively in Giovanni's "Finch' han dal vino" (No. 11), as we saw in Chapter 10.

Sudden chromatic surges upward, such as help characterize the hopes and fears of Elvira at the beginning of the sextet, have less clear meaning than chromatic descents, yet Mozart's audience surely understood these too as affective symbols. An example from the year before *Don Giovanni* was written will help place the figure in context.

For the revival of *Idomeneo* at Vienna in March 1786 Mozart rewrote the love duet to take advantage of a tenor Idamante. Near the end of the piece (K. 489), the lovers sing of their union to the words

Non sa che sia diletto	He knows not what delight is
Chi non provò nel petto	Who has not felt in his breast
Sì fortunato amor.	Such fortunate love.

Between these innocent-sounding lines (which may be by Da Ponte), Mozart al-lows his orchestra a sudden chromatic ascent marked crescendo (Ex. 12.1). This makes the surging emotions of the lovers more explicit than do their words or the melodic lines they sing; indeed, if the same degree of passion were to be expressed in words, one suspects they would not pass the imperial censor.

Part of the power of this chromatic surge comes from placing all the violins in unison in their lowest range. Playing on the bottom G string, they produce a gutty sound, all the more penetrating when reinforced by the violas in unison and the cellos and basses at the octaves below. The combination of the timbre, the crescendo, and the upward-striving chromatic surge bespeaks a sensuality that is at home somewhere below the *petto* mentioned in the words. Idamante's new tenor aria to begin act 2 (K. 490) uses the conventional chromatic descent to illustrate the word *pene* (m. 77) and, as if to complement it, a chromatic rise on the word *core* to introduce the return of the rondo theme (mm. 90–91). But the latter amounts to no more than a graceful ornament. Few of Mozart's chromatic rises have the force or intensity of that in K. 489.

EXAMPLE 12.1. *Idomeneo*, No. 20b

Mozart wrote the two substitute pieces for *Idomeneo* while putting the final touches to *Le nozze di Figaro*, and it would be surprising if there were no audible evidences of their proximity. To simulate pain when illustrating how he injured his foot jumping out of the window, Figaro sings a descending chromatic fourth that links two big sections of the second-act finale. At the beginning of act 3, Count Almaviva, infatuated with his wife's maid Susanna, begins wooing her with reproaches for having made him languish so long: "Crudel, perchè finora farmi languir così?" On the long-held *farmi*, an interior part played by the violas intones a rising chromatic line that seems to portray his lust. As the count repeats his last words the second violins, joined by the first flute, turn the chromatic ascent into a descent, leading down to the key of the relative major, C, where Susanna demurely gives her clever and ambiguous answer, "Signor, la donna ognora tempo ha di dir di sì" ("the lady always has time to say yes"). The count is too overheated by his amorous intentions to hear the bass line pick up the chromatic descent as a counterpoint to what Susanna sings, but the audience should not miss the ironic significance of this symbol of grief to comment on the count's absurdly puerile suffering.

Donna Elvira begins the sextet in a way that ingeniously summarizes her entire story. As in her first piece, the key is E-flat, a tonality laden with expressive meaning for Mozart and his contemporaries. Its very choice conveys that Elvira, the escaped nun who was seduced in a convent by Giovanni, takes herself very seriously—and we should too, even if other aspects of her music give us pause. In her opening aria, "Ah! chi mi dice mai" (No. 3), she sings a melodic line that moves by fits and starts, mainly in dotted rhythm, accompanied by unexpected orchestral fortes in the "wrong" places and skittish quick-note outbursts in the violins. Her phrases are short-breathed, totally lacking the broad cantilena to be expected of a noble lady, a quality that does sound forth from Anna. Mozart reinforces the verbal extravagance of the text—Elvira will tear out Giovanni's heart, unless he returns to her—by improbable melodic leaps and rhythmic-dynamic accents. As a result, Elvira emerges as slightly mad in Mozart's very first portrait of her, and she does nothing to alter this impression with her "Ah! fuggi il traditor!" (No. 8), sung to Zerlina, or by her role in the quartet that follows and the terzetto early in act 2. Both these ensembles, like the sextet, are begun by Elvira, and both have musical features in common with the sextet. The skittish quick-note outbursts in the violins that marked her first entrance on the stage recur in the terzetto, "Ah, taci ingiusto core" (No. 15), and do service once again in the sextet.

The motto of the quartet, "Te vuol tradir ancor," repeated over and over by the the orchestra in the notes with which Elvira sang these words, D–E♭–A–B♭, is present once again in the last words of recitative by which Elvira leads in the sextet, words sung to the man she thinks is Giovanni: "Ah non lasciarmi!" (Ex. 12.2). The winds and strings transpose her tritone down to another, forming a bridge of two bars before she comes in singing "Sola, sola in bujo loco." Her second *sola* corresponds with a strong downbeat, the arrival of the tonic in the third measure. But

EXAMPLE 12.2. *Don Giovanni*, No. 19

the following bar contradicts our expectations of a strong-weak succession by its forte dynamic accent (once again in the "wrong" place) and underscores one of Elvira's favored leaps, the descending seventh. She sings her second line, "palpitar il cor io sento," to the same dotted rhythms as before, but now with rests between the longer and shorter notes, as if gasping for breath, while the orchestra portrays her heartbeat with regular pulses, as it did in "Ah, taci ingiusto core." The third line, "E m'assale un tal spavento," is interrupted in the middle by the quick-note shudder of the violins, descending quickly from high B-flat to low D (the extremities of Elvira's vocal range, which are exploited as such beginning with her initial piece). For the fourth line, "che mi sembra di morir," Mozart has invented yet another kind of accompaniment for the violins, related to the ones in bars three and five but more urgent in its syncopations:[7] the line ends with an interrupted cadence on VI, as sung the first time, allowing Mozart to repeat these words and give a more pungent turn to the kind of "death" that is on Elvira's mind.

Singing "che mi sembra di morir" the second time, Elvira begins with the same descending passage in quick notes as before on *palpitar*, the urgency greatly enhanced by the sustained chord marked *mfp*—the highly charged third inversion of the dominant seventh, which places greatest weight on the dissonant seventh degree, A-flat, in the bass. To reinforce this note, Mozart takes the violins down from their normal range to join the lower strings. The resolution comes softly to low G, so that Elvira's sustained high E-flat will ring out over the orchestra, but the charge released is no less electric for being piano. From this low G (the violins' bottom string, which must be played open, and hence with rather gutty results even when soft), all the strings rise chromatically through a tritone and make a crescendo to forte, quite similar to the chromatic surge in K. 489 (Ex. 12.1). They revert to piano as Elvira descends from her perch to make the cadence.

Abert described the unison chromatic rise as *unheimlich* (uncanny).[8] But surely it is meant to be heard as an intensification of the rather pleasant chromatic rises in thirds, with crescendo, in "Ah, taci ingiusto core," where Elvira is just beginning to give in to her sensual nature. Here she is quite overcome by "all those shameful transports of an earthy and common love" that Molière described when first creating her character.[9] Knowing what we know about the use of chromatic surges and their significance in erotic situations, we hear (providing the conductor pays sufficient attention to Mozart's crescendo to forte) Elvira's inner thoughts, as re-

7. One of the best early critics of *Don Giovanni*, Bernhard Weber, wrote of a performance at Berlin in 1791: "Never can one find in his works an idea that one has heard before; even Mozart's accompaniments are always new" (Deutsch, *Dokumente*, p. 360).

8. Hermann Abert, *W. A. Mozart*, 7th ed. (Leipzig, 1956), 2:436. Abert fails to observe that in Ottavio's "Dalla sua pace," written a year later for the Viennese production, there is an echo of the sextet's chromatic rise with crescendo in the orchestra at mm. 14–15, and once again in response to the idea of death (*morte*), but here in the context of an otherwise pleasant erotic outpouring. Mozart insists on the figure by repeating it twice in the reprise.

9. *Dom Juan, ou Le festin de pierre*, act 4, scene 6: "Le Ciel a banni de mon âme toutes ces indignes ardeurs que je sentais pour vous, tous ces transports tumultueux d'un attachement criminel, tous ces honteux emportements d'un amour terrestre et grossier."

vealed by the orchestra: they are on a certain kind of death—the kind that poets since time immemorial have used as a metaphor for the sexual act. The perceptive listeners among Mozart's audience must have relished this point.

Mozart was not the only composer of the time to indulge in such titillation of his audience. In the finale to act 1 of Haydn's *La fedeltà premiata* (1780), Nerina, a young lady described in the libretto as "volubile in amore," calls for help, saying she is being pursued by satyrs. To depict the satyrs Haydn places a chromatic rise, forte, in his orchestra (Ex. 12.3). The orchestra's leering commentary leaves no doubt about the satyrs' intentions. Unlike Mozart, Haydn repeats the chromatic rise, and not once but twice, so that by the third statement we have lost interest.

Elvira assumes some dignity in the sextet by being contrasted with the buffoonery of Leporello, who sings next, after being introduced by his orchestral calling card, a quick exchange between winds and strings that comes from the end of his opening song, "Notte e giorno faticar." She takes on still more precise coloration by contrast with what the serious figures, Anna and Ottavio, sing following Leporello, which amounts to the most profound and moving music in the whole opera. Only after it has sounded do we fully perceive the distance between Anna and Elvira, who personifies the *mezzo carattere*, standing halfway as she does between buffa (Zerlina) and seria (Anna). In fact, she defines what the concept meant to Mozart to a higher degree than any of his other characters. Who but Mozart could have achieved so many dramatic shades, ranging from low comedy to high tragedy—and to have done so, moreover, within the same ensemble?

EXAMPLE 12.3. Haydn, *La fedeltà premiata*, No. 24

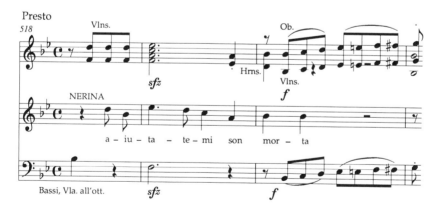

13 · THREE SCHOOLS FOR LOVERS, OR "COSÌ FAN TUTTE LE BELLE"

The success of *Figaro* in Prague led to the commissioning of *Don Giovanni*. Likewise, it was *Figaro*, on its successful revival in Vienna during the summer of 1789, that opened the way for Mozart and Da Ponte to begin their third and last collaboration. The result reached the stage of the Burgtheater in early 1790 as *Così fan tutte, o sia La scuola degli amanti*.

Da Ponte refers to *Così fan tutte* in his memoirs by its second title only—"The School for Lovers." The main title was in fact a late afterthought of Mozart's. Da Ponte says that he wrote the libretto especially for Adriana Gabrieli del Bene, called La Ferrarese, the great soprano who was engaged in Vienna since 1788 and for whom the role of Fiordiligi was created. She sang Susanna in the 1789 revival of *Figaro*, on which occasion Mozart enlarged the part considerably, writing the substitute aria "Al desio, di chi t'adora," an elaborate concertante rondo that is already a study preparatory to creating the role of Fiordiligi. Da Ponte says further that La Ferrarese had a heavenly voice, wonderful eyes, and a lovely mouth, that she greatly pleased the Viennese public, and that he himself was greatly smitten by her lovely charms (to his later regret, when her diatribes succeeded in getting them both dismissed from imperial service). Beyond this he says nothing that would throw light on the genesis of the work, except to call it the third sister of his collaboration with Mozart, thus emphasizing the family ties with the first two. We propose a different filiation: *Così fan tutte* is the daughter of *Le nozze di Figaro* in certain musical and dramatic aspects; but so is *Don Giovanni*, from a different lineage.

Figaro deserves to be called a "School for Lovers" no less than does *Così fan tutte*. It explores a wide gamut of amatory feelings, ranging over the field of what Andrew Porter describes as "love and the effects of love in all their variety—idyllic

Reprinted from "Three Schools for Lovers: The Mozart–Da Ponte Trilogy," *About the House* 6, no. 2 (1981).

tenderness, steady devotion, deceit, infatuation, lust, frivolity, jealousy, obsession." *La folle journée* is Beaumarchais's masterpiece, and it capped a long tradition in French comic theater. Its ancestry can be traced back to Molière, to be sure, his greatness being difficult for subsequent dramatists to escape. But even more important was Marivaux, who embodied a newer and specifically eighteenth-century vein of feeling, one best summed up in the term *galant*.

Most of the thirty-odd comedies by Marivaux concentrated on erotic entanglements between two or more couples, handled deftly and with a lighthearted touch that could be compared with the brush of Watteau, the master of *fêtes galantes*. The bark adorned with flowers, being boarded by pairs of lovers in Watteau's delightful painting *Pèlerinage à l'isle de Cythère* (1717), became a frequent stage property in *galant* comedies and is still found in *Così fan tutte*. One of Marivaux's recurrent themes is the coming to awareness of the state of being in love, particularly in young ladies, found not only in his comedies but also in his influential novel *La vie de Marianne* (1731–41). Sometimes the process of falling in love is rigged and observed with a kind of clinical detachment by an older and "philosophical" type, as in *Les fausses confidences*, a play that was especially popular in Vienna, where it was performed at the Burgtheater in 1776, 1785, and 1790[1]—the very year of *Così fan tutte*, for which it served as one point of departure.

Marivaux was rather hard on the foibles of men, especially their silly pride and vainglory, but he excused women their few frailties (and in this respect he anticipated the culminating speech of Don Alfonso, before he pronounces the motto "Così fan tutte": "Everyone blames women and I excuse them, were they to change their affects a thousand times a day; some call it a vice, others a habit, but to me it appears a necessity of the heart"). Indeed, few looked into the female heart with such sympathy as did Marivaux. For his delicate and original psychological penetration into the nuances of emotion he was compared in his own day to one of his greatest contemporaries, the painter Chardin.[2] Pierre Rosenberg has written of Chardin's 1735 painting, *Une dame qui prend du thé*: "a feeling of gentleness and tenderness emerges that in his century only Chardin knew how to capture on canvas."[3] We might add that only Mozart captured the same so superbly in music.

In both *Figaro* and *Così fan tutte*, the male lovers emerge more or less chastened from the schooling in the emotions that they have undergone. The lesser characters hardly change at all, though buffeted by the abrupt twists and turns of the action to no less a degree. The page Cherubino, for all we know at the end of the drama,

1. Hadamowsky, *Die Wiener Hoftheater*, No. 366.
2. Thomas L'Affichard, *Caprices romanesques* (Amsterdam, 1745), p. 63: "His [Marivaux's] comedies are no comedies; they are novels which now cause laughter, now tears. His style is unique, or rather, his style is not a style; to write as he does, he has to be utterly himself. He writes as *Chardin* paints; it's a special genre, much admired, but beyond anyone else's reach: imitators can only produce monstrosities"; cited after *Chardin, 1699–1779: A Special Exhibition Organized by the Réunion des Musées Nationaux, Paris, the Cleveland Museum of Art, and Museum of Fine Arts, Boston* (Boston, 1979), p. 81.
3. *Chardin, 1699–1779*, p. 218.

is quite likely to grow up and become a real Don Juan, following up on his adolescent successes. Basilio, the sardonic, scandal-mongering priest and music teacher of the former Rosina, now Countess Almaviva, remains an unregenerate scoundrel to the end. Yet it is his music, and his viewpoint, that provide a link between the first and third Mozart–Da Ponte operas.

When Cherubino is discovered hiding in a chair by the count in the first act of *Figaro*, Basilio cackles with delight, while the count blusters his annoyance, believing that Susanna has tricked him, and Susanna makes what excuses she can. In this terzetto Basilio keeps repeating the phrase "Così fan tutte le belle, non c'è alcun novità" ("Thus do all women, there's nothing new about it"), sung to the chattering motif of a written-out trill, followed by a melodic descent to the same rapid notes (Ex. 13.1). Basilio's music will return to end the main theme of the Presto in the overture to *Così fan tutte*, leaving no doubt about the verbal-musical link between the two operas. But that is not the only use Mozart found for Basilio's absurd trilling motif.

In the second act of *Figaro*, two schemes are set in motion to teach the count a lesson. Figaro writes an anonymous letter casting aspersions on the fidelity of the countess and sends it by way of none other than Basilio. Strong medicine perhaps, but it is not unmotivated, coming after the despairing words of the countess about her husband: "systematically unfaithful, generically capricious, and jealous as a matter of pride." Figaro's intention is to throw the count off the track in his attempts to deflower Susanna before her marriage to Figaro. The other part of his plot is to have Susanna give the count an assignation in the garden that very evening, to be kept by Cherubino dressed as a woman. As the ladies are trying out some feminine finery on the page, the count arrives. Cherubino hides in the dressing closet, which the countess refuses to open despite her husband's mounting fury. They depart together at his insistence to fetch another key. Susanna, having overheard the quarrel, takes the place of Cherubino in the closet, and he jumps out the window.

The finale begins at this point, with the return of the count and countess. She admits the truth and pleads for mercy on behalf of Cherubino. The count refuses, then out of the closet steps Susanna, to a graceful little minuet in B-flat, molto andante. The Allegro that follows this section, also in B-flat, is one in which the countess, first breathless and confused, gradually becomes more irate with her boorish consort. "To play such a trick is cruel," says the count to the falling con-

EXAMPLE 13.1. *Figaro*, No. 7

junct thirds in sequence that recall the terzetto in act 1. The recall does not stop with this. When the count asks Susanna to help calm his wife's ire, Susanna begins intoning Basilio's written-out trills to the words "Così si condanna chi può sospet-tar" ("Thus are condemned those who are suspicious"—the very word *così* may have prompted this recall; Ex. 13.2).

In this version, the trill has become a three-part chordal trill. Susanna subse-quently uses the same two tones, B-flat and C, as she implores her mistress, "Si-gnora!" The count servilely follows suit an octave lower singing "Rosina!"—provoking an outburst from his wife: "I am no longer she, but the miserable object of your abandonment." Can it be coincidence that Don Giovanni addresses a lady he has deserted, Donna Elvira, in precisely the same way (Ex. 13.3)?

Mozart was by no means through exploiting Basilio's trill. When the count asks about the anonymous letter, both *belle* confess: "Figaro wrote it, the deliverer was Basilio." At the mention of Basilio's name the whole orchestra sounds the harmo-nized trill, forte, drowning out the count's "Ah! perfidi" (Ex. 13.4). After further imploring on the part of the count, the countess relents and forgives him, but she directs her words toward Susanna: "How soft-hearted I am! Who will ever again believe in a woman's fury?" Susanna responds, "With men, my lady, one must twist and turn, and even so be prepared to fall flat on one's face." She illustrates this shaky condition (recall that the old word for trill was "shake") by singing the three-part trill again, this time taking the lowest part of the harmony, giving it a new color, more somber than before. Women only do what they have to do in order to survive, seems to be her message.

EXAMPLE 13.2. *Figaro*, No. 15

EXAMPLE 13.3A–B.

A: *Figaro*, No. 15   B: *Don Giovanni*, No. 3

By the time "la folle journée" has reached nightfall in act 4, Figaro has become caught up in his own machinations and deludes himself into believing that Susanna welcomes the count's advances. He too must learn the lesson due those who are too readily suspicious. Susanna leads him on in the garden aria (replaced by the formidable rondo for La Ferrarese in 1789), then punishes him in the finale as he is wooing her in the guise of the countess. His newly found mother, Marcellina, had warned Figaro in no uncertain terms about distrusting Susanna, but this scene with its aria is almost always cut owing to the excessive length of the last act. Marcellina's views on women have a curiously contemporary ring: "Every woman must come to the defense of her poor sex, so wrongfully oppressed by ungrateful men." For Marcellina's aria, "Il capro e la capretta," Da Ponte found inspiration in Ariosto's *Orlando furioso*. "Even wild beasts treat the female of the species well," sings Mar-

EXAMPLE 13.4. *Figaro*, No. 15

cellina; "only we poor women, who love men so much, are treated by them as perfidious, and always with cruelty."

One "folle journée" deserved another. Viewed as a battle between the sexes, *Figaro* could be said to end in a draw, for we are by no means sure that the lessons administered have cured the men of their vain follies. The subject was so rich and sprawling that it could be contained in one opera only with difficulty, no matter how tight a rein was kept on the material by the composer and the librettist. *Così fan tutte* provided them an opportunity to take up some of the same issues again, but under more controlled circumstances and with a smaller cast.

Romantic critics dismissed *Così fan tutte* as an amoral clinical experiment, rigged by the heartless scientist Don Alfonso aided by his venal laboratory assistant, Despina. This view is wrong on several counts. The legacy of Marivaux that we have discussed is present, but it is neither cynical nor immoral; rather, it is blithely spiritual. Don Alfonso is an "old philosopher," not a scientist, and one need only put oneself into the frame of the Josephinian Enlightenment to realize that he was a force working for good and truth—like Sarastro, who also used rather harsh teaching devices.

Ferrando and Guglielmo at the beginning of the opera are two young coxcombs who need to be cured of their ridiculous notions about love and honor quite as much as their shallow and stagestruck sweethearts, Fiordiligi and Dorabella. Alfonso's "School for Lovers" is thus compulsory for both sexes, and this is a major difference with *Figaro*, where only the men need to be taught a lesson, the women having come to self-awareness by the time we first meet them. Mozart not only pokes fun at Dorabella's credulity and Fiordiligi's highstrung theatrics, but he makes musical jokes at the expense of their lovers too, and from the beginning. In the three terzettos inaugurating the first act, he has them sing most of the time so as to be indistinguishable the one from the other, which has a very comical effect.

When Don Alfonso, provoked by their bravado, begins the second terzetto by saying, "The faith of lovers is like the Arabian phoenix: it exists, says everyone, but where?—no one knows," the orchestra answers his question "Dove sia?" ("But where?") with a few falling thirds, anticipating the motto "Così fan tutte." And it is to these same unforgettable intervals that the lovers later intone the names of Fiordiligi and Dorabella. Mozart is having his fun at the young men's expense.

The third terzetto, begun by the young men, is bellicose and heroic in vein, up to a point. When the three men raise their glasses in a toast to love, and Mozart takes the voices up to a sustained high chord, the orchestra emits an absurd three-part trill, like a horselaugh, then repeats it, forte. (This is the same device by which Susanna and the countess twit the count about the phony letter brought by Basilio.) The absurd trill later serves hilariously in helping to characterize the phony guises of Despina.

The two sisters from Ferrara begin by being nearly as identical as their male counterparts. Mozart introduces them singing an exquisitely beautiful "falling in love with love" duet in a garden by the Bay of Naples. The piece is in the dulcet key of A (with clarinets), like many Neapolitan love duets, a convention that Mozart is happy to follow in his operas, and which is appropriate, by extension, for attempted seductions (Susanna by the count, Zerlina by Don Giovanni, and Fiordiligi by Ferrando). Note that the keys of Nos. 1–5 are related by falling thirds. When the sisters later sing individually, each reacts in an exaggerated opera seria manner to her imagined distress, giving Mozart delightful opportunities to parody the serious style, and especially his own *Idomeneo*. Yet we are to take neither woman seriously for a moment: it is all an act, a demonstration of how the heroines of the operatic stage behave when abandoned or betrayed. Both young ladies, indeed, seem to have learned more from libretti than from real life. Recall in this connection what Leporello says on first encountering Donna Elvira: "She talks like a printed book." Just as Elvira deepens and changes into a real person in the course of her sufferings, so do the two sisters (and particularly Fiordiligi) come to grips with deep emotions as the opera progresses, probably for the first time in their lives.

That the two women should be described as coming from Ferrara was almost mandatory, since not only La Ferrarese/Fiordiligi but also Louise de Villeneuve (possibly her real sister), the first Dorabella, hailed from that sleepy little northern Italian town, a kind of pun that the Viennese audience would enjoy. Da Ponte originally laid the scene of the opera in Trieste, the Habsburg Empire's commercial "window" on the Adriatic. Mozart must have insisted on the more evocative setting of a grander port of call: Naples. Trieste was hardly a glamorous sojourn for two young ladies from Ferrara. Naples, in contrast, was a great royal capital and the largest city in Europe, the center of the Italian Enlightenment (making it only natural that the philosophical Don Alfonso would dwell there) and the seat of the foremost Italian lyric stage, the Teatro San Carlo. Naples combined all the aspects needed to give the opera a sharp focus: it epitomized the struggle of the senses with the intellect.

The sensual South seduces the prim North—a myth for sure, but like many others an apt idea for the stage. It matters that Donna Elvira comes from Burgos, making her the equivalent in Spanish terms of "a young lady from Boston." She was inevitably doomed by the myth to succumb to the charms of the lustful Don from Seville. The switch on the myth in *Così fan tutte* is this: Ferrando and Guglielmo are no Don Juans—they too only played at being in love before undergoing Alfonso's schooling. What really seduces the women is the irresistible suavity and power of Mozart's music, which is responsible for conjuring up the Bay of Naples, with its gentle breezes, lapping waves, and warm evenings for serenading. The terzettino "Soave sia il vento" is Mozart's transcendental tribute to a long series of "Zeffiro" pieces in Neapolitan opera, and not by chance is its key the rarefied sphere of E major. While the stage painter would have furthered the illusion of this magical garden setting, nothing survives to give an idea of the original

FIGURE 27

Zuliani: Garden scene from
Goldoni's *Arcadia in Brenta*

or early stage designs of *Così fan tutte*. Nevertheless, a suggestive illustration from the Venetian edition of Goldoni's works (1788–95) captures the fashions in formal gardens, hats, and apparel reigning in Italy around 1790, and it also shows the turf seats (*sedili erbosi*) required by the stage directions (Fig. 27). The scene could almost be of Don Alfonso sardonically commenting on the lovers' farewell in act 1.

Perhaps the most haunting visual evocations of southern Italian climes from this time were done by Fragonard, who worked in both Rome and Naples and who was a child of the perfumed south of his own country, having been born at Grasse in Provence. His famous drawings of the Villa d'Este gardens at Tivoli from his first Italian trip (1756–61) evoke the verdant graceful avenues (*viali leggiadri*) through which Ferrando led Fiordiligi, and much else that is in tune with Mozart's remembered experience of southern delights (Fig. 28). Mozart and Fragonard had much in common (besides genius). Each was rooted in the *galant* mainstream of the eighteenth century, yet each went beyond the *galant* to become absolutely original. Each found the decisive artistic wellspring for his creative life south of the Alps. Fragonard sought to renew his sources of inspiration by a second trip to Italy

FIGURE 28

Fragonard: Italian garden

in 1773–74. Even during later years in Paris he could conjure afresh from his memory the radiant effects of the sun on a southern Italian garden.[4] Mozart's last trip to Naples, a voyage of the intellect as well as the senses, is represented by *Così fan tutte*, which becomes a kind of spiritual going-home.

Don Giovanni has fascinated every generation since its creation. In 1787 the Prague theater thought it was going to get another *Figaro*, which in a sense it did, at least as to voice types and casting. More important still, Mozart profited in *Don Giovanni* from the enormous compositional strides he made when working on his first opera with Da Ponte. Unlike *Figaro* and *Così fan tutte, Don Giovanni* is not a

4. As in the drawing signed and dated "frago 1786" in the E. B. Crocker Gallery, Sacramento, California, reproduced in Williams, *Drawings by Fragonard*, No. 52.

"well-made play." It flouts the *bienséances* of the French tradition, offering instead the unruly caprice of a Spanish morality play. This different lineage does not stop the opera from being a "School for Lovers," albeit of a strange sort. Zerlina and Masetto, as well as Ottavio and Anna, emerge knowing more about themselves for having had their little worlds perturbed by the demonic Don. Leporello learns little or nothing. Elvira and Giovanni give us much to ponder.

The original idea of the Spanish play was to teach us a lesson by exposing evil in the person of Giovanni and his unbridled carnal lust. Molière in his version added the character Elvira, who also was a hostage to her carnal desires. Both could be considered as anti-lovers, or an example of how lovers should not behave. A man like Don Giovanni, who runs riot over every moral precept in attempting to satisfy the flesh, is no lover at all; he embodies a negative precept. In going to his eventual doom, he provides sufficient titillation even for enlightened eighteenth-century audiences, which had but the slightest interest in doom and damnation. The moral issue of crime and punishment is not what interested Mozart or his audience most: political overtones related to those in *Figaro* loomed at least as large.

The playwright who more than any other made Don Juan into a political statement was Molière, in his *Dom Juan, ou Le festin de pierre* (1665). In the first scene of the play, Sganarelle/Leporello (played by Molière himself) pronounces what could be the work's motto: "Un grand seigneur méchant homme est une terrible chose" ("A great lord who is a wicked man is a terrible thing"). Besides being a murderer, adulterer, and atheist, Don Juan wishes his father dead, and the latter upbraids his son in no uncertain terms: "Et qu'avez-vous fait dans le monde pour être gentilhomme? Croyez-vous qu'il suffise d'en porter le nom et les armes, et que ce nous soit une gloire d'être sorti d'un sang noble, lorsque nous vivons en infâmes? Non, non, la naissance n'est rien où la vertu n'est pas."[5] The initial question reminds inevitably of one that Beaumarchais puts into the mouth of Figaro, concerning the count: "Noblesse, fortune, un rang, des places: tout cela rend si fier! Qu'avez-vous fait pour tant de biens? Vous vous êtes donné la peine de naître, et rien de plus; du reste, homme assez ordinaire!"[6]

Such sentiments were too strong for opera of course, and had to be deleted. But the point is that, just as everyone knew the play by Beaumarchais, which was translated immediately into several languages and rushed through several editions, everyone seems to have known Molière as well. Beaumarchais and Da Ponte certainly did, as did Mozart, who was able to put back into his music much of the ironic audacity with which both French playwrights passionately condemned misuse of the noble condition. Molière's Elvira suffers such torments of the flesh as no person

---

5. "And what have you done in the world to become a gentleman? Do you believe it suffices to bear the name and the arms, and that it is a glory for us to issue from a noble blood, when we live in infamy? No, no, birth is nothing where there is no virtue"; act 4, scene 5.

6. "Nobility, fortune, a rank, positions; all this makes for so much pride! What have you done for so many benefits? You gave yourself the trouble of being born, and nothing more; beyond that, a rather ordinary man!"; act 5, scene 3.

would have been allowed to enunciate on the imperial stages of Prague and Vienna. Yet Mozart, speaking the universal language, could and did recapture them in his immensely moving portrait of Donna Elvira, the fallen woman. There is no clearer case of his going beyond Da Ponte to achieve a freedom and vision that belongs only to the very greatest creative spirits, allowing them to communicate over vast distances of time and space.

14 · CITATION, REFERENCE, AND RECALL IN *COSÌ FAN TUTTE*

Mozart accustomed his audiences to large-scale musical recall with the sounding again of the Andante from the overture to *Don Giovanni* for the return of the Commendatore. In *Così fan tutte* it is the march with chorus for the feigned embarkation of the two soldier-lovers, "Bella vita militar" (No. 8), that is sounded twice in act 1, then repeated near the end of act 2 to signal the soldiers' return. There are many other musical recalls in the opera, some overt and clearly intended to be recognized as such, others so subtle or modest as to be almost private—like the joking nod to "Così fan tutte le belle" from *Figaro* at the end of the Presto main theme of the overture. Here the textual link leaves no doubt that Mozart was conscious of the reference (as this is best called), though probably few others noticed it.

Da Ponte showed the way by the unusual number of citations in his text. They mainly concern Don Alfonso, whose age and sagacity make it only natural that he should cite proverbs and other sayings, witty or wise. When the two young men think they have already won the wager because of their girlfriends' extravagant behavior in the quintet (No. 6), he chides them with a remark in Latin: "Finem lauda" ("Save your praises for the end"). When Guglielmo thinks that all is over after Dorabella has fallen, but Fiordiligi, with difficulty, has remained steadfast, Alfonso remonstrates: "Folle è quel cervello, che sulla frasca ancor vende l'uccello" ("Mad is the brain that sells the bird while it is still in the bush"). As early as No. 2, in dispute with the young men, Alfonso cites nearly verbatim an entire quatrain from Metastasio's *Demetrio* (1731).

Da Ponte was not the first comic librettist to cite this particular verse. Goldoni used it in *La scuola moderna* (1748), and in a manner that made clear it was a borrowing:

LEONORA: E la fede? . . .	And the faith? . . .
DRUSILLA: Che fede? Io vi rispondo	What faith? I tell you
La mia Leonoretta,	My little Leonora, that,
Come dice il poeta in un arietta:	As the poet says in an aria:
E la fede degli amanti	The faith of lovers
Come l'araba fenice;	Is like the Arabian phoenix;
Che vi sia, ciascun lo dice	That it exists, everyone says
Dove sia, nessun lo sa.	But where, no one knows.

(Act 1, Scene 8)

The more Goldoni and Da Ponte are compared, the more apparent it becomes that Da Ponte learned much from his older countryman. We shall begin, accordingly, by proposing a libretto by Goldoni that should be added to the long list of possible sources for the plot of *Così fan tutte*.[1]

Goldoni's *Le pescatrici* (1752) is a "dramma giocoso per musica" set on the shores of the Gulf of Taranto in the Kingdom of the Two Sicilies. Toward the end it deploys a double-disguise subplot. The seria roles are Lindoro, Prince of Sorrento, and the noblewoman Eurilda, who swear eternal fidelity to each other. Mastriccio, a wise old fisherman, presides over a tableau in the penultimate scene of act 3, an embarkation accompanied by chorus. Setting forth on a voyage of love is one of those *galant* themes that ties the entire century together and of course inspired some of its greatest paintings, from Watteau's nostalgic masterpiece of 1717 to Fragonard's late and troubling *L'isle d'amour*.[2] Goldoni acquits himself simply and beautifully in limning the atmospherics of the scene:

CHORUS: Soave zeffiri	Gentle zephyrs
Al mar c'invitano,	Invite us to the sea,
Son l'onde placide,	The waves are placid,
Non v'è timor.	And there is no fear.
Procelle torbide	Dark clouds
Dal mar spariscono	Disappear from the sea
Quando si naviga	When you are navigating
Col dio d'Amor.	With the God of Love.
LINDORO: Andiam, sposa diletta.	Come, beloved spouse.
EURILDA: Io seguo i passi vostri.	I follow your steps.
MASTRIC.: Oh come i voti nostri	Oh, how everything
Tutto, tutto seconda:	Seconds our desires:
Ciel sereno, aure liete	Serene sky, happy breezes,
e placid'onda.	and calm waves.

1. See Andrew Steptoe, "The Sources of 'Così fan tutte': A Reappraisal," *Music and Letters* 62 (1981): 281–94.

2. Its traditional title, *La fête à Rambouillet*, can be traced back only to the nineteenth century, whereas *L'isle d'amour* was used in the eighteenth century, as shown by Rosenberg in *Fragonard*, pp. 355–57.

Kinship with the terzettino (No. 10) in *Così fan tutte* is evident even in the choice of vocabulary:

Soave sia il vento,	May the wind be gentle,
Tranquillo sia l'onda,	The waves be calm,
Ed ogni elemento	And may every element
Benigno risponda	Respond kindly
Ai nostri desir.	To our desire.

Certain musical conventions went along with poetic ones in numbers of this kind, above all the key of E major. Mozart made this choice for zephyr pieces twice in *Idomeneo* and observed the convention even in his earliest operas. It is instructive to observe what Haydn did when he came to "Soave zeffiri" in his setting of *Le pescatrici* (1770). Instinctively, it would seem, he chose E major, his instincts perhaps helped along by his wide knowledge of Neapolitan composers, whose operas he performed in line with his duties as Esterházy Capellmeister. Yet how different is Haydn's E-major zephyr music from that of Mozart! For lacking from the older master's chorus is any hint of the sensuous charm that Mozart poured into such numbers. It cannot be coincidental that, whereas Haydn had never experienced Naples itself, nor any part of Italy (nor even the sea until late in his life), Mozart had an uncanny affinity for the sights, sounds, and perfumes of southern climes.

In the last scene of *Le pescatrici*, Goldoni brings to an abrupt end the masquerade that the two young fishermen, Burlotto and Frisellino, had been playing, disguised as noblemen in order to test their girlfriends, Nerina and Lesbina (all *parti buffe*). After the disguises come off—to the surprise and anger of the young ladies— Mastriccio scolds the men firmly for even thinking of testing their girlfriends' fidelity. Like Da Ponte's Alfonso, he finds that the fault lies with the men. His remedy for the damage they caused is the same as well: marriage. "Sposarle," replies Alfonso, as Guglielmo rages at the fall of Fiordiligi and asks what the men can do to exact punishment. Mastriccio can be equally pithy, and Goldoni makes a habit of putting in his mouth what sound like folk proverbs:

MASTRIC.: E chi, pazzi, v'insegna	And who taught you, madmen,
Le femmine tentare? In caso tale	To tempt women? In such a case
Che avreste fatto voi,	What would you have done,
Sciocchi che siete?	fools that you are?
Se bene a lor volete	If you wish them well
Sposatele, tacete, e non parlate:	Marry them, be silent, and speak not:
Si strapperà, se troppo la tirate.	What is drawn too tight will break.
BURLOTO: Amico, il giuramento.	Friend, the oath.
FRISEL.: Sì, sì, me lo rammento.	Yes, yes, I remember it.
E voi?	And you?
BURLOTO: Ed io pentito	And I am repentant
Son della trista prova.	About the shabby testing.
MASTRIC.: Chi va il mal cercando,	Who goes looking for trouble
il mal ritrova.	will find it.

Mastriccio unites the original couples by placing hand in hand. The final ensemble, "Discendi, Amore, pietoso," is sung by the reunited couples plus Mastriccio on the shore, and by the noble couple from the bark. "Forgive and forget" in a spirit of generosity is the lesson Goldoni instills by way of his wise old fisherman, who seems to be a country cousin to Don Alfonso. "Chi va il mal cercando, il mal ritrova" is very close to what Alfonso says in warning the arrogantly overconfident lovers in the very first number of *Così fan tutte*:

O pazzo desire	Oh what a mad whim it is
Cercar di scoprire	To go looking for
Quel mal che trovato	Trouble which, when found,
Meschini ci fa.	Will make us miserable.

Goldoni and Da Ponte share a remarkably similar viewpoint as to the moral question at issue here. Even more a child of the Enlightenment than Goldoni, Da Ponte took care to have Don Alfonso explain at the end how his masquerade was staged in a spirit of beneficence:

Ingannai, ma fu l'inganno	I deceived you in order
Disinganno ai vostri amanti,	To undeceive your lovers,
Che più saggi omai saranno	who will henceforth be more wise
Che faran quel ch'io vorrò.	For doing what I asked.
Quà le destre: siete sposi:	Give me your right hands: you are wed;
Abbracciatevi, e tacete.	Embrace each other and be silent.
Tutti quattro ora ridete,	All four now laugh about what
Ch'io già risi e riderò.	I have already laughed and shall again.

Instead of remaining silent, the women accept their original lovers back with renewed protestations of fidelity, sung to sweet chains of thirds, delicate hesitations, and chromatic waverings so characteristic of these affected young ladies. Have they learned nothing from the schooling of Don Alfonso? Maybe they are beyond schooling, but the men are not. They respond to the women's vows of fidelity by saying that they believed them but did not wish to put them to the test ("ma la prova io far non vò"). Similarly, Goldoni's Burlotto expressed his regret for having perpetrated "la trista prova."

Don Alfonso is a philosopher in the modern sense of the French *philosophe*, an enlightened thinker and doer of good. He is a virtuoso with words, dropping little pearls of wisdom here and there. He cleverly adapts the first line of Metastasio's quatrain to his own purposes, misquoting it as "E la fede delle femmine." His borrowed parable brings an outburst first from Ferrando, the more cultivated of the two young gentlemen—"Scioccherie di poeti!" ("Stupidities of poets!")—which serves to acknowledge that he too recognizes it as a quotation. In another passage, Da Ponte actually uses quotation marks in the libretto to single out one of Alfonso's aphorisms. It comes directly after the heavenly terzettino (No. 10), which Alfonso seems to belittle by beginning his monologue with the words "I'm not a bad actor!" ("Non son cattivo comico!"). He speaks of going to meet the two champions of Venus and Mars, then comments on the women's behavior:

. . . quante smorfie,	. . . what grimaces
Quante buffonerie! . . .	What buffooneries! . . .
Tanto meglio per me . . .	So much the better for me . . .
Cadran più facilmente:	They will fall more easily:
Questa razza di gente è la più presta	This kind of person is the fastest
A cangiarsi d'umore: oh poverini!	To change moods: ah, poor men!
Per femina giocar cento zecchini?	Wager a hundred sequins for women?
"Nel mare solca, e nell'arena semina	"He plows the sea and sows in sand
E il vago vento spera in rete accogliere	And hopes to catch the wind in a net
Chi fonda sue speranze in cor di femina."	Who places his hopes in a woman's heart."

Alfonso proves to be right about Dorabella. She will fall, and soon; accordingly, she must be seen to outdo her sister in the grimacing department throughout the farewells, just as she is the first to burst out in an aria about her situation. Fiordiligi is made of sterner stuff. Both poet and composer take pains to make fine distinctions between the women from their first appearance.

Alfonso's concluding citation, "Nel mare solca . . . ," challenges us to identify it—once again Da Ponte is playing literary games.[3] In the case of this Catullus-like dictum on feminine inconstancy, he has resorted to Sannazaro's *Arcadia*.[4] The learned Alfonso and the librettist become as one here, obviously intent on impressing us with both their knowledge and wisdom. Alfonso's *Vernunft* does combat with the lovers' *Empfindsamkeit* and *Schwärmerei*. One reading of the opera has effectively argued this as its main idea.[5] Such an interpretation fits well with Da Ponte's title for the work, *La scuola degli amanti*: he never used any other. Mozart is responsible for the motto title, and he hit on it late in the process of composition.[6] The poster for the premiere gives top billing and a bigger typeface to Mozart's choice (Fig. 29). If Da Ponte can be seen peppering his libretto with literary allusions, Mozart does no less by making his music a commentary on what had been achieved in opera up to 1790, and most especially in his own operas.

3. Kurt Kramer ("Da Ponte's 'Così fan tutte,'" *Nachrichten der Akademie der Wissenschaften in Göttingen*, Philologisch-historische Klasse, 1 [1973]: 1), traces many of Da Ponte's locutions to their Latin, French, and Italian sources, but not this citation.

4. Wolfgang Osthoff, "Gli endecasillabi Villotistici in *Don Giovanni* e *Nozze di Figaro*," in *Venezia e il melodramma nel settecento*, ed. Maria Teresa Muraro (Florence, 1981), 2:293–94; and Daniela Goldin, *La vera fenice: Librettisti e libretti tra sette e ottocento* (Turin, 1985), p. 147n9.

5. Cornelia Kritsche and Herbert Zeman, "Das Rätsel eines genialen Opernentwurfs—Da Pontes Libretto 'Così fan tutte' und das literarische Umfeld des 18. Jahrhunderts," in *Die österreichische Literatur: Ihr Profil an der Wende vom 18. zum 19. Jahrhundert (1750–1830)*, ed. Herbert Zeman (Graz, 1979), pp. 355–77.

6. Alan Tyson, "Notes on the Composition of Mozart's *Così fan tutte*," *Journal of the American Musicological Society* 37 (1984): 356–401 (on the motto, see pp. 371 and 377); reprinted in Tyson, *Mozart: Studies of the Autograph Scores*, where the relevant passages are on pp. 190 and 197.

FIGURE 29

Poster for the premiere of *Così fan tutte*

Mozart began using motivic recalls on a large scale in *Idomeneo*. In *Die Entführung*, the recurrence of Turkish musical elements works to give the opera an overall unity. In *Figaro*, the title role is endowed with a kind of musical calling card, and there are allusions to Paisiello's *Barbiere* and Gluck's *Don Juan*. *Don Giovanni* goes much further (consider the role of chromatic descent from the opening of the overture to the last bars of the opera). The three citations in the banquet scene of *Don Giovanni*, culminating with "Non più andrai" from *Figaro*, predict the three recalls from previous masquerade scenes in the second finale of *Così fan tutte*. As in *Don Giovanni*, citations, allusions, and recalls proliferate in *Così fan tutte* so as to become an entire network from the beginning to the end of the opera.

References to *Figaro* in the overture to *Così fan tutte* do not stop with installing Basilio's silly little trill and descending figure ("Così fan tutte le belle") as the conclusion to the main theme of the Presto. In m. 59 Mozart starts using a stealthy rhythmic figure in conjunction with the minor mode, beginning

EXAMPLE 14.1A–B.

A: Monsigny, *On ne s'avise jamais de tout*, Vaudeville

B: *Così fan tutte*, No. 30

The reference is of course to the beginning of the *Figaro* overture. The forte block (mm. 25–28) of fanfares wavering between the harmonies of I and IV$^6_4$ also has its parallels in the *Figaro* overture, and also introduces a progression that will be crucial throughout the opera. Mozart seems to be telling us from the outset that this third and last collaboration with Da Ponte is going to be an opera about opera. Emperor Joseph's days were numbered when it was being written, and perhaps Mozart foretold that Da Ponte's dalliance with Fiordiligi/La Ferrarese would soon bring their downfall. Stefan Kunze goes so far as to suggest that the aura of nostalgic recollections and farewell hanging over *Così fan tutte* points to Mozart's thoughts being already on his early death;[7] in support of such a view, he cites the despairing letters Mozart wrote to Michael Puchberg from the same time. But surely the web of musical allusions that Mozart spins can be explained as merely an intensification of what he had been doing all along.

There were recent precedents for singing an opera's title as its motto at or near the end. In Paisiello's *Il barbiere di Siviglia, ovvero Le precauzioni inutili* (1782), the characters, after bandying about "the useless precaution" in dialogue, finally come out with it in part-song as a kind of motto summing up the work at the very end. More directly related to what Mozart does in *Così fan tutte* is the concluding motto-title sung in one of the most influential Parisian opéras-comiques, *On ne s'avise jamais de tout* (1759) by Michel Jean Sedaine and Pierre Alexandre Monsigny (Ex. 14.1A–B). Like Monsigny, Mozart constructs his motto as a double statement, ending the first half with a deceptive cadence to the sixth degree, which leads to a repetition with tonic cadence. This same formula can be found in countless instrumental works by Mozart and many other composers. Typically, it is a closing gesture in a fast movement: its very banality renders it particularly incisive and effective as a motto-title bearer.

7. Kunze, *Mozarts Opern*, p. 495.

If the two sisters visiting Naples from Ferrara had been a little more discerning about the world around them, they would have had reason to be suspicious about their lovers' being called to the field of battle by royal command ("Al martial campo ordin reggio li chiama"), as Alfonso tells them. What battle? The Kingdom of the Two Sicilies under Ferdinand I and his Habsburg queen, Maria Carolina, had the good fortune to be free of wars from the 1750s until the late 1790s, when all of Italy became engulfed in the struggles between postrevolutionary France and the Habsburg Empire.

The sisters' gullibility in this little matter helps Da Ponte create the greater gullibility by which they do not recognize their lovers in disguise. Since even the shrewd Despina does not penetrate these disguises, they must be unusually elaborate (and it is very important that Ferrando be fair and blond, Guglielmo swarthy and brunet). The women's failure to see through the disguises could also be taken to mean that they had never really looked all that closely at the men in the first place (only their portraits, perhaps?).

The women are pretty shallow creatures, as Da Ponte portrays them. When Alfonso asks the men after the second number why they are so sure of their fiancées' fidelity, they blurt out, turn by turn, a string of platitudes that include "noble education," "sublime thoughts," "similarity of temperament," "unselfishness," and "immutability of character." How Da Ponte delights in giving the lie to each of these traits! The sisters' education is such that they cannot comprehend the few words of Latin with which Despina as Doctor greets them in the first finale.[8] As for "sublime thoughts" and "unselfishness," their first recitative dialogue shows that their thoughts, like those of most ordinary girls, revolve around getting married as soon as possible. This objective matters more to them than does the specific partner—a premise on which the whole adventure is built. Guglielmo believes he is similar in temperament to Fiordiligi, but events will show that he is not— another central theme of the work. "*Mutability* of character" could, in fact, be the title of the opera.

Much has been written about the differences in character between Fiordiligi and Dorabella, less about those between Ferrando and Guglielmo. Yet both poet and composer were careful to differentiate the men as early as the third number. Ferrando begins by saying he will use his money won in the wager to offer a beautiful serenade to his goddess. Guglielmo counters on a more physical than spiritual level, saying he wants to give a banquet in honor of his Venus. Mozart intensifies the distinction by giving the tenor a noble-sounding cantilena, replete with *galant* melodic turns and spun out in sustained notes over a rustling accompaniment of eighth and sixteenth notes in the strings. (A year and a half later he will give the same opening to Sesto in *La clemenza di Tito*, No. 26; Ex. 14.2A–B.)

---

8. In the libretto, Da Ponte has Despina greet the girls with "Salvete amabiles Bonae puellae," to which they respond, "Parla un linguaggio / Che non sappiamo." In the interest of realism, Mozart changed this correct Latin to "Salvete amabiles bones puelles": clever as Despina is, she is still a chambermaid.

Ferrando has all the earmarks of a seria lover here. He ranks in a class with Sesto, Idamante, Belmonte, and Ottavio. His soaring precadential triad up to G, touching high A before stepwise descent to the tonic, will provide the oboe theme at the beginning of the overture. Ferrando's solo is of great structural importance because Mozart is going to bring it back in a varied reprise at a late, climactic moment in the opera: the love duet with Fiordiligi (No. 29), just before she yields to Ferrando (Ex. 14.2C). Curiously, it is Fiordiligi who starts singing his music, with the melodic turn over the harmonies I$_4^6$–I. The ardent rise in quarter notes of the original (m. 7) now generates two rises (twice as ardent!), and the precadential area is expanded too, but the essentials remain the same. Are we meant to hear the whole passage from the duet as a recall? Certainly, and to take delight in the irony whereby Ferrando's ardor for Dorabella has been redirected, even intensified, while he has been wooing Fiordiligi.

The melodic turn with descent over I$_4^6$–I also occurs in the quintet (No. 6), sung by both women in thirds, and indeed could be said to be the climax of this ensemble (Ex. 14.2D).[9] It comes after a long dominant pedal, the young ladies expressing their increasing desperation at the thought of their lovers' departure. Dorabella will sooner tear her heart out than see her lover go (cf. Elvira's resolve to tear Giovanni's heart out if he refuses to return). Fiordiligi is only slightly more restrained when she follows suit (also melodically) by saying that she wishes to die at her lover's feet. This leads them to the outrageously pompous line "Il destin così defrauda le speranze mortali" ("Thus does fate defraud human hopes"). With its lambent sixteenth-note string accompaniment supporting the long-held and ever-so-sweet parallel thirds of the two sisters, the moment sounds like anything but the tread of destiny. It sounds like the *bella serenata* promised when Ferrando first intoned this music (Ex. 14.2B).

Guglielmo/Benucci gets surprisingly short shrift in the terzetto (No. 3) compared with Ferrando/Calvesi, lacking the quality of breadth and the elegant melodic turns that make Ferrando sound so noble. His melodic line is instead more disjunct, and Mozart accompanies it with a more active bass line, plus a skittering sixteenth-note figure in the first violins that would sound perfectly at home in the Turkish music of *Die Entführung* (Ex. 14.3A–B). Guglielmo comes close to the opera's motto when he repeats "in onor di Citera . . . ," but Mozart probably had not arrived at the motto when he wrote this, and so it only demonstrates anew what a cliché of buffo style this cadential approach and the motto both represent. The unisons are also pure buffo, as are the sudden dynamic contrasts. It may be that Mozart cannot quite forget Benucci's superb comic servant roles (Figaro and Leporello). In any case, Benucci remains a typical primo buffo, singing mostly the bass lines, even when he plays a Neapolitan officer/Albanian nobleman.

---

9. Frits R. Noske ("Musical Quotation as a Dramatic Device: The Fourth Act of 'Le Nozze di Figaro,'" *Musical Quarterly* 54 [1968]: 185–98; reprinted in *The Signifier and the Signified*, pp. 3–17) has an apt explanation for this kind of recurrence: "Actually the characters do not quote each other; it is Mozart, who winks at his audience" (p. 9).

EXAMPLE 14.2A–D.

A: *Clemenza di Tito*, No. 26

B: *Così fan tutte*, No. 3

C: *Così fan tutte*, No. 29

D: *Così fan tutte*, No. 6

A

B

C

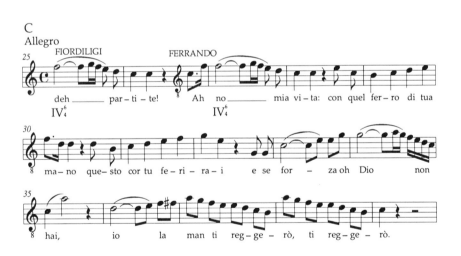

D

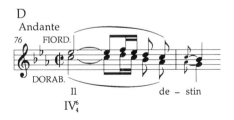

EXAMPLE 14.3A–B.

A: *Entführung*, No. 5b

B: *Così fan tutte*, No. 3

The little touch of Turkish music in the flurry of sixteenth notes could be interpreted as a hint of the disguises to come. Despina takes the men in their outlandish getups for "Turchi" or "Vallachi" (Wallachia was the part of Romania around Bucharest). She guessed well. At the time, Albania, like Romania, had been under Turkish rule for centuries.[10]

Having so early in the opera established Ferrando as an idealizing Romantic compared with the more down-to-earth Guglielmo, poet and composer could pur-

10. It is calculated that over half the Albanian people had abandoned Christianity by the eighteenth century. Da Ponte gives his Albanians non-Christian names, Tizio and Sempronio; when they wake up in the act 1 finale, their first question is whether they are standing before the throne of Jove. Mozart elaborated on the running sixteenth notes of his Turkish music in connection with Guglielmo in Benucci's big act 1 aria (No. 15a), and then, when that was scrapped for No. 15b, several of its features, including trumpets and drums and the running sixteenths, were incorporated into his act 2 aria, No. 26.

sue the distinction and refine it throughout the work. The character of Ferrando comes into sharpest focus in his sublimely beautiful *aria d'affetto* in A major, "Un' aura amorosa" (No. 17), set up so cleverly by Da Ponte. Guglielmo's mind is on food. "Ed oggi non si mangia?" ("Aren't we going to eat today?"), he asks Alfonso. Ferrando steps in with the answer. After they have won the wager, dinner will be all the more savory. This leads into Ferrando's aria, which is about spiritual food:

Un' aura amorosa	An amorous breath
Del nostro tesoro	From our treasure
Un dolce ristoro	Will offer sweet
Al cor porgerà.	Balm to the heart.
Al cor che nudrito	To the heart, which, nourished
Da speme, da Amore	With hope, with Love,
Di un'esca migliore	Has no need of
Bisogna non ha.	Greater allurement.

Metastasio himself would have been proud of this; it has his mellifluous touch and his concision, even his little trick of linking the end of the first stanza with the beginning of the second by verbal repetition.

Mozart responds with an aria that would grace any opera seria. Like most seria arias, it stands outside the action, as do Ottavio's two meditations on his love for Anna, "Dalla sua pace" and "Il mio tesoro." Although Dent pronounced it "quite superfluous," he would not have done so had he considered its musical function in the opera as a whole. It is the median link between three pieces in A major, uniting the "falling in love with love" duet of the ladies (No. 4) and the love duet proper (No. 29). Morever, the three pieces have specific musical features in common besides key. Ferrando's aria, like No. 4, benefits from clarinets in A, and the two pieces share the same opening progression: $I–ii_2^6–vii/I$ or $V^7/I–I$. The ardent rise up to the fourth degree that Ferrando makes in No. 29 (Ex. 14.2C, mm. 29–30) is prefigured in his aria, mm. 34–35, where it is one of the high points of the piece. Another is when Ferrando soars up to high A over a $IV–I_4^6$ progression in approaching the final cadence: this echoes the ending of Belmonte's aria in A (No. 4), which is also about a heart overflowing with love (Ex. 14.4A–B).

What follows the fermata in Ferrando's aria is an extraordinary prolongation of IV for three bars, the voice being accompanied by winds alone, then yielding again to I_4^6 and resolution—a vast plagal cadence. Full orchestra comes in, forte, after Ferrando's final cadence, initiating a postlude that is one of the longest and most meaningful in the entire opera. The melody, climbing high in the first violins, is punctuated by chords in dotted rhythms from the rest of the orchestra, further enhancing Ferrando's noble qualities and somehow endorsing his lofty sentiments. Of course, it is also exit music for Ferrando and Guglielmo (who has been listening to the whole outpouring while thinking about how hungry he is)—but it is so much more than mere exit music.

EXAMPLE 14.4A–C.

A: *Entführung*, No. 4

B: *Così fan tutte*, No. 17

C: *Così fan tutte*, No. 29

A

Andante

B

Andante cantabile

C

Larghetto

Mozart drops the winds back to piano in m. 76 as they sustain a diminished chord against which the violins, imitating Ferrando, softly climb by step up to the tonic, A. To this same diminished chord in No. 29 Fiordiligi is going to yield to Ferrando ("hai vinto . . .") as a solo oboe winds its way up to the high tonic accompanying Ferrando (Ex. 14.4C). The oboe begins by imitating Ferrando's chromatic rise, E–E#–F#, sung to "idol mio" (mm. 88–89); approaching the cadence, it sounds the melodic turn around the fifth degree with descent to the tonic (m. 100), familiar from Ferrando's solo in No. 3 (Ex. 14.3B) and given by Mozart more importance throughout the opera than the motto itself. Fiordiligi had already flirted with this figure in her act 1 aria (No. 14, mm. 19–22), and in her rondo in act 2 she sings it again, at first somewhat unobtrusively (No. 25, mm. 10–11), and then in a very prominent spot: the cadence linking the slow and fast sections (mm. 34–35).

What Fiordiligi's gradual melodic symbiosis with Ferrando tells us is that they were destined to become lovers from the beginning. No wonder Mozart chose this very same melodic figure for the oboe solo at the beginning of the overture: it was his way of saying that romantic, idealistic love figures in the opera just as importantly as the schooling of lovers, no matter what Da Ponte wanted.

Only once does Ferrando seem to fall from the lofty pedestal of idealistic love erected by his sentiments and his music. His cavatina "Schernito, tradito" (No. 27), sung after he learns of Guglielmo's success with Dorabella, begins in c minor, the opening words about his being scorned and betrayed rendered explosively to short, disjunct musical utterances. But this opening is quickly contrasted with the soaring and smoothly conjunct lines in the major mode, expressive of hope and very much in the vein of a seria lover. Belmonte's opening song in *Die Entführung* is closely akin—it too comes as a statement of hope in major, after being adumbrated, but in minor, in the middle of the overture. The tessitura of both numbers is nearly identical (cf. the pedal high G in the voice which moves up to A for the climax of both pieces).

A more problematic piece is Ferrando's aria "Ah lo veggio" (No. 24). It began life as the projected rondo finale of the Clarinet Quintet, K. 581, dated 29 September 1789. As an aria it has several features of the two-tempo rondo that the primo uomo was expected to sing in serious operas, gavotte rhythm being one of them, concertante wind writing another. The main melody betrays its instrumental conception all too clearly: it requires tremendous agility, taking the tenor up to high B-flat both by step and by skip. Mozart allows the opening Allegretto in cut time to meander on for nearly a hundred bars before he reaches the Allegro and the final section of the text. Here the rondo theme goes into the orchestra, and Ferrando sings, "Ah cessate," dropping a sixth from F to A and then resolving up to B-flat (mm. 100–101). (This is a literal echo of Belmonte's "Ach Constanze" [mm. 19–20] in No. 15 of *Die Entführung*, which is also in B-flat and a two-tempo rondo. Obviously Mozart was thinking back to Belmonte when shaping the ardent and earnest Ferrando.) From the vocal writing in "Ah lo veggio" it appears that Calvesi outdid even Adamberger in fluid technical control over the entire range of his voice. Mozart put a note in his autograph sanctioning the cutting of this tour de force for tenor; if he was finally willing to sacrifice all the work that went into Ferrando's rondo, it may have been not only because the opera was becoming overlong, but also because it anticipated too many features of the next piece, Fiordiligi's great rondo "Per pietà, ben mio" (No. 25).

Guglielmo's part gave Mozart and Da Ponte more trouble than any other. Benucci, as the veteran primo buffo of the troupe and its mainstay, clearly deserved every possible consideration. Indeed, they may have been overeager to please him and to use his great acting abilities; it is otherwise difficult to explain how Mozart's shrewd discernment about texts failed him when he permitted Da Ponte to let stand such a motley collection of oddities as the original Guglielmo aria (No. 15a),[11] in which Da Ponte careens wildly from myth, to history, to geography, to Boiardo's *Orlando innamorato*, throwing in references to bird song and a contemporary dancer for good measure. Mozart composed it from beginning to end and fully orchestrated it before he brought himself to admit how wrong it was where it stood. The piece is in D major, with trumpets and drums—features of the impending first finale. Yet Mozart had always reserved trumpets and drums as well as the key of the finale by not using them in the immediately preceding numbers.

From the music itself it is pretty clear that Mozart was bent on creating another triumph for Benucci along the lines of "Non più andrai" in *Figaro*. There is even a hint of Figaro's rousing aria in the way Mozart begins the vocal line here with accents on the first beats (both arias are Allegro in common time) and then, as Guglielmo turns to Dorabella in m. 22, switches to gavotte rhythm (just as in m. 15 of the earlier aria). To get through so much text he has to forsake any musical reprises and compose the lines straight through, like a narrative. By the time he gets to the punchline—"E qualche altro capitale / Abbiam poi che alcun non sa" ("And we have some other assets that no one knows about")—he has traversed several keys and well over a hundred measures in attempting to do justice to this catalog of absurdities. Da Ponte's ending is clever, because it allowed Benucci, by the hint of a gesture, or perhaps only a leer, to suggest where the unknown assets might be located. The strategy is not unlike the ending of Figaro's last aria ("Il resto nol dico, / Già ognuno lo sa").

Precisely because Benucci was known for not overacting could he be trusted with such a piece, or so Mozart must have thought. Benucci preserved his vocal and acting perfection into the 1790s, as a Berlin review of 1793 indicates: "He [Benucci] combines with his unforced, excellent acting an extremely round, beautiful, and full bass voice. He is as much a complete singer as he is a choice actor. He has the rare and very commendable custom of never exaggerating."[12] Benucci's deserved fame and high standing with both the emperor and the Viennese public were essential to the success of the new opera. Mozart knew this full well and acted accordingly. Only in this light is it possible to understand so great a miscalculation as "Rivolgete a lui lo sguardo." Perhaps the aria would have had the desired success

---

11. For the text of No. 15a and its replacement, No. 15b, see the Appendix to this chapter.

12. "Er vereinigt mit seinem ungezwungenen vortrefflichen Spiel eine äusserst runde, schöne, volle Bassstimme. Er ist ein ebenso vollkommener Sänger, wie er ein trefflicher Schauspieler ist. Er hat die seltene, sehr löbliche Gewohnheit, dass er nichts übertreibt"; *Berliner musikalische Zeitung*, 1793, p. 138; cited in Bitter, *Wandlungen in den Inszenierungsformen des "Don Giovanni,"* p. 54.

with the public, but only to the detriment of the opera as a whole. A piece taking six minutes or more was out of place here, in what had already become a very long first act. Out it went, and one senses the chagrin with which Mozart entered separately in his work catalog, under December [1789]: "Eine arie welche in die oper Così fan tutte bestimmt war. für Benucci. . . ."

Poet and composer went to work again, producing the short but very effective substitute aria "Non siate ritrosi" (No. 15b). It is an Andantino in 2/4 time and in the key of G major, allowing it to connect directly, without need of transition, to the little laughing trio in the same key (No. 16). Economy was served, but there remained seventeen numbers before the first finale, whereas in *Figaro* there were fourteen, in *Don Giovanni* twelve.

Mozart allowed himself to dwell at length on the farewells and parting of the lovers in the first half of act 1, which created problems for the rest of the act. Arriving at the short but perfect aria for Benucci, a process that was undoubtedly painful for all involved, was not the only crisis. More cutting had to be undertaken. A drastic cut removed the music in d minor that Ferrando quotes in the second finale, by means of which he had introduced himself to Fiordiligi as an Albanian nobleman (Ex. 14.5A). Alan Tyson suggests that Ferrando lost an aria just before or after Fiordiligi's "Come scoglio" (No. 14),[13] but this makes little sense because it would have been too close to his crucial aria in A (No. 17). Others have suggested that there was originally a duet number for the Albanians.[14]

We suggest that the missing model for Ferrando's recall was in a section cut from the sextet (No. 13). As it stands, the sextet is very long, and is so much like a finale in construction, with contrasting meters and keys, that it threatens to steal some of the thunder of the finale proper. From the dramatic point of view, it is odd that there should be no answer somewhere in the sextet to the question Despina raises as to whether the strange men are Turks or Wallachians. We must wait until the marriage contract is made at the end of the opera to find out that they are merely posing as Albanians (i.e., quasi-Turks). Also odd is the way Despina simply steps aside at the beginning of the second section, as the music moves from C to F and into an Allegro in 3/4, allowing the men to be discovered by Fiordiligi and Dorabella, without benefit of introduction.

Here would seem to be the place for Ferrando to present himself as an Albanian nobleman to Fiordiligi, bowing elaborately as he does so, followed by Guglielmo

13. Tyson, "Notes on the Composition of Mozart's *Così fan tutte*," p. 376 of original article; p. 196 in *Mozart*.

14. William Mann, *The Operas of Mozart* (New York, 1977), pp. 540–41. The proposal is described as "a piece of joint detective work by Stanley Sadie, R. B. Moberly," and the author. Stefan Kunze, who devoted nearly a hundred pages to the work in *Mozarts Opern*, on p. 487 dismisses the issue as if he were unaware of the problem: "Mit weiteren Zitaten, die den Mädchen einige Episoden aus der Maskerade in Erinnerung rufen, wird die Demaskierung vollendet" ("With further citations, which recall for the young ladies several episodes from the masquerade, the unmasking is complete"). In the other two recalls, Guglielmo sings the beginning of his duet with Dorabella, "Il core vi dono" (No. 23), and both men sing the Despina-as-Doctor music with the absurd trill from the first finale.

EXAMPLE 14.5A–B.

A: *Così fan tutte*, No. 31

B: *Così fan tutte*, No. 13

presenting himself to Dorabella. The minor mode is an appropriate choice and figures as an important element in Mozart's Turkish arsenal (cf. the "alla Turca" finale of the Sonata in A, K. 331, or the theme from *Le gelosie del seraglio* ballet, K. 135a, in the finale of the Violin Concerto in A, K. 219). Combined with the stiff and pompous dotted rhythms in which he declaims, not to mention the affectedly courtly language, such as addressing Fiordiligi as "bella damina," Ferrando's d minor sounds exotic and calculated to enhance the men's bizarre visual appearance. But with the cut, the women react on visual appearance alone, which is not enough to explain or provoke their outbreak of cackling indignation. Having the men properly introduce themselves here would also haved helped to prepare their next approach, as they try getting down on their knees along with Despina, begging forgiveness in a little trio in a minor.

The music of Ferrando's recall alone contains a few hints that it belongs in the sextet and not elsewhere. Dotted rhythms and explosive accents in the middle of the bar characterize the sextet from the very beginning, Alfonso setting the tone as he presents his exotic friends to Despina ("Alla bella Despinetta"). An unexpected dynamic accent also occurs mid-measure in Ferrando's short solo (m. 498). More striking still is the correspondence between this solo and the final section of the sextet, Molto allegro in cut time (Ex. 14.5B). The unison D in the strings sounded forte in Ferrando's passage corresponds to the accented unison C that starts off the Molto allegro, where accents on the downbeat also do battle with accents on the upbeat (i.e., with the second half of the measure in cut time). The sudden, forceful downbeat appears several times in the opera, most notably in the women's duet of choosing, "Prenderò quel brunettino" (No. 20, m. 54), where it conveys a decision that has been taken, and in the Allegro molto of the second finale (No. 31, m. 592), by which time all is decided. In the latter case, the first heavy downbeat is on V, and so it is too at the beginning of No. 3, after the wager has been decided upon.

For the scenes in which the two young ladies from Ferrara take themselves most seriously and act like tragic heroines, Mozart turned to his beloved *Idomeneo*. Despite his many efforts to bring *Idomeneo* to the stage in Vienna, he succeeded in gaining only a semiprivate performance of it in the palace theater of Prince Auersperg during Lent 1786; thus it would not have been as well known to the Viennese public as *Die Entführung, Figaro*, and *Don Giovanni*. At the heart of the tragic conflict in *Idomeneo* is the sacrifice a father must make of his son. It is a memorable moment when King Idomeneo recognizes his son on the shore (act 1, scene 8): the violins in unison rocket up to high D at Idamante's words "E il padre mio!" then they do the same over the fourth degree (see Ex. 3.11). These are gestures so central to the opera that Mozart puts them in the overture (mm. 23–26). In act 1, scene 8, the loud outbursts give way to a softening both in dynamics and in harmonic direction, as the music veers far toward the flat side, hinting at tears of pity that come welling up after the heroic moment of tragic awareness. The lead into Idamante's grand rondo of 1786, "Non temer, amato bene," goes through the very same motions to recall the tragic conflict (see Ex. 3.12).

Astonishingly, Mozart used a similar lead into Dorabella's "Smanie implacabili" (No. 11). "Stand back," Dorabella warns Despina, "and tremble before the outbreak of my desperation!" At the words "disperato affetto" the first violins rush up and down the scale of D, forte, followed by the same in d minor, then over the fourth degree in g minor. These runs up and down are to be compared to the eerie scales in the Andante of the overture to *Don Giovanni*, or those at the moment when Count Almaviva wills Cherubino's death ("Mora, mora," No. 16, mm. 83–108). After the heroics comes the softening, with a descent into a protracted E-flat sixth chord (Ex. 14.6). "Who scoffs at my sorrow?" asks Dorabella, suggesting that Despina was smiling rather than trembling at the tantrum up to this point. The little wavering motions in dotted rhythm are also familiar from *Idomeneo*; their equivalent is found in Ilia's opening recitative at the words "Oh sorte!" ("Ah fate!" No. 1, mm. 36–37). They occur also at the end of the quintet (No. 6) in *Così*, where the operative word is *destin*.

Dorabella's moving chromatic rise and fall of a fourth for "who will console me?" recall what Fiordiligi sang in the quintet (No. 9) at "Mi si divide il cor" ("My heart is torn asunder," mm. 15–17). This beautiful turn of phrase also comes from *Idomeneo*; Idamante sang it in the lead-in to his rondo, pleading with Ilia: "You were my first love and will be my last" (see Ex. 3.11). The hurtling of the strings in

EXAMPLE 14.6. *Così fan tutte*,

Act 1, Scene 9, Recitative

opposite directions, forte, is pure *Idomeneo* as well.[15] The answer to Dorabella's question as to who would console her comes from the music alone, in Mozart's favorite stringed instruments, the velvet-toned violas, which hold steady while the other strings resume their wavering. Use of the violas as the most sustained line of all, often the only sustained line, came to the fore especially in *Idomeneo*. The most stunning instances of it are in *Così fan tutte*, in the quintet (No. 9) and the terzettino (No. 10).

Despina may smile at Dorabella, but Mozart is warmly sympathetic to her imagined distress. He puts himself into her frame of mind by thinking back to the sufferings of Ilia and Idamante, thus getting into the mood for her ensuing aria about the Furies. There are textual similarities between "Smanie implacabili" and the final aria for Electra in *Idomeneo*, "D'Oreste, d'Aiace ho in seno i tormenti." The earlier aria, in c minor, has a little turning figure, repeated incessantly in the strings like a haunting obsession, which probably gave Mozart the idea to do some-

15. Cf. the converging lines in the violins at the beginning of Ilia's opening recitative (mm. 4–5), which are recalled in the lead-in to Idamante's rondo (No. 10b, mm. 44–45).

EXAMPLE 14.7A–C.

A: *Così fan tutte*, No. 11

B: *Così fan tutte*, No. 20

C: *Così fan tutte*, No. 22

thing similar in accompanying the raving Dorabella. In her case, the violins take up a five-tone murmuring figure and pursue it throughout the aria, now high, now low, now soft, now loud, stopping only to let the winds accompany Dorabella down to her private hell at the words "col suono orribile" in mm. 89–93. Are we to laugh or cry at this portrait of the fearsome Eumenides? Certainly we should be allowed to smile at the parody of love sighs at the end, since the more serious Fiordiligi herself parodies the parody in a lighter moment, in the duet (No. 20); and Despina, as might be expected, does no less, in the quartet (No. 22; Ex. 14.7A–C). Alfonso has already made fun of the women's sighs in the opening argument, along with their tears, caresses, and swoons ("Pianti, sospir, carezze, svenimenti . . . Lasciatemi un po' ridere!"). He laid the groundwork for everything that followed with great care, for which Da Ponte deserves much credit. No one but a Mozart could shed tears with Dorabella even as he was laughing at her, along with Despina and Don Alfonso.

The two sisters echo each other in more important ways than their musical sighs. Tonal maneuvers related to *Idomeneo*, by which Mozart heightened the tension before Dorabella's aria, he used again before Fiordiligi's "Come scoglio" (No. 14). A rising orchestral outburst in D (m. 50) leads to the same in g minor (m. 54), followed by a retreat to an E-flat sixth chord, piano, for the words "l'intatta fede," followed by the little wavering figure in dotted rhythm. The vocal lines are similar, too.

Once again Mozart puts himself in the *Idomeneo* mode as a way of entering into the emotions that the character, in this case Fiordiligi, believes she is experiencing. And these emotions are heroic in the extreme: she will be faithful until she dies, in spite of the world, in spite of fate. The aria is of the simile variety: "Like an immobile rock standing firm against the winds and the tempest" (cf. "Velut . . . rupes immoto resistat" in Virgil's *Aeneid*). Opera seria is the proper home of such similes, and Metastasio their greatest master. Musically, "Come scoglio" bears resemblance to Idamante's first aria, "Non ho colpa," at its opening, including their shared key of B-flat. By the time of the Più allegro in "Come scoglio," the orchestral outbursts and answering vocal fireworks (mm. 76–89) begin to sound like another demonstration of constancy and fortitude—Constanze at her most fiery in "Martern aller Arten" (cf. especially the Allegro assai, mm. 160ff.).

These are resemblances between the arias in question, not references. But the *Idomeneo* material before both Dorabella's and Fiordiligi's arias in act 1 is so specific that it may not be amiss to hear it as a reference to that tragic opera. This is how people sound when they take themselves very seriously, like the heroes and heroines of a tragedy—such is the general import if these passages are heard as references. When Fiordiligi girds herself for another heroic outpouring in scene 6 of act 2, Mozart repeats nearly verbatim some of the music leading to "Come scoglio." At the passage that accompanies "l'intatta fede" ("her fidelity [to Guglielmo] intact"), she sings to Ferrando, "Tu vuoi tormi la pace" ("You would take away my peace"). The irony of this accurate prediction cannot be missed.

Just before the three recalls of masquerade music in the finale of act 2 there is a more subtle quotation of a melody from near the beginning of the opera. Fiordiligi points her finger at Despina and Don Alfonso, blaming them as deceivers: "Per noi favelli, il crudel, la seduttrice" ("They tricked us, the cruel man and the seductress"), singing it to the outlines of a melody she has sung before, only a half-tone away (Ex. 14.8A–B). The lesson from this instance of recall is clear: in *Così fan tutte*, it is the music that does the seducing. At the same time, there is also an unmistakable reference to the entrance aria of the tricked and seduced Donna Elvira (Ex. 14.8C). A close study of the second finale will reveal many other links with the music that sounded earlier in both this opera and the previous operas.

The ending of the opera, as the ladies go back to their original fiancés, has occasioned more discussion than any other part of it. Yet it was ordained by tradition that the opera should end this way, as we saw in the case of Goldoni's *Le pescatrici*, where forgiveness was also swift and complete. Did Mozart and Da Ponte at any point consider breaking with operatic tradition in this matter? They must have been tempted by a different ending, since they made Ferrando and Fiordiligi into such a splendid pair of seria lovers. This factor justified Da Ponte in calling his libretto, like that for *Don Giovanni*, a *dramma giocoso*. Mozart called both an "opera buffa" in his work list.

EXAMPLE 14.8A–C.

A: *Così fan tutte*, No. 31   B: *Così fan tutte*, No. 10   C: *Don Giovanni*, No. 3

Critics have been understandably loath to see the high-spirited Fiordiligi go back to the grumbling Guglielmo. Leaving aside the question of matching temperaments, we arrive on musical grounds alone at the verdict that the new pairing is better than the old. Fiordiligi belongs with the tenor Ferrando because by all the laws of opera, if not of Heaven, high voices should be paired together.[16] In some other type of opera this argument might weigh less. In an opera about opera, the prima donna surely deserves to contemplate going through life into eternity singing love duets with the tenor, not the bass.

Did poet and composer eventually argue this very point? If they did, the viewpoint of Da Ponte/Alfonso won out in the end. His philosophy of reason and optimism permeates the final ensemble:

Fortunato l'uom che prende   Fortunate is the man who takes
  Ogni cosa pel buon verso,   Everything for its good side,
  E tra i casi e le vicende   And in all circumstances and trials
  Da ragion guida si fa.   Lets himself be guided by reason.

A notable literary ancestor lurks behind these sentiments as well. Molière's *Le misanthrope* is a case study of a person who takes everything for its bad side; his opposite, the worldly-wise Philinte, remonstrates:

16. Johann Adam Hiller, in his *Wöchentliche Nachrichten und Anmerkungen, die Musik betreffend* 2 (1767): 118, says that the highest and lowest voices should never sound together in a duet, unless it is comic ("da sich, ausser dem comischen, diese beyden äussersten Stimmen nie zu einem Duett schicken").

Je prends tout doucement les hommes comme ils sont,
J'accoutume mon âme à souffrir ce qu'ils font;
Et je crois qu'à la cour, de même qu'à la ville,
Mon flegme est philosophe autant que votre bile.[17]

The self-possessed and phlegmatic Don Alfonso could not have said it any better. Perhaps Da Ponte was content to stop there, but Mozart needed another quatrain with which to build some musical contrast into the final ensemble, allowing it to attain a suitable valedictory length.

Quel che suol altrui far piangere	Something that only makes others weep
Fia per lui cagion di riso,	Gives him cause to laugh,
E del mondo in mezzo turbini	And amid the storms of this world
Bella calma troverà.	He will find perfect peace.

Bella calma literally means a "beautiful serenity." These two words sum up the mood induced by the opera as well as any words could. Dent, as usual, pronounced the definitive twentieth-century evaluation: "*Così fan tutte* is the best of all Da Ponte's librettos and the most exquisite work of art among Mozart's operas."

APPENDIX

*Original Act 1 Aria for Guglielmo (No. 15a),
as Printed in Libretto 1, pp. 29–30*

Rivolgete a lui lo sguardo (*a Fiord.*)	Turn your gaze toward him
E vedrete come sta:	And you will see how it stands:
Tutto dice io gelo, io ardo;	All of him says: I freeze, I burn,
Idol mio, pietà pietà.	My idol, have pity!
E voi cara un sol momento (*a Dor.*)	And you, dear, for only a moment
Il bel ciglio a me volgete,	Turn your beautiful eyes on me,
E nel mio ritroverete	And in mine you will find
Quel che il labbro dir non sa.	What my lips cannot express.
Un Orlando innamorato	An enamored Roland
Non è niente in mio confronto	Is nothing compared with me;
Un Medoro il sen piagato	The wounded breast of a Medor
Verso Lui per nulla io conto:	I count as null next to him;
Son di foco i miei sospiri,	My sighs are like fire,
Son di bronzo i suoi desiri.	His desires are of bronze.
Se si parla poi di merto	If, then, one speaks of merit,

Certo io sono, ed egli e certo,	I am sure, and so is he,
Che gli uguali non si trovano	That our equal cannot be found
Dall' Sebeto all Canadá.	From Naples to Canada.
Siam due Cresi per ricchezza,	In wealth we are like Croesus,
Due Narcisi per bellezza,	In beauty, like Narcissus;
In amor i Marcantoni	In love, even the Marc Antonys
Verso noi sarien buffoni	Compared with us would be buffoons.
Siam più forti d'un Ciclopo,	We are stronger than a Cyclops,
Letterati al par di Esopo,	Cultivated as much as Aesop;
Se balliamo un Pich ne cede	If we dance, a Pique would yield,
Si gentil, e snello è il piede:	So delicate and fleet are our feet.
Se cantiam col trillo solo	If we sing, with a single trill
Facciam torto all' uscignuolo;	We outshine the nightingale.
E qualch'altro capitale	And we have some other assets
Abbiam poi che alcun non sa.	Which no one knows about.
(Qui le ragazze partono con collera.)	*(Here the young ladies leave in anger.)*
(Bella, bella, tengon sodo:	(Lovely, lovely, they are holding firm,
Se ne vanno, ed io ne godo;	They are leaving, and I am glad of it!
Eroine di constanza,	Heroines of constancy,
Specchi son di fedeltà.) *(Con summo giubilo.)*	They are paragons of faithfulness.) *(With the greatest joy.)*

I am indebted to Phyllis Benjamin, cand. phil. Harvard University, for calling my attention to the existence (unknown to specialists) of this first version of the printed libretto during a visit to Vienna in June 1987. It must date from no later than December 1789, by which time Mozart entered the rejected Guglielmo aria in his work list. As in the case of the definitive libretto (Libretto 2), the only copy known is preserved in the Stadtbibliothek, Vienna. In his musical setting (K. 584) Mozart deviates slightly from the text as printed, correcting *sarien buffoni* to *sarian buffoni*, and *uscignuolo* to *usignuolo*. He also parts company with Da Ponte on one major point, replacing the oft-repeated cadential line "Dall' Sebeto a Canadà" with "Da Vienna al Canadà." Not surprisingly, he demurred at the obscure word *Sebeto*—he had his Viennese public to keep in mind, after all, a public that expected to understand and savor every word sung by Benucci (who may also have complained). "Sebeto" was an old poetic name for Naples, one that went back to antiquity, like "Partenope," which was considerably less obscure, at least on the operatic stage. The case reveals another instance of the delight Da Ponte took in making this particular libretto literary and learned.

Replacement Aria for Guglielmo (No. 15b)

Non siate ritrosi	Do not be shy,
Occhietti vezzosi	Charming little eyes,
Due lampi amorosi	Two loving flashes of lightning;
Vibrate un po quà.	Flash a bit in this direction.

Voi siete forieri	You are the harbingers
Di dolci pensieri	Of sweet thoughts;
Chi guardavi un poco	Who looks at you a little
Di foco si fa.	Becomes inflamed.
Non e colpa nostra	It is not our fault
Se voi ci abbruciata	If you are burning us:
Morir non ci fate	Don't make us die
In sì buona età.	At such a young age.
Felici rendeteci,	Make us happy,
Amate con noi,	Love us in return,
E noi felicissime	And we, overjoyed,
Faremo anche voi;	Will make you happy too;
Guardate, toccate,	Look, touch,
Il tutto osservate;	Observe all of us;
Siam due cari matti	We are two endearing madmen,
Siam forti, e ben fatti,	We are strong and well made,
E come ognun vede,	And as anyone can see,
Sia merito, o caso,	Be it by merit or chance,
Abbiamo bel piede,	We have nice feet,
Bell'occhio bel naso;	Nice eyes, nice noses;
E questi mustacchi	And these moustaches
Chiamare si possono	May be called
Trinofi degli uomini	The triumphs of men,
Pennachi d'amor.	Plumes of love.
(Qui le ragazze partono con collera.)	*(Here the young ladies leave in anger.)*

The definitive libretto was printed in January 1790 (Libretto 2). Before this replacement text, which is found in it on pp. 29–30, the printer included by error the line "Rivolgete a lui lo sguardo. *(A Fiord.)*" from the original aria. Mozart found the replacement text still not short enough and simply omitted setting the second and third quatrains.

15 · LA CLEMENZA DI SARASTRO:
MASONIC BENEFICENCE
IN THE LAST OPERAS

"In ogni cosa ci vuol filosofia."
Don Alfonso

*E*manuel Schikaneder, the producer, director, and librettist of *Die Zauber-flöte*, in which he created the part of Papageno, was a friend of long standing to Mozart. He requested permission for his troupe of wandering actors to visit Salzburg in 1778 and may in fact have played there; it is also possible that he played Salzburg from mid-July to mid-August 1780, and he is known for sure to have played there from 17 September 1780 to 27 February 1781.[1] With a company of thirty-four, reinforced by local musicians lent by the prince-archbishop of Salzburg, Schikaneder offered quite an advanced repertory of plays, including works by Gozzi, Lessing, Voltaire, Beaumarchais, and Shakespeare, plus comic operas by Johann André, Hiller, Umlauf, and Vogler, among others.[2] Schikaneder was a composer himself, moreover, as well as a librettist and actor-singer. His setting of his own libretto, *Die Lyranten*, was performed in Salzburg on 18 September 1780.

Mozart and his sister Nannerl were regular visitors to the shows in the small court theater across the square from where they lived (on the site of the present Landestheater). Nannerl made lists of the plays and operas performed and noted in her diary that she often went to the morning rehearsal as well as the evening performance. She kept her brother informed of the troupe's offerings after he left for Munich in early November to finish composing *Idomeneo* for the court theater there. Before leaving, Mozart had promised Schikaneder to compose a piece for

Revised and expanded from "La Clemenza di Sarastro: Masonic Benevolence in Mozart's Last Operas," *Musical Times* 124 (1983).

1. Friedrich Johann Fischer, "Emanuel Schikaneder und Salzburg," *Jahrbuch der Gesellschaft für Wiener Theaterforschung* 15–16 (1966): 179–216.

2. Sibylle Dahms, "Das musikalische Repertoire des Salzburger Fürsterzbischöflichen Hoftheaters (1775–1803)," *Österreichische Musikzeitschrift* 31 (1976): 340–55. Works by Duni (*Les deux chasseurs et la laitière*) and Piccinni (*La schiava*) were also given by Schikaneder. Beaumarchais's *Le barbier de Séville* was given with Friedrich Ludwig Benda's stage music. Concerning the building of the court theater in Salzburg, see Ernst Hintermaier, "Das fürsterzbischöfliche Hoftheater zu Salzburg," *Österreichische Musikzeitschrift* 30 (1975): 351–63.

insertion in Carlo Gozzi's *Le due notte affannose*, given in German translation as *Peter der Grausame, oder Die zwei schlaflosen Nächte*. He kept his promise, somehow finding time amid all the labor of composing *Idomeneo* to write the recitative and aria (now lost), "Warum, o Liebe, treibst du jenen grausamen Kurzweil—Zittre, töricht' Herz und leide" (K. 365a). In a letter of 2 December 1780, Leopold Mozart reported to his son that the comedy was very good and the aria was well produced and well sung.

Schikaneder's troupe did not return to Salzburg until the spring of 1786, when they offered another work with words and music by their principal, *Das urianische Schloss*. Mozart was then busy in Vienna preparing for the premiere of *Le nozze di Figaro* in the Burgtheater, but before this the paths of the two friends had crossed in Vienna. In 1783, while playing Pressburg, Schikaneder had impressed Joseph II, resulting in an invitation to Vienna, where he opened his season in the Kärntnerthor Theater by reviving Mozart's *Entführung aus dem Serail*. In early 1787, Schikaneder took over the theater in the Bavarian city of Regensburg, the region where he was born in 1751. He returned to Vienna in June 1789 and was appointed director of one of the suburban theaters, the Freihaustheater auf der Wieden (later replaced by the Theater an der Wien). Here *The Magic Flute* had its premiere on 30 September 1791. Thus Mozart, who had previously written operas only for court theaters, was confronted during the last months of his life with composing for a popular genre, the machine comedy, and for a lower-class public than that at the court theater. It is no wonder, then, that the music he wrote, especially that for his friend Schikaneder as Papageno, outdoes any other from his pen in its folklike simplicity.

Another long-standing bond between Mozart and Schikaneder seemed destined to bring about their collaboration on a work like *The Magic Flute* as well: both were Freemasons. A secret society confined to males, Freemasonry originated in England (where Voltaire was initiated as a young man in the 1720s) and spread throughout the Continent, mainly by way of France. With a typically Gallic twist, Parisian Masons added a parallel (but less exalted) order for women, called Les Loges d'Adoption.[3] Francis of Lorraine, husband of the empress Maria Theresa, was a Mason, but after his death in 1765 she clamped down on Freemasonry. When their son Joseph became sole ruler in 1780 on the death of his mother, he pursued more liberal and tolerant policies that allowed the Masons to enjoy five years of growing strength and openness. The number of lodges in Vienna increased from six to eight, with membership more than tripling, from 213 to 764.[4]

Mozart was admitted as an apprentice to the "Beneficence" ("Wohltätigkeit") Lodge in December 1784, and during the year that followed he took a very active part in this and other Viennese lodges. Haydn signed a letter of application to join "True Concord" ("Wahre Eintracht") on 29 December 1784 and was admitted in

---

3. René le Forestier, *Maçonnerie féminine et loges académiques* (Milan, 1979).
4. Elizabeth Grossegger, *Freimaurerei und Theater, 1770–1800: Freimaurerdramen an den k. k. privilegierten Theatern in Wien* (Graz, 1981), p. 99.

early 1785.[5] Ignaz von Born (1742–91) was Master of the Chair of "True Concord." A famous mineralogist and director of the imperial museum, he was a man of wisdom and leadership who has often been suggested as the prototype of the wise Sarastro. He died on 24 July 1791, by which time most of *The Magic Flute* had been written; to those Masonic brothers witnessing the first performances of the opera in the fall of 1791, it could well have served as his epitaph.

There is not the slightest doubt that Mozart's cantata "Die Maurerfreude" (K. 471) was written to honor Born. Its text, by Franz Petran, refers to Born's being crowned with laurels by Joseph the Wise, and in fact the emperor raised him to the degree of *Reichsritter* on 24 April 1785 for having discovered a new method of amalgamation for separating metals. On the same day, "Die Maurerfreude" was first performed at a banquet given by the "Crowned Hope" Lodge. It consists of a virtuoso aria for tenor and a final tenor solo with three-part male chorus, connected by an orchestrally accompanied recitative in the middle. Mozart wrote this demanding tenor part for his fellow Mason Adamberger, the first Belmonte. He chose the key of E-flat major, which, with its three accidentals, had special Masonic significance. Certain other musical features of the cantata also seem to foreshadow *The Magic Flute* (for instance, the conjunct falling sixth in the melody together with Papageno's panpipes rhythm in mm. 44–45 at the first climax of the opening Allegro). Artaria published the cantata in August 1785 with a preface explaining how and where it originated. Then on 9 December 1785, "Crowned Hope" put on a gala concert to which all the Viennese sister lodges were invited; featured was not only the cantata in honor of Born, sung again by Adamberger, but also a piano concerto with Mozart as soloist and "Phantasien von dem w. Br. Mozard" ("improvisations by the worthy brother Mozart").[6] Little could the brothers have known that this occasion represented the high-water mark of Freemasonry in the Habsburg domains.

The openness that Freemasonry enjoyed in Vienna around 1785, evident in the printing of "Die Maurerfreude," went so far as to allow Masonic initiation rites to be discussed and shown on the stage of the imperial theater. A play by the great actor Friedrich Ludwig Schröder entitled *Die Freymaurer* ("The Lady Mason") concerns a woman who tries, wearing male attire, to penetrate a lodge; she is finally frightened away by being told about the *Prüfungen* (trials), at which she must be disrobed and confront a glowing sword and human skull.[7] Eighteenth-century engravings confirm that would-be apprentices were partially disrobed in order to

5. Joachim Hurwitz, "Haydn and the Freemasons," *Haydn Yearbook* 16 (1985): 5–98. This lengthy article is scrupulously careful to distinguish fact from conjecture, and it supersedes all previous accounts of Viennese Freemasonry in the 1780s.

6. For the complete program, see Deutsch, *Dokumente*, p. 226.

7. Grossegger, *Freimaurerei und Theater*, p. 34. There is a conflicting attribution of the play to Johann Christian Wagenseil, which Grossegger convincingly argues against (p. 31*n*1). The sword and the skull are displayed together on a table in the famous painting of a Masonic lodge meeting in 1790, which is the subject of H. C. Robbins Landon's monograph *Mozart and the Masons: New Light on the Lodge "Crowned Hope"* (London, 1982); see his Illustration no. 41 on p. 44.

ascertain their sex. There were seven performances of *Die Freymaurer* in the Burg-theater during 1784, and it was revived for four more in late 1785 and early 1786,[8] after which it disappeared completely—understandably so, in the light of a change in opinion at the highest level of authority.

Joseph II, for reasons that have yet to be fully explained, decided to put severe limits on Freemasonry within his domains, a decision formulated in the so-called *Freimaurerpatent* of 11 December 1785.[9] The eight Viennese lodges were ordered to combine immediately into two or three, with the total number of members not to exceed 360. "True Concord," "Palm Trees," and "Three Eagles" combined to form "Truth," while "Beneficence" combined with "Crowned Hope" and others to form "Newly Crowned Hope." Lists of the remaining members were to be made avail-able to the police. Mozart's name, along with an indication that he had achieved the third degree (Master), appears on such a list for "Newly Crowned Hope" in 1786. Bickering and confusion beset the lodges in their efforts to conform to the imperial decree. Not even Ignaz von Born could bring order out of the chaos and restore harmony. He resigned from the order in 1786, an action followed by many other prominent members, including Joseph von Sonnenfels, but not Mozart. The decline and fall of Austrian Freemasonry seemed all but inevitable.

Leopold II succeeded his childless elder brother on the latter's death in February 1790. What had pleased Joseph displeased Leopold, and vice versa, as Da Ponte complained in his memoirs; Leopold dismissed Da Ponte and laid plans to rein-troduce opera seria and full-scale pantomime ballets to the imperial capital—the very genres that Joseph had banished.[10] With regard to Freemasonry, Leopold showed himself tolerant up to a point. His censors were strict with plays intended for the Burgtheater, but more lenient if it was a question of a Singspiel for one of the suburban theaters. Thus August von Kotzebue's *Die Sonnenjungfrau* for the Burgtheater in 1791 could be performed only after it had been purged of Masonic elements,[11] but *Das Sonnenfest der Braminen*, a "heroisch-komisches Singspiel" by Karl Friedrich Hensler, with music by Wenzel Müller, got away with denunciations of religious intolerance; indeed, it has been called "a strikingly high-minded ratifi-cation of Enlightenment ideals of fraternity, humanism, and freedom from super-

8. Hadamowsky, *Die Wiener Hoftheater*, No. 409.
9. He retreated back to a point of view closer to that of his mother: secret societies were a potential political threat in an absolutist state. The question has been posed by Denyse Dalban (*Le comte de Cagliostro* [Paris, 1983], p. 162) whether the disgrace of Cagliostro, Grand Master of the Egyptian Rite, in the affair of the diamond necklace (1785) that compromised Marie Antoinette, did not have something to do with her brother's turning against the Masons. Another factor often cited is the emperor's pique at not being supported by Bavarian Masons in his attempts to exchange the Austrian Netherlands for Bavaria. This decisive turning point in the emperor's reign will undoubtedly receive full treatment in the monumental biography by Derek Beales in progress, the first volume of which appeared as *Joseph II: In the Shadow of Maria Theresa, 1741–1780* (Cambridge, 1987).
10. John Rice ("Emperor and Impresario: Leopold II and the Transformation of Viennese Musical Theater, 1790–1792," Ph.D. diss., University of California, Berkeley, 1987) brings to light much new archival material on the subject. The changed climate for opera seria in Vienna encouraged the Bohe-mian Estates to request an opera seria in celebration of the coronation of Leopold as king of Bohemia. Leopold was hailed as "the new Titus" (ibid., 1:323).
11. Grossegger, *Freimaurerei und Theater*, p. 113.

stition anticipatory of Schikaneder's *Die Zauberflöte* of a year later."[12] It went on the stage of the suburban Theater in the Leopoldstadt in September 1790 and enjoyed an enormous success. Müller's exploitation of Viennese popular music was not lost on Mozart, any more than Hensler's testing of the waters with Emperor Leopold's censors was lost on Schikaneder—or, of course, Mozart, who, as always, actively participated in shaping the libretto.

Schikaneder's relationship to Freemasonry is less well documented than Mozart's, but he is known to have belonged to a lodge when in Regensburg. The libretto to *The Magic Flute* testifies to an intimate knowledge of the order's initiation rites and symbolism. Ignaz Alberti, a lodge brother of Mozart's who was a printer and engraver, was responsible for the engraved frontispiece of the printed libretto, which he also printed. It shows the approaches to a temple, with implements for stonemasonry, a five-pointed star, and an impressive urn (Fig. 30). This scene, representing the Vault of the Pyramids (act 2, scene 20), is depicted very similarly in one of the six early engravings by Joseph and Peter Schaffer (Fig. 31). Thanks to recent detective work by art historians, we know that the related stage picture and frontispiece were formed by making a composite of two plates by Jean-Laurent Legeay, one from his series of *Vasi* (no date) and one from his series of *Rovine* (1768).[13] Legeay, a French artist working in Rome, already uses many of the same Masonic symbols in the two pictures in question, which is perhaps what attracted Alberti to them in the first place.

The libretto itself also has French connections. Its serious Masonic side has long been known to derive from Abbé Terrason's *Sethos* (Paris, 1731). The other side—fairy queen sends boy on quest with a magic flute to rescue girl from an evil magician—comes from A. J. Liebeskind's fairy tale "Lulu, oder die Zauberflöte," collected in Wieland's *Dschinnistan* (vol. 3, 1789). Conflating these two sources produced a few loose ends, but it is no longer necessary to believe, as did Dent, that the plot was radically changed by abandoning one for the other. Andrew Porter explains what happened in terms of confluence and views the change of direction and resulting ambiguity as one of the work's great strengths: "When Tamino, before the temples, learns that nothing is quite what he—and we—have been led to believe, he takes his first step towards Enlightenment, and the opera moves to sublimity."[14]

As the libretto was being hammered out between Schikaneder and Mozart in the spring of 1791, another librettist of renown arrived in Vienna to take up temporary duties in the Burgtheater, replacing Da Ponte. He was the Dresden court

12. Thomas Bauman, in his introduction to Wenzel Müller, *Das Sonnenfest der Braminen*, vol. 16 of *German Opera 1770–1800*, ed. Thomas Bauman (New York, 1986). The librettist, Hensler, was a Mason and the author of *Maurerrede auf Mozarts Tod*, which he read at a lodge meeting of "Newly Crowned Hope," then had printed by another Mason, Ignaz Alberti (Vienna, 1792).

13. *Piranèse et les Français, 1740–1790: Colloque international*, ed. Georges Brunel (Paris, 1976), 1:199–212.

14. Introduction to Porter's edition and English translation of *The Magic Flute* libretto, published by Faber (London, 1980).

poet Caterino Mazzolà, who had welcomed Da Ponte ten years earlier in Dresden, when he first arrived from Italy. Mazzolà had contributed to the wedding festivities for Prince Anthony of Saxony in 1781 *Osiride*, a "dramma per musica" set by Naumann in which the ancient Egyptian mysteries provide a background for the trials of two young lovers. Mazzolà was paid one hundred florins a month for May, June, and July 1791, after which his interim appointment ended and Bertati arrived to take up his duties as regular theater poet.[15] As the Burgtheater saw no new productions and only two revivals during June and July, it is difficult to explain how Mazzolà earned his salary, unless he was hired with the tacit understanding that he would be working on the coronation opera for the "German Titus," as Leopold was called.

Guardasoni, the impresario at Prague, got his opera contract signed with the Bohemian Estates only on 8 July 1791, but one of its stipulations suggests that he already had an opera based on Metastasio's *La clemenza di Tito* in the planning stages. The Bohemian Estates wanted outstanding Italian singers, and specifically "un Primo Musica di prima sfera"—meaning a soprano castrato, of which four were named in example—and a prima donna of equal rank. Count Rottenhan, the highest civic authority in Bohemia (*Burggraf*), had given Guardasoni two subjects for the opera, and the impresario was in no position to disregard so powerful a person. The second point of the contract shows how he got around this problem:

> Secondly, I obligate myself to have the poetry of the libretto written, on the model of one of the two subjects given to me by his excellency the Burggraf, and to have it set to music by a famous master, but in case this is impossible because of the limitations of time, I promise to procure an opera newly composed on the subject of Metastasio's *Tito*.[16]

The contract signed, Guardasoni left immediately for Vienna.

Salieri claims in a letter to Prince Anton Esterházy that Guardasoni pestered him to set the libretto, which is not impossible, for Salieri was still Capellmeister, even though he stood less high in the favor of Leopold than he had of Joseph;[17] but since Salieri was also busy making excuses as to why he could take on no additional work for Esterházy, we need not necessarily believe him. One circumstance in fact contradicts Salieri. Mozart's first sketches for the music of Sesto were for a tenor. Perhaps he believed that the part would go to Antonio Baglioni, the fine tenor who had created the role of Don Ottavio. In any event, this suggests that Mozart

---

15. The payment records are given in Rice, "Emperor and Impresario," 2:393.

16. "2do Mi obligo di far comporre la Poesia del Libro, anorma dei due Sogetti datimi da S. A. gran Burgravio e di farlo porre in Musica da un cellebre Maestro, in caso però che non fosse affatto possibile di ciò effetuare per la Strettezza del tempo, mi obligo di procurar un Opera nuovamente composta sul Suggetto del Tito di Metastasio"; Tomislav Volek, "Über den Ursprung von Mozarts Oper 'La clemenza di Tito,'" *Mozart-Jahrbuch 1959*, p. 281.

17. [János Hárich et al.], "The Acta Musicalia of the Esterházy Archives (Nos. 101–152)," *Haydn Yearbook* 15 (1984): 153–54 (No. 141).

was involved with setting *Tito* before he knew that the first stipulation on the contract was for a soprano castrato. As it turns out, Guardasoni procured a primo uomo in Domenico Bedini, a prima donna in Maria Marchetti-Fantozzi, and Baglioni sang the role of the emperor. All three principals excelled.

Mozart is believed to have immersed himself in work on *The Magic Flute* (perhaps the libretto mostly at first) by the middle of April 1791, after finishing his last string quintet (K. 614, dated 12 April). By 11 June he was far enough along that he could cite a line ("Tod und Verzweiflung war sein Lohn") from No. 11 in act 2 in a letter to his wife, Constanze, who was taking the cure at Baden. Then on 2 July he requested back from his pupil and copyist Süssmayr the vocal score of act 1 so that he could begin orchestrating it. He entered the opera in his work catalog in July (without a precise date) as consisting of twenty-two numbers, followed directly by *La clemenza di Tito* with twenty-four.

Most of *Tito* was composed after *The Magic Flute*; thus it is his last opera. While great haste was necessary, the time was not nearly as short as the eighteen days claimed by Niemetschek. Mazzolà was on hand in Vienna to perform the radical surgery Mozart required on the old libretto. He was on hand in Prague too, where Mozart arrived on 28 August. Since Mazzolà did not return to Dresden until after the premiere on 5 September, we may assume that he performed the poet's customary function of training the singers in the action. Friedrich Rochlitz explains what he regarded as weaker moments in the score due to the time pressure Mozart was under: "He saw himself forced, since he was no god, either to produce an entirely mediocre work, or one in which the main pieces alone were very good, the less interesting ones lightly written and conforming to present-day tastes among the populace. He rightly chose the latter path." [18] What Rochlitz means by the popular preference for light music is of course music in the Italian style, and it was surely no mistake on Mozart's part to pluck what he could from Paisiello and Cimarosa, since the sovereign being honored had spent twenty-five years in Italy and was a decided partisan of Italian composers.

Imagining how *La clemenza di Tito* might have been different given more time, we lose sight too easily of the monarch Mozart was trying to please. To achieve his goal it was crucial that he capitalize on the two principal singers imported from Italy at great expense. Zinzendorf noted in his diary about the premiere that Marchetti sang quite well: "The emperor was enthusiastic about her." [19] In his letter to his wife of 7–8 October, Mozart relays the news, written to him from Prague by

18. "Er sahe sich mithin gezwungen, da er kein Gott war, entweder ein ganz mittelmässiges Werk zu liefern, oder nur die Hauptsätze sehr gut, die minder interessanten ganz leicht hin und blos dem Zeitgeschmack des grossen Haufens gemäss zu bearbeiten. Er erwählte mit Recht die Lezte"; Friedrich Rochlitz, "Verbürgte Anekdoten aus Wolfgang Gottlieb Mozarts Leben: Ein Beytrag zur richtigeren Kenntnis dieses Mannes, als Mensch und Künstler," *Allgemeine musikalische Zeitung* 1 (1798/99): col. 151. Later in the same passage Rochlitz praises Mozart for suppressing Metastasio's act 2 and concentrating the action of the drama in two acts with ensembles and finales. He was unaware of Mazzolà's collaboration, which is in fact not mentioned in the printed libretto. In 1775 Mozart had set Metastasio's three-act *Il re pastore* in a condensed two-act form.

19. H. C. Robbins Landon, *1791: Mozart's Last Year* (New York, 1988), p. 115.

FIGURE 30

Alberti: Vault of the Pyramids
from the libretto of *Die Zauberflöte*

FIGURE 31

Schaffer brothers: Vault of the
Pyramids

Stadler, about the opera's triumphant last performance in which the primo uomo
"sang better than ever" ("der Bedini sang besser als allezeit"). The opera did not
fail, as has sometimes been claimed.

On his return to Vienna, Mozart composed the march of the priests and the
Ouverture (Mozart's spelling) for his German opera, entering them in his catalog
on 28 September, two days before the premiere. Since compositional work on the
two operas overlapped to a considerable extent, it is not surprising that their music
should show many affinities.

Die Zauberflöte, though always held up by critics as a model of German purity,
nevertheless shares many stylistic features with Mozart's Italian operas. Tamino's
"Ich fühl es" in the portrait aria (No. 3), sung to expressive rising appoggiaturas,
was first perfected by the composer in another aria in E-flat: Ilia's "Se il padre
perdei" in *Idomeneo*—a fact that Mozart's contemporaries did not fail to notice, as
we shall see below (see the Epilogue to Chapter 18). The portrait aria also has links
with *Tito*: its counterpoint of interlocking groups of three beats between voice and
orchestra at "Ich fühl es" and later, as Tamino reiterates "die Liebe" (mm. 29–32),

resounds often in *Tito*.[20] All three terzettos feature it, and it is used in summary fashion at the end as the emperor stands out in counterpoint against all the others (No. 26, mm. 89–101).

The single terzetto (No. 19) in *The Magic Flute* proves especially prone to "Ti-toisms." Sesto's habit, established in the very first number, of slurring eighth notes together in pairs turns up in Tamino's music as well. (The habit is evident in the early sketch of No. 1 with Sesto as a tenor; see Ex. 15.1A–B.) Their lines are so similar in tone in these two cases that Tamino's phrase would work well as a consequent to Sesto's antecedent.[21] In the same ensemble, Mozart allows Pamina extraordinary moments of vocal acrobatics à la *Clemenza* (Ex. 15.2A–B). The figure sung by Tito here occurs repeatedly in the Prague opera, and in Sesto's great rondo (No. 19) he sings the same arpeggiated descent to words about going to his death in desperation (see Ex. 18.1 below). Pamina warns Tamino of deathly danger in her sudden fall. Vocal extravagance of this sort risked pushing Pamina into seeming to be too much the daughter of her mother, the Queen of the Night, and in general Mozart avoided it in her part. In this case, the textual similarity drew both operas close.

The prima donna of *Tito*, Vitellia, is characterized by nervously disjunct and wide-ranging melodic lines, but hers is not a coloratura part like that for the Queen of the Night (except for one flaring triad up to high D and back at the climax of No. 11; cf. Ex. 18.6B). Even so, the climactic drive to the cadence in Vitellia's rondo (No. 23) was projected by a rising harmonic progression with sforzandi (mm. 172–74) that is nearly identical to one in the Queen of the Night's short but hair-raising second aria (No. 14, mm. 43–45), and the orchestral postludes are also similar (cf. No. 14, m. 48, with No. 23, m. 178).

A week after the premiere of *The Magic Flute*, Mozart returned to witness a performance. He reported to his wife, who was once again taking the cure at Baden, that the house was packed as usual, the success enormous, with several numbers encored, "but what pleases me most is the *silent applause*" (Mozart's emphasis).[22] Silence was one of the virtues hymned in Mozart's Masonic cantatas and songs, and instilled with success in Tamino (but not in Papageno). In the same letter, indeed in the same sentence, Mozart expressed his equal delight at the simultaneous success of *The Magic Flute* in Vienna and *Tito* in Prague.[23]

20. The overlapping groups of three beats between voice and accompaniment were used earlier in K. 489 (see Ex. 12.1) and in Ferrando's rondo in *Così fan tutte* (No. 24, mm. 37–39 and passim, for the repetition of "tu cedi"). Ferrando's rondo anticipates another characteristic of *Tito*: syncopated treble over pendulum bass in quarter notes (mm. 57–65). It should be recalled that Mozart cut this aria, providing all the more reason for plundering its "buried treasures."

21. Kunze (*Mozarts Opern*, p. 533) is of a different opinion: "kein Ton Sestos könnte von Tamino stammen" ("not a note sung by Sesto could stem from Tamino").

22. "— was mich aber am meisten freuet, ist, der *Stille beifall!*"; letter of 7–8 October 1791.

23. Ibid.: "das sonderbareste dabei ist, das den abend als meine neue Oper mit so vielen beifall zum erstenmale aufgeführt wurde, am nehmlichen abend in Prag der Tito zum leztenmale auch mit ausserordentlichen beifall aufgeführt worden. — alle Stücke sind applaudirt worden" ("The strangest thing is that the evening my new opera received so much applause at its first performance, on that same evening in Prague *Tito* was performed for the last time, also to extraordinary acclaim — all pieces were applauded").

EXAMPLE 15.1A–B.

A: *Clemenza di Tito*, No. 1

B: *Zauberflöte*, No. 19

EXAMPLE 15.2A–B.

A: *Zauberflöte*, No. 19

B: *Clemenza di Tito*, No. 6

On the next night Mozart was once again in the theater for a performance. As he related to Constanze, whom he wrote daily and sometimes twice a day (just as Dorabella insisted in the quintet of parting), he could not resist playing a trick on his old friend Schikaneder. He stole behind the scenes and improvised on the Glockenspiel in "Ein Mädchen oder Weibchen" (No. 20):

> Today I had such a yen to play the Glockenspiel myself I went on stage. Just for fun, at the point where Schikaneder has a pause, I played an arpeggio. He was startled, looked into the wings and saw me. When he had his next pause I played no arpeggio. This time he stopped and refused to go on. I guessed what he was thinking and again played a chord. He then struck the magic bells and said, "Shut up!" This made everyone laugh. I think this joke taught many of the audience for the first time that he does not play the instrument himself.[24]

To be sure, there is so much of Mozart's playful nature in the music of *The Magic Flute* that it tends to obscure the solemn and serious side of the work. Yet in the same letter he related his displeasure with a member of the audience who applauded everything most heartily.

> He, the know-it-all, showed himself to be such a thorough Bavarian that I could not remain or I should have had to call him an ass. Unfortunately, I was there just when the second act began; that is the solemn scene. At first I was patient enough to draw his attention to a few speeches. But he laughed at everything. Well, I could stand it no longer. I called him a Papageno and left. But I don't believe the idiot understood even this.[25]

There is an irony in calling such an undiscerning spectator a "thorough Bavarian"—or rather, two ironies. Schikaneder/Papageno was of course a Bavarian, and Mozart himself, as a Salzburger, was closer to being a Bavarian than an Austrian.[26]

During his last decade in Vienna, Mozart transcended not just his roots in Salzburg, but all that was local or limiting. Still, the combination of moral earnestness, comedy, and farce in *The Magic Flute* could have happened only at Vienna, where it crowned a century of German popular theater and a decade of Josephinian Enlightenment.

---

24. "nur gieng ich auf das theater bey der Arie des Papageno mit dem GlockenSpiel, weil ich heute so einen trieb fühlte es selbst zu Spielen. — da machte ich nun den Spass, wie Schickaneder einmal eine haltung hat, so machte ich eine Arpeggio — der erschrack — schauete in die Scene und sah mich — als es das 2:te mal kamm — machte ich es nicht — nun hielte er und wollte gar nicht mehr weiter — ich errieth seinen Gedanken und machte wieder einen Accord — dann schlug er auf das Glöckenspiel und sagte *halts Maul* — alles lachte dann — ich glaube dass viele durch diesen Spass das erstemal erfuhren dass er das Instrument nicht selbst schlägt"; 8–9 October 1791.

25. "aber Er, der allwissende, zeigte so sehr den *bayern*, dass ich nicht bleiben konnte, oder ich hätte ihn einen Esel heissen müssen; — Unglückseeligerweise war ich eben drinnen als der 2:te Ackt anfieng, folglich bey der feyerlichen Scene. — er belachte alles; anfangs hatte ich gedult genug ihn auf einige Reden aufmerksam machen zu wollen, allein — er belachte alles; — da wards mir nun zu viel — ich hiess ihn *Papageno*, und gieng fort — ich glaube aber nicht dass es der dalk verstanden hat"; ibid.

26. Salzburg was a part of Bavaria for centuries before it became an independent bishopric in the Middle Ages. Its territory was awarded by Napoleon to Austria in 1802, but Bavaria regained it briefly before it was definitively assigned to Austria in 1816.

Mozart's very last letter, written to his wife from Vienna on 14 October 1791, shows that the sparks of divine radiance and forgiveness emanating from *The Magic Flute* had overcome him to the point where he spoke in a kindly tone even about Salieri, about whom he had rarely, if ever, said a kind word. He took Salieri, Cavalieri, and his young son Carl to the opera, along with his mother-in-law, Madame Weber.

> You can hardly imagine how charming Salieri and Cavalieri were, how much they liked not only my music, but the libretto and everything. They both called it an *operone*, worthy of being performed at the grandest festival or before the greatest monarch, and said that they would go often to see it, as they had never seen a more beautiful or delightful show. Salieri listened and watched most attentively and from the overture to the last chorus there was not a single number that did not call forth from him a *bravo!* or *bello*! It seemed as if they could not thank me enough for my kindness. They had intended to go in any case to the opera yesterday. But they would have had to be in their places by four o'clock. As it was they saw and heard everything in comfort in my box. . . . Carl was absolutely delighted at being taken to the opera.[27]

Carl had just turned seven. One of the amazing truths about *The Magic Flute* is that, from the very beginning, it has enchanted children of all ages, as well as the Salieris and the Goethes of this world.

What Mozart calls "the solemn scene" begins with a spoken dialogue so simple that even it is within a child's ken. "Does he possess Virtue [*Tugend*]?" asks the First Priest about Tamino at the beginning of act 2. "Tugend!" answers Sarastro. "Also the ability to maintain Silence [*Verschwiegenheit*]?" asks the Second Priest. "Verschwiegenheit!" answers Sarastro. "Is he a Doer of Good [*Wohltätig*]?" asks the Third Priest. "Wohltätig!" answers Sarastro, who then asks for the priests' assent, which they give symbolically at the sounding of the threefold fanfare. This ritual sets the tone for the solemn aria with chorus "O Isis und Osiris" (No. 10). We are privy to Masonic teachings here—but Mozart had more in mind than just Masonic lore.

Mozart's ideas on the subject of women, and their place in society, went quite beyond those taught by Freemasonry. This is evident above all in his treatment of Pamina. In her duet with Papageno, "Bei Männern, welche Liebe fühlen" (No. 7), he undercuts Papageno's simplistic and typically masculine sentiments by giving

---

27. "Du kannst nicht glauben, wie artig beide waren, — wie sehr ihnen nicht nur meine Musick, sondern das Buch und alles zusammen gefiel. — Sie sagten beide ein *Operone*. — würdig bey der grössten festivität vor dem grössten Monarchen aufzuführen, — und Sie würden sie gewis sehr oft sehen, den sie haben noch kein schöneres und angenehmeres Spectacle gesehen. — Er hörte und sah mit aller Aufmerksamkeit und von der Sinfonie bis zum letzten Chor, war kein Stück, welches ihm nicht ein bravo oder bello entlockte, und sie konnten fast nicht fertig werden, sich über diese Gefälligkeit bei mir zu bedanken. Sie waren allzeit gesinnt gestern in die Oper zu gehen. Sie hatten aber um 4 Uhr schon hinein sitzen müssen — da sahen und hörten Sie aber mit Ruhe. . . . Dem Carl hab ich keine geringe Freude gemacht, dass ich ihm in die Oper abgehohlt habe"; 14 October 1791.

FIGURE 32
Schinkel: Stage set for the final
scene of *The Magic Flute*

more musical weight to Pamina. There is no precedent in Masonic doctrine for
raising women to the level of equality and enlightenment achieved by Pamina at
the end of the opera. Not only does she undergo the trials to become one of the
initiates, but she leads Tamino through them as well. As the powers of superstition
and darkness are overthrown once and for all and Sarastro announces his triumph
to the words "Die Strahlen der Sonne vertreiben die Nacht" ("The beams of the
sun drive out night"), the stage direction in the original libretto specifies: the stage
is transformed into a sunburst; Sarastro appears on high; Tamino and Pamina are

DER SCHLUSS SCENE DER OPER DIE ZAUBERFLÖTE.

in priestly robes, surrounded on both sides by the Egyptian priests; the Three Boys offer flowers.[28]

The climactic triumph of light over darkness is also the triumph of the keynote, E-flat major, over its rival, c minor. (In *The Creation*, Haydn's God granted light to the world in the Masonic key of C major.) The artist who perhaps came closest

28. Both the final set and the Fire and Water decor used the full stage. Schikaneder's nephew, who was present at the original production, claimed that Papageno's attempted suicide, which was played on a short stage against a garden decor, was only inserted so that there would be time to prepare the "imposanten Sonnentempel" of the final scene. See Deutsch, *Dokumente, Addenda und Corrigenda* (Kassel, 1978), pp. 99–100.

to capturing the sublimity of light's triumph in *The Magic Flute* was Karl Friedrich Schinkel in his final stage design for the Berlin production of 1816 (Fig. 32). At this supreme moment in the opera its creators chose to show Pamina in priestly robes; and when the final chorus places an eternal crown on Beauty and Wisdom, it is in fact crowning the perfect couple in Pamina and Tamino. The notion that women, once enlightened, should participate in all things, and perhaps even enter the priesthood, was far in advance of Mozart's day. Several titles might have been given to the opera besides the one Mozart and Schikaneder gave it. One heads this chapter. Another might be "Aufklärung durch Liebe" ("Enlightenment Through Love"). But the most tellingly appropriate, given Mozart's infinite care to create strong and deeply moving female characters in the course of writing all his operas, would be the simplest of all: "Pamina."

Mozart sketched an early version for the beginning of the overture to *The Magic Flute* that was quite different from his final solution. It began with an Andante in cut time in which a pair of flutes softly answered the syncopated forte beginning of the strings (Ex. 15.3). The proximity of *La clemenza di Tito* is very much apparent in these opening bars. A syncopated treble against the bass sounds prominently at the beginning of the overture to *Tito* and in the opera's orchestral postlude at the very end. The descent in thirds of the two flutes, moreover, corresponds to the second theme of the overture to *Tito*. But the ensuing Allegro moderato leaves no doubt of its allegiance to the world of Tamino and Pamina. The syncopations in the treble remain, but the ascent by a leaping sixth then filled in by stepwise descent corresponds to Tamino's ecstatic song about Pamina's picture (No. 3). Choice of Tamino's phrase here cannot surprise; there are echoes of it at crucial moments throughout the work, most notably when Pamina sings "Tamino mein" before she leads him through the trials, making the phrase one of the most emotionally charged and memorable moments among the opera's many melodic high points. The jagged descent of the second violins in mm. 9–10 (and first violins in diminution in m. 12) is related to the bass line of the sorrowful orchestral postlude to Pamina's "Ach ich fühl's" (No. 17, mm. 38–41; see Ex. 16.3 below), which is related ultimately to the "*duol* motif" in *Idomeneo* (see Ex. 1.1). Mozart discarded these ideas for the overture, deciding to rely not on melodic references but on subtler harmonic means and the craft of fugato. Yet he did not give up all reliance on the sister overture to *Tito*, the beginning of which also rises majestically through the triad, and the middle of which pursues a complicated contrapuntal course (as if conveying the trials to come) before the triumphant return to the keynote.

The Magic Flute is a mirror image of *La clemenza di Tito* in terms of tonality. Both are centered around the polar relationship between E-flat and C, the two main keys Mozart used in his Masonic songs and cantatas. Every choice of key he had to make in both operas was affected by his placing the finales in the keynote (act 2) or in the polar rival key (act 1). The first return to the keynote after the overtures underscores a highly dramatic or symbolic moment in both operas: Ta-

EXAMPLE 15.3. *Zauberflöte*,

Sketch for earlier version of Overture

mino's picture aria (No. 3) and the identically placed duettino for Sesto and Annio (No. 3) in praise of friendship.[29] The latter is so much in the vein of a German Lied that it could easily slip into *The Magic Flute* and seem quite at home there; indeed, its concluding phrase echoes the concluding phrase of the duet between Pamina and Papageno (No. 7) as they sing "Mann und Weib, und Weib und Mann." Sesto and Annio sing about friendship in their similar phrase. Loyalty to friends, betrayal, and forgiveness—these are the central issues of *La clemenza*. No matter how tiny the duettino, it is as central to the drama as its counterpart in *The Magic Flute*.

The common bonds between the two operas are most evident in the two figures of responsibility who stand apart from the others, Tito and Sarastro. On the surface they are different because one is a temporal, the other a spiritual, ruler. And yet Sarastro reigns over his flock with at least as much temporal might as the prince-

29. In *Così fan tutte* also, Mozart comes back to the keynote in the third number.

archbishop of Salzburg, whose absolute power Mozart experienced personally, to his great dismay. As Roman emperor, Titus was a religious as well as secular figure. By invoking his memory and his vaunted clemency, the creators of the coronation opera were offering a parable to his successor, the Holy Roman emperor, Leopold II. Sarastro serves justice ("Gerechtigkeit" is what the chorus praises him for in the finale of act 1) quite as much as Titus the Just: "Tito il giusto, il forte," sings the chorus in act 1. Each takes a forgiving rather than a vengeful attitude after experiencing the wrongdoing of others. Tito eventually forgives Sesto, and even Vitellia, who instigated the plot on his life. Sarastro dismisses Monostatos without punishment after the Moor threatens Pamina with a dagger, because the weapon was forged by the Queen of the Night, source of the evil. He then forgives the queen her horrid plot to have him killed by Pamina's hand, singing his slow strophic air, "In diesen heil'gen Hallen kennt man die Rache nicht" ("These sacred halls know not revenge"). And to Papageno he ultimately concedes Papagena, even though the trials proved Papageno unworthy of his reward.

Clemency was a virtue ardently espoused by the Enlightenment, an age during which Montesquieu, Beccaria, and Voltaire led the fight against penal torture. Forgiveness was written into the code of Freemasonry as one of its first principles. It figures in the second point of "Charakter und Eigenschaften eines echten Freimaurers" ("Character and Qualities of a True Freemason"), the first being that a member should be a freeborn male, raised in the Christian religion, and not less than twenty years of age:[30] "Er soll ein redliches, treues, menschenliebendes, sanftes und gefühlvolles Herz habe, mitleidig gegen das Unglück anderer, nachgebend, fern von Hass und Rache und bescheiden" ("He should have an honest, true, humanity-loving, tender, and feeling heart, sympathetic to the misfortunes of others, compliant, far from hate and revenge, and modest"). The very vocabulary of this prescription echoes throughout Schikaneder's libretto.

To find a work that matches the concentrated dose of humanity and clemency in Mozart's twin operas of 1791 we need search no further than *The Tempest*. The beauty of forgiveness has never been sung more profoundly than in the Bard's farewell to the stage, unless it is in Sarastro's own swan song, "In diesen heil'gen Hallen." There is more than a hint of Prospero and his magic in Sarastro. Caliban and Papageno, both creatures of nature and limited in intellect, are somewhat alike too: both would populate the world with little Calibans and little Papagenos/Papagenas. Caliban is also, like Monostatos, the false servant who deserts and goes over to the forces that would destroy his master. Pamina has not a few things in common with Miranda; and Ferdinand, like Tamino, must prove himself worthy before becoming half of the divinely ordained perfect couple. Prospero yields his powers to the young couple at the end, and so, we assume Mozart intended, if only because of the exact parallel with the end of *Idomeneo*, does Sarastro.

30. This set of prescriptions dates from the second half of the eighteenth century and is printed in Grossegger, *Freimaurerei und Theater*, pp. 11–12.

There is a numinous tone, both sad and sweet, about the works of Mozart's last year, a beautiful calmness, an air of resignation, that pervades the Clarinet Concerto (K. 622) as well as both operas. It draws together the two representatives of wisdom, Tito and Sarastro. Their closeness in Mozart's mind is evident from the way he treats them musically. "If I am deprived of showing mercy, what is left to me?" asks Tito before his first aria (No. 6), and in Metastasio's lovely aria text comes the answer (John Hoole's English translation, published in 1767, furnishes a poem exuding period flavor, while very free):

Del più sublime soglio	This fruit the monarch boasts alone,
L'unico frutto è questo:	The only fruit that glads a throne:
Tutto è tormento il resto,	All, all besides is toil and pain,
E tutto è servitù.	Where slav'ry drags the galling chain.

The beginning of Tito's vocal line and of Sarastro's air are brought into the same key and meter in order to facilitate comparison in Exx. 15.4 and 15.5. Tito starts his solo before the orchestra enters, which enhances his lonely eminence, while Sarastro is preceded by a short orchestral statement that encapsulates the whole piece (Ex. 15.4A–B). The opening melodic figures, falling gently from the fifth degree, then reversing direction, are similar. And in his continuation Mozart makes the music, and hence the characters, even more similar. Both passages start from a unison and gradually increase the number of voice parts in the texture, an opening outward that is like a flower coming into bloom (Ex. 15.5A–B). Tito, being a tenor, can reach up to the high F in answer to the protracted melodic sigh (B-flat to A) high in the violins, imitated a measure later in the basses. Sarastro, a bass, turns back on the D above middle C, but the violins two octaves above continue marching on up to the high F and then emit their sighing fall.

The exquisite contrapuntal writing in each piece is emblematic in its own way, like the development sections in the overtures of both operas. Counterpoint be-

EXAMPLE 15.4A–B.

A: *Clemenza di Tito*, No. 6
B: *Zauberflöte*, No. 15

A
Andante
TITO   1

Del più su – bli – me so – glio l'u–ni–co frut–to è que–sto

B
Larghetto
2   SARASTRO

In die – sen heil' – gen Hal – len kennt man die Ra – che nicht!

A: *Clemenza di Tito*, No. 6

B: *Zauberflöte*, No. 15

stows solemnity and wisdom on these worthy specimens of humanity. A heritage from ages past, it suits the ancient Roman and Egyptian venerability of the proceedings and seems to invoke the splendors of the Golden Age. The gilded wooden flute that Tamino plays is carved out of a thousand-year-old oak tree, and its Orphic feats are nothing short of a tribute to the wondrous powers of music.[31]

Mozart's last completed work, the Masonic Cantata in C (K. 623), shares many features with both operas of 1791, but more with *Tito*, as might be expected from the identity of key. It begins with a rousing three-voiced chorus for men in gavotte rhythm (Ex. 15.6) that resembles a passage in yet another opera—the toast to love proposed by the three men in the third number of *Così fan tutte* ("E che brindisi replicati far vogliamo al Dio d'Amor"). How could Mozart draw on so profane a passage when setting exalted sentiments appropriate to the consecration of a Masonic temple? They both involve men in the act of celebrating, and in Mozart's mind the jolly party envisaged by Don Alfonso at the end of his much-needed

31. On the kinship of *The Magic Flute* to the Orpheus myth, see Frederick W. Sternfeld, "Orpheus, Ovid and Opera," *Journal of the Royal Musical Association* 118 (1988): 172–202.

EXAMPLE 15.6. Eine kleine
Freimaurer–Kantate, K. 623

lesson to the two lovers must be closer to Masonic ideals than appears on the surface. "Let there be philosophy in all things" says Don Alfonso at one point (words that would not be strange from the lips of either Tito or Sarastro). Callow youths have to be put to the test and come to know themselves before they are worthy or capable of true love. In this light Alfonso's "experiment" is not so far from the hard testing of Tamino, and especially of Pamina, who is torn from her mother without knowing why and later experiences rejection by her beloved (or so she believes). Joseph Richter wrote an epitaph for the reforming emperor Joseph II in 1791 that helps explain what Alfonso and Sarastro were up to: kings are forced to do people harm, he reflected, so that good may emerge.[32]

A more precise parallel with imperial politics can be made as well. In 1784, Emperor Joseph had his nephew Francis taken from his parents at the tender age of sixteen and brought to Vienna so that he could be tutored by the sages of the imperial court in preparation for his future rule. Just so is Tamino the prince who will come to rule. Sarastro says outright to him: "If you will one day wish to rule as a wise monarch, may the gods accompany you further" ("Und wünschest du einst als ein weiser Fürst zu regieren, so mögen die Götter dich ferner begleiten"). As it happened, Emperor Leopold, to whom the lessons in magnanimity of *La clemenza di Tito* were directed, was succeeded by his son Francis after a reign of only two years. The troubled times confronting the Habsburg Empire were not such as to promote magnanimity. Most of the Josephinian reforms that had not been set aside by Leopold were dismantled by Francis, who closed down the Masonic lodges for good in 1794–95. Austrian Freemasonry then entered the period known as "hohe Mitternacht."

32. Paul D. Bernard, *Jesuits and Jacobins: Enlightenment and Despotism in Austria* (Urbana, Ill., 1971), p. 182.

16 · AT THE NORTH GATE: INSTRUMENTAL MUSIC IN *DIE ZAUBERFLÖTE*

by Thomas Bauman

From the very first, *The Magic Flute* has generated divergent and often contradictory traditions of interpretation. Early Austro-Germanic exegeses established several camps—the Masonic, the revolutionary, and the conservative—as Paul Nettl points out.[1] During the 1790s, Masons in northern Germany saw at once in the opera an allegory of the brotherhood's secrets. The director of the National Theater in Berlin, Johann Jakob Engel, who did not approve, intrigued to keep it off the royal stage there in 1792 despite the keen interest of the mystic and music-loving King Friedrich Wilhelm II.[2] Goethe, who did approve, produced the opera at Weimar, later began a sequel to it, and claimed that it took more education to praise the libretto than to condemn it.

The early decades of the nineteenth century saw the search for a key to the opera's meaning carried out in other quarters, and very often in the spirit of the contemporaneous roman à clef. In the Rhineland, which was at the time overrun with Jacobins, one writer could see a perfect cipher of the French Revolution; simultaneously, in Biedermeier Vienna, another divined a patriotic defense of the Holy Roman Empire. But no significant appeal to the music itself was made in elaborating these interpretations of the text's meaning. This holds true even for the quaint, latter-day attempt of Egon Komorzynski to foist on Schikaneder's libretto an allegory of the conflict between Italian and German opera in Vienna at the time when *The Magic Flute* was written.[3]

1. Paul Nettl, *Musik und Freumaurerei* (Esslingen, 1956); the essays relative to Mozart appeared in English translation as *Mozart and Masonry* (New York, 1970). Nettl builds on the work of the indefatigable Emil Karl Blümml, "Ausdeutungen der 'Zauberflöte,'" *Mozart-Jahrbuch* 1 (1923): 109–46.

2. Engel declared in a letter to the king that "the public, unacquainted with certain mysteries and unable to peer through the heavy, dark veil of allegory," could not possibly take any interest in the opera; see my *North German Opera in the Age of Goethe* (Cambridge, 1985), p. 264.

3. Egon Komorzynski, *Emanuel Schikaneder: Ein Beitrag zur Geschichte des deutschen Theaters* (Vienna, 1951), pp. 215–18. The cast is interpreted as follows: Papageno (Schikaneder himself), Pamina (German opera), the Queen of the Night (Italian opera), Tamino (the German musician—Mozart), Sarastro (Joseph II), and Monostatos (who else?—Salieri!).

Recent insights into the opera's possible meanings differ sharply from the early Austro-Germanic *Deutungen*. They come mostly from non-German writers, for one thing, and they prefer the psychological and philosophical to the social-political. In 1959, the British art historian Michael Levey offered a new view of Pamina, at least partly in response to the apparent misogyny in the opera and in much of the literature touching on her. "Not only is Pamina very different from . . . the rest of Mozart's female characters," he writes, "but she is a novel conception in operatic history and perhaps in eighteenth-century literature." She appears first as a normal operatic heroine, a passive creature destined as a prize for Tamino's heroics. But she sheds this role, inspired not by Tamino but by a more abstract, almost Platonic ideal of love as the agency of personal growth. Her fate, Levey remarks of her suicide scene, "far outweighs our interest in that of Tamino. From this point onwards Tamino ceases explicitly to be a character in his own right; his fate is merged with Pamina's."[4]

The idea of merged fates (later amplified to merged personalities, as we shall see shortly) figured little if at all in the Masonic study of Jacques Chailley a decade later.[5] His attempt to apply Masonic symbolism to every detail of the opera's structure led him to lay heavy stress on the antagonistic duality represented by the Queen of the Night and Sarastro, under which Tamino and Pamina are to be comprehended. Chailley even suggested that the duality's embodiment in the opera had more than a little to do with the antipathy of Vienna's male lodges toward their female counterpart, the so-called lodges of adoption.

Joscelyn Godwin took a broader view in a provocative article published in 1979, "Layers of Meaning in *The Magic Flute*." Godwin reads into the opera's story a historical allegory of esoteric organizations in general. Although he begins like earlier exegetes with an attempt to read *The Magic Flute* as historical allegory, he interprets the opera's possible relationship to esoteric cults from an inner, psychological perspective. Specifically, he applies the Jungian concept of the *animus* and the *anima* to Tamino and Pamina. From Tamino's standpoint, Pamina represents his soul or *anima*, in Jungian terms his own inward feminine qualities, lacking in his masculine conscious attitude. At the beginning of his spiritual journey, Tamino simply projects his *anima* onto Pamina (in the opera, we may recall, he falls in love not with Pamina herself but with her portrait). "Pamina's relationship with Tamino," Godwin states, "cannot be described by a simple reversal of terms," since her inward qualities are also feminine.[6] The *animus* she projects onto Tamino in-

4. Michael Levey, "Aspects of Mozart's Heroines," *Journal of the Warburg and Courtauld Institutes* 22 (1959): 132–56; the section on Pamina comprises pp. 132–43, with quotes here from pp. 133 and 140. For a particularly absurd specimen of male chauvinism on the subject of Pamina and Tamino, see Alfred Heuss, "Liebt—auf Grund der 'Zauberflöte'—die Frau oder der Mann tiefer und stärker?" *Zeitschrift für Musik* 92 (1925): 72–79.

5. Jacques Chailley, *"The Magic Flute": Masonic Opera*, trans. Herbert Weinstock (New York, 1972); originally published as *"La flûte enchantée," Opéra maçonnique* (Paris, 1968).

6. Joscelyn Godwin, "Layers of Meaning in *The Magic Flute*," *Musical Quarterly* 65 (1979): 471–92; quote p. 487.

vests her consciousness with a capacity for reflection and self-knowledge. In this interpretation, then, the opera's central love interest is seen principally in terms of relatedness, incompleteness, and interchange.

Following similar lines, Dorothy Koenigsberger has suggested "that all the main characters of *The Magic Flute* are also joint participants in one being, one psyche, or one soul," the major theme played out through this metaphor being "the human quest for self-perfection."[7] Leaning heavily on alchemical lore, she describes a rite of purification that takes place in stages within Sarastro's temple, which itself stands as the body of the one being.

Early interpretations had assumed that *The Magic Flute* lay under a cipher, and that the key to this cipher, once it was found, would unlock a single, unified meaning. Implicitly, they seem to share many of the assumptions underlying E. D. Hirsch's epistemological conception of valid interpretation as the explication of a verbal meaning that is reproducible, stable over time, and intended by the author (or in this case, authors).[8] Recent writers, in contrast (with the notable exception of Chailley), speak less of a single, determinate meaning and more of complexes or "layers" of meaning. Neither do they shrink from retrojecting Freudian and Jungian modes of thought onto the work. All this Hans-Georg Gadamer would probably find both heartwarming and deliciously ironic—heartwarming in that the work's critical *Rezeptionsgeschichte* appears as *Wirkungsgeschichte*, that is, as a series of mediated, co-determined meanings erected largely on earlier interpretations and contemporary prejudices; ironic in that *The Magic Flute* itself, as a child of the Enlightenment, came into being in an age that proclaimed open warfare on the prejudices Gadamer considers an indispensable condition of true understanding.[9]

It is significant, though not uncharacteristic, that the recent studies discussed above do not have much to say about the music of the opera.[10] Indeed, it is most curious. After all, *The Magic Flute* has flourished and fascinated because of the genius of Mozart's music, not the mythic power of Schikaneder's cobbled text. Whether one agrees or not with Gadamer that we cannot escape our own prejudices in the hermeneutic act of understanding, in the case of *The Magic Flute* the least we can do is test our interpretations against the part of the work that really counts.

What follows is a preliminary attempt at incorporating at least one portion of Mozart's music into recent interpretations of *The Magic Flute*, and in particular into ideas about Pamina and Tamino as co-equal, merged personalities. The role of

7. Dorothy Koenigsberger, "A New Metaphor for Mozart's *Magic Flute*," *European Studies Review* 5 (1975): 229–75; quote p. 231.

8. E. D. Hirsch, *Validity in Interpretation* (New Haven, Conn., 1967); see esp. chap. 2.

9. Hans-Georg Gadamer, *Wahrheit und Methode*, 4th ed. (Tübingen, 1975), 2.2.1; translated from the 2d edition as *Truth and Method* (London, 1975) by Garrett Barden and John Cumming.

10. Chailley offers a number-by-number analysis, but one single-mindedly limited to possible Masonic symbolism in the score.

instrumental utterance seems a propitious point of focus: it operates on all levels, from the slightest inflection within a number, to the opera's imposing overture; it also opens up a position outside the work's immediate verbal meanings, a new and essentially musical vantage point from which to assess the aesthetic relevance of those meanings—all of which seems useful in confronting an opera where appearance and reality are so clearly at issue.

As Mozart himself did, we shall leave the overture for last, and turn first to the role of the closing ritornello in *The Magic Flute*. Normally, this device acts as a convention, as a musical signal that a number has ended. When it serves in this way, nothing more than a perfunctory cadence or two is needed, or perhaps a repetition of the closing bars of the sung portion. To be sure, Mozart made use of these well-worn procedures here and there in *The Magic Flute*; but at other times in the opera he transforms this potentially mechanical routine into something much more artful.

Edward Cone, in his book *The Composer's Voice*, analyzes the interacting roles that voice and accompaniment play in solo vocal music, using the German Lied as his field of study.[11] The sophisticated relationship he describes derives ultimately from Mozart, and not from his Lieder but from his operas and concert arias. Here, the independence of the orchestral part was a primary reason early listeners tended to find Mozart's style overwrought and confusing. In his operas, the technique was little short of revolutionary, for it established a distinctive and wholly music-dramatic "persona" (to use Cone's word), a voice separate from the character's. Mozart's closing ritornellos in effect transfer responsibility for creating a sense of an ending from the text and its singer to this other voice. And the ritornello's last thoughts are almost always conceived in the spirit not of the number's autonomous musical workings, but of the dramatic situation in which it is fixed.

For a simple example, look at the end of Tamino's famous picture aria, "Dies Bildnis ist bezaubernd schön" (Ex. 16.1). By the normal standards of tonal-motivic analysis, this is run-of-the-mill work: the pitches are not particularly distinctive, nor are the harmonies they arpeggiate. But rhythmic and dynamic features are a different matter. Tamino has just sung five variations on "Und ewig wäre sie dann mein" ("And then would she be mine forever"). The underlying rhythm of these variations—an upbeat to a dotted eighth followed by three sixteenths—shapes the ritornello's cadence figure. With Tamino's fivefold closing utterance fresh in our ears, we hear his words as the "inner text" of the ritornello, as indicated above the

11. Edward Cone, *The Composer's Voice* (Berkeley and Los Angeles, 1974), esp. chap. 1 on Schubert's setting of Goethe's "Erlkönig."

EXAMPLE 16.1. *Zauberflöte*, No. 3

first violins in Ex. 16.1. Notice as well that the ritornello's pattern is stated first forte, then piano. The forte statement flushes with Tamino's joyous anticipation, but the piano one that follows offers a pensive afterthought that seems to hang hesitantly on the subjunctive *wäre*.

With these few strokes we have Tamino's whole character before us—not just the knight ready to dash off, half cocked, to rescue a damsel in distress, but a mind also given to reflection. (This is Mozart's creation, incidentally, for there is little if any depth to the hero as presented by Schikaneder.) Other closing ritornellos in act 1 tend toward similar expository goals with respect to characterization. In act 2, however, their function changes. Consider Sarastro's aria with the chorus of priests, "O Isis und Osiris." The closing ritornello (Ex. 16.2A) again suggests an "inner text" by echoing the closing bars sung by the chorus of priests, who themselves are echoing Sarastro's concluding prayer, "Nehmt sie in euren Wohnsitz auf" ("Take them into your dwelling-place"). But again Mozart has worked a subtle change: the ritornello takes up harmonies of the chorus's concluding statement but modifies the melodic cadence along the lines of one heard earlier, in the act 1 duet "Bei Männern welche Liebe fühlen" (Ex. 16.2B). We are now much further along in the opera, caught in an ever richer tapestry of associations; the linkage provided here by the orchestra's closing bars is no longer just to the immediate situation, but to a vital strand even deeper in the opera's fabric. In the immediate context of the aria, the ritornello speaks of the union of Tamino and his companion Papageno

EXAMPLE 16.2A–B.

A: *Zauberflöte*, No. 10

B: *Zauberflöte*, No. 7

with the gods should the trials end with their death; but we also hear in a broader context an appeal to the duet's aphoristic dictum, "Nichts edlers sei als Weib und Mann" ("Nothing is nobler than wife and husband"). It is not to the present, physical pair of Tamino and Papageno that the ritornello directs our attention, but to the ideal pair, Tamino and Pamina.

To think not of immediate appearances but of larger significance is the principal lesson both Tamino and Pamina must learn in the opera. And Mozart's music asks us to think in similar terms about the meaning of seemingly slight details when taken in a larger context. It is a long-recognized part of the opera's individual style that its score is strewn with musical interconnections of all kinds. Rather than worrying these interconnections into a single arcane reading, however, we should acknowledge the invitation they extend to multilayered interpretation—the same sort of interpretation the libretto has received in recent years.

Nowhere is the interplay of detail and larger context richer than in the four measures that close Pamina's g-minor aria in act 2. Bending to the strictures of his trials, Tamino has refused to speak to Pamina and, with a sigh, has motioned her away. The aria embodies her response, cast as a classical lament, in the minor mode and with a predominance of descending conjunct motion and affective chromatic inflections.

The closing orchestral ritornello, of surpassing expressive eloquence, differs from all other ritornellos in the opera, analogous to the way in which the sublime is distinguished from the beautiful. We have reached the crux of the opera's fundamental human relationship—a moment of deepest despair for Pamina, who sings, and for Tamino, who is bound to silence. As classical rhetoric had taught since the days of Longinus, and as Burke and Kant had stressed in the eighteenth century, the sublime defies conventional expectations. In various ways, earlier ritornellos had established what those expectations are. One thing they all share is reliance on a close *rhythmic* association with a key phrase in the foregoing number. Pamina's aria, however, appears to offer no such connection. Quite the opposite, in fact. After a breathless moment of silence, the ritornello abruptly abandons the aria's 6/8 heartbeat pattern for an entirely new one of far greater metric complexity (Ex. 16.3). The new pattern begins on the weak beat of m. 38 and continues out of metric joint until disrupted by a compression of activity at the Neapolitan in the middle of m. 40.

As so often happens in *The Magic Flute*, silence is used as expressively as the notes themselves. Silence is one of the virtues the Three Youths urge on Tamino, and a virtue that Mozart detected with pleasure in the opera's first audiences. After writing to Constanze of the most applauded numbers at an early performance, he added: "But what pleases me the most is the *silent applause*: one can see how much

EXAMPLE 16.3. *Zauberflöte*, No. 17

(Sieh Ta - mi - no   Ta - mi - no Ta - mi - no Ta - mi - no. . .)

this opera continues to grow."[12] Silence is a crucial ingredient in the opera—dramatically and musically. An important function of the silence following Pamina's last cadence is to distance the ritornello from its potential role as a simple echo of the aria's closing thought and enjoin deeper reflection on the moment. Further, it helps erase any lingering sense of metric continuity, so that the singular metric-rhythmic features of the ritornello strike us more forcefully.

Yet beneath all of this distancing, the closing ritornello is deeply indebted to the aria it concludes. The opening two measures trace the same descending octave outlined by Pamina's first words, "Ach, ich fühl's, es ist verschwunden" (Ex. 16.4). More important, the melodic motif employed here is a direct elaboration of her interjection "Sieh, Tamino!" from the passionate middle section of the aria. Harmonically, the ritornello falls by thirds through the descending D-to-D octave, I–VI–iv, as shown in Ex. 16.3. When the flutes, bassoons, and oboes enter, the dynamic level increases to forte, and a new set of falling thirds begins on B-flat, III–i–VI. At the end of this second set of thirds (on the fourth eighth-beat of m. 40), several things happen to break the ritornello's pattern. A second octave descent from D that began at the end of m. 39 breaks off; the dynamics shift back to piano; and the displaced metric pattern slips abruptly back into the regular 6/8 meter of the aria. Then, in place of the expected subdominant, a Neapolitan sixth

12. "— was mir aber am meisten freuet, ist, der *Stille beifall!* — man sieht recht wie sehr und immer mehr diese Oper steigt"; letter of 7–8 October 1791.

EXAMPLE 16.4. *Zauberflöte*, No. 17

chord produces sudden harmonic darkness at this moment of metric compression. Under this dark shadow, the "Tamino" motif disintegrates into the final linear descent to the tonic.

For whom does the orchestra speak in these moving final measures? The obvious answer would be Pamina. As in earlier ritornellos, this passage derives a psychological subtext from key verbal phrases in her aria. In this case, however, the process is far more thoroughgoing. Tamino's name seems to repeat itself obsessively in Pamina's mind, and through the octave descent (see Ex. 16.4) his name is linked with her aria's opening thoughts of lost happiness.

Or does the "inner text" sound instead in Tamino's mind? The moment of silence that separates this passage from the aria proper offers a stark manifestation of the excruciating vow of silence under which he suffers, and the cry that echoes in the ritornello—"Sieh, Tamino"—was after all addressed to him. There is a certain exquisite uncertainty about whether he, she, or both are laying claim to our sympathies in the aria's closing ritornello. We have seen how the lovers have been viewed in modern literary interpretations of *The Magic Flute* as merged entities, as joint participants in a single soul. Both come to understand some such higher reality in the course of the opera, and it is this reality that we can begin to hear in these despairing final measures. In a clear departure from convention, Pamina and Tamino never sing a love duet anywhere; rather, each acts as a silent partner in the single aria granted to the other by Mozart and Schikaneder. In his aria, Tamino accepted appearance for reality—Pamina's mute picture for herself—just as he soon after accepts the Queen's interpretation of events for the events themselves. Here in Pamina's aria, she too accepts appearance for reality—Tamino's silence and apparent indifference for a lack of love. In both arias the same key phrase covers the deception: "ich fühl's," Tamino had sung on gazing at her portrait; "Ach, ich fühl's," Pamina sings when greeted by his silence.

This silence torments both equally. Each is fighting the same battle for self-mastery, and each battle hangs in the balance at Pamina's last, despairing allusion to death, followed by a breathless moment of silence. In the closing ritornello Pamina's anguish becomes Tamino's own as he hears his name die with her last hopes in the final orchestral strains. The forte eruption in mm. 39 and 40 cries out briefly in protest, then resigns to the downward pull of the dark Neapolitan cadence. It is not hard to imagine the stage gestures that might accompany this music. As in the closing ritornello of Tamino's aria, where piano similarly follows forte (as illustrated above in Ex. 16.1), reflection now succeeds fervor, thought masters feeling.

The closing orchestral rumination is more than a last thought in this case: it is an afterthought, for Mozart's autograph indicates that he added these measures after completing both the outer voices and the filling-in of the aria proper. Perhaps he appended it out of frankly dramaturgical concern; Pamina must make a slow, disconsolate exit after she finishes singing, and without these final bars, applause from the audience might work utter ruin on this supreme moment. Here, if ever, the opera demands the "silent applause" of its audiences.

It is generally agreed that *Don Giovanni* is Mozart's greatest operatic achievement, indeed to most minds the "opera of all operas." But critical opinion has not extended an analogous honor to its overture. Among Mozart's mature operas, Nissen pointed instead to the overture to *The Magic Flute* as Mozart's greatest instrumental prologue and, more than that, as the "Ouverture aller Ouverturen."[13] Possibly a form of reverence for last utterances guided Nissen's choice. Written down on the eve of the inaugural performance of *The Magic Flute* in September 1791, the overture, together with the march of the priests from act 2, represents Mozart's farewell to the musical stage.

In writing out the overture last, Mozart was continuing a practice followed in all the other operas he composed after *The Abduction from the Seraglio*. German scholars in particular have sought to fashion from this fact a view of the Mozartian opera overture as the summary that is greater than its parts, as a distillation of the work's deepest meaning unfettered by dependent ties to word or action on the

---

13. Nissen, *Biographie W. A. Mozarts*, Anhang, p. 117.

stage. This view has a long history in German Romantic thought. In the early nineteenth century, the poet Wackenroder went so far as to propose that the overture to a theatrical work be played last, where the music's sublime accents could idealize the work's spiritual message after its imperfect visual-verbal rendering by the actors.[14]

A similar idealistic tone continues to suffuse modern musical discussions of the overture to *The Magic Flute*. For Hermann Abert—to take the most magisterial example—the counterpoint of the overture's Allegro symbolizes "the highest idea of the piece, the triumph of complete and noble humanity over the resistance of all antagonistic powers." And, lest this be taken too literally, he adds: "The overture betrays nothing at all of the following dramatic conflict itself." Instead, as the last piece of the opera written by Mozart, it is to be regarded as "a sort of lyric general confession of Mozart's on his whole inner relationship to his work. For one last time the artistic experience of the opera stormed through his soul; now, however, it is no longer *Die Zauberflöte* in its concrete form but *Zauberflötenstimmung* that inspires him to this piece."[15]

Abert was unable or unwilling to hear the overture's abstract musical argument in terms of the drama that so deeply informs the close of Pamina's aria. Do we need a dramatic context beyond the movement itself in order to interpret its meaning? The music does not seem to cry out for such a context, at least compared with many works from the century that followed. In fact, the overture to *The Magic Flute* is universally acknowledged to be a masterpiece of formal design, with a degree of coherence and unity unusual even by Mozartian standards.

The question, then, is not whether we *need* a dramatic context, but how we interpret the fact that we have one. Indeed, how do we reconcile the overture's formal perfection with the opera it introduces? To my knowledge, no one has ever called the story of *The Magic Flute* a masterpiece of design. Quite the contrary—the libretto has been generally regarded, in Dent's words, as "one of the most absurd specimens of that form of literature in which absurdity is regarded as a matter of course." Does the overture stand apart or, better, above all this? We know that throughout Mozart's creative life, his operatic overtures became more and more intimately related to the drama that each introduces. Yet why has it proved so difficult to draw more than the most general associations of mood (Abert's *Zauberflötenstimmung*) between the overture to *The Magic Flute* and the opera's rich store of symbolic meanings?

One way to go about answering this question is to consider the proposition that compelling formal coherence does not preclude a metaformal dimension to the overture's musical argument—indeed, that we experience this dimension precisely

14. Wilhelm Heinrich Wackenroder, *Phantasien über die Kunst für Freunde der Kunst*, ed. Ludwig Tieck (Hamburg, 1799); quoted from Wackenroder's *Werke und Briefe* (Heidelberg, 1967), p. 257.
15. Abert, *W. A. Mozart* 2:635.

in and through such coherence. The metaformal dimension distinguishes itself from the formal by thematizing phenomena and processes that contribute to formal clarity: the hierarchy of levels on which several of the overture's basic features can be perceived, for example, or the technique of interruption or delay. Formal analysis explains how the overture's argument is carried on in such musical terms; metaformal analysis explains how the argument is also *about* those terms and, on that basis, what analogies we might fruitfully and responsibly draw to the essential characteristics and processes we have isolated. We shall return to this problem after looking at some of these characteristics and processes.

When the principal theme bolts from the closing cadence of the overture's Adagio, the world of fugue with all its associations seems to rush in with it. Like every good fugue subject, this one was no doubt crafted with much care. In this respect its oft-cited resemblance to the main theme of a sonata written a decade earlier by Muzio Clementi can only be regarded as unfortunate, for it has branded the subject as little more than humble raw material, a stock in trade (Ex. 16.5A–B).

It is hard to make much out of Clementi's theme; Mozart's, in contrast, rouses the listener from comfortable habits immediately with its incessant sforzandi on the weak fourth beat of every measure. Abert shunted these crucial dynamic markings aside in phrasing the subject across each bar (Ex. 16.6). We must disagree. How can a sforzando *gruppetto* ending in a leading tone to tonic possibly be considered an upbeat to a piano dominant in the next measure? On the contrary, Mozart seems to have introduced the sforzando precisely to insulate the two pitches from each other, the tonic torqued into place with a conclusive blur of sixteenth notes at the end of the first measure, the dominant at the end of the next. These two primal degrees sound at the beginning of the subject as two distinct tonal poles.

In the third measure of the subject a pair of rising fourths carries forward the repeated-note pattern and weak-beat accentuation of the first two measures. Mozart reiterates this G–C–F–B♭ pattern in the fourth measure, as well he might. Its circle-of-fifths trajectory and linear longing for descent to the tonic broach major issues for the rest of the overture. For the present, this longing does not find fulfillment: other fugue subjects with which this one has been compared (shown in Ex. 16.7A–B) complete the expected sequential descent to the tonic. The subject of the overture to *The Magic Flute* does not.

After this initial statement in the second violins, the first violins reply with a tonal answer. Meanwhile, the seconds add to the metric conflict already brewing with a suspension figure that injects a new sforzando, this one on the second beat (Ex. 16.8). With the third entry, the subject drops to a lower register and aural attention shifts to an important counterpoint based on the descending scale that we shall for convenience call the countersubject.

EXAMPLE 16.5A–B.

A: *Zauberflöte*, Overture

B: Clementi: Piano Sonata in B-flat, Op. 41, No. 2

A

B

EXAMPLE 16.6. *Zauberflöte*, Overture, after Abert

EXAMPLE 16.7A–B.

A: Bach, *Das wohltempierte Klavier*, Book 2, Fugue 7

B: Mozart, Fantasy and Fugue in C, K. 394

To this point we have heard the subject in the tonic, then a tonal answer, then the subject once again in the tonic. With the entry of the fourth voice, however, Mozart quite exceptionally writes a *real* answer (Ex. 16.9). Why? In the four-voiced fugues with tonal answers in the *Well-tempered Clavier*, Bach never once resorted to such a pattern. If he did not choose to make the fourth entry a tonal answer, he opted instead for a restatement of the subject in the tonic. In the overture to *The*

EXAMPLE 16.8. *Zauberflöte*, Overture

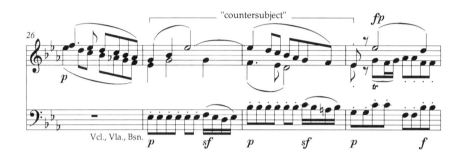

EXAMPLE 16.9. *Zauberflöte*, Overture

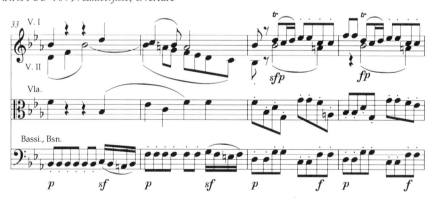

EXAMPLE 16.10. *Zauberflöte*, Overture

Magic Flute, however, both the slow introduction and the fugue subject itself force the issue of tonic-dominant polarity, and like other musical details throughout the opera, this polarity is projected onto an ever-broadening scale as the piece unfolds.

The very nature of a normative fugal exposition of course insures a higher-level expression of the stratification of I and V already embodied in the Allegro's subject. On an even larger plane, so does sonata form. But at this point, how do we know that what we are hearing *is* a sonata form? It is precisely Mozart's setting of the fourth entry as a real answer that first alerts us to the fact that not fugue but a higher level of harmonic polarity, that of eighteenth-century sonata form, will govern the overture's overall architecture. Mozart's real answer in the dominant sets up one of the trustiest patterns for anchoring the tonic in an Exposition's primary group—a dominant prolongation issuing in an assertive, forte restatement of the main theme. Six measures of dominant introduced by the fourth entry's real answer prepare for the return of both subject and countersubject at m. 39. But this restatement of the themes is not literal. The subject has shed its third and fourth bars—the ones with the anxious rising fourths—as well as its weak-beat sforzandi; this confident, triadic, metrically stable new version of the subject is now wedded to the countersubject at the octave in invertible counterpoint (Ex. 16.10).

How might these events, so beautifully integrated in their own right, be related to the opera that follows? The fugue subject, which grows into the vigorous, self-assured entity we just heard, first appeared in a different guise, disjunct, buffeted back and forth, and harried by weak-beat accents. The countersubject added several things lacking in the original manifestation of the subject: clear downbeats and purposive descending conjunct motion down to the tonic. The interaction of these musical ideas is tantamount to that of two complementary personalities. Let us resist the temptation to construe them as stand-ins for Tamino and Pamina (a blatant example of what Ludwig Finscher has called "vulgar hermeneutics") [16] and

---

16. Ludwig Finscher, "'Zwischen absoluter und Programmusik': Zur Interpretation der deutschen romantischen Symphonie," in *Über Symphonien: Beiträge zu einer musikalischen Gattung* (Tutzing, 1979), p. 108. Finscher distinguishes the "Vulgarhermeneutik der Konzertführer" from his own interpretive concept of "transmusikalische Inhalt." But "transmusical content" must equally be distinguished from the metaformal, but still essentially musical, dimension we have spoken of here.

instead consider the subject and countersubject in their own right as an ideal *musical* couple, having analogies to the world of the opera, but of a metaphorical rather than allegorical nature.

It appears that at one time Mozart thought of connecting the overture's principal theme directly with Tamino. He had originally planned a different overture for the opera, which he later rejected (K. Anh. 102; see Ex. 15.3 above); its theme shows unmistakable affinities with Tamino's picture aria and virtually none with the final overture as we know it. The autograph of this passage has disappeared from the Mozarteum in Salzburg, but its continuation is preserved on an autograph leaf at Berlin. The paper on which it is written was not used by Mozart before he had returned from Prague in September of 1791.[17] Until quite late in the compositional process, then, he appears to have had a very different plan for the overture in mind, one involving a direct link to Tamino and the central love interest.

Such a connection was by no means unprecedented. In his earlier German opera, *The Abduction*, Mozart had linked the overture to the opera's hero in no uncertain terms, quoting Belmonte's opening arietta in the minor mode as the central section of the opera's overture. Why did he not pursue his initial idea of linking the overture to *The Magic Flute* with Tamino? Can it possibly be that Mozart opted in the end for what Abert perceived—an overture that "betrays nothing at all of the following dramatic conflict itself"?

We might notice that these musical personalities are not presented to us as separate entities—as, say, the contrasting themes of the Exposition's two key areas—but in almost continuous counterpoint with each other. Godwin's application of the Jungian *anima* and *animus* and Levey's efforts to promote the significance of Pamina and her trials as at the very least commensurate with Tamino's seem analogous here to the musical principles underlying the overture's thematics. Perhaps in abandoning his earlier idea for the overture and its obvious affinities with Tamino's aria, Mozart was looking beyond the male protagonist to a deeper level, to a musical narrative of contrapuntally conjoined personalities who are developed and reshaped by their common experiences.

The Magic Flute wears its didactic heart on its sleeve. It is not a love story but rather a parable about love and its role in the human quest for self-betterment. One of the opera's key musical numbers states its motto: "Mann und Weib und Weib und Mann / reichen an die Gottheit an" ("Husband and wife, and wife and husband, reach toward the divine"). The interchange of nouns is not to be overlooked. It is linguistic testimony to the reciprocal relationship of the ideal pair. The aphorism, we may notice, is not uttered for the sake of the couple who sing it—Pamina and Papageno—for they come from different spheres and pursue different paths. It celebrates instead the principle of growth in mutuality, the same principle that underlies the opera's overture.

17. Tyson, *Mozart: Studies of the Autograph Scores*, p. 341n23.

EXAMPLE 16.11. *Zauberflöte*, Overture

In the opera this principle is tested through the instrument of trials. Virtually every model of personal growth from Freemasonry to Freud acknowledges the need for impediments which, once overcome, lead to a higher plane of consciousness or fulfillment. In the overture, the first hint of any obstacle comes at the end of the transition section. Normally Mozart allowed for a rhetorical pause on V of V here, followed by the second group. Instead he has interpolated a six-bar sequence (Ex. 16.11). While these six measures could conceivably have been omitted with no lapse in musical logic, without them the secondary theme would lose a significant degree of musical meaning. For this six-bar sequence interjects a tentative, quizzical dialogue between the two principal motives. The subject has lost its anxious sforzandi and has gained a sense of direction: it is now clearly phrased across the bar. The countersubject undergoes a contrary transformation, now inverted and chromatic instead of descending and diatonic.

Owing to the interpolated sequence, the dominant comes into focus only by degrees. And these degrees have a familiar ring. The harmonic motion of the sequence brings back the pitch relations of the subject's restless third and fourth bars: G to C, F to B-flat, followed by a IV–V–I cadence in the new key. We noticed earlier how the subject had shed these fourths when wedded to the countersubject at the octave. Yet although these two bars of rising fourths never appear again as part of the subject, they do not disappear from the overture. Rather, they take on an antagonistic role as the harmonic underpinning of progressively broader and darker sequential passages, beginning with this six-bar interpolation.

Another kind of interpolation, more admonitory in character than these six bars, occurs after the double bar with the ceremonial intonation of the Threefold Chord. This represents the one direct quotation of musical material from the opera itself. The Threefold Chord—three groups of three forte bursts of a B-flat–major triad scored for winds and brass—was a last-minute addition to the opera, written down on a separate leaf and inserted into the score near the beginning of act 2, where it announces the start of the trials. It occupies the same position and the same key in the overture, where it performs an analogous function with respect to the subject and countersubject. Their trials begin in earnest with the Development. It is organized thematically and harmonically as shown in Table 9.

Mozart normally favored an unsegmented plan for his Development sections. Here, however, he divided it with a measure-long rhetorical pause in m. 127 that cuts short an anticipated cadence in g minor. Like a parabola, this dark Development, cast almost entirely in the minor mode, moves from b-flat minor to g minor, then back again to B-flat major. The rhetorical pause acts as the vertex of the parabola: it is approached through a broad forte sequence that carries an intense canon through the entire gamut of g minor, a canon in which the subject struggles against itself.

At the beginning of the canon we again encounter the pitch collection of the main theme's rising fourths (g–c–F–B♭). Already directly implicated in moments of anxiety and obstruction in the overture, it returns here at the movement's darkest moment. The canon's circle back to g minor is forestalled at the vertex of our metaphorical parabola by the bar of silence. Among the overture's many interruptions, this is the profoundest of them all. As we saw earlier, silence stands at the midpoint of the trials of Tamino and Pamina, as the ultimate test of the bonds uniting them. Here too in the overture's drama, silence is made to represent its point of furthest remove, both harmonically and expressively.

The second half of the Development reacts to the silence with another circle of fifths. The most troubled forms of the principal motifs appear in this half of the Development. The subject redoubles its off-beat sforzandi in a pungent diminished-octave cross-relation; the countersubject, now disconnected from the subject, seems to lose its bearings as it wanders up and down, looking for a way out of each successive dominant seventh. This sixteen-bar passage following the bar of silence invokes for the last time the same four pitches that began the canon, G–C–F–B♭, now on the grandest scale of all.

By progressive expansion this small motivic feature from the subject has been projected onto ever larger fields. And by extension, the anxiety and lack of fulfill-

T A B L E 9.
Thematic-harmonic Scheme
of the Development, Overture to *The Magic Flute*

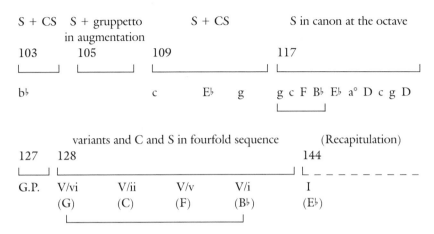

S + CS	S + gruppetto in augmentation		S + CS			S in canon at the octave								
103	105		109			117								
b♭			c	E♭	g	g	c	F	B♭	E♭	a°	D	c	g D

	variants and C and S in fourfold sequence				(Recapitulation)
127	128				144
G.P.	V/vi (G)	V/ii (C)	V/v (F)	V/i (B♭)	I (E♭)

ment these fourths represented in the subject have expanded to large-scale instability. Now, however, the inability of these fourths to descend to E-flat is at last overcome. It is, in the end, the recovery of the countersubject's diatonic bearings and its descent along the tonic major scale that leads to the quiet victory of the Recapitulation.

Although the tortuous path followed by the Development section might seem to suggest labyrinthine disorder, it is actually among the most carefully planned in all of Mozart's works, hence the geometric metaphor of the parabola. The symmetry, as shown in Table 10, extends beyond the plunge deep to the flat side, the rise to the canon and pause in g minor, and the return to the threshold of e-flat minor. There is also the aural pattern created by the insistent repeated notes of the subject's first bars. In the first half of the Development, the subject moves through

T A B L E 10.
Key Scheme of the Development,
Overture to *The Magic Flute*

Bar:	103	109	117		127	128	132	136	140
Flats: 2	(B♭)			g (canon) PAUSE					
3		c				V$_7$/c			(E♭)
4							V$_7$/f		
5	b♭							V$_7$/b♭	
6									V$_7$/e♭
Reciting note of subject:	B♭–F	C–G				G	C	F	B♭

a retrograde of the four-note pitch collection G–C–F–B♭, and then in the second half through the same collection in their proper order. The modal shift from B-flat major to b-flat minor at the start is similarly mirrored by a leap from an expected e-flat minor to E-flat major at the end of the Development.

Symmetrical planning around a central focus in music, because it unfolds in time to the ear rather than appearing, as here, synoptically to the eye, is dynamic rather than static, Euripidean rather than Euclidian. An especially powerful example in late Mozart appears toward the close of *La clemenza di Tito* with Vitellia's recitative and rondo (Table II). The recitative, "Ecco il punto, o Vitellia," is a profound self-examination that begins in D, then moves through a series of questions about her conduct leveled by Vitellia at herself, falling remorselessly to ever darker tonal regions, until at b-flat minor she realizes the futility of her position: "Ah! mi vedrei sempre Sesto d'intorno" ("Ah! I would find myself always near Sesto").

The pattern thus begun informs every subsequent element under its curve. Vitellia pauses on the climb from b-flat at F major for her great rondo, "Non più di fiori," the basset horn weaving poignant garlands as she sings of wedding hopes now vanished, and even the Allegro beginning with a dark turn to f minor and A-flat major. But most astonishing in its power and grandeur is the arrival of the G-major chorus "Che del ciel, che degli Dei," the greatest compliment ever paid to the aspirations of Metastasian opera to idealize the worth and dignity of those who hold temporal power. Poised at the end of this broad tonal trajectory, the chorus and the sovereign it celebrates assume a far-reaching scope of vision that extends back over the preceding darkness, as if the whole course of Vitellia's agonized self-searching lay already within Tito's ken—a benign omniscience that in *The Magic Flute* is invested in Sarastro.

Less directly, one feels something of the same omniscience in the overtures to both operas. Each is a masterpiece of instrumental design and expression yet at the same time deeply implicated in the central conflicts of the opera it introduces. Chapter 18 discusses how intimately the overture to *La clemenza di Tito* is related to the music of the entire opera. *The Magic Flute*, in contrast, makes a different claim of kinship. As befits the character of the opera itself, the affinities appear deeper and more mysterious.

Walter Wiora, in his classic essay "Between Absolute and Program Music," has observed that "an opera overture partakes of the basic mood, the atmosphere, the overall qualities . . . of the opera, and possesses corresponding functional and characteristic traits. But if such a piece is performed as an independent instrumental work, then these traits recede into the background, if they do not disappear altogether."[18] In light of our discussion, this last statement needs a gentle correction: it is not the functional and characteristic traits themselves that recede or disappear,

18. Walter Wiora, "Zwischen absoluter und Programmusik," in *Festschrift Friedrich Blume zum 70. Geburtstag*, ed. Anna Amalie Abert and Wilhelm Pfannkuch (Kassel, 1963), p. 383.

TABLE 11.
Key Scheme of Vitellia's Final
Recitative and Rondo in *La clemenza di Tito*

Flats:	*Recitative*										*Rondo (trans.)*					*Chorus*
−2	D														D	
−1		G													G	G
0			a											C		
1				F–d									F			
2					Bb							Bb				
3						c					c–Eb					
4							Ab		f							
5								bb								

but their correspondence with analogous traits in the opera itself. The meanings that arise in experiencing this overture, or any piece of music, do not inhere in the notes themselves, but depend on the context in which we apprehend them.

For an overture, of course, that context is the way it relates to the opera being introduced. The initial plot of *The Magic Flute*, one of the most popular of its day, is the romance of quest and rescue. This plot, however, is supplanted by another, higher one. In the act 1 finale, Tamino swerves from the knightly mission so familiar to audiences at Schikaneder's Theater auf der Wieden and embraces a different quest: the topos of trials and initiation replaces the topos of crusade and rescue. In the process, the inherent inequality and stereotyping of the sexes that the rescue topos perpetuates are superseded by a new order.

The overture too begins with one apparent plot and turns to another. The slow introduction and fugal exposition speak of an old order of harmonic and thematic organization and discourse; but that order yields to sonata form with its higher modes of organization. They are higher, I think, because they do not banish those of the old order but subsume and redirect their energies. It bespeaks a higher mode as well that overt musical correspondences with the opera itself are all but absent from the overture; in that way, its musical discourse adumbrates the spirit of the work less directly but more fully: it speaks in parables. Prior to the lifting of the curtain we in the opera house, like Tamino at the start of act 2, stand at the North Gate of the kingdom, and the overture begins our musical initiation into the mysteries of the opera that follows.

17 · MOZART AND HIS ITALIAN CONTEMPORARIES

*M*ozart's *La clemenza di Tito* is often dismissed with the summary remark that it is a mere opera seria, the implication being that the genre per se rendered the work unworthy and moribund—beyond rescue even by Mozart. Such remarks are made in the bliss of ignorance. Truth is, the serious operas of the Neapolitan school between Vinci and Paisiello remain the greatest unknown field of eighteenth-century studies. So uncharted is this realm, even the very nomenclature remains nebulous. The designation *opera seria* was not common at the time, and neither was *opera buffa*, although both terms occur in the correspondence of the Mozart family.

The two qualifying designations referred less to genres than to types of singers. Thus in the Goldoni librettos of ca. 1750 there are often "parti buffe" and "parti serie." The arrival of a troupe of "buffoni" at Paris in 1752 and the works they played (such as Pergolesi's intermezzo *La serva padrona*) gave rise to the celebrated "Querelle des Bouffons," as a result of which the expression *opéra bouffe* became common in French. Rousseau, in his *Confessions*, speaks of the "opere buffe" he saw when in Italy, using the proper Italian plural form. In his *Traité du melo-drame* (Paris, 1772), Laurent Garcins contrasted "opéras bouffes" with "opéras serieux" as Italian genres. Yet Planelli's *Dell'opera in musica*, printed the same year at Naples, contains no reference to "seria" and "buffa" types of opera. The most influential writer on opera at the time, Algarotti, refers in his *Saggio sopra l'opera in musica* (Venice, 1755) to "opere buffe" and "opere serie" but in a context of the disputes in the early 1750s.

Did the traditional distinction that everyone accepts without question actually get started in French criticism? It probably did. In Italy the comic genre was called "operetta," "bernesca," "burletta," "ridicola," and a few other names, but rarely

Reprinted from "Mozart and His Italian Contemporaries: 'La clemenza di Tito,'" *Mozart-Jahrbuch 1978/79*.

"buffa." Gianmaria Ortes, in his *Riflessioni sopra i drammi per musica* (Venice, 1757), contrasted the comic and serious genres by using the terms *serio* and *burlette*. In a letter to the court of Lisbon in 1769, Jommelli promised to supply annually "un' opera Seria, ed un' altra grottesca." The same year, at Vienna, Gassmann brought out his comic parody called *L'opera seria*, a name that suggests the term had become common by this time, at least outside Italy.

By 1783 Arteaga, who that year published the first volume of his *Le rivoluzioni del teatro musicale italiano dalle sue origini fino al presente*, accepted the terms *seria* and *buffa*, but he broadens and weakens their significance by including under the former everything from the Florentine Camerata on and under the latter whatever is mainly comic, starting with madrigal comedies. For him, the serious genre reached its height with Metastasio and his composers, the comic one with Goldoni and his composers. I propose that we accept these two paragons among poets as a way to define what we mean by opera seria and opera buffa. So defined, opera seria betokens the kind of serious drama in Italian built up around exit arias, a type that Metastasio perfected in the 1720s. It flourished with undiminished vigor right up to the end of the century, and lasted even beyond. In the case of *La clemenza di Tito*, we are fortunate to have Mozart's own description of the work in his catalog: "Opera seria . . . ridotta a vera opera dal Signor Mazzolà." So it is at once an opera seria and more than one, because of the revisions introduced by the librettist.

La clemenza di Tito, like most of Metastasio's dramas, attracted dozens of settings. It was not set so often as his *Artaserse* or *Olimpiade*, yet some forty different composers took it up in one form or another between Caldara's original setting in 1734 and Arena's in 1839. No composer after Caldara ever composed the libretto exactly as the poet wrote it, that is, with its twenty-five arias and thousands of lines of recitative. When Hasse set it for Verona in 1738 he substituted several aria texts, specifically to achieve more metric variety than Metastasio offered. Hasse made at least three additional settings, in which he went back to some of the original arias while making substantial cuts in the recitatives.[1]

Cutting back the number of arias is a gradual process that can be observed in this and other Metastasian dramas throughout the century. Gluck at Naples in 1752 reduced the arias to twenty-three by diminishing the part of the seconda donna, Servilia.[2] He also eliminated the choruses in acts 1 and 3 because the San Carlo at that time did not provide choristers (the simple *coro* at the end, sung by the soloists, remained). Furthermore, he set a dialogue that was somewhat emasculated, palliating the cruelty and cunning of the prima donna, Vitellia—as if the original character conceived by the poet were too strong for courtly sensibilities at

---

1. Fredrick Millner, "The Operas of Johann Adolph Hasse," Ph.D. diss., University of California, Berkeley, 1976, pp. 241ff.
2. William Weichlein, "A Comprehensive Study of Five Musical Settings of *La clemenza di Tito*," Ph.D. diss., University of Michigan, 1957, pp. 88–89. See also Helga Lühning, *Titus-Vertonungen im 18. Jahrhundert: Untersuchungen zur Tradition der Opera seria von Hasse bis Mozart* (Regensburg, 1983).

Naples. Such changes were treated like a matter of state in the Kingdom of the Two Sicilies, as we know from the case in 1760 where the tenor Raaff wished to substitute a final aria by Domenico Alberti in Jommelli's *Attilio Regolo*, a request that went to the impresario, to the prime minister, and finally to the king, and back.[3] When Jommelli set *Tito* for Stuttgart the following year, the arias were reduced in number to eighteen, with cuts in all roles. By the time of Anfossi's setting for Rome in 1769 the arias numbered only seventeen, and they were further cut by Holzbauer at Mannheim in 1780.

Thus, a long trend is at work providing the precedent by which Mozart and Mazzolà reduced the arias to only eleven. Massive rewriting and substitution was the rule, not the exception, with this libretto. The local poet was called on, though rarely named (out of deference to Metastasio), to adjust and "tailor" the roles to the singers at hand, to the occasion, and perhaps lastly to the composer. At Turin in 1760, for example, the court poet Vittorio Cigna provided four substitute arias, including three for the part of Vitellia, sung by Caterina Gabrielli; it may be suspected that her wishes were being served by the alterations as much as or more than those of the composer, who was Galuppi.[4] For this same production Fabrizio Galliari made stunningly beautiful set designs in the early neoclassical style (Fig. 33).

The revisions of Metastasio's librettos made in the theater would provide material for several volumes. Few composers came close to setting the poet's every word. The elderly Hasse was the most faithful (but the young Hasse had been willing to set hastily and poorly contrived revisions). Jommelli was also devoted to the poet and complained only that he did not supply enough new works. He complained also when other composers set mangled versions of the original, as occurred with the setting of the *Adriano in Siria* by Carlo Monza that he witnessed at Naples in 1769, of which he wrote: "The drama has been despoiled and adorned not in heroic but in Harlequin's dress—blunders that would be avoided even by a born goatherd."[5] As the operas traveled from town to town, they gathered more accretions and ever more complicated relationships to the original.

Through all the cuts and substitutions, Metastasio's original dramas generally remained a source of strength for composers. This is the case in Mozart's setting of *La clemenza di Tito*. Aside from being well made and mellifluous in language, as always with Metastasio, *La clemenza di Tito* had the advantage of a fascinating

3. Ulisse Prota-Giurleo, "Alcuni musicisti d'oltralpe a Napoli," *Analecta musicologica* 2 (1965): 136–37.

4. Turin was one place that liked its operas on the long side, apparently. Galuppi wrote twenty-five numbers, including the overture. As late as 1798, when Ottani set the libretto anew for the same court, Metastasio's original remained substantially intact; a concession to modern taste was made by turning the confrontation between Titus and Sextus in act 3 into a duet.

5. Original letter in the Music Library of the University of California, Berkeley. This and many other unpublished letters of Jommelli are edited and translated in Marita Petzoldt McClymonds, "Niccolò Jommelli: The Last Years," Ph.D. diss., University of California, Berkeley, 1978. The passage in question is quoted on p. 625A.

FIGURE 33

F. Galliari: Stage designs for act 1
of *La clemenza di Tito*

character in Vitellia, who makes up in hauteur and sheer hubris what she lacks in nobility and sentiment. No wonder that her partner, Sesto, bends to her headstrong lead. *La clemenza di Tito* is dominated by the prima donna from beginning to end. She sings first at the opening, setting the action in motion; she has the first aria in act 1, as well as the last, which Metastasio preceded with an impressive monologue—"Aspetta. (Oh dei!)"—set by most composers after Caldara as an elaborately accompanied orchestral recitative. Mazzolà transforms this scene into a terzetto using the same words—or rather, into a solo aria for Vitellia, with occasional vocal accompaniment from Annio and Publio, who between them have exactly one line of text, expressing befuddlement at her erratic behavior ("Oh come un gran contento confonde un cor").

Metastasio also gave Vitellia the last aria both in his act 2 and in act 3—that is to say, the last aria in the opera, which had to be the musical climax of the work, and certainly is with Mozart. After her aria there is nothing left but the ultimate clemency of Tito, hardly unexpected and therefore somewhat less than dramatically overpowering. It is Vitellia, finally, who confesses all, managing thus to dominate

FIGURE 34

J.-A. Martin: The encounter of
Tito and Sesto in act 3 of
La clemenza di Tito

even the pardon scene. Sesto, by contrast, is more sympathetic by virtue of his
long-suffering abuse at her hands. He is not strong in dramatic terms even by the
standards of Metastasio's often vacillating heroes. He leaves the stage twice without
an aria, a distinct oddity for a primo uomo. His biggest dramatic scene is the head-
to-head meeting with Tito, whom he has attempted to assassinate at Vitellia's instigation. Mozart relegated the confrontation to simple recitative, the way Metastasio intended. In the sumptuous Paris edition of the poet's works (1780–82), this
very scene, which Voltaire had praised, was singled out for illustration (Fig. 34).

The addition of ensembles, for which Metastasio characteristically made no provision, goes back to the beginning of the libretto's history. When setting *Tito* for London in 1737, Veracini composed two ensembles. For Verona the following year, Hasse placed a terzetto for Vitellia, Servilia, and Annio in place of the big solo scene for Vitellia in the last act. Ensembles found less favor in Italy, with the exception of love duets, than they did in the outposts of Italian opera like London and Vienna.[6] This situation did not change very much until toward the end of the century, when more and more operatic fashions from the outposts and from French opera began to flow into Italy.

Mozart's last decade in Vienna was a constant struggle for domination in the world of opera. In the first part of the decade, before the German troupe disbanded in 1783, it was opéra-comique sung in translation that most pleased the audiences at the Burgtheater, to judge from the number of performances. Thereafter the most-performed operas were by Italians like Paisiello, Cimarosa, Guglielmi, Anfossi, Sarti, and Salieri, and the Italian-trained Martín.[7] Mozart missed none of the comedies of his Italian contemporaries, nor did he fail to take stock, season by season, of what novelties and fashions most pleased the Viennese. Chapter 8 above shows how he profited from Paisiello, whose *Barbiere di Siviglia* became the delight of audiences at the Burgtheater in 1783–84. Paisiello himself stopped in Vienna in mid-1784, as we have seen, and set Casti's *Il Rè Teodoro in Venezia* for the Burgtheater. His subsequent career as *maestro di cappella* at Naples will occupy us next, to provide some idea of the typical operatic climate during the years from 1785 to 1790. For Vienna was not typical.

On his triumphal return to Naples, Paisiello first showed himself to the public with Metastasio's *Antigono*, given at the San Carlo for the Carnival season of 1785. Later the same year he brought out Palomba's comedy *La grotta di Trofonio* at the smaller Teatro dei Fiorentini, which specialized in comic operas. In 1786 he set Metastasio's *Olimpiade* for the San Carlo during Carnival and a comedy, *Le gare generose* (by Palomba), for the Fiorentini. In 1787 he set Gamerra's serious libretto *Pirro* for the San Carlo and Lorenzi's comedy *La modista* for the Fiorentini. In 1788 Salvioni's serious libretto *Fedra* provided the Carnival opera for the San Carlo, and Palomba's *L'amor contrasto, ossia La molinara*, a comedy, was played at the Fiorentini. In 1789 he set Metastasio's *Catone in Utica* for Carnival at the San Carlo and *I zingari in fiera* by Palomba at the Teatro del Fondo, another of the smaller theaters at Naples. For the summer palace at Caserta this same year he set a pastoral opera that Carpani and Lorenzi arranged after a French libretto by Marsollier for

6. The most telling example of this difference is found in Galuppi's *Artaserse*. As written for Vienna in 1748 the first act ends with a great dramatic quartet, the text of which is made by collapsing several arias and recitatives; as revived in Padua in 1751 the quartet gave way and the singers reclaimed their arias. For more detail, see Daniel Heartz, "Hasse, Galuppi, and Metastasio," in *Venezia e il melodramma nel settecento*, ed. Maria Teresa Muraro (Venice, 1978), 1:309–40.
7. See Table 1 in Michael F. Robinson, "Mozart and the Opera buffa Tradition," in Tim Carter, *W. A. Mozart: "Le nozze di Figaro,"* Cambridge Opera Handbooks (Cambridge, 1987), p. 12.

Dalayrac, *Nina, ossia La pazza per amore*. In 1790 he set Sertor's *Zenobia in Palmira* for the San Carlo and Lorenzi's comedy *Le vane gelosie* for the Fiorentini.

We could go on year by year through the 1790s, but the pattern remains the same: serious operas for the big theater, comic ones for the smaller houses. It is the same with Paisiello's chief rivals in Naples at this time, Guglielmi and Cimarosa, and with Sarti, who worked at Milan and Venice before he left for Russia to replace Paisiello. Indeed, it is the same all over Europe where Italian opera flourished, whether at London or St. Petersburg, at Dresden, Munich, or Berlin—everywhere, that is, except Vienna, where Joseph II refused to pay the high wages exacted by seria singers. Since music historians have tended to see everything, even opera, in the prism of Vienna, they believed that opera seria, being absent there, was out of fashion everywhere.[8] How do they then imagine that serious opera passed from the hands of Cimarosa and Paisiello to the young Italian composers coming to the fore around 1800? At issue partly is a blind spot in Mozart scholarship. We have presumed that Mozart by age twenty-five or so was immune to further outside "influences," at least in the field of opera. This presumed immunity has been taken as a license by scholars, exempting them from paying much attention to his Italian contemporaries in the 1780s.

Sarti's *Giulio Sabino* offers a convenient point with which to begin an assessment of Italian opera seria in the 1780s. It was written for the San Benedetto at Venice in 1781. This theater, like the San Giovanni Grisostomo before it and the Fenice after it, was the large house for serious operas and the greatest voices, while comic operas played at the several smaller theaters. Unlike most Italian operas, *Giulio Sabino* was printed in full score (not at Venice, but at Vienna).[9] There are six characters: the hero Sabino (a role created for the castrato Pacchiarotti), who is in hiding on account of former offenses against the emperor Tito's son, who loves Epponina, not knowing she is the wife of Sabino; the three secondary characters only complicate the central drama and stretch it out to the requisite length. Each singer receives one aria apiece in both acts 1 and 2, but in the last act only the three principals sing arias, accounting for fifteen arias in all. There are no choruses, and ensembles are restricted to a duet at the end of act 1, a terzetto at the end of act 2, and the traditional *coro* sung by the soloists to end the opera. Tonally, the keys are restricted to very few, never passing beyond three accidentals. There is some evidence of broad tonal planning. It emerges especially in the role assigned to A major, which sounds directly after the overture in C major, and again for the most expressive piece in the opera, the rondo sung by Sabino prior to the concluding *coro* in C major. Thus the tonal relationship of a minor third is emphasized.

8. Henry Raynor offers a perverse switch on the usual misinformation in his *Social History of Music* (London, 1972), p. 292: "The German and Austrian courts kept opera seria . . . alive long after the Italian opera houses, in which opera seria grew up, had left the form to die."

9. See John A. Rice, "Sarti's *Giulio Sabino*, Haydn's *Armida*, and the Arrival of Opera seria at Esterháza," *Haydn Yearbook* 15 (1984): 181–98.

Most of the arias are in binary form, and some are so short that they provide a marked contrast with the very long ones, just as in Mozart's *La clemenza di Tito*. Multitempo arias occur several times in *Giulio Sabino*; they progress from slow to fast, giving an overall stringendo effect that is the direct ancestor of the nineteenth-century cantabile-cabaletta combinations. The final rondo is marked Largo-Allegro-Presto. Only the prima donna and the primo uomo are allowed to sing rondos, a type of piece that had quite clearly become the favorite showpiece of Italian opera. Manfredini, in his *Difesa della musica moderna* (1785), gives an apt definition of the sentimental rondo in two tempos: "Those arias resembling in part the rondo are not all true rondos, but sublime and grand airs containing two motives or subjects, one slow, the other spirited, each stated only twice, which arias are certainly better than what used to be called an aria cantabile, because they are more natural, more true, and more expressive."[10]

By saving the hero's big rondo for the penultimate scene of *Giulio Sabino*, Sarti made it the dramatic and musical high point of the work, just as is Vitellia's "Non più di fiori" in Mozart's *La clemenza di Tito*. Sarti leads up to his piece by having the hero conducted to his death by the strains of a richly scored "Marcia lugubre" in c minor.[11] In the following obbligato recitative, fragments of the march break in on Sabino's monologue, a distortion that prefigures the ending of the Marcia funebre of the "Eroica" Symphony. With tension raised to a very high point, the tender and slow strains of the rondo in A commence, with wonderfully poignant effects. After the two statements of the Largo theme, the Allegro ensues, its theme also repeated. Then comes what must have been a surprise to everyone in the opera house: Epponia bursts in and turns the same piece into a short duet, Presto, as she tries to join her husband in death. The inevitable clemency of Tito then saves the day and allows the opera to come to a happy end, as most critics, if not all, preferred at the time.

The sentimental rondo in two tempos became the most prominent feature in Italian opera during the 1780s. Mozart himself took up the aria type in his operas only after *Idomeneo*. While the first version of that masterwork had no such piece, he took pains to include one for the performance at Vienna in 1786, as we have seen in Chapter 3. This was not the only two-tempo rondo during the year of *Le nozze di Figaro*. *Der Schauspieldirektor* received one; the garden aria of Susanna, "Deh vieni, non tardar," was first sketched as a rondo of the type, in E-flat, on the text

10. "Non tutte quelle Arie somiglianti in parte ai Rondò, son veri Rondò; ma son Arie grandi, e sublimi, che contengono due motivi, o soggetti, uno lento, e l'altro spiritoso, replicato due volte solamente, le quali Arie sono certamente migliori delle così dette Arie cantabili antiche, perché più naturali, più vere, e più espressive"; on the relationship between the grand two-tempo vocal rondo of the 1780s and the old ritornello rondo characteristic of the previous two decades, see Helga Lühning, "Die Rondo-Arie im späten 18. Jahrhundert: Dramatische Gehalt und musikalischer Bau," *Hamburger Jahrbuch für Musikwissenschaft* 5 (1981): 219–46.

11. Ernst Bücken, *Der heroische Stil in der Oper* (Leipzig, 1924), gives the funeral march in excerpt, pp. 56–57 and 33.

"Non tardar amato bene" (see Ex. 8.15). Belmonte's "Wenn der Freude Tränen fliessen" in *Die Entführung aus dem Serail* offers an earlier example of the type, and shows that it was equally at home in the opéra-comique/Singspiel kind of sentimentality. When writing to his father to describe Belmonte's aria, Mozart used the French spelling, "rondeau" (letter of 20 July 1782). *Don Giovanni* and *Così fan tutte* both received their rondos, placed late in the opera as climactic pieces.

When Cimarosa set *Olimpiade* for the opening of the new theater at Vicenza in 1784, Metastasio had been dead two years. Had he been alive and witnessed the event, he would have been surprised at what still passed under his name. Whereas the first act, ending with the great duet for Aristea and Megacle, is left almost intact, acts 2 and 3 have been collapsed and combined into a single act, one in which a lot of text not found in the original was required. This represents a major structural change in opera seria, one that was becoming widespread in the 1780s. Mazzolà, before putting *La clemenza di Tito* into two acts for Mozart, had written two-act serious librettos for Naumann at Dresden.

In Cimarosa's *Olimpiade* there are eight numbers in act 1, not counting the splendid overture for large orchestra, and eleven in the new second and final act—an economy effected by cutting arias in every part, while one role, Alcandro, has been eliminated altogether. Aminta and Licida receive only two arias apiece, and one of Aminta's is a little song of only thirty measures; the other characters get three arias apiece. Only the prima donna, Aristea, and the primo uomo, Megacle, are allowed rondos. These are long pieces in two tempos, and the longer of the two goes to the hero in the penultimate scene of the opera, as in Sarti's *Giulio Sabino*. Also like Sarti, Cimarosa's two rondos are marked by gavotte rhythm in both slow and fast sections. The two pieces are in A major and F major respectively, which seem to have been favorite keys of this type, and remained so down to Mozart's rondos for Sesto and Vitellia. Their main themes are shown in Ex. 17.1A–B.[12]

Cimarosa had no chorus at his disposal in Vicenza, so the pastoral chorus in act 1, "Oh care selve," was turned into an aria, as often happened in Italy ever since Pergolesi's influential *Olimpiade* setting of 1735. The sacrificial chorus in the last act Cimarosa replaced with a lugubrious orchestral march. Throughout the score he makes generous and telling use of the orchestra in many obbligato recitatives (just what Metastasio reproved in his well-known letter to Hasse concerning *Attilio Regolo*). The anonymous poet at Vicenza administered the coup de grâce with his ending to *Olimpiade*: he turned Metastasio's dénouement, intended to be set as a recitative, into a complex finale, that is to say an action finale such as had grown up in opera buffa. In setting it, Cimarosa resorted to several different keys, tempos, and meters, making for quite an imposing ensemble to end the opera. When he

12. The text for the Larghetto of "Grandi, è ver" is by Metastasio, but that for the Allegro is not. Typically, the new rondos required three strophes. Eight-syllable lines were preferred, perhaps because they gave a natural gavotte pattern when set as eight quarter-note beats. Neither part of Megacle's rondo "Nel lasciarti" comes from Metastasio.

EXAMPLE 17.1A–B.

Cimarosa, *Olimpiade*, principal themes from 2 rondos

got through, he wrote in the autograph (preserved at the Naples Conservatory) the number of measures, as was his custom: "233 Finis Laus Deo."

Paisiello rejoined the operatic scene in Italy shortly after Cimarosa's *Olimpiade*. The librettos of Metastasio that he worked for the San Carlo had to be adapted in ways similar to what we have just observed, and there was no dearth of poets at Naples who could perform the operation. Calzabigi was there, among others, and he would eventually collaborate with Paisiello on his two final operas, *Elfrida* in

1792 and *Elvira* in 1794. The non-Metastasian librettos, *Pirro* and *Fedra*, as set by Paisiello, will show some of the elements being added that helped diversify the stock of situations and devices available to serious operas just prior to 1790. *Pirro* of 1787 begins, after the overture, with a lengthy ensemble involving the main characters in debate and dispute—in other words, an *introduzione*. The origin of this device is again opera buffa. Act 1 of *Pirro* ends with an enormous finale involving all the singers. Here the librettist, Gamerra, went so far as to show an attempted assassination on the stage, an outrage precluded by the Metastasian niceties (which are none other than the *bienséances* of French classical tragedy). The grim event inspires some powerful and somber music from Paisiello, who chooses E-flat major, as one might expect, with contrasting episodes in g minor and c minor, and one memorable passage clothing the words "A morte!" in the flat submediant, C-flat major. Act 2 ends with an even longer finale, by which time we have reached No. 17 in the score. No. 14 is a "Rondeau" in g major for the prima donna. There is a third act (or rather, the vestigial remains of one) consisting only of some dialogue, a terzetto, the dénouement (in recitative), and concluding *coro*; in subsequent productions it was amalgamated with the second act.

Paisiello's *Fedra* of the following year is a different kind of opera altogether. What it shares with *Pirro* is a relatively high volume of violence and anguish. Salvioni, in a preface to his libretto, mentions his indebtedness to Euripides and Racine, and a printer's note adds that he should have cited Frugoni as well. Indeed he should have, for the libretto was nothing other than an adaption of Frugoni's *Ippolito ed Aricia* (after Racine and Pellegrin), produced at Parma with music by Traetta (and Rameau)[13]—the first attempt in Italy to effect a marriage between opera seria and Ramellian *tragédie lyrique*. What French opera texts offered, besides a generally high literary quality, was spectacle on the grand scale, such as had been typical of Italian seventeenth-century opera. The story of *Fedra* moves back and forth to Hades, the gods of which are much in evidence, as is Diana, who descends from the skies to set things aright not once but twice. Besides this there is a grand hunting chorus, a very picturesque disembarkation scene, then a great storm, "un' orrida tempesta," with thunder and lightning, plus a sea monster. The stage engineer at the San Carlo must have been busier than he had been in anyone's memory, for Metastasio had eschewed all this recourse to the "merveilleux."

In music, spectacle such as this required abundant orchestral tone painting, lots of pantomime ballet music, and many choruses. With his demonic music for the underworld scene, Paisiello shows that he knew and respected Gluck's *Orfeo*.[14] The emphasis on the spectacular worked to reduce further the number of the arias. Not

13. See Daniel Heartz, "Operatic Reform at Parma: Ippolito ed Aricia," in *Atti del convegno sul settecento Parmense nel 2° centenario della morte di C. I. Frugoni* (Parma, 1969), pp. 271–300.
14. In his earlier opera buffa *Socrate immaginario* (Naples, 1775), Paisiello had parodied the same Gluck scene; the poet set this up by using the same "quinari sdruccioli" that were characteristic for scenes of horror. See Wolfgang Osthoff, "Die Opera buffa," in *Gattungen der Musik in Einzeldarstellungen: Gedenkschrift Leo Schrade* (Berlin, 1973), 1 : 702–3.

that the popular aria types were forsaken. Aricia sings a long rondo at the beginning of the second and last act. It begins with the words "Parti, ma pensa," directed to Ippolito. The force of the Italian aria tradition was such that her initial word, *depart*, had almost invariably called forth a melodic descent of a fourth or fifth as far back as Hasse's first setting of "Parto" in *Tito*. Paisiello, like Mozart, proved no exception: he followed the tradition.

The renewal of opera seria from the materials of *tragédie lyrique* was such a general current at the time that it perhaps requires no further comment, except this one in the form of a question: are we dealing here with something that should be identified under the rubric opera seria? It applies to Mozart's *Idomeneo* as well as to Paisiello's *Fedra*.[15] The "Lärm und Getümmel" that was characteristic of Mannheim opera,[16] and which achieved such terrifying results at the end of act 2 in *Idomeneo*, stems ultimately from French opera. With regard to Mozart's *La clemenza di Tito*, the point is that crowd scenes and tumultuous choruses such as enliven the finale of act 1 come not from Metastasio, but from the hybrid operas blending French spectacle and Italian music. Rochlitz praised this very scene, drawing parallels with *Idomeneo* and *Don Giovanni*: "a composition which, as already remarked, is modeled on the whole after a scene in his *Idomeneo*, and unmistakably reveals Mozart's Shakespearean, all-powerful strength in the grand, stately, frightful, fearful, and shocking, here demonstrated to a hair-raising degree, so that even the famous first-act finale of *Don Giovanni* scarcely equals it."[17]

The ending of Paisiello's *Fedra* makes up for the nearly unrelieved gloom of the tale. Rameau, like Racine, and following Greek and Roman precedent, was content to let Ippolito perish. Frugoni and Traetta had mitigated the calamity by having the goddess Diana intervene to rescue him from the monster and restore him to Aricia. Salvioni and Paisiello went even further by bringing the reunited lovers together in a final reconciliation with Teseo, who, enlightened by the truth at last, pardons their transgressions and blesses their union. To go beyond this it would be necessary to rehabilitate the self-convicted Fedra and explain her incestuous passion for Ippolito—so far as that no one went even during those most enlightened times. Clemency was one of the virtues that Planelli proffered as the reason why modern opera with its "lieto fine" was superior to the carnage of ancient tragedy: "This passage made by tragedy from a sad to a happy ending is a certain

15. It is necessary to specify which composer of *Idomeneo* is meant here. Galuppi wrote an opera of the same name (Rome, 1756), as did several other Italian composers in the course of the period ca. 1750–1810. Paisiello himself composed an opera *Il ritorno d'Idomeneo in Creta*, qualified as "Rappresentazione tragica" on a libretto of S. Salzi, for Perugia in 1792.

16. See Roland Würtz, "Die Erstaufführungen von Mozarts Bühnenwerken in Mannheim," *Mozart-Jahrbuch 1978/79*, pp. 163–71.

17. "eine Komposition, die, wie schon bemerkt worden, im Ganzen zwar nach einer Scene seines *Idomeneo* angelegt ist, aber Mozarts shakespear'sche, allmächtige Kraft im Grossen, Prachtvollen, Schrecklichen, Furchtbaren, Erschütternden so unverkennbar, und so bis zum Haaremportreiben darlegt, als kaum das berühmte Finale des ersten Akts seines *D. Giovanni*"; Friedrich Rochlitz, "Anekdoten aus Mozarts Leben," col. 152. Kunze (*Mozarts Opern*, p. 667n22) suggests that Rochlitz is referring to No. 17 in *Idomeneo*, but Rochlitz made it clear in an earlier installment that he was comparing Nos. 23–24 in *Idomeneo* with Nos. 10–12 in *Titus*. See the Epilogue to Chapter 18 below.

proof of the progress made by humanity in matters of placidness, urbanity, and clemency, no matter what is said by our misanthropes."[18]

Paisiello's serious dramas and those of his most important Italian contemporaries around 1790 received many productions up and down the peninsula, some even beyond. Did Mozart know them? The singular restrictions that Joseph II imposed on the Burgtheater made sure that only comedies were staged there. But concert performances of music from the latest Italian serious operas took place at Vienna, including substantial selections from Paisiello's *Fedra*, given in the Burgtheater on 16–17 April 1791, a concert in which Mozart participated. The comedies that the emperor and the Viennese public preferred were those of the Italian composers, as we have seen. Since the language of comic and serious opera was merging more and more, the very distinction began to lose meaning: big, serious pieces like the sentimental rondo in two tempos could appear in comic operas, and remarkably slight and songlike pieces could appear in serious operas, along with rousing ensemble finales. Given Mozart's intense interest in everything to do with the world of opera, it would be surprising if he did not keep abreast of what his major Italian rivals were doing in their scores, just as he is reputed to have studied the French operas of Grétry, Gluck, Piccinni, and Salieri.[19]

Paisiello's pastoral opera *Nina*, having swept north in triumph, reached the stage of the Burgtheater to extraordinary acclaim in the spring of 1790. For Paisiello, this libretto was something out of the ordinary. In the first place, it had almost no plot: an abandoned girl, driven mad by her despair, waits and waits until her lover Lindoro finally returns and gradually restores her to sanity. With no subplots, no incidents, no ornaments of any kind to enhance this drama of pure sentiment, much was demanded of the composer. Paisiello instinctively found the right tone in his setting. The simple, almost naive melodic statement with which he clothes Nina's first song, "Il mio ben," represents a concentration of his expressive language to its essence (see Ex. 17.2). The effect this almost legendary piece had on contemporary sensibilities passed all bounds of moderation; audiences wept profusely, and individuals were heard to shout their consolations to poor Nina.

Formally, "Il mio ben" is a rondeau in the old sense, with one tempo. It could also be called a *romance*. Cultivated naïveté marked this epochal newcomer to the operatic stage (Rousseau started the fashion in his *Devin du village* of 1752), and archaic-sounding modal turns, such as the arrival at the cadence on the mediant in the middle of the Paisiello example, were among its special properties (Ex 17.2). Rousseau described the *romance* in his *Dictionnaire de musique* (1768) as follows: "As the romance must be written in a style that is simple, touching, and a little

18. "Questo passaggio fatto per la Tragedia dal tristo al lieto Fine è una pruova ben certa del progresso fatto dal genere umana nella placidezza, nella urbanità, nella clemenza, che che si dicano i nostri misantropi"; Antonio Planelli, *Dell'opera in musica* (Naples, 1772), pp. 72–73. On the cultural-political ramifications of choosing a clemency scene in connection with the coronation of Leopold II, see Adam Wandruzka, "Die 'Clementia austriaca' und der aufgeklärte Absolutismus: Zum politischen und ideellen Hintergrund von 'La clemenza di Tito,'" *Österreichische Musikzeitung* 31 (1976): 186–93.

19. As reported by his student Joseph Frank; see Deutsch, *Dokumente*, p. 476.

EXAMPLE 17.2. Paisiello,

Nina, ovvero La pazza per amore, No. 5

antique in taste, the tune ought to respond to the character of the words: no ornament, nothing mannered, but a sweet, natural, rustic melody."[20] Given the
amount of ornamental filigree characteristic of most Italian arias of the time (cf.
Cimarosa in Ex. 17.1), Nina's song can be said to be without ornament or mannerism. Particularly expressive is the return to an absolutely straightforward melodic
style at the beginning of the second half, on the words "di bei fior."

20. "Comme la Romance doit être écrite d'un style simple, touchant, et d'un goût un peu antique,
l'Air doit répondre au caractère des paroles; point d'ornemens, rien de maniéré, une mélodie douce,
naturelle, champêtre"; see Daniel Heartz, "The Beginnings of the Operatic Romance: Rousseau, Sedaine, and Monsigny," *Eighteenth-Century Studies* 15 (1981/82): 149–78.

Perhaps it is no coincidence that when Vitellia begins her last aria, which is also about garlands of flowers (or their absence), Mozart achieves a similarly elegiac mood—something that goes beyond the obvious similarity of key, meter, tempo and the melodic turn of phrase that links "di bei fior" with "Non più di fiori." The resemblance is all the more striking when, on the second statement by Vitellia of the slow rondo theme, the basset horn accompanies her in slow triplet figurations such as Paisiello gives his second violins.

Several other features of Paisiello's *Nina* suggest parallels in Mozart's last Italian opera. The Neapolitan master was known for his speed in composing, which was

EXAMPLE 17.3. Paisiello,

Nina, ovvero La pazza per amore, No. 10

incredible, even by the then-prevailing standards in Italian opera. He could compose whole operas in a few days, partly because he relied on very few types of orchestral accompaniment and on a texture that was unusually thin, with lots of unison passages and rarely more than two to three real parts. His favorite accompanimental device in *Nina* is the alternating third, played by the basses in eighth notes. An example is the aria of Susanna, Nina's governess (Ex. 17.3). Charles Burney called attention to this very accompaniment in connection with Italian opera, labeling it "shorthand" (i.e., stenography) and showing its origins in Galuppi's serious operas as far back as the 1740s.[21]

Paisiello was not the only Italian of his time to use such an economical accompanying figure, of course, but he was so successful in generating catchy melodies above it that the device became one of his trademarks. Mozart uses the same "economy-style" orchestration in several places, Tito's second aria in act 1, "Ah, se forse intorno al trono" (No. 8), being a particularly striking example, since much of the piece relies on the same bass. This piece is known to be among those written after Mozart's arrival at Prague a few days before the premiere,[22] and hence under conditions that demanded utmost economy of time.

21. Charles Burney, *A General History of Music*, ed. Frank Mercer (New York, 1957), 2:850.

22. Alan Tyson, "*La clemenza di Tito* and Its Chronology," *Musical Times* (1975): 221–27; see p. 223; reprinted in *Mozart: Studies of the Autograph Scores*, pp. 48–60; see p. 49. Tyson's conclusions supersede other work on the opera's chronology, which he cites in his note 1 (note 3 in *Mozart*).

Sometimes Paisiello forgoes using his "shorthand" bass during the first stages of a piece, so that he can bring it in near the end so as to generate excitement (and applause); an example is the end of Lindoro's aria in act 2. Mozart turns to the device for a similar heightening of rhythmic drive toward the end of the terzetto (No. 18); he resorts to it also for climactic effect in Vitellia's first aria (No. 2) and in Sesto's rondo (No. 19). When Paisiello wants to convey tension and struggle, he sometimes uses his "shorthand" bass together with a syncopated treble. In the finale of act 2, for example, as Nina struggles to regain her memory, he combines these features with a modulatory passage, further enhancing the unsettled quality (Ex. 17.4).

EXAMPLE 17.4. Paisiello,
Nina, ovvero La pazza per amore, No. 16

To find a similar passage in Mozart's *La clemenza di Tito* we return to the cynosure of the work, Vitellia's rondo (No. 23), which was probably composed as an independent concert aria before the rest of the opera.[23] The syncopated treble against bass "shorthand" first comes in as she utters the words "Infelice! qual orrore!" (mm. 50–54), a transition process that provides a fluid and astonishing link between the slow and fast rondo themes, passing from F major to A-flat by way of f minor. The force of the syncopated passage then returns with even greater intensity at the dissonant orchestral shrieks interpreting the words "Stretta fra barbare" (mm. 86–90), another transition passage, just after Mozart has extended and deepened the piece by bringing back the slow theme and its text in the fast part of the rondo—an almost unprecedented departure in this genre so dependent on precedents. The massive strokes of Mozart's orchestra here still do not exceed two real parts. In this economy of means and amplitude of effect Mozart is already using some of the orchestral sonorities that will become characteristic of Italian opera in the following two decades, with the generation of Simone Mayr, Spontini, and Weber (who held *Tito* in high regard). Had Mozart lived to rival the same, he would undoubtedly have shown them much more to admire along these lines.

23. Landon, *1791: Mozart's Last Year*, pp. 91–97.

That Mozart's *La clemenza di Tito* enjoyed more international success than any of his other operas during the last years of the eighteenth century and early years of the nineteenth should occasion no surprise.[24] It was the most modishly up-to-date work that he left. The simplified orchestral accompaniments were employed not only to save effort, which they did do, but also because Mozart was trying, for a final time, to challenge Paisiello and the Italians on their own terms. And he succeeded. Moreover, *La clemenza di Tito*, unlike their operas, is all of a piece in inspiration (with the sole exception of the simple recitatives, which, lamentably, had to be entrusted to another hand). The clue to its unity of style lies in Vitellia's great rondo, together with Sesto's equally fine one, which embodied so much of the opera's essence that Mozart resorted especially to them when, at the last minute, he had to put the magnificent overture to paper.

24. For the early "Wirkungsgeschichte" of the opera, see Daniel Heartz, "Mozarts 'Titus' und die italienische Oper um 1800," *Hamburger Jahrbuch für Musikwissenschaft* 5 (1981): 255–66.

18 · THE OVERTURE TO
LA CLEMENZA DI TITO
AS DRAMATIC ARGUMENT

When composing his operas Mozart deferred writing down the overture (except in the case of *Die Entführung*) to the last possible moment. While he may have conceived the overture from the very beginning, along with the central idea of the whole drama, by way of practical necessity he put off scoring what could wait the longest. Recitatives, arias, ensembles, and choruses had to be in the hands of the performers ahead of time for study and rehearsal; the overture could be almost indefinitely postponed, for it required only a run-through by the orchestra—if indeed it got that. Even incidental orchestral pieces such as marches had to figure in the score and parts during rehearsals because they usually involved scene changes and stage action and had to be timed to the second accordingly. But an overture involved no stage action (except in the case of the three-movement overtures to Mozart's *Ascanio in Alba* and *Lucio Silla*, where the action began in the middle). All his later overtures were played with the curtain down and were not part of the drama in the most literal sense; nonetheless, they were central to Mozart's scheme of dramatic exposition, for they presented at once, and with the greatest concentration of emotional and intellectual content, the crux of the drama. They fulfilled in a supreme degree Gluck's admonition, expressed in the preface to *Alceste* (1769), that the overture serve as dramatic argument.

Critical appreciation of the Mozartian overture as dramatic argument has not been lacking, at least for the masterworks from *Idomeneo* on. Constantin Floros has brought together early views on the subject and added many insights of his own as to how each overture emerges from the material of its opera.[1] A few points can be added to supplement his discussion. One has to do with Mozart's practice of tying

Reprinted, with a new epilogue, from "The Overture to *Titus* as Dramatic Argument," *Musical Quarterly* 64 (1978).

1. Constantin Floros, "Das 'Programm' in Mozarts Meisterouvertüren," *Studien zur Musikwissenschaft* 26 (1964): 140–86.

the overture together with the end of the opera, a not unnatural consequence of their having been written within a short time of each other. Another concerns the importance of tonality and tonal progressions, which Floros plays down in favor of thematic relationships. And finally, the overture to *La clemenza di Tito* receives but brief treatment by Floros even on thematic grounds—a state of affairs typical of the underevaluation accorded this festival opera until recently, when it has come into its own again.

The first decison that Mozart faced after accepting a libretto concerned the key-note of the opera (and consequently its overture). The second most important tonality had to be chosen from the outset as well, for it also affected the whole interior organization. This polarity of key became ever more distinct in the operas of the last decade of his life, until in *Tito* and *The Magic Flute* it assumes the clearest and simplest formulation. Not only are these two operas complementary in that the composition of one intertwined with the other; they also mirror each other tonally, as we have seen. Recall that *Tito* is a C-major opera with E-flat as its most important rival goal. *The Magic Flute* is an opera in E-flat major, with C, major and minor, as its most important rival goal. The rival keys prevail in the finales of both first acts, and hence enjoy their greatest supremacy midway through each drama. Thus in the broadest sense both operas are governed by a third relationship. In the five preceding operas, in contrast, a second relationship obtains through the two polar keys, as Table 12 shows.

La clemenza di Tito passes from C to E-flat and back; its ultimate tonal effect is the purging of the minor third, as in a *tierce de Picardie*. How satisfying, then, that Mozart makes E-flat not only the center of the opera, but the center of its overture as well. It arrives suddenly and unexpectedly at the beginning of the overture's Development, following hard on the dominant, G, and providing the material that informs the whole section, which is elaborately worked out as a contrapuntal tour de force.

"Ma fin est mon commencement," Machaut's charming *rondeau à 3*, could serve as a general commentary on Mozart's operas. The last orchestral passage of *The Magic Flute*, after the chorus has ceased celebrating E-flat and bestowing an eternal crown on Beauty and Wisdom, may seem at first no more than an afterthought. It had already inaugurated the final section, but the last statement of this little contre-danse is rendered even more insouciant by being punctuated by the winds' "pah pah," all marked piano. The dance is there to set up the "message" that follows, marked forte: the treble instruments ascend the triad of E-flat over the progression I–V_6–VI, answered by the cadential resolution I_6–IV(or II_5^6)–V–I. A rising triad over I–VI–I_6 initiates the opera's overture. But only at the end of the opera is there a rise through the triad to complete an octave.

There are other instances in which some melodic figure or modulation at or near the end of the opera has given Mozart the beginning or main idea of the overture. To put it more prudently, there are other cases where a late or even final musical

TABLE 12.

Polar Keys in Five Mozart Operas

	Idomeneo	*Abduction*	*Figaro*	*Giovanni*	*Così*
Keynote:	D	C	D	d–D	C
Principal rival key:	E♭	D	E♭	C	D
	(Quartet, Act 3)	(Finale, Act 2)	(Finale, Act 2)	(Finale, Act 1)	(Finale, Act 1)

gesture in the work became, at some point in the compositional process impossible to determine, the nucleus of the overture. The most obvious example is perhaps in *Così fan tutte*; there Mozart transfers the well-known motto, sung to the words of the opera's title on the outcome of the wager, to the first part of the overture. In *Don Giovanni*, the entire climactic scene at the Stone Guest's arrival becomes the slow introduction to the overture (minus the sepulchral trombones, which are appropriate only after the Commendatore has passed to the other world). The descending chromatic figure underlying this passage has sounded in many contexts throughout *Don Giovanni* (just as the harmonic progression to VI at the beginning and end of *The Magic Flute* recurs repeatedly in that work). It is especially connected with mortality and sounds a final time in the second violins at the very end, a blithe little orchestral tag that compares with the ending of *The Magic Flute* (see Ex. 9.2). In the *Figaro* overture, the rapid motion in the strings at the beginning suggests scurrying about, and of a surreptitious nature to boot because of the dynamic: pianissimo. A similiar motive occurs in the orchestra at the end of the Allegro assai section of the act 4 finale, at the words "Corriam tutti."

The overture to *Tito* proves no exception. Unison slides on the G string up to middle C allow the violins to deploy their gruffest tones, producing an effect powerful enough to launch a great symphony (the "Jupiter") or close a brilliant act ending (Figaro's "Non più andrai"). Here they begin and end the overture, and the end of the overture duplicates the end of the entire opera. To a greater extent than any of Mozart's other overtures, the one to *Tito* is a compendium of musical ideas from passages throughout the drama. The circumstances of its composition may help explain this fact. Mozart had even less time than usual to complete the opera.

As has been shown recently by conclusive studies, the overture was written, along with several other pieces, after the composer arrived in Prague, just a few days before the opera's premiere on 6 September 1791.[2] Mozart saved himself time by not scoring the reprise of the overture's main section. Instead, he indicated to the copyist "D.C. 26," directing him to write out again at this spot the first twenty-six measures. As the recapitulation was in reverse order, with the initial fanfare and following main theme placed last, he only needed to add a final twelve measures of

---

2. Tyson, "La clemenza di Tito and Its Chronology."

orchestral jubilation in order to complete the overture. More of the final measures of the opera turn up here: the slide up to the fifth and then up to the tonic. Overture and opera alike end up with the slide up to C in all the strings and winds, punctuated with the final threefold hammerstroke of the tonic. The device is as simple and majestic as the fine neoclassical building in which it first sounded (Figs. 35 and 36; the Nostitz Theater was subsequently subject to ruinous enlargement and redesign).

Trumpets and drums, fanfares, and majestic dotted rhythms betoken the imperial ambience in *La clemenza di Tito*, and in this sense the world of the opera is created from the beginning of the overture. Not just the title role is involved in having to bear the burden of the imperial state. Vitellia, the daughter of an emperor, resents not being an empress herself, and her overweening pride creates the central conflict of the drama. She plays on her lover, Sesto, so as to betray friend and country alike—both embodied in the person of the emperor. Mozart lavished his most expressive and demanding music on Vitellia, as had many composers before him

FIGURE 36

Pluth: Detail from the coronation
ball for Leopold II in the Nostitz
Theater (1791)

(the opera was always a showcase mainly for the prima donna),[3] although Sesto,
the primo uomo, does not fall far behind her in psychological interest or in the
vividness with which Mozart portrayed him. The climax for both characters arrives
in their long and incredibly powerful rondos toward the close of act 2, "Deh per
questo istante" (No. 19) and "Non più di fiori" (No. 23).[4]

Consciously or not, Mozart was still steeped in the two great rondos while composing the overture. A reminder is in order about this most fashionable aria type
in Italian opera during the last third of the eighteenth century. It consisted of a
slow theme, repeated after a contrasting section, and then a fast theme, often
melodically related to the slow one, which was repeated at least once after the
contrasting material. Mozart refined and deepened the type, among other ways by
creating a sense of fluid transition between the slow and fast sections, especially in
these two rondos. In Sesto's rondo the transition begins with a scurrying passage

3. The libretto's history prior to Mozart's setting is the subject of Lühning, *Titus-Vertonungen*.
4. Kunze (*Mozarts Opern*, p. 539) inexplicably says that Sesto's showpiece is not called a rondo.

(related to the beginning of the overture to *Figaro*) after which the music plunges boldly from A major, the key of the piece, to C major. Reversion to the keynote of the opera here has an undeniably heroic effect. The composer rises to the ringing words of the hero's resolve to go to his death in desperation but not in fear.

The passage is all the more remarkable as it comes as a later effort, Mozart having rejected the first(?) thought, which was to set "Vado disperato a morte" to a rather neutral idea that did not involve modulation at all but remained in A major.[5] He remembered the modulatory transition when he composed the overture. The rising scales against descending ones form the climactic section of the overture's long "Mannheim crescendo" (mm. 24–27 and, in the reprise, mm. 154–57). Moreover, he took over the same harmonic progression, I–VI–IV (harmonies falling by thirds reminds us of this overture's similarity to *The Magic Flute*). The violin's rising-fourth figure onto the downbeat at the word "morte" of the aria is also used in the overture and becomes one of the most prominent motives in the development (mm. 65–70 and 78–85). The grandiloquent dotted rhythms in the orchestra as Sesto halts on the word "traditor," just prior to the enunciation of the second rondo theme, have their parallel in the dotted rhythms preceding the fermata and the second theme of the overture (mm. 28–29). Similar dotted rhythms are used elsewhere in the opera to give rhetorical force to a question or pronouncement, both in the orchestrally accompanied recitatives and in the set pieces. Use of the flat sixth in the second measure of Ex. 18.1 resembles its treatment in m. 10 of the overture.

Another dramatic transition passage in Sesto's rondo has ramifications beyond its immediate context and calls here for a short digression. The transition occurs after the Allegro theme has been heard for the first time as the first violins jump from a dissonant B-flat up to the higher octave, marked by a sforzando, then descend in a flurry of sixteenth notes, the B-flat having been reinterpreted as the dominant seventh of F (Ex. 18.2). If this rising cry of anguish in the violins has a familiar ring, it is because something quite similiar is heard in the finale to act 1: a sforzato D-flat half note, arrived at by a leap, after which there are shivering descending sixteenth notes, the D-flat having turned into a dissonant minor ninth against a measure-long dominant seventh chord in the other strings (Ex. 18.3). The destination to F is the same in both examples, but in the latter it is minor rather than major. Similar as well are the vocal phrases with which Sesto and Publio respond. Publio at this point in the first-act finale makes public the traitorous conspiracy against Tito for the first time. Recurring late in the drama in Sesto's rondo, this orchestral gesture assumes the force of a stab of conscience: for the conspiracy is mainly his doing. Its recall brings home to him the full magnitude of his betrayal. He is, as he says, "unworthy of pity."

5. The draft is quoted in the Revisionsbericht of the Alte Mozart-Ausgabe; and in Abert, *Mozart* 2:614. It is not included in the Neue Mozart-Ausgabe, although many sketches are. They show how much trouble Mozart took arriving at just what he wanted in the musical numbers.

The finale to act I serves as a nexus of the work and has ties to both the beginning (the overture) and the ending. At the most obvious level are the three-note slides in the bass, used in Ex. 18.3 to emphasize the (temporary) dominant and tonic. They had been introduced a little earlier in the strings at an important structural point, the arrival of the "polar" key of c minor; their impact, coupled with the massively doubled minor chords in the winds, must be sufficient to make convincing Servilia's reaction: "Ah che tumulto orrendo!" Toward the end of the finale, cadences are repeatedly thwarted by the arrival of powerful diminished seventh

EXAMPLE 18.1. *Clemenza di Tito*, No. 19

chords in which all the forces join—solo voices, chorus, and orchestra (see mm. 144, 148, 152). The impact of these surprising tonal detours may be compared to the recurrent use of the same diminished chords in the overture, especially toward the end of the Development—for example, the surprise arrival and resolution in mm. 92–94. The polychoral overlapping echo between the soloists and chorus as they sing "Oh nero tradimento" (mm. 131–33) and later just "tradimento" (mm. 152–54) occurs first as a rhythm in the terzetto No. 10 (mm. 36–39, 65–80), then in the terzetto No. 14 (mm. 63–65, Sesto against the strings), and most prominently in the last finale, as chorus and soloists interact with Tito (mm. 89–91; repeated in mm. 98–99).[6] This link between first- and second-act finales is particularly strong and appropriate because it erases all memories of "tradimento" with protestations of fealty and vigilance to ensure a happy end to the emperor's life.

6. For anticipations of this peculiar rhythmic Gestalt in earlier Mozart, see Chapter 15, note 20.

EXAMPLE 18.2. *Clemenza di Tito*, No. 19

EXAMPLE 18.3. *Clemenza di Tito*, No. 12

Vitellia's rondo does what it must do: it surpasses the one sung by Sesto. Mozart's language for struggle and distress, expressed in many kinds of dissonances in conjunction with syncopations at various levels and surprising modulations, reaches its most intense level in this opera with her "Non più di fiori." In it the transition from the slow theme to the faster one again becomes an area of quickly rising tension. The key of F, projected so simply and with unclouded sweetness in the first part, a Larghetto in 3/8, is replaced by the parallel minor with the onset of the Allegro in common time, a fluid section led off by the solo of the obbligato basset horn (Ex. 18.4).[7]

The solo melody is already a little disconcerting because it introduces a three-measure phrase, followed by another, upsetting the absolute rule of the four-measure phrase obeyed up to this point. Moreover, it introduces the element of dissonance, the D-flat in m. 45 being a minor ninth above the dominant. Vitellia picks up the end of the phrase only, responding "Infelice!" to a falling third from the fifth to the third degree. When the phrase is repeated with modulation to A-flat, her words are "qual orrore!" To this Mozart had his orchestra react, its outbursts, forte, coming at two-measure intervals, with syncopated descents in the violins against the insistent eighth notes of alternating thirds in the basses and violas and sustained chords in the winds. The syncopations will occur later in the aria as very dissonant upward-resolving minor-second appoggiaturas (mm. 86–90), a kind of orchestral shriek that Mozart rarely, if ever, equaled. This moment is made all the more poignant by coming after a startling and heartrending return to the initial pastoral theme, now adapted to the common-time Allegro and serving as an episode in the subdominant. Emphasis on A-flat in the first transition (Ex. 18.4) foreshadows an entire later section of the piece (mm. 105–21) in which the Allegro theme is in this key. Special emphasis on the relationship of thirds is thus a prominent feature of both rondos, and in both instances it is the minor third above the tonic. The overweening prominence of E-flat in a C-major overture does not seem unnatural in the light of the two great outbursts of anguish projected in the final arias of Sesto and Vitellia.

"Non più di fiori," with its strident violin syncopations, left its mark on more than one part of the work. The eighth-note syncopation returns at the very end of the opera, after the chorus stops singing its praises; here the violins, doubled by winds, ascend and descend the tonic and dominant seventh chords against the steady quarter-note pulse of the bass (No. 26, mm. 119–22). We should hear this passage as related also to the troubling syncopations that beset the opening of the

7. This solo was played by Mozart's friend Anton Stadler, for whom the Clarinet Concerto and Clarinet Quintet were written. Equal treatment of the prima donna and primo uomo insured that both Vitellia and Sesto not only were provided with a rondo but also were given a concertante aria with Stadler; the one for Sesto is the well-known "Parto" (No. 9). The solo in Ex. 18.4 is nearly identical with one in the Clarinet Concerto (K. 622), first movement, mm. 78–80 and 272–76. In his letter of 7–8 October 1791, Mozart mentions news from Prague that Stadler was cheered by both the audience and the orchestra for his solos.

EXAMPLE 18.4. *Clemenza di Tito*, No. 23

overture, mm. 10–11, where they introduce the first darkening use of chromatic and minor color, the A-flat in the violas, doubled in the winds.[8] Syncopations in the violins against the basses are also prominent in the passage of the overture corresponding to Sesto's rondo (mm. 88–109). By using this figure associated with the first theme so extensively at the end of the Development, Mozart found himself in a situation where a normal reprise would present a problem: his imperial flourishes and fanfares were used up for the moment. He solved this difficulty by first bringing back the lightly scored second theme, then gradually leading, via the Mannheim crescendo, up to the return of the opening heroics. The result was rather similar to what Stamitz and other Mannheimers had done many times in the opening Allegro movements of their symphonies.[9] This is not to suggest that Mozart remembered or consciously imitated such older symphonic movements when, a few months before his death, he came to write *La clemenza di Tito*; but he may have remembered some of his own experiences with reverse recapitulations that he had made for the same reasons. (An example is the opening movement of the Piano Sonata in D, K. 311, written at Mannheim in 1777.)

A brief recounting of the overture's thematic and tonal content is now in order. The main theme begins in m. 8, after the introductory fanfare rising through the octave (similar to the beginning of the *Idomeneo* overture).[10] The theme could hardly be simpler, consisting of nothing more than a decorated tonic in the rhythm of the dotted half note followed by five quarter notes: C – – E / D C B C /, the first violins being accompanied by the seconds at the sixth below. It is lightly scored for strings alone at the beginning of the first chord, without basses, and marked piano. The gruff two-measure rejoinder, an orchestral tutti marked forte, introduces the syncopations. What Mozart makes of this menacing rejoinder in the course of the overture passes all bounds of expectation. The flat sixth, planted in the ear along with the syncopations, becomes obsessive after the piece has come to a temporary rest on the dominant, the more expansive second theme having been

8. Floros ("Das 'Programm' in Mozarts Meisterouvertüren," p. 81) correctly relates the suspended bass tone of the overture's m. 10 to the majestic bass suspensions at the beginning of the chorus, No. 24. He neglects to point out that suspensions become a prominent feature of the overture's Development section and help to account for its tremendous forward-moving propulsion, especially after the climactic arrival at c minor, forte, midway through the section (m. 78). He does point out the resemblance of the cadential formula in the orchestra's second theme (mm. 35–36) to that in the chorus (No. 15, mm. 19–20); here it is a question of a very common *galant* mannerism more than a thematic relationship.

9. Eugene K. Wolf, *The Symphonies of Johann Stamitz* (Utrecht, 1981), pp. 155–56. Floros ("Das 'Programm' in Mozarts Meisterouvertüren," p. 184) recognizes the inversion in the recapitulation, but he mistakenly says that the last measures of the Development (mm. 102–12), over a dominant pedal, "function to a certain extent as the development and beginning of the reprise." Such an error betrays a thematic rather than a thematic-tonal conception of sonata form.

10. Floros ("Das 'Programm' in Mozarts Meisterouvertüren," p. 181) points out this similiarity. He neglects to note that (1) the second theme of the *Idomeneo* overture is followed by a modulation from a to C that parallels a passage in the love duet of act 3 (original version, No. 21a in the Neue Mozart-Ausgabe, m. 11); (2) the "Mannheim rockets" of the violins up to high D over the triads of D and G also occur at highly significant points of the drama, such as the recognition of father and son in act 1 and the admission of Idomeneo's guilt at the end of act 2; and (3) the long descending passage at the end of the overture, with its many suspended dissonances (cf. Ex. 1.1), bears a resemblance to the use of dissonance in the chorus concluding act 2, and the overture's final measures come from the recognition scene in act 1.

heard twice. The first theme then sounds in the winds (mm. 45–46), over the dominant: G – – B / A G F♯ G /. Such a recurrence has overtones of the concerto in its ritornello-like return of the main theme at places other than the tonic. A tutti rejoinder similar to the one elicited the first time ensues, but now more furious—a dissonant diminished chord over a G pedal in which the first violins keep rapidly rising to a high E-flat while the seconds provide the syncopations.[11]

As at the opening, the four measures are repeated, leading to a reaffirmation of G with chords and dotted rhythms for emphasis. Then comes an uncanny strategy, begun by the violins and joined by the rest of the strings and the bassoons in a unison passage making the rapid move via A-flat and a circular scalar passage down, then up to E-flat. It is like a first-ending lead-back that went astray. The arrival at E-flat is marked forte, in contrast to the piano of the scalar passage. Attempts to achieve the flat sixth above the dominant by assault, as it were, the violins hammering their way up to it repeatedly, give way to another strategy, equivalent to slipping through the rear defenses. It is not just E-flat that arrives, but the first theme: E♭ – – G / F E♭ D E♭ /, played in unison by all the violins without accompaniment, as if they were proposing a subject for consideration. It then becomes a subject, as the second violins intone it against the eighth-note countersubject in the violas, and the quasi-fugal proceedings are under way. Arrival at the main theme in E-flat after a quick departure from G has a parallel in one of the vocal pieces of the opera. The resemblance is such as to suggest that Mozart, whether he knew it or not, was reliving a dramatic moment connected with Vitellia when he conceived this passage.

Vitellia sings an aria in G (No. 10) prior to the finale of act 1, "Vengo . . . aspettate . . . Sesto . . . Ahime!" Actually, it is called a terzetto because two other characters, Annio and Publio, comment uncomprehendingly on her strange behavior. But Vitellia provides all the musical and dramatic interest as she struggles with herself in a newly evolved situation: she has been named empress by Tito, whom she has just sent Sesto to assassinate. The piece is an Allegro in common time, like the overture and like the second part of her rondo in act 2. In it her agitation emerges from the sudden forte-piano exchanges and vigorous leaping figures, characteristic of Vitellia, that are deployed with unrelenting energy, in the manner of an obbligato recitative.[12] These occupy the first violins and provide an obsessive kind of continuity, against which she utters her disjointed words to unconnected scraps of melody, while in the winds there is a layered series of long dissonant suspensions above. Suddenly she summons forth a collected musical thought, and the piece plunges in one measure from G to E-flat as she tells of her mortal shame

11. Floros (ibid., p. 181) calls attention to the close similiarity of this passage to one in the overture of *The Abduction from the Seraglio*. He also points out the similarity of mm. 64–70 in the *Tito* overture to mm. 198–201 in the overture to *The Magic Flute*.

12. A close parallel to this piece in another Mozart opera is the great obbligato recitative "Crudeli" for Sandrina in *La finta giardiniera*. The emotions of terror and indecision are common to both.

and insane fury (Ex. 18.5A). As if the motion from G to E-flat were not enough to identify this moment with the crucial one in the overture, there is in addition the melodic motif of the falling conjunct third: G–F–E♭.

Vitellia's conniving and boundless jealousy, here interpreted musically as an astonishing tonal detour, are responsible for everything that happens in the drama. It is therefore only appropriate that Mozart chose to make its musical equivalent so central a part of the overture. To emphasize further the sudden move from G to E-flat in No. 10, he has Vitellia leap from low F-sharp to high B-flat on the word "orror" at the end of her part, while the strings enter with a forte E-flat on the second beat and the winds harmonize the chord (Ex. 18.5B). To give more power and a darker color to the E-flat, Mozart has the violins play it on the low G string

EXAMPLE 18.5A–B.

Clemenza di Tito, No. 10

A

B

(marking the passage "una corda"). The road back from E-flat to tonic G is swift, via a chromatic descent in the bass line. On the first eruption of E-flat near the beginning of the piece, this same tonal route occupied twelve measures. Never were Mozart's powers of reducing a broad musical gesture into an intensely concentrated capsule greater than here.

Sesto, as acted on by Vitellia, engendered some further musical thoughts that eventually found their way into the overture. We have seen how his rondo (No. 19) used the ascending and descending scales as well as the harmonic progression I–VI–IV that caps the two occurrences of the crescendo passage in the overture (Ex. 18.1). When the scalar figures begin in m. 16 of the overture, they are constituted by a simple descent in sixteenth notes through the octave from C in the second violins, accompanied by sixths in the violas; succeeding flurries begin on ever higher chord tones, a rise through the triad that is related to the fanfare at the beginning of the overture. Each downbeat is punctuated by the three-note slide up to the tonic. The gradually increasing orchestral sonority gains further interest by having the descending scale sound simultaneously against an ascending one (mm. 22–26) similar to the passage borrowed from No. 19.

The effect of the long crescendo is that of bells and the ringing of changes. It is used again with a most joyous result in the familiar concertante aria "Parto" (No. 9), which Sesto sings to Vitellia. He will do her bidding if only she will bestow a glance on him. The actual glance must come with the Allegro assai in m. 96 as the orchestra launches into the peal-like scalar figures in sixteenth notes, first descending, then descending and ascending at once. This offers a fine example of Mozart's music giving an "implied stage direction."[13] The composer brings the joyous noise once again in the conclusion of the aria in order to achieve an applause-inducing *stringendo al fine*. He had anticipated this effect even earlier in act 1. In the duetto (No. 1) between Vitellia and Sesto, as the latter says "Your fury is already setting me afire," the peal of a descending C-major scale in sixteenth notes is heard first in the first violins, the second violins then chiming in with what the firsts just played (mm. 27–28). The overture prepares us not only for the heroism of Sesto (Ex. 18.1) but also for his infatuation with the fiery Vitellia (Nos. 1 and 9). Since in the drama these are the dominant sides of his character, they could not have been better chosen if the overture is to represent the conflict within his personality.

Also suggestive for the overture was the great solo scene for Sesto just prior to the finale of act 1. This obbligato recitative is so elaborate that it is assigned its own number, No. 11 (as is the case with Vitellia's No. 22 and Tito's No. 25). Beginning in c minor, to which the G major of Vitellia's No. 10 acts as a dominant, it deploys an energetic figure in the violins, rising first to the third and then to the fifth, each destination being marked with a sforzando, and then finally to the octave, all in regular two-measure segments (Ex. 18.6). Violins rising through the triad starting from middle C in symmetrical two-measure segments are also employed at the beginning of the overture.[14]

The rhythm of Ex. 18.6 corresponds to that of the overture's main theme. Importance of rhythmic shape, aside from melodic content, emerges in the overture's Development section, where the main theme eventually sheds its tune but persists as a rhythmic impetus (mm. 78–85). Harmonically, mm. 78–87 traverse the circle-of-fifths progression c–g–d–a–E, with suspended dissonances of the major ninth layered above every new chord (except the last). A similar layering of dissonances in long suspensions occurs in the winds at the beginning of No. 10, as Vitellia blurts her disjointed thoughts, and also in the reprise (mm. 48–53). Given the direct tonal connection between Nos. 10 and 11, which makes the two pieces function as a unit (extended further by the finale, No. 12, which arrives as a tonic E-flat prepared by its dominant B-flat, on which No. 11 ended), it is not surprising that this area of the opera offered not one but several ideas that were eventually used in the overture.

13. The phrase is that of Robert Moberly, "The Influence of French Classical Drama on Mozart's 'La Clemenza di Tito,'" *Music and Letters* 54 (1974): 291.
14. The rising fanfare figure is also used to introduce the march (No. 4) in a passage in which the timpani alternate between tonic and dominant. This perhaps suggested what was to become a prominent bass figure in No. 11.

EXAMPLE 18.6. *Clemenza di Tito*, No. 11

Preoccupation with the darker, flat side of the tonal spectrum is particularly evident as the catastrophe nears—in the recitative for Sesto (No. 11) and the finale that grows out of it (No. 12). As he becomes more and more horrified at the perfidy he is about to commit, the tonalities sink deeper and deeper, leaving c minor for f minor (No. 11, m. 25). The word "traditor" is sung by him first in m. 40, bringing the music back to f minor after an episode in E-flat. Four measures later the word is repeated to the flat sixth, D-flat. As if to hammer the point home, a half-note D-flat unison appears four measures later in the orchestra, sforzando. It sounds all the more raw for arriving as a dissonance, the bass motion being from G to D-flat. The resulting tritone cries out for resolution to A-flat and C, though this does not occur in satisfactory form and sufficient weight until the return to Tempo primo at measure 57, with the whole orchestra stating the ritornello (Ex. 18.6) in A-flat, forte, then repeating the passage with even stronger syncopations in f minor (N.B.:

the I–VI–IV progression). Mozart finds another use for his ritornello figure, as its staccato eighth notes explode all the way up to high C (mm. 69–71), a pictorial effect carefully described in the score: "Flames are seen to engulf the Capitol and leap higher by degrees."

It is now too late to turn back. Sesto reaches the climax of the recitative and its melodic peak, G-flat, which he sustains for five beats ("ahi! tardo") to a diminished-seventh harmony while the violins rise in syncopated chord tones, similiar to those at the end of the opera. The lingering G-flat, left unresolved in its own register at the end of the recitative, has a bearing on the subsequent finale. From its beginning in E-flat, Sesto quickly pushes to an uncanny tonal destination, a cadence on G-flat major (m. 26). What was a melodic goal has become a harmonic one. When Annio reacts by saying that Sesto is incoherent, his remark applies to more than just the hero's disjointed words. Yet there is a certain haunting logic about the sound of the tonal degree a minor third above the tonic here; it is the *Tito* sound that has been observed in both rondos and in the overture.

The overture's second theme is closely related to its main theme, being composed of not one but two descending conjunct thirds. Or to express it differently, the descending parallel sixths of the first theme need only be inverted to become the descending thirds of the second theme. The latter is broader in layout, a four-measure phrase answering its counterpart, instead of the two-measure segments of statement and rejoinder comprising the main theme. The answering four-measure phrase in the second theme is first rendered by the lowly bassoons, which enter with an upbeat triadic figure that sees further use in the Development, as the countersubject against the main theme. This conjunction tends to bring the second theme into even closer relationship with the main theme.

An oddity about the second theme that probably struck Mozart's contemporaries was the relegation of the violins to an accompanying role, for at first they provide their "pah pah" on offbeats two and three. Even this tiny detail is taken up in the Development (by the winds, mm. 72, 74, 76, resulting in a further amalgamation features from the second theme with the main theme). To the answering four-measure phrase in the bassoons, the violins at first provide only an accompanimental echo on offbeats two and four. They were reduced to a similar role in another very prominent spot in the opera: the winding down of the first finale, eight measures before the end of act I.

Each of the four statements of the second theme is differently orchestrated, but it remains the showplace for the winds, the strings always being accompaniment. The mission of the second theme as a foil to the first is achieved by its light texture, more expansive proportions, and the exchange of roles that sees the usually subservient voices (winds) replace those that usually predominate (strings). As for the theme itself, no close parallels embodying all its salient features exist in the opera. But the fall from the fifth to the third degree by step has been remarked in

Vitellia's part (Ex. 18.4), which is also similar in rhythm; and Sesto sings in his rondo to a rhythm even closer to the second theme (Exx. 18.1 and 18.2, beginning of the voice part).

La clemenza di Tito is in many ways the simplest and most grandiose opera in the Mozartian canon. The raw materials of its construction are such primal ones as the cadential progression IV–V–I, a sequence heard not only at the beginning of the opera—Nos. 1, F; 2, G; 3, C—but also at its end—Nos. 23, F; 24, G; 26, C (No. 25 being the brief obbligato recitative for Tito that prepares for the final ensemble and chorus of praise). The cadential progression between numbers operates on the other scale degrees as well. After the imperial march and chorus (Nos. 4 and 5) establishing the polar eminence of E-flat, which follows directly on C major without transition, we hear the cadential sequence of keys confirming the tone between the two polar ones—Nos. 6, G; 7, A; 8, D.[15] The tritone sequence between numbers that Mozart had relied on with such effect in the last act of *Idomeneo*[16] and the second act of *The Abduction* also sees use. The terzetto in E-flat (No. 18), one of the weightiest pieces in act 2, is succeeded by the equally weighty rondo of Sesto in A (No. 19), providing a tonal conflict to match the dramatic impasse at this moment of the plot. It is of course resolved as a tritone should be. Tito renews his determination to be clement (No. 20, B-flat); Servilia pleads with Vitellia to rescue Sesto (No. 21, D).

From this moment on, the focus of the drama is Vitellia, and she inaugurates the final cadential sequence with her rondo in F. Such a sequence between numbers may seem like an obvious means of establishing tonal stability on the grand scale, appropriate to beginning and ending an opera. Yet Mozart had done nothing of the kind prior to *Tito*. In *The Magic Flute* he was more intent on strategic deployment of the relative minor (No. 1, Tamino's plight, and the penultimate section of the act 2 finale, where the forces of darkness are finally routed), in keeping with the initial progression of that opera's overture. *Così fan tutte* begins by playing on the descent of a seventh by thirds (Nos. 1–4), in keeping with the opera's motto-title.

The overture to *Tito* does not fall behind its companions in setting forth the characteristic progression of the opera. Its first departure from the tonic, after the C-major fanfare and beginning of the main theme, is to the subdominant (expressed as II_{2}^{6}) then to the dominant en route back to the inevitable tonic. The opera's first harmonic progression is also its last. The flat sixth that troubles the subdominant realm at the beginning of the overture, taken in conjunction with the turbulence of the syncopations that accompany it, sums up much of the world of emotion that attracted Mozart in this time-honored libretto: romantic ardor, betrayal of friendship because of it, and resolution through magnanimity. To be more specific, the flat sixth betokens the hero's treachery, as Mozart made abun-

15. No. 8 is another very late addition to the opera, written at Prague, as Tyson shows in his article "*La clemenza di Tito* and Its Chronology."
16. See Heartz, "Tonality and Motif in *Idomeneo*" and "The Great Quartet in Mozart's *Idomeneo*."

dantly clear in Nos. 11 and 12 at the end of act 1. It has to be purged through his steadfastness, and ultimately it is, when all the dark shadows of this opera have passed and the glory of C major is proclaimed over and over, with winning simplicity and grandeur.

A masterpiece of "pure music" such as the overture to *Tito* needs no guide to the drama in order to be understood. But if it is enjoyed along with and in the context of the stage drama, the experience can only be enhanced by understanding its indebtedness to the music of the entire opera. The imperium and the title character who embodies that power sound forth most obviously with the pomp and ceremony of the beginning and ending. The elaborate contrapuntal course taken by the extensive Development section bears on another imperium, the Habsburg. By extension, the Habsburg being crowned at Prague in 1791, and fêted with this opera, was a Holy Roman emperor. Counterpoint and fugue came to play an almost emblematic significance in identifying the house of Habsburg and setting it apart from others.[17] Sesto, the hero in spite of himself, inspired Mozart to create an unforgettable human portrait. Vitellia, the scheming femme fatale, one of the most fascinating characters in the gallery of Mozartian female roles, worked her ways on the composer as well. She touched the deepest wellsprings of the opera, and consequently its overture.

EPILOGUE

Mozart's *Tito* enjoyed considerable critical acclaim and popular success during the period after its premiere. Constanze Mozart instigated many performances of it as benefit concerts for herself and the children, taking the work on tour throughout Germany and Austria. Some of the best contemporary criticism we have of any Mozart opera was written about *Tito*. In a review of a performance at Prague on 3 December 1794, Franz Niemetschek wrote with sensitivity about the opera's particular coloring, while invoking the ideals of classical antiquity:

> There is a certain Grecian simplicity, a quiet sublimity, in the entire music that strike a sensitive heart gently yet all the more deeply; these qualities fit the character of Tito, the times, and the entire subject so well that they do honor to Mozart's delicate taste and his powers of observation. At the same time the cantilena, especially in the Andantes, is of a heavenly sweetness, full of emotion and expression; the choruses are stately and sublime—in short, Gluck's nobility is united to Mozart's original art, his flowing feelings and his totally enchanting harmonies. Unsurpassable, and perhaps a *non plus ultra* of music, is the last trio and finale of the first act. Connoisseurs

---

17. This idea runs like a leitmotif through Warren Kirkendale's *Fuge und Fugato in der Kammermusik des Rokoko und der Klassik* (Tutzing, 1966); revised and expanded edition in English translated by Margaret Bent and Warren Kirkendale: *Fugue and Fugato in Rococo and Classical Chamber Music* (Durham, N.C., 1979).

are in doubt whether even *Don Giovanni* has been surpassed by *Tito*. Guardasoni gave us this heavenly work of the immortal genius on 3 December before a full house and to the unanimous applause of the public.[18]

Quite apparent here is the influence of Winckelmann's "noble simplicity and calm grandeur," proclaimed as hallmarks of ancient Greek art in the 1760s, that is, during the time when Gluck wrote his epochal *Orfeo ed Euridice* and *Alceste*. Niemetschek's parallel between Mozart and Gluck is well taken. The vision of antiquity projected in *Tito* (and also in *Idomeneo*) owes much to Gluck.

Niemetschek returned to the issue of *Tito* and its particular coloration at greater length in his biography of Mozart published in 1798. He had the advantage of having witnessed the premiere under the composer's direction, a circumstance that lends special force and eloquence to his observations:

> *La clemenza di Tito* is esteemed the most perfect work Mozart completed, from the aesthetic viewpoint of a beautiful work of art. With fine sensitivity Mozart seized the simplicity and the quiet nobility of Tito's character, and of the whole action, and conveyed it entirely in his composition. Every part, even the most modest instrumental voice, embodies this trait, and combines to enhance the most beautiful unity of the whole. Since it was written for the celebration of a coronation and for two specially hired singers from Italy, Mozart had to write brilliant arias for these two roles. But what arias they are! How high do they stand above the usual crowd of bravura arias![19]

In his 1794 review Niemetschek disparaged the Italian virtuosi who created the original Vitellia and Sesto in 1791, but as we have seen, Emperor Leopold was impressed with the first, Anton Stadler wrote glowingly about the second, and Mozart complained about neither. In his continuation, Niemetschek singles out the choruses concluding both acts and, not surprisingly, Vitellia's rondo for special praise:

> The other pieces betray in all things the great spirit from which they flowed. The last scene or finale of the first act is certainly the most perfect work by Mozart: expression, character, feeling [*Empfindung*] vie with each other to bring forth the greatest possible effect. The singing, the instrumentation, the variety of harmony, the calls of the chorus in the distance cause such a moving and illusive effect in every performance, that its like is a rarity in opera. Among all choruses that I have heard, none is so flowing, so sublime and full of expression, as the closing chorus of the second act; among all arias, none is so pleasing, so full of sweet sadness, so rich in musical beauties, as the entire rondo in F with obbligato basset horn, "Non più di fiori," in the second act.[20]

18. Paul Nettl, "Prager Mozartiana," *Mitteilungen der Internationalen Stiftung Mozarteum* 9 (1960): 4. In *1791: Mozart's Last Year* (pp. 117–18), Robbins Landon falsifies his translation from Nettl by having the last sentence we quote refer to *Don Giovanni*, to which purpose he must suppress the rest of the review, as Niemetschek goes on writing about *Tito*.
19. Niemetschek, *Leben des k. k. Kapellmeisters Mozart*, p. 73.
20. Ibid., pp. 73–74.

Another critic who wrote about *Tito* in 1798 was Friedrich Rochlitz, first editor of the *Allgemeine musikalische Zeitung*. Like Niemetschek, but independently of him, he greatly admired the end of act 1, and he also drew specific parallels between it and *Idomeneo*. Rochlitz gathered his anecdotes from Mozart himself, whom he met at Leipzig in 1789, and from the widow and friends of the composer after his death. Mozart, says Rochlitz, treasured most highly among his operas *Idomeneo* and *Don Giovanni*. He quotes the composer directly on *Don Giovanni*: "The opera is written for Prague, not for the Viennese, but most of all for myself and my friends."[21]

Rochlitz describes *Idomeneo* as a product of particularly happy circumstances—a generous, music-loving princely patron being not the least among them. Mozart's love for this child of his first maturity is demonstrated, claims Rochlitz, by the number of ideas it supplied him in his last works:

> His preference for this child he shows also by taking several of its ideas as the foundation—or even more than just the foundation—in some of his best later works. Compare, for example, the overture to *Idomeneo* with that to *Tito*, or the incomparable scene "Volgi intorno lo sguardo, o sire" [No. 23] in *Idomeneo* with the equally outstanding finale of act 1 in *Tito*, the moving aria of the first "Se il padre perdei" with the aria "Dies Bildnis ist bezaubernd schön," and the Andante of the aria "Zum Leiden bin ich auserkoren" in *The Magic Flute*; or the march in act 3 of *Idomeneo* with the beginning of the second act of *The Magic Flute*; and so forth. He has been reproached for this, I believe unjustly. Mozart could rightfully make use of his earlier work thus, not only because it was so magnificent, but also because, as long as he lived, it lay hidden, like a buried treasure.

He might have added that Sesto's "Parto" (No. 9) echoes several elements in Idamante's "Non ho colpa" (No. 2), and that the postlude of Pamina's "Ach ich fühl es" resembles a passage in *Idomeneo* (cf. Ex. 1.1B, mm. 83–84, with Ex. 16.3). Particularly astute on Rochlitz's part is his detection of a minor-mode passage in Ilia's aria "Se il padre perdei" (No. 11, mm. 33–39) that was transferred to the Queen of the Night's first aria (No. 4, mm. 40–44), which shows that he knew well the three operas in question.

That there is a special bond between the two operas of 1791, treated here and elsewhere by contemporaries on a basis of absolute equality, and the opera that caught the first full rays of Mozart's musical genius a decade earlier gives us much to ponder. Such a bond strengthens our contention that all seven master operas of Mozart's last decade belong to the same family. They constitute an interrelated cycle within the larger corpus of his works.

---

21. "Für die Wiener ist die Oper nicht, für die Prager eher, aber am meisten für mich und meine Freunde geschrieben"; Rochlitz, "Anekdoten aus Mozarts Leben," cols. 51–52.

WORKS CITED

Abert, Hermann. *Mozart's "Don Giovanni."* Translated by Peter Gellhorn. London, 1976.

———. *W. A. Mozart.* 7th ed. 2 vols. Leipzig, 1956.

Albrecht, Heinrich, ed. *Die Bedeutung der Zeichen Keil, Strich und Punkt bei Mozart.* Kassel, 1957.

Algarotti, Francesco. *Saggi.* Edited by Giovanni da Pozzo. Bari, 1963.

Allanbrook, Wye Jamison. "Pro Marcellina: The Shape of 'Figaro' Act IV." *Music and Letters* 63 (1982): 69–84.

———. *Rhythmic Gesture in Mozart: "Le nozze di Figaro" and "Don Giovanni."* Chicago, 1983.

Anderson, Emily. *The Letters of Mozart and His Family.* Rev. ed. London, 1985.

Arneth, Alfred Ritter von. *Beaumarchais und Sonnenfels.* Vienna, 1868.

Bauman, Thomas. *North German Opera in the Age of Goethe.* Cambridge, 1985.

———. *W. A. Mozart: "Die Entführung aus dem Serail."* Cambridge Opera Handbooks. Cambridge, 1987.

Beales, Derek. *Joseph II: In the Shadow of Maria Theresa, 1741–1780.* Cambridge, 1987.

Beaumarchais, Augustin Caron de. *Théâtre: "Le barbier de Séville." "Le mariage de Figaro." "La mère coupable."* Edited by René Pomeau. Paris, 1965.

Beer, A., and J. von Fiedler, eds. *Joseph II und Graf Ludwig Cobenzl: Ihr Briefwechsel.* 2 vols. Vienna, 1901.

Bernard, Paul D. *Jesuits and Jacobins: Enlightenment and Despotism in Austria.* Urbana, Ill., 1971.

Bitter, Christof. *Wandlungen in den Inszenierungsformen des "Don Giovanni" von 1787 bis 1928.* Regensburg, 1961.

Blümml, Emil Karl. "Ausdeutungen der 'Zauberflöte.'" *Mozart-Jahrbuch* 1 (1923): 109–46.

Brown, Bruce Alan. "Christoph Willibald Gluck and Opéra-Comique in Vienna, 1754–1764." Ph.D. diss., University of California, Berkeley, 1986.

Brunel, Georges, ed. *Piranèse et les Français, 1740–1790: Colloque international.* 2 vols. Paris, 1976.

Bücken, Ernst. *Der heroische Stil in der Oper.* Leipzig, 1924.

Burney, Charles. *A General History of Music.* Edited by Frank Mercer. 2 vols. New York, 1957. (1st ed. 4 vols. London, 1776–89.)

———. *Memoirs of the Life and Writings of the Abate Metastasio in Which Are Incorporated Translations of His Principal Letters.* 3 vols. London, 1796; facsimile reprint New York, 1971.

Carse, Adam. *The Orchestra in the XVIIIth Century.* Cambridge, 1940.

Carter, Tim. *W. A. Mozart: "Le nozze di Figaro."* Cambridge Opera Handbooks. Cambridge, 1987.

Chailley, Jacques. *"La flûte enchantée," Opéra maçonnique.* Paris, 1968. English translation by Herbert Weinstock: *"The Magic Flute": Masonic Opera.* New York, 1972.

Chardin, 1699–1779: A Special Exhibition Organized by the Réunion des Musées Nationaux, Paris, the Cleveland Museum of Art, and Museum of Fine Arts, Boston. Boston, 1979.

Charlton, David. *Grétry and the Growth of Opéra-Comique.* Cambridge, 1986.

Cone, Edward. *The Composer's Voice.* Berkeley and Los Angeles, 1974.

Courville, Xavier de. *Luigi Riccoboni, dit Lélio.* 3 vols. Paris, 1943–58.

Crow, Thomas E. *Painters and Public Life in Eighteenth-Century Paris.* New Haven, Conn., 1985.

Dahms, Sibylle. "Das musikalische Repertoire des Salzburger Fürsterzbischöflichen Hoftheaters (1775–1803)." *Österreichische Musikzeitschrift* 31 (1976): 340–55.

Dalban, Denyse. *Le comte de Cagliostro.* Paris, 1983.

Da Ponte, Lorenzo. *An Extract from the Life of Lorenzo Da Ponte, with the history of several dramas written by him, and among others, Il Figaro, Il Don Giovanni & La Scuola degli Amanti set to music by Mozart.* New York, 1819.

———. *Memorie.* Edited by G. Gambarin and F. Nicolini. 2 vols. Bari, 1918.

Dean, Winton, and John Merrill Knapp. *Handel's Operas, 1704–1726.* Oxford, 1987.

Dent, Edward J. *Mozart's Operas: A Critical Study.* 2d ed. London, 1947.

Deutsch, Otto Erich. *Mozart: Die Dokumente seines Lebens.* Neue Mozart-Ausgabe, series 10, workgroup 34, supplement. Kassel, 1961. English translation by Eric Blom, Peter Branscombe, and Jeremy Noble: *Mozart: A Documentary Biography.* London, 1965.

———. *Mozart . . . Addenda und Corrigenda.* Kassel, 1978.

Diderot, Denis. *Entretiens sur "Le fils naturel."* Paris, 1757.

Dietrich, Margret. "'Wiener Fassungen' des *Idomeneo.*" *Mozart-Jahrbuch* 1973/74, pp. 56–76.

Eggebrecht, Hans Heinrich. *Versuch über die Wiener Klassik: Die Tanzszene in Mozarts "Don Giovanni."* Wiesbaden, 1972.

Einstein, Alfred. "Das erste Libretto des 'Don Giovanni.'" *Acta musicologica* 9 (1937): 149–50.

———. *Mozart: His Character, His Work*. Translated by Arthur Mendel and Nathan Broder. Oxford, 1945.

Fekete de Galántha, Johann Graf. *Wien im Jahre 1787: Skizze eines lebenden Bildes von Wien, entworfen von einem Weltbürger*. Translated and edited by Victor Klarwill. Vienna, 1921.

Fellinger, Imogen. "Brahms's View of Mozart." In *Brahms: Biographical, Documentary, and Analytical Studies*, edited by Robert Pascall, pp. 41–57. Cambridge, 1983.

Ferrero, Mercedes Viale. *La scenografia del '700 e i fratelli Galliari*. Turin, 1963.

Finscher, Ludwig. "'Zwischen absoluter und Programmusik': Zur Interpretation der deutschen romantischen Symphonie." In *Über Symphonien: Beiträge zu einer musikalischen Gattung*, pp. 103–15. Tutzing, 1979.

Fischer, Friedrich Johann. "Emanuel Schikaneder und Salzburg." *Jahrbuch der Gesellschaft für Wiener Theaterforschung* 15–16 (1966): 179–216.

Floros, Constantin. "Das 'Programm' in Mozarts Meisterouvertüren." *Studien zur Musikwissenschaft* 26 (1964): 140–86.

———. "Stilebenen und Stilsynthese in den Opern Mozarts." *Hamburger Jahrbuch für Musikwissenschaft* 5 (1981): 155–68.

Francis, John W. *Old New York, or, Reminiscences of the Past Sixty Years*. New York, 1865.

Gadamer, Hans-Georg. *Wahrheit und Methode*. 4th ed. Tübingen, 1975. English translation from the 2d edition by Garrett Barden and John Cumming: *Truth and Method*. London, 1975.

Galeazzi, Francesco. *Elementi teoretico-pratici di musica*. 2 vols. Rome, 1791–1796.

Gnau, Hermann. *Die Zensur unter Joseph II*. Strassburg, 1911.

Godwin, Joscelyn. "Layers of Meaning in *The Magic Flute*." *Musical Quarterly* 65 (1979): 471–92.

Goldin, Daniela. *La vera fenice: Librettisti e libretti tra sette e ottocento*. Turin, 1985.

Goldoni, Carlo. *Mémoires de M. Goldoni pour servir à l'histoire de sa vie et à celle de son théâtre*. [Originally published 1787.] Edited by Paul de Roux. Paris, 1965.

———. *Tutte le opere di Carlo Goldoni*. Edited by Giuseppe Ortolani. 14 vols. Milan, 1935–56.

Gottlieb-Billroth, Otto, ed. *Billroth und Brahms in Briefwechsel*. Berlin, 1935.

Grasselli, Margaret Morgan, and Pierre Rosenberg. *Watteau 1684–1721*. Catalog of the Tercentenary Watteau Exhibition. Washington, D.C., 1984.

Grimm, Friedrich Melchior von. *Correspondance littéraire, philosophique et critique par Grimm, Diderot, Raynal, Meister et al*. Edited by M. Tourneux. 16 vols. Paris, 1877–82.

Grossegger, Elizabeth. *Freimaurerei und Theater, 1770–1800: Freimaurerdramen an den k. k. privilegierten Theatern in Wien*. Graz, 1981.

Guilcher, Jean-Michel. *La contredanse et les renouvellements de la danse française.* Paris, 1969.

Haas, Robert. "Josse de Villeneuves Brief über den Mechanismus der italienischen Oper von 1756." *Zeitschrift für Musikwissenschaft* 7 (1924): 129–63.

Hadamowsky, Franz. *Die Josefinische Theaterreform und das Spieljahr 1776/77 des Burgtheaters: Eine Dokumentation.* Quellen zur Theatergeschichte, vol. 2. Vienna, 1978.

———. *Die Wiener Hoftheater (Staatstheater) 1776–1966, Teil 1: 1776–1810.* Vienna, 1966.

Hamm, Charles. *Music in the New World.* New York, 1983.

[Hárich, János, et al.] "The *Acta Musicalia* of the Esterházy Archives." *Haydn Yearbook* 13 (1982): 5–96; 14 (1983): 9–128; 15 (1984): 93–180.

Heartz, Daniel. "The Beginnings of the Operatic Romance: Rousseau, Sedaine, and Monsigny." *Eighteenth-Century Studies* 15 (1981/82): 149–78.

———. "The Creation of the Buffo Finale in Italian Opera." *Proceedings of the Royal Musical Association* 104 (1977/78): 67–78.

———. "The Great Quartet in Mozart's *Idomeneo*." *Music Forum* 5 (1980): 233–56.

———. "Hasse, Galuppi, and Metastasio." In *Venezia e il melodramma nel settecento*, edited by Maria Teresa Muraro, 1:309–40. Venice, 1978.

———. "Idomeneus Rex." *Mozart-Jahrbuch 1973/74*, pp. 7–20.

———. "Mozart, His Father, and *Idomeneo*." *Musical Times* 119 (1978): 228–31.

———. "Mozarts 'Titus' und die italienische Oper um 1800." *Hamburger Jahrbuch für Musikwissenschaft* 5 (1981): 255–66.

———. "Nicolas Jadot and the Building of the Burgtheater." *Musical Quarterly* 68 (1982): 1–31.

———. "Operatic Reform at Parma: Ippolito ed Aricia." In *Atti del convegno sul settecento Parmense nel 2º centenario della morte di C. I. Frugoni*, pp. 271–300. Parma, 1969.

———. "Raaff's Last Aria: A Mozartian Idyll in the Spirit of Hasse." *Musical Quarterly* 60 (1974): 517–43.

———. "Terpsichore at the Fair: Old and New Dance Airs in Two Vaudeville Comedies by Lesage." In *Music and Context: Essays for John M. Ward*, edited by Anne Dhu Shapiro, pp. 278–304. Cambridge, Mass., 1985.

———. "Tonality and Motif in *Idomeneo*." *Musical Times* 115 (1974): 382–86.

———. "Traetta in Vienna: *Armida* (1761) and *Ifigenia in Tauride* (1763)." *Studies in Music from the University of Western Ontario* 7 (1982): 65–88.

———. "*Vis comica*: Goldoni, Galuppi, and *L'arcadia in Brenta* (Venice, 1749)." In *Venezia e il melodramma nel settecento*, edited by Maria Teresa Muraro, 2:33–69. Florence, 1981.

Heitner, Robert R. "The Iphigenia in Tauris Theme in Drama of the Eighteenth Century." *Comparative Literature* 16 (1964): 289–309.

Henze-Döhring, Sabine. *Opera seria, Opera buffa und Mozarts "Don Giovanni": Zur Gattungsconvergenz in der italienischen Oper des 18. Jahrhunderts.* Laaber, 1986.

Heuberger, Richard. *Erinnerungen an Johannes Brahms: Tagebuchnotizien aus den Jahren 1875–97.* Edited by K. Hoffmann. Tutzing, 1971.

Heuss, Alfred. "Liebt—auf Grund der 'Zauberflöte'—die Frau oder der Mann tiefer und stärker?" *Zeitschrift für Musik* 92 (1925): 72–79.

Hildesheimer, Wolfgang. *Mozart.* Frankfurt, 1977. English translation by Marion Faber. London, 1982.

Hiller, Johann, ed. *Wöchentliche Nachrichten und Anmerkungen, die Musik betreffend.* 4 vols. Leipzig, 1766–70.

Hilton, Wendy. *Dance of Court and Theater: The French Noble Style, 1690–1725.* Princeton, N.J., 1981.

Hintermaier, Ernst. "Das fürsterzbischöfliche Hoftheater zu Salzburg." *Österreichische Musikzeitschrift* 30 (1975): 351–63.

Hirsch, E. D. *Validity in Interpretation.* New Haven, Conn., 1967.

Hodges, Sheila. *Lorenzo Da Ponte: The Life and Times of Mozart's Librettist.* London, 1985.

Hogarth, William. *The Analysis of Beauty with the Rejected Passages from the Manuscript Drafts and Autobiographical Notes.* Edited with an introduction by Joseph Burke. Oxford, 1955.

Hurwitz, Joachim. "Haydn and the Freemasons." *Haydn Yearbook* 16 (1985): 5–98.

Kelly, Michael. *Reminiscences of Michael Kelly.* 2 vols. London, 1826.

Kirkendale, Warren. *Fuge und Fugato in der Kammermusik des Rokoko und der Klassik.* Tutzing, 1966. Revised and expanded ed., translated by Margaret Bent and Warren Kirkendale: *Fugue and Fugato in Rococo and Classical Chamber Music.* Durham, N.C., 1979.

Koenigsberger, Dorothy. "A New Metaphor for Mozart's *Magic Flute.*" *European Studies Review* 5 (1975): 229–75.

Komorzynski, Egon. *Emanuel Schikaneder: Ein Beitrag zur Geschichte des deutschen Theaters.* Vienna, 1951.

Kramer, Kurt. "Antike und christliches Mittelalter in Varescos *Idomeneo,* dem Libretto zu Mozarts gleichnamiger Oper." *Mitteilungen der Internationalen Stiftung Mozarteum* 28 (1980): 1–15.

———. "Da Ponte's 'Così fan tutte.'" *Nachrichten der Akademie der Wissenschaften in Göttingen,* Philologisch-historische Klasse, 1 (1973): 1.

———. "Das Libretto zu Mozarts 'Idomeneo': Quellen und Umgestaltung der Fabel." In *Wolfgang Amadeus Mozart. Idomeneo 1781–1981.* Munich, 1981.

Krause, Christian Gottfried. *Von der musikalischen Poesie.* Berlin, 1752.

Kritsche, Cornelia, and Herbert Zeman. "Das Rätsel eines genialen Opernentwurfs—Da Pontes Libretto 'Così fan tutte' und das literarische Umfeld des 18. Jahrhunderts." In *Die österreichische Literatur: Ihr Profil an der Wende vom 18. zum 19. Jahrhundert (1750–1830),* edited by Herbert Zeman, pp. 355–77. Graz, 1979.

Kunze, Stefan. *Don Giovanni vor Mozart: Die Tradition der Don-Giovanni-Opern im italienischen Buffa-Theater des 18. Jahrhunderts*. Munich, 1972.

———. *Mozarts Opern*. Stuttgart, 1984.

———, ed. *Arien, Szenen, Ensembles und Chöre mit Orchester*. Neue Mozart-Ausgabe, series 2, workgroup 7, vol. 1. Kassel, 1967.

Kurfürst Clemens August Landesherr und Mäzen des 18. Jahrhunderts. Brühl, 1961.

L'Affichard, Thomas. *Caprices romanesques*. Amsterdam, 1745.

Lambranzi, Gregorio. *Neue und curieuse theatralische Tantz-Schul*. Nuremberg, 1716. English translation by Derra de Moroda, edited with a preface by Cyril W. Beaumont: *New and Curious School of Theatrical Dancing*. New York, 1966.

Landon, H. C. Robbins. *Haydn: Chronicle and Works*. 5 vols. Bloomington, Ind., 1976–80.

———. *Mozart and the Masons: New Light on the Lodge "Crowned Hope."* London, 1982.

———. *1791: Mozart's Last Year*. New York, 1988.

Le Forestier, René. *Maçonnerie féminine et loges académiques*. Milan, 1979.

Legband, Paul. *Münchener Bühne und Litteratur im achtzehnten Jahrhundert*. Oberbayerisches Archiv für vaterländische Geschichte, vol. 51. Munich, 1904.

Leux-Henschen, Irmgard. *Joseph Martin Kraus in seinen Briefen*. Stockholm, 1978.

Levey, Michael. "Aspects of Mozart's Heroines." *Journal of the Warburg and Courtauld Institutes* 22 (1959): 132–56.

———. *Giambattista Tiepolo: His Life and Art*. New Haven, Conn., 1986.

Litteratur- und Theater-Zeitung. Edited by Christian August von Betrams. 7 vols. Berlin, 1778–84.

Lühning, Helga. "Die Rondo-Arie im späten 18. Jahrhundert: Dramatische Gehalt und musikalischer Bau." *Hamburger Jahrbuch für Musikwissenschaft* 5 (1981): 219–46.

———. *Titus-Vertonungen im 18. Jahrhundert: Untersuchungen zur Tradition der Opera seria von Hasse bis Mozart*. Regensburg, 1983.

McClymonds, Marita Petzoldt. "Niccolò Jommelli: The Last Years." Ph.D. diss., University of California, Berkeley, 1978.

Mann, William. *The Operas of Mozart*. New York, 1977.

Massin, Jean, and Brigitte Massin. *Wolfgang Amadeus Mozart*. Paris, 1970.

Metastasio, Pietro. *Tutte le opere di Pietro Metastasio*. Edited by Bruno Brunelli. 5 vols. Milan, 1943–54.

Michtner, Otto. *Das alte Burgtheater als Opernbühne: Von der Einführung des deutschen Singspiels (1778) bis zum Tode Kaiser Leopolds II (1792)*. Vienna, 1970.

Mies, Paul. "Die Artikulationszeichen Strich und Punkt bei Wolfgang Amadeus Mozart." *Musikforschung* 11 (1958): 428–55.

Millner, Fredrick. "The Operas of Johann Adolph Hasse." Ph.D. diss., University of California, Berkeley, 1976.

Moberly, Robert. "The Influence of French Classical Drama on Mozart's 'La Clemenza di Tito.'" *Music and Letters* 54 (1974): 286–98.

Mosel, Ignaz von. *Ueber das Leben und die Werke des Anton Salieri, k. k. Hofkapellmeisters*. Vienna, 1827.

Mozart: Briefe und Aufzeichnungen. Gesamtausgabe. Edited by the Internationale Stiftung Mozarteum; collected and annotated by Wilhelm A. Bauer and Otto Erich Deutsch. 4 vols.: documents; 2 vols.: commentary; 1 vol.: indices. Basel, 1962–75.

Müller, Wenzel. *Das Sonnenfest der Braminen*. Vol. 16 of *German Opera 1770–1800*, edited by Thomas Bauman. New York, 1986.

Nettl, Paul. *Mozart in Böhmen*. Prague, 1938.

———. *Musik und Freimaurerei*. Esslingen, 1956. Essays concerning Mozart appeared in English as *Mozart and Masonry*. New York, 1970.

———. "Prager Mozartiana." *Mitteilungen der Internationalen Stiftung Mozarteum* 9 (1960): 2–6.

Niemetschek, Franz. *Leben des k. k. Kapellmeisters Wolfgang Gottlieb Mozart*. Prague, 1798. English translation by Helen Mautner: *Life of Mozart*. London, 1956.

Nissen, Georg Nikolaus von. *Biographie W. A. Mozarts*. Edited by Constanze von Nissen. Leipzig, 1828.

Noske, Frits. *The Signifier and the Signified: Studies in the Operas of Mozart and Verdi*. The Hague, 1977.

Osthoff, Wolfgang. "Gli endecasillabi Villotistici in *Don Giovanni* e *Nozze di Figaro*." In *Venezia e il melodramma nel settecento*, edited by Maria Teresa Muraro, 2:293–311. Florence, 1981.

———. "Die Opera buffa." In *Gattungen der Musik in Einzeldarstellungen: Gedenkschrift Leo Schrade*, 1:678–743. Berlin, 1973.

Payer von Thurn, Rudolf, ed. *Joseph II als Theaterdirektor: Ungedruckte Briefe und Aktenstücke aus den Kinderjahren des Burgtheaters*. Vienna, 1920.

Pezzl, Johann. *Skizze von Wien: Ein Kultur- und Sittenbild aus der josefinischen Zeit*. Edited by Gustav Gugitz and Anton Schlossar. Graz, 1923.

Piozzi, Hester Lynch. *Observations and Reflections Made in the Course of a Journey Through France, Italy, and Germany*. Edited by Herbert Barrows. Ann Arbor, Mich., 1967.

Planelli, Antonio. *Dell'opera in musica*. Naples, 1772.

Pomeau, René. *Beaumarchais, ou la bizarre destinée*. Paris, 1987.

Porter, Andrew. "Haydn and 'La fedeltà premiata.'" *Musical Times* 112 (1971): 331–35.

Prota-Giurleo, Ulisse. "Alcuni musicisti d'oltralpe a Napoli." *Analecta musicologica* 2 (1965): 112–43.

Rasch, Wolfdietrich. *Goethe's "Iphigenie auf Tauris" als Drama der Autonomie*. Munich, 1979.

Raynor, Henry. *A Social History of Music*. London, 1972.

Reichart, Sarah Bennett. "The Influence of Eighteenth-Century Social Dance on the Viennese Classical Style." Ph.D. diss., City University of New York, 1984.

Rice, Howard C., Jr. *Thomas Jefferson's Paris.* Princeton, N.J., 1976.

Rice, John A. "Emperor and Impresario: Leopold II and the Transformation of Viennese Musical Theater, 1790–1792." Ph.D. diss., University of California, Berkeley, 1987.

———. "Sarti's *Giulio Sabino*, Haydn's *Armida*, and the Arrival of Opera seria at Esterháza." *Haydn Yearbook* 15 (1984): 181–98.

Richter, Joseph. *Bildergalerie weltlicher Misbräuche: Ein Gegenstück zur Bildergalerie katholischer und klösterlicher Misbräuche, von Pater Hilarion, Exkuzuzinern. Mit Kupfern und anpassenden Vignetten.* Frankfurt and Leipzig [actually published in Vienna], 1785.

Rochlitz, Friedrich. "Verbürgte Anekdoten aus Wolfgang Gottlieb Mozarts Leben: Ein Beytrag zur richtigeren Kenntnis dieses Mannes, als Mensch und Künstler." *Allgemeine musikalische Zeitung* 1 (1798/99): cols. 17–24, 49–55, 81–86, 113–17, 145–52, 177–83, 289–91, 480, 854–56; 3 (1800/1801): 450–52, 493–97, 590–96.

Rosenberg, Pierre. *Fragonard.* New York, 1988.

Ruf, Wolfgang. *Die Rezeption von Mozarts "Le nozze di Figaro" bei den Zeitgenossen.* Wiesbaden, 1977.

Rushton, Julian. *W. A. Mozart: "Don Giovanni."* Cambridge Opera Handbooks. Cambridge, 1981.

Sadie, Stanley, ed. *The New Grove Dictionary of Music and Musicians.* 20 vols. London, 1980.

Sahut, Marie-Catherine, ed. *Carle Vanloo: Premier peintre du roi.* Nice, 1977.

Saint-Foix, Georges de. "Le théâtre à Salzbourg en 1779–1780." *Revue de musicologie* 16 (1935): 193–204.

———. *Wolfgang Amédée Mozart: Sa vie musicale et son oeuvre. Essai de biographie critique.* 3d ed. 5 vols. Bruges, 1958.

Scheel, Hans Ludwig. "*Le mariage de Figaro* von Beaumarchais und das Libretto der *Nozze di Figaro* von Lorenzo da Ponte." *Musikforschung* 28 (1975): 156–72.

Schikaneder, Emanuel. *The Magic Flute.* Translated by Andrew Porter. London, 1980.

Schindler, Otto G. "Das Publikum des Burgtheaters in der josephinischen Ära." In *Das Burgtheater und sein Publikum*, edited by Margret Dietrich, 11–95. Vienna, 1976.

Schink, Johann Friedrich. "*Die Entführung aus dem Serail*: Komische Oper in drei Aufzügen, von Brezner, die Musik von Mozart." In *Dramaturgische Fragmente*, 4:1001–25. Graz, 1782.

Schubart, Christian Friedrich Daniel. *Ideen zu einer Ästhetik der Tonkunst.* Edited by Ludwig Schubart. Vienna, 1806.

Schuler, Manfred. "Mozarts 'Don Giovanni' in Donaueschingen." *Mitteilungen der Internationalen Stiftung Mozarteum* 35 (1987): 63–72.

Sonnenfels, Joseph von. *Briefe über die wienerische Schaubühne aus dem Französischen übersetzt*. Vienna, 1768.

Squarzina, Luigi. *Teatri e scenografia*. Milan, 1976.

Steblin, Rita. *A History of Key Characteristics in the Eighteenth and Early Nineteenth Centuries*. Ann Arbor, Mich., 1983.

Steptoe, Andrew. "The Sources of 'Così fan tutte': A Reappraisal." *Music and Letters* 62 (1981): 281–94.

Sternfeld, Frederick W. "Orpheus, Ovid, and Opera." *Journal of the Royal Musical Association* 118 (1988): 172–202.

Stone, John. "The Making of 'Don Giovanni' and Its Ethos." *Mozart-Jahrbuch 1984/85*, pp. 130–34.

Strunk, Oliver. *Source Readings in Music History*. New York, 1950.

Tyson, Alan. *Mozart: Studies of the Autograph Scores*. Cambridge, Mass., 1987.

Ungarese, F. "*Die Entführung aus dem Serail*: Ein deutsches Singspiel in 3 Aufzügen." *Zeitung für Theater, Musik und Poesie* 3 (1808): 361–65.

Volek, Tomislav. "Prague Operatic Traditions and Mozart's *Don Giovanni*." In *Mozart's "Don Giovanni" in Prague*. Divadelní ústav [Theater Institute], no. 334, pp. 23–27. Prague, 1987.

———. "Über den Ursprung von Mozarts Oper 'La clemenza di Tito.'" *Mozart-Jahrbuch 1959*, pp. 274–86.

Wackenroder, Wilhelm Heinrich. *Phantasien über die Kunst für Freunde der Kunst*. Edited by Ludwig Tieck. Hamburg, 1799.

Wagner, Richard. "Über die Ouverture." In *Gesammelte Schriften und Dichtungen*, edited by Wolfgang Golther, 194–206. Berlin, 1913.

———. *Wagner Writes from Paris . . . Stories, Essays, and Articles by the Young Composer*. Edited and translated by Robert L. Jacobs and Geoffrey Skelton. London, 1973.

Wandruzka, Adam. "Die 'Clementia austriaca' und der aufgeklärte Absolutismus: Zum politischen und ideellen Hintergrund von 'La clemenza di Tito.'" *Österreichische Musikzeitung* 31 (1976): 186–93.

Weber, Carl Maria von. *Sämtliche Schriften von Carl Maria von Weber*. Edited by Georg Kaiser. Berlin, 1908.

———. *Writings on Music*. Translated by Martin Cooper; edited by John Warrack. Cambridge, 1981.

Weichlein, William. "A Comprehensive Study of Five Musical Settings of *La clemenza di Tito*." Ph.D. diss., University of Michigan, 1957.

Weiss, Piero, and Richard Taruskin, eds. *Music in the Western World: A History in Documents*. New York, 1984.

Williams, Eunice. *Drawings by Fragonard in North American Collections*. Washington, D.C., 1978.

Wilson, W. Daniel. *Humanität und Kreuzzugsideologie um 1780: Die "Türkenoper" im 18. Jahrhundert und das Rettungsmotiv in Wielands "Oberon," Lessings "Nathan" und Goethes "Iphigenie."* New York, 1984.

Wiora, Walter. "Zwischen absoluter und Programmusik." In *Festschrift Friedrich Blume zum 70. Geburtstag*, edited by Anna Amalie Abert and Wilhelm Pfannkuch, 381–88. Kassel, 1963.

Witzmann, Reingard. *Der Ländler in Wien: Ein Beitrag zur Entwicklungsgeschichte des Wiener Walzers bis in die Zeit des Wiener Kongresses*. Vienna, 1976.

Wolf, Eugene K. *The Symphonies of Johann Stamitz*. Utrecht, 1981.

Wolfgang Amadeus Mozart: Neue Ausgabe sämtlicher Werke. Edited by the Internationale Stiftung Mozarteum Salzburg. Kassel, 1955–. Opera volumes (series 2, work group 5):

Lucio Silla, vol. 7:1–2. Edited by Kathleen Kuzmick Hansell. 1986.

Il re pastore, vol. 9. Edited by Pierluigi Petrobelli and Wolfgang Rehm. 1985.

Idomeneo, vol. 11:1–2. Edited by Daniel Heartz. 1972.

Die Entführung aus dem Serail, vol. 12. Edited by Gerhard Croll. 1982.

Le nozze di Figaro, vol. 16:1–2. Edited by Ludwig Finscher. 1973.

Don Giovanni, vol. 17. Edited by Wolfgang Plath and Wolfgang Rehm. 1968.

Die Zauberflöte, vol. 19. Edited by Gernot Gruber and Alfred Orel. 1970.

La clemenza di Tito, vol. 20. Edited by Franz Giegling. 1970.

Würtz, Roland. "Die Erstaufführungen von Mozarts Bühnenwerken in Mannheim." *Mozart-Jahrbuch 1978/79*, pp. 163–71.

INDEX OF MOZART'S WORKS

Born, Ignaz von, 257, 258
Boucher, François, 5–6, 57, 112–13, 200–201
Brahms, Johannes, 8 n.15, 129 n.10
Bretzner, Christoph Friedrich, 67, 70–87
Brissot, Jacques-Pierre, 131
Brockmann, Johann, 73
Brown, Bruce Alan, 143 n
Buffa. *See* Opera buffa
Buffa, Baron, 78
Buffo finale. *See* Finale
Buffo patter, 145
Bulgarelli, Marianna, 90
Burke, Edmund, 283
Burney, Charles, 90 n, 91, 94, 314
Bussani, Francesco, 124, 126

Cabaletta, 306
Cafarelli, 94
Cagliostro, Count, 258 n.9
Cahusac, Louis de, 192
Caldara, Antonio, 300
Callot, Jacques, 207
Calvesi, Vincenzo, 237, 242
Calzabigi, Raniero de, 27, 33, 75, 139, 308–9
Campra, André, 2, 16
Canal, Count Josef Emanuel, 157
Canciani, Nadal, 95
Cannabich, Christian, 33
Carl Theodor, Palatine elector and duke of Bavaria, 15–17, 33, 47, 341
Carpani, Giuseppe, 304–5
Casti, Giambattista, 98, 99–101, 125, 127, 134, 304
Cavalieri, Catarina, 69, 70, 71, 76–77, 152–54, 267
Cavatina, 26, 80, 117–18, 127, 140–42, 149, 242
Chapman, John, 41–42
Chardin, Jean Siméon, 218
Charles VI, Emperor, 89
Cicognini, Giacinto Andrea, 165
Cigna, Vittorio, 301
Cimarosa, Domenico, 127, 198–99 n, 202, 304, 305, 307–8
Clementi, Muzio, 288
Cobenzl, Count Ludwig, 138
Colloredo, Hieronymus, Archbishop of Salzburg, 65–66, 74

Colman, George, 75
Coltellini, Marco, 4, 199
Commedia dell'arte, 137, 165, 179–80, 187–89, 207
Cone, Edward, 280
Contat, Mlle, 113
Corneille, Thomas, 35, 73, 74 n.15
Crébillon (père), 2

Dalayrac, Nicolas, 304–5
Dal Bene, Gabriella (La Ferrarese), 152, 217, 223
Dal Prato, Vincenzo, 21, 49
Dance bands, 183, 189, 190, 192, 193
Dance halls, 192–93
Dance types: branle, 185; chaconne, 21, 43–44; contredanse, 157–58, 182, 185–91; Deutscher (German dance), 157–58, 182, 190; gavotte, 59, 146, 147, 274–75; Ländler, 49, 190 n.10; minuet, 180, 182–84, 185, 219; polonaise, 183; waltz, 190
Danchet, Antoine, 2, 5, 16, 18, 20, 21, 22, 23, 27, 28, 31
Danzi, Innozenz, 47
Da Ponte, Lorenzo: arrival in Vienna, 97–98; disgrace and dismissal from Vienna, 235, 258; Epistle to Casti, 99–101; *Extract from the Life of,* 101, 133–38, 147, 158–60; librettos for Mozart. *See* librettos in Index of Mozart's Works, K.492, K.527, and K.588; librettos for other composers, 97–98, 101, 102, 103, 127, 128–29; *Memorie,* 101, 108, 133–38, 147, 159, 200, 202; Metastasio as model for, 60 n, 240; Mozart's first impressions of, 126–27; originality questioned by Casti, 98–99; as stage director, 89, 102, 103–4
Dean, Winton, 89 n
Dent, Edward J., 79 n.20, 148 n.21, 150 n.23, 208, 240, 251, 258, 287
Destouches, Philippe Néricault, 199
De Wilde, Samuel, 152
Diderot, Denis, 4, 111, 192
Dramma giocoso, 96–97, 162–63, 195–202, 203, 249
Du Barry, Madame, 107
Duni, Egidio, 255 n.2
Durazzo, Count Giacomo, 124

Mayr, Simone, 316

Mazzolà, Caterino, 97, 125, 259–60, 261, 300, 307

Merk, Johann Heinrich, 180

Metastasio, Pietro, 22, 33, 38–39, 40, 42, 60n, 89–94, 95, 97–98, 139, 160, 203, 229–30, 232, 240, 249, 260, 261n.18, 300–304, 307–9

Meude-Monpas, J. J. O. de, 44

Micelli, Caterina, 160, 168

Migliavacca, Giovannambrogio, 94

Molière (Jean-Baptiste Poquelin), 74n.15, 139, 160n.4, 165, 200, 208, 214, 218, 226–27, 250–51

Monsigny, Pierre-Alexandre, 235

Montesquieu, 272

Monza, Carlo, 301

Mosel, Ignaz von, 154

Mozart: attitude toward women, 208–9, 218, 220, 267–69, 270, 278; composing habits, 32, 69, 136, 286; dancing, 157, 179–80, 182, 192–93; distinct color of each of his major operas, 32, 43, 58, 72, 234, 338–39; European tours, 15, 38; Freemasonry, 256–59, 267–70, 274–75; and Gluck, 4, 6–9, 27–28, 34, 164, 165, 339–40; librettists defer to, 32, 70, 100, 119, 136, 147, 169, 172, 200, 261; and Mannheim, 15–18, 33–34, 37n.1, 331; marriage, 74–75, 84; and nature, 24–26, 47, 97, 223–24, 231; and Paisiello, 128, 140–46, 148–49, 311–17; personal honor, 65–66, 77–78; and Prague, 42, 101–2, 157–58, 169, 200, 225, 259–62, 321, 341; relative strengths in comedy and tragedy, 37, 215; romantic love as his inspiration, 47, 55, 60, 79, 242, 281–83, 292; and Salzburg, 17–18, 67, 255–56, 266; seria versus buffa, 16, 43, 76, 174–76, 198, 204–5, 215, 231; and Vienna, 65, 67, 256, 263, 266. *See also* Index of Mozart's Works

Mozart family: Bäsle (Maria Anna Thekla, cousin), 87; Carl Thomas (son), 267; Constanza (née Weber, wife), 74–75, 84, 157, 180, 261–62, 266, 267, 339; Leopold (father), 15, 16, 18, 21, 28, 29, 33, 35, 38, 65–70, 73–74, 75, 77–78, 136, 179–80; Maria Anna (mother), 15; Nannerl (Ma-

ria Anna, sister), 28–29, 65, 136, 255; Raimund Leopold (son), 180

Müller, Johann Heinrich, 180

Müller, Wenzl, 258–59

Naumann, Emil, 260, 307

Neoclassical art and architecture, 24n, 115, 301–3, 322–23

Nicolai, Friedrich, 124

Niemetschek, Franz, 42–43, 108, 261, 339–40

Nissen, Georg Nicklaus von, 72n.10, 180, 286

Noske, Frits R., 150n.23, 237n

Opera buffa, 43, 73, 133–34, 195, 249, 299–300

Opéra-comique, 49n, 235, 304, 307

Opera seria, 37, 38, 40–43, 89–94, 95, 97, 174–76, 196–97, 198, 240, 299–300

Ortes, Gianmaria, 300

Ortolani, Giuseppe, 94n.7, 97

Osthoff, Wolfgang, 233n.4

Ottani, Bernardo, 301

Pacchiarotti, Gasparo, 305

Paisiello, Giovanni, 75, 108, 118, 125, 126, 127, 128, 138, 140–46, 148–49, 151, 169, 235, 304–5, 309–11, 311–16

Palomba, Antonio, 196n.3, 304

Pantomime, 20, 32, 258

Panzachi, Domenico de', 21–22, 28, 58

Pasquini, Giovanni Claudio, 91

Paul Petrovich, grand duke of Russia, 67

Pellegrin, S.-J., 309

Pergen, Count Johann Anton, 131, 135, 137

Pergolesi, Giovanni Battista, 138, 299, 307

Petran, Franz, 257

Petrosellini, Giuseppe, 108, 125, 140–41, 199

Pezzl, Johann, 74, 124–25

Piccinni, Niccolò, 33, 197–99, 255n.2, 311

Piozzi, Hester Thrale, 131

Piranesi, Giambattista, 259n.13

Planelli, Antonio, 299, 310–11

Ponziani, Felice, 160, 168, 172

Porpora, Nicola, 95

Porta, Nicola, 161

Porter, Andrew, 198–99n, 217–18, 259

Puchberg, Michael, 235

Designer: Steve Renick
Compositor: G & S Typesetters, Inc.
Text: 10/14 Galliard
Display: Galliard
Printer: Malloy Lithographing, Inc.
Binder: John H. Dekker & Sons